Contents

Notes on Contributors

Kate Alexander holds the South Research Chair in Social Change and is director of the Centre for Social Change at the University of Johannesburg in South Africa. She has published widely in comparative labour history and social movement studies. In recent months she has been active in the South Africa's C-19 People's Coalition.

Nicolás Arata teaches history of education at the University of Buenos Aires in Argentina. He is also director of Training and Editorial Production of the Latin American Council of Social Sciences. His last book is *Latinoamérica: la educación y su historia* (2020), co-edited with Pablo Pineau.

Kathya Araujo is Professor of Sociology at the Institute for Advanced Studies at the Universidad de Santiago de Chile and Director of the Millennium Nucleus Centre on Authority and Asymmetries of Power. She has published over 20 books, including *El miedo a los subordinados* (2016) and *Hilos Tensados. Para leer el octubre chileno* (2019).

Michelle Bachelet has served as the United Nations High Commissioner for Human Rights since 2018. She served as president of Chile twice, from 2006 to 2010 and again from 2014 to 2018 for the Socialist Party, the first woman to occupy the position. Previously, she was the first executive director of the United Nations Entity for Gender Equality and the Empowerment of Women.

Supurna Banerjee has a PhD in sociology from the University of Edinburgh and is Assistant Professor at the Institute of Development Studies in Kolkata. She is the author of *Activism and Agency in India: Nurturing Resistance in the Tea Plantations* (2017).

Karina Batthyány is the executive secretary of the Latin American Council of Social Sciences and Professor of Sociology at the Republic University of Uruguay. She conducts research in the area of care, gender and social welfare.

A feminist activist, with extensive experience in women's movements and organizations, she has written or edited more than 20 books.

Ilán Bizberg is Professor at the Colegio de México, based at the Centre for International Studies. He has a PhD in Social Sciences at the École des Hautes Etudes en Sciences Sociales and also obtained a Humboldt Stiftung Scholarship in Germany. His latest book in English is *Diversity of Capitalisms in Latin America* (2019).

Breno Bringel is Professor of Sociology at the Institute of Social and Political Studies at the Rio de Janeiro State University and Senior Fellow (Programa Talento Investigador) at the Universidad Complutense de Madrid. He is the current president of the International Sociological Association Research Committee on Social Classes and Social Movements (ISA RC-47) and director of the Latin American Sociological Association. He also collaborates with several Latin American social movements and participates in activist research initiatives. His latest book in English is *Critical Geopolitics and Regional (Re)configurations* (2019).

Hillary Caldwell is a Ph.D. candidate in environmental psychology at the City University of New York Graduate Centre and co-founder and assistant director of the Community Change Studies Programme at City College. A specialist in community-based research and popular education around land and housing issues, she has worked with the Morris Justice Project, Picture the Homeless, and the New York City Community Land Initiative.

Stéphanie Cassilde is a researcher involved in the Social Movements in the Global Age Research Group at the University of Louvain, a research scholar at the Ronin Institute for Independent Scholarship and an on-site researcher at the social centre Comme Chez Nous in Charleroi, where she currently reinforces the team of volunteers for social work.

Chris Chan has a PhD in sociology from the University of Warwick. He is an associate professor at the Department of Sociology and co-director of the Centre for Social Innovation Studies at the Chinese University of Hong Kong. He works closely with trade unions, NGOs and activists' groups to promote labour rights and social equality in Hong Kong, China and beyond.

Jean De Munck is Professor at the Catholic University of Louvain. His work focuses on the epistemology of evaluative sociology, specially applied to institutions, and on changes to normativity in contemporary societies in the legal and political fields. He has also conducted research on the critical discourse of consumerism and on a sociological account of participation inspired by a discussion of the Capability Approach of Amartya Sen and the communicative turn of Jürgen Habermas.

Olivier De Schutter is the United Nations Special Rapporteur on Extreme Poverty and Human Rights. He is also Professor at the University of Louvain and at SciencesPo Paris, besides formerly the UN Special Rapporteur on the right to food and a member of the UN Committee on Economic, Social and Cultural Rights.

Boaventura de Sousa Santos is a (retired) professor of sociology from the University of Coimbra in Portugal and a distinguished professor at the Institute for Legal Studies of the University of Wisconsin-Madison in the United States. He is the author of over 30 books, translated into several languages, on legal sociology, the global left, Southern epistemologies and social theory. His latest book in English is *The End of the Cognitive Empire: The Coming of Age of Epistemologies of the South* (2018).

Donatella della Porta is Professor of Political Science and Dean of the Institute for Humanities and the Social Sciences at the Scuola Normale Superiore in Florence, Italy, where she also leads the Centre on Social Movement Studies. In 2011, she was the recipient of the Mattei Dogan Prize for distinguished achievements in the field of political sociology. She is the author of dozens of reference books on social movements and recently published with Bristol University Press the book *Contesting Higher Education: Student Movements against Neoliberal Universities* (2020).

José Maurício Domingues holds a PhD in sociology from the London School of Economics. He teaches at the Institute of Social and Political Studies at Rio de Janeiro State University and is author of over 30 books on social theory and political sociology, including recently *Critical Theory and Political Modernity* (2019). He is also the recipient of the Alexander von Humboldt Anneliese Maier Research Award for 2018–23.

Arturo Escobar is the Kenan Distinguished Professor of Anthropology at the University of North Carolina, Chapel Hill, and Research Associate with the Culture, Memory, and Nation group at the Universidad del Valle and the Cultural Studies Group at Universidad Javeriana. Over the past 25 years, he has worked closely with several Afro-Colombian social movements in the Colombian Pacific, particularly the Process of Black Communities. His last book is *Pluriversal Politics: The Real and the Possible* (2020).

FASE (Federation for Social and Educational Assistance) was founded in 1961. It is a non-profit, non-governmental organization, active in different regions of Brazil with its headquarters in Rio de Janeiro. Since its inception, it has devoted itself to the grassroots organization and popular education and development of communities and associations. The Rio de Janeiro team that authored this article consists of Aercio Barbosa de Oliveira, Bruno França, Caroline Rodrigues, Emanuelle Anastasoupoulos, Milla Gabrieli dos Santos Faria, Monica Oliveira and Rachel Barros.

Michele Ford is the director of the Sydney Southeast Asia Centre at the University of Sydney, Australia. Her research focuses on the international labour movement and trade unions in Asia, including their responses to migrant workers and the rise of the gig economy. Her most recent books include *From Migrant to Worker: Global Unions and Temporary Labor Migration in Asia* (2019) and *Labor and Politics in Indonesia* (2020, with Teri Caraway). She has also co-edited several volumes including *Activists in Transition: Progressive Politics in Democratic Indonesia* (2019).

Tommaso Gravante is Researcher at CEIICH of the Mexican National Autonomous University in Mexico City. He researches and writes about emotions and social movements. He is the author of several articles and chapters on emotions and grassroots activism. In 2018, he won the Seventh Worldwide Competition for Junior Sociologists, organized by the International Sociological Association.

Sari Hanafi is Professor of Sociology at the American University of Beirut and the president of the International Sociological Association. His last book is *Knowledge Production in the Arab World: The Impossible Promise* (2016, with R. Arvanitis). In 2019, he was awarded an Honorary Doctorate of the National University of San Marcos in Peru.

Pauli Huotari is a PhD candidate in world politics, University of Helsinki. His research interests include the role of economics, economists and economic ideas in societal change and continuity. Most recently, he has been teaching Global Political Economy at the University of Helsinki. Huotari has long been involved in various civic movements.

Alexandra Kassir has a PhD in sociology from the Ecole des Hautes Etudes en Sciences Sociales in Paris. Her primary areas of research focus are social movements, religion, secularism and migration. She is a postdoctoral researcher at the Centre for Lebanese Studies and a lecturer in sociology at the American University of Beirut.

Anastasia Kavada is Reader in Media and Politics in the School of Media and Communication at the University of Westminster. She is co-leader of the Arts, Communication and Culture Research Community and of the MA in Media, Campaigning and Social Change. Her research focuses on the links between digital media, social movements, participatory democracy and campaigning for social change.

Ashish Kothari is the founder of Kalpavriksh, an Indian non-profit organization working on environmental and social issues at local, national and global levels. He was trained at the Indian Institute of Public Administration and coordinated India's National Biodiversity Strategy and Action Plan. He served on the board of Greenpeace International. He is part of the coordination team of Vikalp Sangam, the Global Tapestry of Alternatives and Radical Ecological Democracy. He is the (co-)author of several books including *Churning the Earth* (2012) and a co-editor of *Pluriverse: A Post-Development Dictionary* (2019).

John Krinsky is Professor of Political Science at the City College of New York and the City University of New York Graduate Centre. He is the author and editor of several books and articles on urban neoliberalism and social movements, and is on the editorial board of *Metropolitics*. He founded and directs the Community Change Studies Programme at City College and is a founding board member of the New York City Community Land Initiative.

Kamal Lahbib is a Moroccan activist and intellectual. Former political prisoner, he is a founding member of several associations including the Forum des Alternatives Maroc, Transparency Maroc, the Moroccan Observatory of Public Freedoms, the Moroccan Truth and Justice Forum, the Moroccan Coalition for Climate Justice, and the Collectif Associatif pour l'Observation des Elections. He is a member of the International Council of the World Social Forum and a key member of the Maghreb Social Forum.

Elísio Macamo is Professor of Sociology with a focus on Africa at the University of Basel. He was born and grew up in Mozambique. He studied in Maputo, London and Bayreuth. He was Fellow in Bayreuth, Research Fellow at the Centre for African Studies in Lisbon, AGORA Fellow at the Wissenschaftskolleg zu Berlin and Guest Lecturer at the Eduardo Mondlane University in Mozambique. He regularly offers methodological workshops for lusophone African PhD students for the Council for the Development of Social Science Research in Africa, based in Dakar, Senegal.

Paulo Henrique Martins is Professor of Sociology at the Federal University of Pernambuco in Brazil. He is former president of the Latin American Association of Sociology (2011–13) and founder and editor of *REALIS (Journal of AntiUtilitarian and Post-Colonial Studies)*. Author of several books including *Critical Theory of Coloniality* (2019) and *Itineraries of the gift: Theory and Sentiment* (2019).

Stefania Milan is Associate Professor of New Media and Digital Culture at the University of Amsterdam. Her work explores the interplay between digital technology, activism and governance. She is the principal investigator of several projects, such as DATACTIVE (data-activism.net). She is the author of *Social Movements and Their Technologies: Wiring Social Change* (2013/2016) and co-author of *Media/Society* (2011).

Clément Petitjean has a PhD in sociology from the Université Versailles Saint-Quentin. He teaches political science there, and is a member of the Laboratoire Printemps (Professions, Institutions, Temporalités). His research focuses on social movements, representation, group-making, political socialization and professional trajectories. He is currently working on a book project on a critical history of community organizing in Chicago.

Geoffrey Pleyers is FNRS Senior Researcher and Professor of Sociology at the University of Louvain in Belgium. He is the Vice-President for Research of the International Sociological Association and the past-president of its Research Committee on Social Movements. He chairs the Research Programme 'Social movements in the global age' at the Collège d'Études Mondiales and at the University of Louvain. He is the author of *Alter-Globalization. Becoming Actors in the Global Age* (2011) and *Movimientos sociales en el siglo XXI* (2018).

Alice Poma is Researcher at the Social Sciences Institute at the Mexican National Autonomous University in Mexico City. She is the author of the book *Defendiendo territorio y dignidad: emociones y cambio cultural en las luchas contra presas en España y México* (2017) and several articles and chapters on the role of emotions and environmental social movements.

Bandana Purkayastha is Professor of Sociology and Asian American Studies at the University of Connecticut, USA. She has over 75 publications on migration, gender/race, human rights and violence and peace. She received many honours and awards, including the Jessie Bernard award from the American Sociological Association. Her last book is *Human Trafficking: Trade for Sex, Labor, and Organs* (2019).

Guy Ryder is the director general of the International Labour Organization. He studied Social and Political Sciences at the University of Cambridge and then Latin American Studies at the University of Liverpool. Previous to his current position, he was general secretary of the International Trade Union Confederation (ITUC) between 2006 and 2010.

Montserrat Sagot is Professor of Sociology and Chair of the Women's Studies Research Centre at the University of Costa Rica. She was the chair of the CLACSO's Working Group on Feminisms, Resistance and Emancipatory Processes in Latin America. She has published widely about violence against women, femicide as necropolitics, and the feminist movement in Central America.

Leanne Sajor is from the Philippines and has dedicated 12 years to feminist organizing working with grassroots groups and transnational advocacy networks in New York and member-led human rights networks internationally to address inequalities and build solidarities for socioeconomic justice. She previously managed the Economic Policy and Human Rights Programme at the International Network for Economic, Social and Cultural Rights. She is Senior Atlantic Fellow for Social and Economic Equity in the International Inequalities Institute, London School of Economics.

Rita Laura Segato is Emeritus Professor at the University of Brasilia in Brazil and Professor at the National University of San Martín in Argentina. She is the author of numerous books including *Las Estructuras Elementales de la Violencia* (*The Elementary Structures of Violence*) (2003 and 2013), *La Nación y sus Otros* (*The Nation and Its Others*) (2007) and *La Guerra contra las Mujeres* (*The War against Women*) (2018).

Nara Roberta Silva is a sociologist with a Ph.D. from the State University of Campinas, Brazil. She is a core faculty member at the Brooklyn Institute for Social Research in New York, where she researches and teaches about social movements and democracy, global Marxism, post/anti-colonialism, and social theory.

Teivo Teivainen is Professor of World Politics at the University of Helsinki in Finland. He lived for many years in Peru and was a visiting scholar in Brazil, Canada and the United States. He is an active participant in public debate in Finland and received various honours and awards for his work. In recent years he directed a project at the Helsinki Collegium for Advanced Studies on non-state forms of politics.

Emiliano Treré is Senior Lecturer in Media Ecologies and Social Transformation in the School of Journalism, Media and Culture at Cardiff University, UK. He is a member of the Data Justice Lab and the co-founder of the 'Big Data from the South' Initiative. His latest book, *Hybrid Media Activism* (2019), won the Outstanding Book Award of the ICA Interest Group 'Activism, Communication and Social Justice'.

Anna Tsui is Researcher at the Centre for Social Innovation Studies at the Chinese University of Hong Kong, dedicated to fostering research on civil society in Greater China. Its focus is on assembling basic academic archives to support practitioners, research officers, NGOs and foundations in gaining a comprehensive and systematic understanding of civil society in the context of Chinese society.

Pablo Vommaro teaches history and sociology at the Universidad de Buenos Aires. He is a researcher at CONICET and is the Director of Research at CLACSO. He is also the chair of the Youth and Policy Studies Group at the Gino Germani Research Institute. His research focuses on youth, public policies, inequalities, social movements and Latin American history. He is the director of the *Las Juventudes Argentinas Hoy* book collection, which has had 29 books published since 2015.

Lesley Wood is Associate Professor and Chair in Sociology at York University in Canada. She researches and writes about social movements, diffusion and protest policing. She is active in anti-poverty, anti-capitalist and decolonizing movements in Toronto, and is one of editors of *Interface: A Journal for and about Social Movements*. She is the author of *Crisis and Control* (2014) and co-author of *Social Movements: 1768–2018* (4th edition) (2018).

Sabrina Zajak is Professor for Globalization Conflicts, Social Movements and Labor at the Ruhr-University Bochum and leads the Department of Consent and Conflict at the German Centre for Integration and Migration Research. She is a founding member of the Institute for Protest and Social Movement Research in Berlin, and the Vice-President of the Research Committee on Social Classes and Social Movements at the International Sociology Association.

Joy Y. Zhang is Senior Lecturer in Sociology at the University of Kent. Her work has fed into the policymaking of the Royal Society in the UK and China's Ministry of Science and Technology. She authored two monographs: *The Cosmopolitanization of Science: Stem Cell Governance in China* (2012) and *Green Politics in China: Environmental Governance and State–Society Relations* (2013).

Introduction: A Global Dialogue on the Pandemic

Breno Bringel and Geoffrey Pleyers

The COVID-19 pandemic has put the world on hold during 2020 and 2021. Beyond all macrodimensions, it is a global event that has changed the daily routines and lives of every human being on the planet, with multiple impacts for the future. Billions of people have been confined at different stages. Others, however, can not afford this luxury and continue to work in the health sector, in production, food supply, social work, transport, cleaning and at various other tasks which, although defined as 'essential services' in our societies, are not sufficiently recognized and valued. In turn, workers in the informal economy, those living from day to day or those who lost their jobs, have become concerned not only about a virus but also about rapid impoverishment and deterioration of living conditions in a context full of uncertainties.

Faced with the threat of COVID-19, local and national governments turned to doctors, biologists, virologists and epidemiologists to try to contain the pandemic, design policy responses and search for a vaccine. Social sciences also mobilized in all parts of the world, although not always with the same weight. Would this have anything to do with the lesser legitimacy of social sciences as compared to the so-called life sciences? A prestigious physician accompanying a crisis committee sounds relevant, but would one say the same if this committee also included sociologists, psychologists or philosophers who provide other readings of the health crisis and could convey their proposals for governments and society as a whole? A curious division, by the way: on one side, life; on the other, the 'social' or 'human'. Health, however, is one of those issues that does not understand disciplinary and knowledge boundaries. Although in practice the division may be reinforced by the political hierarchization of knowledge and 'expertise', much progress has been made, mainly in the Global South, towards a holistic, multidimensional and collective understanding of health as understood far beyond an individual physiological dimension.

Although the virus itself is a biological agent that can infect any of us, we have been deeply unequal in the face of the pandemic. Therefore, the emphasis on the ecosystemic and social nature of the pandemic is essential to remind us of the profound global asymmetries and inequalities of class, race and gender, as well as to link the health crisis to other previous crises – environmental, social and political – that are only deepening today. One of the main contributions of social sciences to the contemporary public debate is precisely a broadening of the vision of health and risk, something that is crucial in order to produce more accurate diagnoses about the origins of the pandemic, more effective policies for its containment and strategies aimed at providing a glimpse of the post-pandemic world.

The COVID-19 pandemic comes at a historic moment of natural resource depletion and climate and environmental emergency in which capitalism shows its most predatory face. It is a time of setbacks for democracy and human rights, and of mistrust and rejection of political systems. We also live in societies that have been torn apart by huge inequalities (both North/ South and within national societies) and whose public services have been dismantled by decades of neoliberalism, which, beyond the economy, also strongly permeates individual and collective subjectivities. Meanwhile, the digitalization of society has enabled greater interaction between people and a greater flow of information about the pandemic, but this has been accompanied, before and beyond COVID-19, by a process of growing individualization, circulation of fake news and production of devices for surveillance and social control.

The pandemic also acts as a magnifying glass. It intensifies social and economic problems, as well as political failures, and makes them more visible. The critical analyses of the 46 authors from 27 countries that we bring together in this book make intelligible the local, national and global impacts and challenges generated by the pandemic, while also pointing to problems that the pandemic has amplified or revealed. Read together, these chapters written from all continents and different points of view create a truly global dialogue on the current crisis and the contemporary world, on the way in which inequalities are being exacerbated and forms of social control diversified, but also on how new solidarities and possibilities of other worlds are opening up.

Thinking globally

The analytical perspective that led us to put these texts together articulates four convictions. Firstly, we understand the pandemic as a *critical global event* that marks a historical turning point. Although there have been previous pandemics, the global resonance of this one is unprecedented. The virus does not stop at borders, even when governments decide to close them. It reveals how deeply connected and inter/ecodependent we have become. It generates impacts that will have global consequences. For this reason, it seems essential to articulate diverse scenarios and temporalities of analysis, imagining the short, medium and long term.

Secondly, the pandemic affects people and places in very different ways. In time of pandemic, it is more urgent than ever to *think globally*. This does not only imply a more comprehensive view but also the considering of phenomenon from different places, articulating scales and worldviews to compose a broad and diverse mosaic that takes into consideration the dynamics and conflicts that resonate in the world in a more transversal way, beyond parochial politics. It is crucial to capture the inequalities and diversity of situations and positions. It is essential to unveil issues, territories and experiences that remain barely visible in the mainstream media coverage of the pandemic and are not taken into account by public policies. Without denying the experience of the Western or Westernized middle and upper classes during the pandemic, it is fundamental to 'provincialize' them, integrating them into a global perspective with other experiences in different cultural, geographical and social environments. Learning from other realities opens new analytical and critical horizons with which to understand the world as a whole, as well as to rethink our own daily experience.

Thirdly, we suggest a dynamic perspective of the social and political reality. This perspective opposes teleological readings or deterministic perspectives, which see in the pandemic the confirmation of their previous analyses and are launched into hasty predictions about the structural impact of the crisis. The future is in dispute and possible scenarios are multiple. There is no *telos*, no inevitable logic or predetermined path that will lead us to a better world or, on the contrary, to the exacerbation of the authoritarian drifts and the collapse. The consequences of historical events are contingent and depend on disputes over the meaning of crises and the ability of various actors to impose political lines to address these multidimensional crises and their possible outcomes. This perspective places at the centre the actors and social movements as producers of society and—with this objective—also as producers of knowledge and know-how. *Thinking with the actors* requires incorporating diverse and disputed rationalities and subjectivities, something essential to getting a glimpse of the immediate reactions to the health crisis, but also the projections of the future.

Our fourth premise is a *committed and public sociology* that accompanies and contributes to the struggles for a fairer world. Such sociology should generate both academic knowledge and content accessible to a wide audience based on empirical research and critical analyses. Spaces of articulation between universities and social movements are crucial to the co-production of knowledge. As for its diffusion, this perspective has been materialized in our Open Movements editorial project, hosted by the leading international digital platform Open Democracy. For the last six years, Open Movements has promoted the publication and circulation of short and direct texts by activists and researchers from all over the world. It is a way of trying to translate the results of collective experiences and research into diverse sectors of society, beyond academia and the movements themselves, reaching out to citizens, journalists and public policymakers. In times that are marked by attempts to delegitimize and criminalize critical thinking by various authoritarian governments, the way out cannot be to get defensive and turn inwards to the scientific community.

From pandemic to social change

Since the outbreak of the global pandemic, thousands of articles, essays and books have been published about COVID-19 and the contemporary world. In the first stage of the pandemic, the intellectual and political debates ranged from a 'corona-optimism' to a 'corona-pessimism'. The first stance celebrates the renewed displays of solidarity, the umpteenth death of capitalism, the positive lessons that the experience of the pandemic could generate (such as living better with less or the more equitable distribution of care) and the rearticulation of local initiatives and collective actors. The second emphasizes the deleterious effects of the pandemic: selfishness and utilitarianism, greater social control, restrictions of freedom and deterioration in living conditions.

Two other features of the global debate are the *urgency of the present* and the *shortsightedness of the visible*. Rapid and peremptory interpretations of the extraordinary situation multiply. There seems to be no limit to the overinterpretation of the consequences of the rising pandemic in the virtual conversations and forums: 'Modernity is over', 'Nothing will be the same again', or, in a more exaggerated and ironic version, 'World history from now on will be divided between a new *Anno Domini:* BC and AC: before corona and after corona'.

On the other hand, following wider trends in the press and official stances, analyses have ended up focusing too much or almost exclusively on data, graphs and tables. Counting the number of new infections and deaths and comparing them with other cities, countries or regions has become an obsession. Many would summarize the policy to face the pandemic as the management of the health crisis and its effects. In that picture, social protests and resistance are limited to digital activism and *cacerolazos* on the balconies. In short, faced with an invisible virus, columnists and commentators have ended up being hijacked by the more 'visible' dimension of the pandemic associated with the control of the health crisis.

We challenge these trends for three reasons. First, although there are solid arguments among both the corona-optimists and the corona-pessimists, we have to assume the deeply contradictory nature of this historical moment. There are many threats, but also some opportunities. The pandemic may serve as an alarm, but the derivations of its signals will always depend on the actors and their ability to influence the course of the coming world. These actors develop contentious actions and different interpretation of the crisis, making its outcomes unpredictable. In this way, the 'new normality' is, in itself, a project of reconstruction of capitalism that builds on the wish of many people to recover sociability and employment.

Second, we tend to overestimate the capacity for systemic changes when we are immersed in events and critical junctures that shape new directions. While windows of opportunity are real, we tend to magnify them and believe that everything will change radically, for better or worse. This is not necessarily so. It is essential to be open to new horizons, but also to try to capture the continuities, adaptations, hybridizations and innovations. To leave behind the urgency of the present as a short-term view opens a path for broader interpretations of the actors and the process of social and political life. Our challenge is to distinguish the specific feature of the time of a pandemic from what may remain afterwards. Of course, some urgency cannot be denied. It is notably related to the need to save lives, to defend public health and to prioritize eco-social justice in a context that tends to accentuate inequalities or to incorporate, once again, the 'green' as a make-up without concern for equity and social and environmental justice. But the urgent cannot make us forget about long-lasting outcomes and challenges, nor can it tie us to a spiral that prevents us from building transitions and utopian horizons.

Finally, a third reason refers to tracking society's tectonic plates, the dissatisfactions that emerge from diverse communities and collectivities but which barely make it into the mainstream news headlines. We have to go beyond the most visible part of the iceberg and integrate living experiences that have been 'invisibilized', or actively made invisible, in times of the pandemic. In our work, and in much of this book, we seek to reconstruct these from the agendas, dynamics and community protests, as well as from diverse forms of activism and social movements. This perspective allows us to point to emerging conflicts, but also to innovative solutions to get out of the crisis.

Challenges in the global pandemic
COVID-19 governance, politics and the ambivalence of states

The first part of the book brings together contributions that analyse the ways political regimes, states and governments have dealt with the virus outbreak and the health crisis, and how this reveals ambivalences, weaknesses and possibilities in the fight against COVID-19. Some global and regional analyses are combined with some specific national cases, like those of China, Indonesia and the Philippines.

Nation states have imposed themselves as the main actors in dealing with the pandemic, calling for national unity and intervening daily on TV channels. At the beginning of the pandemic, even the defenders of neoliberalism called for massive state intervention. This increased interventionism was implemented in historic stimulus packages to support businesses and companies, urgent expansion in social and health policies and also increasing social control, with police and sometimes military controls in the streets, sometimes involving cases of people beaten to death for not respecting the restrictions. Curfew or lockdown measures are necessary to mitigate the spread of the virus, but in some circumstances they may also pave the way for increasing social control and authoritarian measures, even in democratic regimes.

Permanent surveillance (from the most classic forms to digital tracking and drones), the control and handling of big data, new facial recognition devices and other sophisticated forms of social control were not just strengthened to fight a virus. Power-concentration measures adopted to fight COVID-19 may even be necessary to enable public healthcare and the 'protection' of the population, however there is a very tenuous line between these and authoritarian practices. Over the last decade, we have witnessed the emergence and strengthening of populist leaders and authoritarian governments that have put hatred, nationalism, regressive agendas and the militarization of life at the centre of the world's political agenda. In the face of the pandemic, they have not taken a step back, but in most cases have become more radical. At the same time, they have also been challenged, since the virus cannot be reduced to a simple flu as Donald Trump or Jair Bolsonaro suggested, nor can it be encapsulated in fake news.

The pandemic has therefore revealed not only the strengths but also the limitations of states and national political systems. The inefficiency of a national government or the repeated stances of state leaders mocking the pandemic and science have resulted in hundreds or thousands of additional deaths. Despite countless warnings, most governments failed to assess the size of the pandemic in time and to provide basic sanitary protections to public health workers and the overall population. In the face of the health crisis, each government has established its own necropolitics. They have provided fewer opportunities for some people to cope with the virus than others. Even in the cases of those who say that every life matters, we see people dying on the periphery, in their homes or in nursing homes, sometimes without even appearing in the national statistics.

State responses have been diverse. In some cases authoritarian state capitalism and repression prevailed. In others the pandemic has opened paths to defend the social face of the welfare state and to propose to extend social protection, as our authors argue. Much of the analysis of states' management of the crisis seeks to highlight cases of 'success' and 'failure'. The main variable is the containment of cases of infection and deaths. Some strategies have been more successful than others in containing the spread of the virus. Denialism allied with incompetence (on these matters, it is difficult to beat Bolsonaro and Trump) has led to human disasters in both the Global North and Global South. We should not forget, however, that for dependent states on the global periphery or semi-periphery, confronting the pandemic is even more challenging. Public health systems are weak or practically non-existent, the right to water undermined, state capacity limited and housing in the urban peripheries precarious and overcrowded, as the second part of our book shows.

Crisis, inequalities and solidarities

The virus can affect every human being. However, the pandemic affects us at very different levels, and the way the virus is treated is closely related to social factors. COVID-19 exacerbates inequalities between countries and within society, notably when it comes to class, race and gender. In the second part of this book, social scientists highlight these inequalities, the multiple impacts of COVID-19 in different realms of social life and also the emergence of solidarity networks in this difficult context.

On all continents, minorities and impoverished sectors have been much more affected by the virus. Many governments, along with the World Health Organization, have tried to differentiate between the existing data on infection and death by age, place and gender. The concentration of cases in peripheral places–strongly racialized and with a concentration of people with low revenues–unveils the social and particularly unfair reality of the pandemic. The older population is usually referred to as the most vulnerable, but it is rarely said that being Black in Brazil or African American in the United States means belonging to a 'population at risk'. In fact, in the United States, several studies have estimated that Latinos and Asians are 1.5 times more likely to be affected and to die from the virus than White people, while in the case of African Americans the chances are twice as high.

Therefore, an intersectional perspective is crucial to understanding how the crisis is experienced in places that remain largely invisible and forgotten in government policies to tackle the virus. Social systems of discrimination, oppression and domination have to be studied with both objective data of the pandemic and with subjective experiences of the multidimensional crisis. Authors in Part II provide accounts of life during the pandemic in the favelas of Rio, working-class neighbourhoods in Latin America and disadvantaged communities in India, as well as of minorities in the United

States and homeless people in Belgium. They show us that the pandemic is unfair and actually widens the gap of social inequalities, generating new forms of poverty (such as the 'data poverty', discussed in Chapter 9 of this section), invisibility and segregation.

Targeting growing inequalities is crucial to unveiling the centrality of the social dimensions of the crisis and for setting policies that can minimize its impacts on those who struggle to cope with the rent or have fallen below the poverty line and whose concern is to get a daily meal. Proactive policies have also proliferated during the pandemic, such as solidarity-based taxation policies like taxes on inheritance, large fortunes and megaprojects, or social aid policies such as universal basic income to try to remedy extreme poverty and the adversities of the crisis. These and other proposals, such as those that seek to advance change in an absolutely unjust agro-food system and to foster food sovereignty, result from the combination of social movements and social science advocacy work.

Social movements, mutual aid and self-reliance during the pandemic

Social movements build or strengthen solidarity, resilience and resistance in communities, popular neighbourhoods and cities. In many cases, this has been boosted by pre-existing groups and movements. Other social movements have underlined the centrality of environmental and climate justice in coping with the pandemic, as well as supporting and developing networks linked to the solidarity economy and agro-ecology, which insist on the need to radically change and relocate the economy and the food system. Feminist movements have also played a key role in placing care at the centre of life and putting it at the core of sociopolitical agendas after unveiling the unequal distribution of care tasks during the pandemic.

On the other hand, conservative and reactionary movements have also been very active during the lockdown and beyond, as some of the chapters of this section argue. Racism has increased in all regions of the world since the beginning of the pandemic, targeting migrant workers in India and China and African Americans and Asian Americans in the United States, and throughout the world refugees, minorities and poor people have been accused of spreading the pandemic by not maintaining physical isolation. Conspiracy theories have spread through social media, resulting in an unprecedented 'infodemic'. Far-right activists attack migrant workers or slum dwellers for allegedly spreading the virus. Counter-movements have protested in various parts of the world against physical isolation policies, even when the pandemic was at its peak. In the United States, there were demonstrations, supported by Trump, against the closure of businesses in most state capitals. In Brazil, President Bolsonaro not only encouraged, but also participated in protests against health measures imposed by state governors.

In Germany, the group of protesters included anti-vaccine, anti-Semitic and ultra-liberal activists who framed the lockdown as the first step in an alleged 'coup' instigated by Angela Merkel.

Finally, the health crisis and restrictions on mobility have accentuated the digitization of many aspects of our daily lives, from friendship to work and forms of protest. While digital activism had already become an increasingly important component of social movements in the last two decades, the pandemic has increased the digitization of social movements and protests. It has played an important role in fostering collective actions and organizing. The mass diffusion of smartphones has made social media a crucial tool for neighbourhood solidarity. Although digital networks are impregnated with fake news, they also offer a space for disseminating alternative analyses and counter-information on practices that are deeply territorialized. In this way, even in times of pandemic, it is important to consider *online* activism in its interweaving with the experiences of activists, constructed sociabilities and the *offline* dimensions of mutual aid projects.

In sum, the authors of this book's third section examine the reconfiguration of the social movement landscape, the transformative possibilities and limits of social movements in the face of the multidimensional crisis and the contemporary fragmented social life. A wide range of cases are discussed, ranging from neighbourhoods and communities in the Global North and in the Global South, from Canada to India, from the COVID-19 mutual aid networks in British neighbourhoods to new alliances among grassroots movements and NGOs in South Africa and the resilience and resistance practices in New York City.

'COVID-19 will not kill the revolution': Protest movements in the pandemic

The COVID-19 outbreak has interrupted a historic worldwide wave of citizen mobilizations. Since the beginning of 2019, weekly protests had invaded the streets of towns and capital cities around the world, as was the case with the *Hirak* movement in Algeria and the yellow vests in France, and pro-democracy demonstrations in Hong Kong reached global news headlines. Iraqi youth also occupied squares and streets every week to demand work opportunities and more democracy, and brave people from Sudan put an end to a fierce dictatorship. Lebanese protestors demanded the end of a corrupt confessional political system. In Latin America and the Caribbean, massive popular protests took place in Bolivia, Colombia, Ecuador, Haiti, Peru, Puerto Rico, Nicaragua and, mainly, in Chile against neoliberalism and inequality.

The pandemic and measures of physical distancing and confinement put a halt to these weekly protests. However, as the authors of the fourth part of the book show, protests and grassroots activism in a broad sense have continued in Lebanon, France, Chile and many other countries. In most cases, and particularly in Hong Kong, the Philippines and France, these mobilizations faced the increasing repression of the state. In the Philippines and in Colombia, it has had deadly consequences, with a rising number of extrajudicial killings that notably target activists. In Hong Kong and in the Arab world, the repression and state social control has managed to crush the revolt of broad popular movements.

Even under authoritarian reprisals by governments, many popular movements and activists have reached the conclusion that 'sexism and racism kill more than the virus'. Protest and revolt have spread through some catalytic events, even at unlikely times such as during a pandemic. This was the case with the brutal murder of an African American man, George Floyd, by a White policeman in Minneapolis, on 25 May 2020. This triggered a cycle of anti-racist protests in the United States unprecedented since the civil rights struggles, impacting the entire world.

It is still too early to assess the nature of a new global protest cycle after the pandemic. At this stage, it's important to understand the connection between movements unleashed before the health crisis and their continuities, discontinuities and innovations with the protest and solidarity dynamic that has emerged in the pandemic. While the pandemic has deactivated in some places and countries the most visible forms of protest, it has not extinguished the claims and the will that moved these demonstrations and which begin to be combined with new agendas and social forces.

Critical thinking and emerging theoretical challenges

The need to rethink the meaning and the paths of emancipation in the 21st century, as well as how we understand the main risks and threats, our vulnerabilities and resilience capacity, represents a crucial challenge for social sciences and critical thinking. In other words, the pandemic has unveiled a fertile ground for crucial issues that need to be addressed, and deepens the ongoing renewal of theoretical debates that has taken place in the last decades.

On one side, the intellectual 'confinement' of provincial perspectives helps little. It reproduces exogenous and often colonial and Eurocentric visions. For example, the pandemic has unleashed a broad debate around the notion and experience of 'risk'. However, what is often presented as a 'global risk' in the intellectual debate is the construction (as global and universal) of a particular conception of risk in Western societies, impregnated with local imaginaries of 'normality'. Moreover, the 'normality' of some has always implied the crisis of others. The security of some is often acquired at the expenses of the insecurity of others. In other words, risk in the Western world has been constructed under an elitist and restricted illusion that protects some while excluding others.

On the other side, beyond diagnosis and denunciation, the critical voices that allow us to understand the multidimensional crisis need to place themselves in a permanent dialogue with emancipatory movements and actors, accompanying actively and permanently the actors of resistance. On this basis, it is the challenge and responsibility of contemporary critical thinking to advance in this field, but also to seek multiple articulations of theoretical-political constellations and new forms of a *collective praxis*, of the relationship between theory and practice. Critical thinking has often remained tied to specific political conceptions, closing itself sometimes in a dogmatic way. It is crucial to maintain its independence, as well as its permanent connection with the concrete problems faced by people and popular movements.

The fifth part of the book gathers contributions from a wide range of critical perspectives, from sociological theory to political philosophy. The reader will have access in this section of the book to several theoretical and often abstract proposals, that whare not disconnected from some of the main contemporary societal challenges. In some chapters, the main focus is on the tensions between the individual and collectivity and on the intersections between scales. In others, the emancipation horizon is discussed together with social regulation as a form of domination. In any case, we make no definitive statements but rather put forward theoretical proposals that seek to reformulate questions and consolidate assumptions by accepting uncertainty honestly, but also courageously.

The paradigm of the gift, for example, has found new resonance as a counterweight to a world that praises competition and short-term profits. Feminist activists and intellectuals have provided key concepts and tools with which to analyse the current crisis and alternative futures by placing care and intersectionality at the core of critical thinking, worldviews and concrete alternatives. The battle for a better, greener and less unequal world, capable of combining redistributive justice with environmental, ethnic and gender justice, is a long shot. The pandemic has opened new paths for critical perspectives, and strengthened existing ones. The following section of the book deepens this discussion by examining some of the disputed scenarios that emerge with the pandemic.

Post-pandemic transitions and futures in contention

As a global crisis of unexpected consequence and dimension, the COVID-19 pandemic has opened up new horizons of possibility. It has been seized upon as an opportunity to reshape the world in a different way. Claims and imaginaries that had little space before the pandemic have gained visibility.

Activists and public intellectuals have emphasized the need for a fairer world that is attentive to human rights, care and community, as well as stronger public health systems. This is the backdrop for the sixth and final part of the book, which focuses on disputes over the future.

Interpreting the current critical moment as a step in a broader civilizational crisis opens the way to a very different perspective from the repeated discourses that invite us to come back to 'normality'. The pandemic questions our relation to nature and acts as a reminder of the urgency to change our economic, social and political systems if we want to put a halt to the destruction of nature. An increasing number of communities, movements and intellectuals put a global ecological perspective at the core of their worldview and of their understanding of this multidimensional crisis. The deep connection between the political and ecological crises requires us to understand the world in a different, more integrated way in order to respond to different individual and collective priorities.

As much as we highlight critical voices, the way the pandemic has been handled so far has privileged competition over solidarity both in society and among nations. The richest are even richer and stronger for the crisis. Instead of greater solidarity at national and international levels, the pandemic may lead individuals and states to prioritize the protection of their own community over the common good. Beyond opening new horizons and trying to challenge the dominant meanings of the crisis, mobilizations, advocacy and global political articulation are required. Unveiling the interests behind the political-economic project of the 'new normal' is the first challenge of social movements and committed intellectuals.

Grasping the tensions and disputes, the glimpses of the possible scenarios and blind spots, is a crucial mission. We maintain that the attention paid to concrete actors and local emancipatory projects should not be incompatible with a global perspective. Hence, this last part of the volume, and the book as a whole, is an invitation to an open intercultural dialogue and to revisit different intellectual and political traditions in the light of the multi-dimensional crisis generated by the pandemic.

Acknowledgements and platforms for a global dialogue

The seeds of this book emerged with the Open Movements editorial project that started in 2015 as a collaboration between the International Sociological Association Research Committee on Social Classes and Social Movements (ISA RC-47) and Open Democracy. We have published more than 250 articles by authors from all regions of the world, animated by a will to 'open' the debate on social movements in five different directions: towards societal changes; towards dialogue with the South; towards the combination of scales and levels of analysis in forging a global sociology; towards learning and acting with and from movements; and towards public sociology.

Initial versions of some articles included in this book were previously published by Open Movements. Most have been updated and developed for this book. Other chapters have been written specifically for it. All the authors were asked for short and direct analyses, written in a language accessible to a wide audience, in which they could synthesize their arguments and research. Their contributions are based on qualitative research and rooted in concrete realities and experience on different continents. They provide us with tools to understand the crisis and the challenges it raises.

We are very grateful to our extraordinary and committed editor in the Open Movements project, Rosemary Bechler, for all her support, as well as to Francesc Badia for his kindness and permanent collaboration with Democracia Abierta. Margot Achard was decisive in the logistical support of this complex editorial project, which involved so many authors in three languages. In this regard, Adriana Santos, as always, contributed with her insightful and lively translation of some pieces. This book also resulted from an increasing collaboration dynamic between the International Sociological Association (ISA), the Latin American Sociological Association (ALAS) and the Latin American Council of Social Sciences (CLACSO), which made possible the publication, in September 2020, of a previous and slightly different version of the book in Spanish under the title *Alerta Global*. We thank Sari Hanafi, Jaime Ríos Burga and Karina Batthyány, the highest authorities of these institutions, for their support, and Nicolás Arata, Pablo Vommaro and María Fernanda Pampín for their crucial role in bringing this project to a successful conclusion.

Last but not least, we would like to thank Shannon Kneis, Bahar Celik Muller, Rich Kemp, Dawn Preston and the team at Bristol University Press (BUP) for their support and enthusiasm for this book. The editors and many authors of this book have also suffered and been affected, in different ways, by the pandemic. This unfortunately slowed down the book production process. Even in the face of so many adversities, the BUP team was always very understanding and sensitive to us. We really appreciate that attitude.

The path towards a fairer way to manage the pandemic and the multidimensional crisis it has triggered requires fostering global dialogues among scholars, intellectuals, political actors, activists and citizens. Building this global perspective is not only a matter of adding a few countries in the list of authors and readings. We need to actively promote the circulation of knowledge and debate of ideas and proposals and build in experience and analyses rooted in different regions of the world. If this book may contribute to this global dialogue, the credit goes mainly to the colleagues who so kindly provided their articles and analyses.

PART I

COVID-19 Governance, Politics and the Ambivalence of States

COVID-19 Governance: State Expansion, Capitalist Resilience and Democracy

Pauli Huotari and Teivo Teivainen

COVID-19 governance is a new field of power that articulates attempts by states and other institutions to control the pandemic crisis. Within the European Union, it includes a bigger role for central banks and suppression of democratic rights and freedoms in various forms, including tightening external and internal border controls. Finland, where we are based, has had one of the most leftist governments in the European Union and imposed some of the strictest border controls of all the member states during the first months of COVID-19 governance.

What does the sudden expansion in state-led governance mean for democratic visions and practices? Our main interest is on horizons that could radicalize democracy, the possibility for the people to take equal part in decisions that concern the basic conditions of their lives. On the one hand, radicalized democracy refers to attempts to bring economic institutions such as capitalist corporations and central banks under greater democratic control. These attempts typically rely on an understanding of democracy that regards parliaments and other democratically elected authorities – and sometimes also popular initiatives or referenda – as the most legitimate source of accountability. At least initially, the effects of the COVID-19 on democracy (in the conventional parliamentary sense) might not be very significant (Rapeli and Saikkonen, 2020).

On the other hand, according to less state-centric understandings, radicalized democracy also includes democratic practices in more autonomous spheres of social life, sometimes characterized by the anarchist tradition of mutual aid. In other words, democracy can be radicalized by expanding its current institutional forms to areas dominated by other logics of power or, alternatively, by creating new social spaces according to democratic principles. If radicalized democracy is also defined to include extension of freedom, we can count in policies that help increase civic autonomy. Such policies can include universal basic income and reduction of working hours.

Resilience of capitalism

There are reasons to be sceptical of the democratic possibilities opened by COVID-19 governance. As argued by Naomi Klein already in *The Shock Doctrine* (2007), the opportunities of sudden crises are often seized by the capitalists and other elites. During the COVID-19 crisis this has meant, for example, what Robert Brenner (2020) calls escalating plunder. Corporate bailouts in the US have outnumbered financial relief provided for ordinary citizens. This has happened in spite of the widespread dissatisfaction with how the 2008 financial crisis was handled with no-strings-attached corporate bailouts. After the first shock of COVID-19, capitalism has demonstrated remarkable resilience in the crisis.

Capitalist accumulation often demands depoliticized predictability, which can be provided by various means including investment protection clauses and strict mandates for economic and monetary policy. Predictability can also be provided by formally authoritarian regimes such as China. During the pandemic, the Chinese government has managed to tame the spreading of the virus quite efficiently, even if it has also been faced with increased world political tensions especially vis-à-vis the United States. The efficiency may provide new reasons for an increasing resilience of capitalism in authoritarian political forms.

Also within what is conventionally called *creative destruction*, now in a disaster-driven form that has led to bankruptcy of many small and medium-sized firms, there exists a tendency towards more centralized economic regimes. The dominance of various platform-based tech corporations has become stronger. In theory, this could make their power more visible in ways that makes their political role more evident and could lead to public demands to democratize corporate power. In practice, market-distorting and other effects of these companies had been a growing concern already, but we have seen little evidence that the mainstream public debates about the COVID-19 crisis have significantly deepened this concern.

Nevertheless, a shock caused by a pandemic may also allow previously marginalized ideas to enter the public discourse. This has happened in the past as well. For example, during the 'mad cow disease' outbreak some demands external to the elite discourse managed to temporarily enter the political arena. These included public health and consumer protection demands

(Aaltola, 1999). Long-term effects, however, were limited, as shown by the apparent lack of preparedness for the new pandemic.

There have been changes in the public discourse this time as well. The most radical attempts to redefine where we are and which way we ought to go have appeared, as usual, in writing, but there have been concrete policy changes and social reorganizing as well. Most visibly, national budgets suddenly became more flexible and provided new policy space for Keynesian-inspired arguments to increase state intervention to mitigate the shock. Especially in Europe, but also elsewhere, central banks have become increasingly important facilitators for the new role of the state. There is also at least some evidence that this has opened new debates about the political role of central banks and a renewed focus on their lack of democratic accountability.

Politicization of central-bank capitalism

COVID-19 governance has amplified what the Finnish economist Jussi Ahokas (2019) and others have called central-bank capitalism. The role of central banks had been growing already before the current crisis, especially since the financial crash of 2008. Under the European COVID-19 governance, markets have been increasingly considered too weak to maintain sufficient aggregate demand, and central banks have been injecting liquidity into the markets in an unprecedented volume. The European Central Bank (ECB) was already operating in ways that were arguably reaching the limits of its mandate. COVID-19 governance is taking this to a next level. The legality of ECB's actions has been challenged on several accounts.

The fiscal capacities of the individual eurozone countries are restricted due to a lack of monetary sovereignty, which complicates deficit spending needed in the pandemic crisis. Direct monetary financing would be against the mandate of the ECB. In fact, the current institutional framework of the EU may play into the pockets of wealthy asset owners and the rentier class, because active fiscal policies have mostly been substituted with monetary easing that benefits them (Seccareccia, 2017; Montecino and Epstein, 2015). There are technical suggestions that could allow bending the existing monetary policy rules. Examples include debt conversion as well as minting coins of very high nominal value and depositing them to central bank accounts.

There have also been similar debates on whether the Bank of England has been engaging in direct monetary financing of the government to cover some immediate costs of the COVID-19 crisis, which would be a dramatic shift in central bank policy. In the United States, the Federal Reserve announced it would give more attention to its mandate to promote full employment, apart from the inflation target. Even if the ECB is institutionally more clearly focused on price stability, its mandate also permits other goals, such as maintaining employment levels, as long as the primary goal is not compromised (Sanbu, 2020).

Compared to the power of big corporations, the role of central banks has become more openly politicized during the COVID-19 crisis. One of the main justifications for shielding central banking, especially in Europe, from mechanisms of democratic governance has been their mandated independence from the changing preferences of elected politicians, based mostly on their assumed propensity to irresponsible behaviour if their policies are subject to preferences of elected politicians (Teivainen, 1997). It is possible that the politicization of central banks may lead to demands for new institutional arrangements that would make them formally more accountable to established forms of democracy, at least in the limited sense that existed in the EU before the creation of the ECB.

For the emergence of more comprehensive supranational democratic governance in the EU, one thorny question has been the difficulty of creating mechanisms to share responsibilities for debts. During the first months of the COVID-19 crisis, Southern European governments were asking for such mechanisms, but in the EU North the governments of Austria, Denmark, Sweden, the Netherlands and Finland were reluctant to assume such expressions of solidarity. In these countries, the recovery programme agreed upon in August 2020 was often perceived to benefit the Southern member states. . Actually, it may also further increase inequalities within the EU by, for example, adding to the debts of already more indebted southern member states (Wahl and Dräger, 2020). Especially in Sweden and Finland, with Social Democratic prime ministers, the lack of substantial solidarity of the governments with the EU South demonstrated the weakness of party-socialist internationalism in times of crisis.

As there are few short-term prospects for a stronger European Union based on democratic values, many have deposited their hopes in the possibility that the crisis would force national governments to assume increasingly active financial policies. This would require extending the fiscal capacities of governments, which in itself would not necessarily mean radically more democratic governance even if it could open new democratic possibilities.

The installation of more democratic principles of public finance faces many kinds of institutional obstacles. The rules of public finance will play a significant role in the aftermath of the crisis, somewhat analogous with the rebuilding of societies after wars. Although this pandemic will not leave behind destroyed physical infrastructure, it will probably lead to massive unemployment. Some suggest that a publicly funded green rebuilding of societies could be the answer, and, for example, South Korea has significantly increased its Green New Deal commitments. In many parts of the Global South, however, neocolonial shackles may prevent these kinds of policies

(Lenferna, 2020). In the eurozone, there are rules that need to be transgressed to enable substantial funding of green rebuilding policies.

State-facilitated expansion of civic autonomy

The democratic implications of the recent expansion of state regulation are ambiguous. The non-democratic power of many big corporations has been boosted, especially but not only in the sphere of platform capitalism, and democratically unaccountable central banks have become more important. Yet, states have also carried out policies that have the potential to increase the autonomy of the people. These include basic-income schemes.

One motivation for temporary basic-income-type policies has been to alleviate suffering and boost consumer demand in ways that prevent significant challenges to governmental and capitalist power. In the US during the electoral year of 2020, various kinds of relatively unconditional relief checks have been delivered to people. For a country enjoying a significant degree of monetary sovereignty, it has not presented a major financial problem. In Spain, facing more financial constraints, the government said at the beginning of the crisis that it would implement a basic-income programme as soon as possible. In June 2020, Spain started a basic-income-like experiment, including around 850,000 poor households in the country (Arnold, 2020). In the Republic of Korea, different basic-income schemes have appeared, and during the pandemic some money was directly handed out for citizens. In the Korean province of Gyeonggi, the local government has been experimenting with a local-currency-based basic income to support local businesses (Hyun-ju, 2020).

There is no guarantee that such exceptional practices will result in long-term transformation, but the crisis can make more radical demands more socially acceptable. One new justification for more permanent basic-income schemes is that they could help prevent contagion in future pandemics, since people could stay home more easily. There are several previous motivations for basic-income policies. It makes a difference whether the focus is on boosting employment, supporting the poor or increasing labour's bargaining power. Even if unconditional monetary income may help people depend less on exploitative labour relations as workers, they can also tie people more deeply into commodifying markets as consumers. For this reason, some prefer expansion of universal basic services and job-guarantee-type policies.

These approaches, however, are not necessarily as mutually exclusive as it is often assumed. We need more debate on the goals of policies such as expansion of universal basic services, democratic creation of work and basic income. Especially where the scarcity is clearly artificial or easily overcome, expansion of public services might be the most equitable solution. Furthermore, it is more efficient to share resources than for everyone to use their basic income to acquire, for example, their own books or tools. In any case, the experiments triggered by the crisis can provide useful experiences for establishing democracy-enhancing combinations of these approaches.

Apart from financial empowerment of citizens through basic income or other mechanisms, state policies can increase freedom in other ways as well. One example is the Finnish prime minister Sanna Marin's recent proposal to explore the possibility of a six-hour work day. Although a shorter work day is a long-standing demand of the left and not directly connected to the COVID-19 crisis, one of Marin's justifications for reproposing it was that COVID-19 times had made people think about what is important in life. Not likely to be realized soon, her proposal is one example of how cracks in the present are brought into the language of governmental party politics.

The crisis has also made visible some collective demands of historically marginalized people. Examples from the first months of the pandemic include how rough sleepers in London were accommodated by public authorities in empty hotel rooms once they were deemed to pose a health threat to other residents in their neighbourhoods. In Portugal, many paperless people have been given temporary citizenship rights for similar reasons. Both of these actions can be considered to enhance democracy in the sense of equality and freedom. There is little evidence that these policies will endure, but they provide new reference points that might make similar and more enduring practices more feasible in the future.

Autonomous organizing in pandemic times

Apart from the incipient democratic possibilities brought about through state regulation, the crisis has also triggered more autonomous non-state forms of collective organization. These are often based on prefigurative principles according to which the creation of a democratic society is inherent in the organizing process (Teivainen, 2017). Some of these experiments trigger bigger movements, others remain local or fade away.

The Finnish Social Forum, taking place annually since 2002, was for the first time organized online in 2020. While especially some of the older participants expressed difficulties communicating through new platforms, the organizers noted that there was more participation by some distant communities that had not been previously able to travel to the capital city for the event. Also, for the first time ever, the International Council of the World Social Forum had a comprehensive meeting with national, regional and thematic social forums in September 2020. Overall, pandemic restrictions on physical travel have energized communication between social-forum activists in various parts of the world. In online debates, there has also been new enthusiasm to renew the organizational structures of the World Social Forum process that have been in decline over many years.

Mutual aid, emphasized historically by many anarchists, has become concrete in many localities. The term itself has become more widely used outside of anarchist activism (Graeber and Grubacic, forthcoming). There are examples of pandemic solidarity all over the globe (Sitrin and Colectiva Sembrar, 2020). Especially in the beginning of the crisis, newly founded mutual aid groups were coming up with ways to help people in their neighbourhoods. As pointed out by Geoffrey Pleyers (2020), neighbours do not always join these groups with a political or activist purpose. A Facebook group in Helsinki expressed its purpose as linking 'those in quarantine, the sick, and the vulnerable with community members near them who can run errands and deliver necessary supplies (or whatever needed)'. It remains to be seen to what extent this kind of organizing could develop into more enduring forms of non-state political community-building.

While people have been furloughed in big numbers and others have been working from home, some people have had more time to get involved in community action (Tiratelli and Kaye, 2020). Divisions of race, class and gender mean that not all have the same possibilities. Basic-income schemes could enable more equal conditions for such involvement, in times of crisis and beyond. As we have noted, basic-income proposals have various limitations, but they may open new possibilities for practice and political theory in which reformist public policies could be articulated with more radical and autonomous democratic organizing.

Politicization of economy and (radicalization of) democracy

In times of crisis, it is often easy to overestimate the prospects for long-term radical changes. At the turn of the millennium, it seemed that the power of international economic institutions entered into a serious crisis of legitimacy as they were challenged by social movements and even some media in various parts of the world. After a few years, the challenge seemed to fade away. In 2008, the financial crisis led to fears and hopes that the global financial architecture would be reorganized. In many ways, things soon went back to normal, even if Keynesian economic ideas gained more permanent presence. What about this time?

Hopes and fears about changing the structures of governance, and the structures themselves, have various short-term cyclical features. There is, however, one issue that has steadily increased its importance in the way the world functions and the way the public becomes aware of it. Climate change is not going away and the climate movement is constantly gaining more attention. The COVID-19 crisis is yet another example of how environmental questions are getting increasingly entangled with other crises. Ideas such as the Green New Deal have received more attention during the crisis, in Finland also among the trade unions. The economic rescue packages of the EU have even had conditionalities related to climate targets. On the other hand, the desire to get back to (the imagined) business as usual is likely to be used as an argument to emphasize more immediate material needs over climate concerns. Be that as it may, climate change is likely to be a constantly growing politicizing issue.

Within the limits we have pointed out, COVID-19 governance challenges some of the depoliticizing assumptions about capitalism. In the EU, various forms of heterodox economic rethinking got boosted by the 2008 crisis and have been made more visible by the escalating climate crisis. In the COVID-19 crisis, the political nature of capitalist economy and technocratic governance has become more evident, even if only partially. Politicization of central bank power might be easier than politicization of corporate power, also because part of the intellectual right is critical of central banks as well, although democratization is obviously not on their agenda. According to this critique, central banks are distorting market signals and efficient allocation of capital. On the other hand, business elites realize that they cannot survive the crisis without states and central banks. The suddenly increased political role of the state helps reveal the dependence of capitalism on politically maintained stability.

Possibilities of radicalized democracy lie in the politicization of what is deemed normal. Politicization can be understood as bringing options to the table. COVID-19 governance has meant the rethinking of social and managerial practices. Arguably, many options might be just patch solutions. Nevertheless, politicization is a precondition for a radicalized democracy. It opens room for various kinds of democratizing practices, even if it does not guarantee their successful outcome.

References

Aaltola, M. (1999) *The Rhythm, Exception, and Rule in International Relations: The Case of Mad Cow Disease*, Doctoral dissertation, University of Tampere, Tampere.

Ahokas, J. (2019) 'Kapitalismin muodot ja institutionaalinen muutos – Kohti keskuspankkikapitalismia', *Politiikasta*, [online] 8 August, available from: https://politiikasta.fi/kapitalismin-muodot-ja-institutionaalinen-muutos-kohti-keskuspankkikapitalismia/

Arnold, C. (2020) 'Pandemic speeds largest test yet of universal basic income', *Nature*, 10 July.

Brenner, R. (2020) 'Escalating plunder', *New Left Review*, 123, [online] May/June, available from: https://newleftreview.org/issues/II123/articles/robert-brenner-escalating-plunder

Graeber, D. and Andrej, G. (forthcoming) 'Introduction', in P. Kropotkin (ed) *Mutual Aid: An Illuminated Factor of Evolution*, Oakland, CA: PM Press.

Hyun-ju, O. (2020) 'Gyeonggi Province sets example for universal basic income', *The Korea Herald*, [online] 11 August, available from: http://www.koreaherald.com/view.php?ud=20200811000938

Klein, N. (2007) *The Shock Doctrine: The Rise of Disaster Capitalism*, Toronto: A.A. Knopf.

Lenferna, A. (2020) 'The solution to the coronavirus recession is a global green new deal', *Jacobin*, 17 April.

Montecino, J.A. and Epstein, G. (2015) 'Did quantitative easing increase income inequality?', Political Economy Research Institute, University of Massachusetts Amherst, Working Paper Series, No. 407.

Pleyers, G. (2020) 'The pandemic is a battlefield: Social movements in the COVID-19 lockdown', *Journal of Civil Society*, 16(4): 295–312.

Rapeli, L. and Saikkonen, I. (2020) 'How will the COVID-19 pandemic affect democracy?', *Democratic Theory*, 7(2): 25–32.

Sanbu, M. (2020) 'ECB must follow the Fed's embrace of a second mandate', *Financial Times*, [online] 31 August, available from: https://www.ft.com/content/380e6290-ded1-4050-aa5f-9c3d1b9ed2bd

Seccareccia, M. (2017) 'Which vested interests do central banks really serve? Understanding central bank policy since the global financial crisis', *Journal of Economic Issues*, 51(2): 341–50.

Sitrin, M. and Sembrar, C. (2020) *Pandemic Solidarity: Mutual Aid during the COVID-19 Crisis*, London: Pluto Press.

Teivainen, T. (1997) 'The independence of the European Central Bank: Implications for democratic governance, in P. Minkkinen and H. Patomäki (eds) *Politics of Economic and Monetary Union*, Dordrecht: Kluwer Academic Publishers, 54–74.

Teivainen, T. (2017) 'Occupy representation and democratize prefiguration: Speaking for others in global justice movements', *Capital & Class*, 40: 19–36.

Tiratelli, L. and Simon Kay, S. (2020) *Communities vs. Coronavirus: The Rise of Mutual Aid*, London: New Local Government Network.

Wahl, P. and Dräger, K. (2020) 'Europe's coronavirus recovery program will make it even more unequal', *Jacobin*, [online] 9 June, available from: https://www.jacobinmag.com/2020/09/european-union-coronavirus-recovery-program

2

Three Political Regimes, Three Responses to the COVID-19 Crisis

Jean De Munck
(Translated by Lee Gilette)

How are we to manage the pandemic? What will happen in its wake? Some believe the COVID-19 crisis will lead spontaneously to a virtuous awareness of the dead ends of anarchic globalization. They dream of an end to the crisis which will also be, in one fell swoop, the end of deregulated capitalism.

Such optimism is dubious. No end to capitalism is on the horizon. Meanwhile, and unfortunately, authoritarian and populist political tendencies are immune to COVID-19. There is no single automatic, rational political outcome inherent to this crisis. Democracies will be severely tested, not only by the health crisis but also by the economic crisis to come.

When it comes to crises, Europe has ample experience. After 1945, Europe responded with a model of practical synergy between the state and capitalism. The welfare state's architecture, boldly rebuilt, can inspire a unique response to the current crisis. The economist Eloi Laurent is right when he says, 'The most useful lesson of the beginning of this crisis is also the most universal: the welfare state is the strategic institution for the 21st century'.[1] But two dominant models challenge the welfare state today: the authoritarian state capitalist model and the right-wing populist model. They shape the policies responding to the COVID-19 crisis.

Response 1: Authoritarian state capitalism

Authoritarian state capitalism combines an authoritarian, centralized mode of government with aggressive capitalism. China and Russia are the obvious examples.

In response to the COVID-19 crisis, these countries are tightening control over public space, silencing dissenting voices and imposing authoritarian measures.[2] The crisis has made it possible for them to expand and perfect extremely intrusive electronic surveillance systems, including facial recognition. The state apparatus is centralized, bureaucratic and supported by a loyal army. Against COVID-19, these states, unlike democracies, don't have to improvise a 'state of emergency' because that's how they rule all the time. As demonstrated by the case of China, brutally managing the health crisis is particularly useful in generating regime propaganda.

Direct control over civil society is a legacy of 20th-century totalitarian regimes. The ideological state apparatus impels citizens to suffer their fate silently, and controls daily life according to the imperatives of order and productivity. State capitalism goes to great lengths to seize world market shares, especially in niches pried open by the health crisis (masks and drugs, for example). Such regimes intend to take advantage of the looming economic crisis as a means to extend their influence over global institutions, competing with Westerners at their own game: accumulating capital.

Response 2: Right-wing populism

Right-wing populism emerged after 2008 and has become established since the electoral victories of Trump in the United States in 2016 and Bolsonaro in Brazil in 2018 (De Munck, 2018). In this model, the relationship between the state and capitalism is reconstructed around reaffirming the state's role (which clearly distinguishes this model from neoliberalism). The state remains formally democratic but assumes a fierce, authoritarian attitude. The ruling bloc aggressively takes over the public media space, in part by incessant scapegoating. It transforms elections into popular plebiscites for programmes centred on the defence of sovereignty against internal and external enemies.

However, unlike the first model, this type of government doesn't seek to control civil society directly. It doesn't deploy an omnicompetent administration – on the contrary, it destroys the government's public services expertise and capacity for action and instead seeks to allow *companies* to take full control of society. Thus this autocratically inclined state supports, according to a seeming paradox, economic, health, educational, social and environmental deregulation on a massive scale. It doesn't seek to control or replace private-sector leaders but rather to promote them and allow them to operate freely throughout all levels of society.

Like the first model, the second can flourish and expand during the COVID-19 crisis. The state goes all in on policies of tight borders and police management of public security. The crisis is the perfect opportunity to re-advertise the 'wall', which supposedly stops migrants and the virus along with them. While systematically denigrating experts and intellectuals, the government saturates media with chaotic, aggressive speeches. Meanwhile, the pandemic is an opportunity to eliminate regulations (labour, environmental, tax) supposedly unkind to business.

Thus we'll see the kind of policy observed after hurricanes Katrina in 2005 and Harvey in 2017 in the United States. Naomi Klein (2007) calls it 'shock doctrine': transforming disasters into opportunities to reinforce capitalism. For example, the US 'corona stimulus bill' (March 2020) didn't aim to launch a new nationally managed healthcare and prevention programme. In fact, it has been devastating for American workers and (what remains of) social security while being extremely business-friendly. At the same time, Trump White House suspended all environmental regulations on its territory, for an indefinite period. It's taking advantage of the crisis to impose pro-free market solutions, which in normal circumstances can't be imposed.[3]

A Western European response: a mixed model?

Erdogan's Turkey represents an interesting mix of the two models. The dictator inherited a totalitarian state apparatus, which inclined him towards the first model, but adopted a political style that clearly goes in the other direction. In Europe, meanwhile, the second model seduces the Polish, Hungarian, English and Israeli elites, and attracts extreme-right parties in Flanders, France and Italy.

The current fortunes of both models testify to the fact that it's simply no longer possible to continue shrinking the state, as neoliberalism tried to do from 1990 to 2016. Both models reinvest the state's power, not to move beyond capitalism but to save it, at the expense of fundamental freedoms, social justice and public deliberation.

A third model is available, however. The welfare state was born in Europe out of the great social crisis caused by industrialization, and was institutionalized after the total disaster of the Second World War. It tries to preserve the rational core of each of the irrational formulas. From the authoritarian state model, the welfare state borrows the idea that the response to dysfunction and crises requires the intervention of a strong (but legitimate) state with powers that penetrate civil society. It mitigates this by embracing the rule of law. An interventionist state is not necessarily anti-democratic; on the contrary, under certain conditions it can be favourable to individual freedoms. At the same time, like right-wing populism, the welfare state holds that the market can be a form of effective coordination, but it rejects the idea of a generalized commodification of life, which leads to dictatorship by private companies and mass inequality. It also rejects the policies of scapegoating, exclusion and incessantly manipulating public debate.

We are entitled to expect European governments to immediately revive this third model. Unfortunately, they're not demonstrating such lucidity.

They remain intellectually bound to the neoliberal ideology. They impose ever more drastic cuts in what they have learned to call 'social costs' (instead of 'investments' in education or health). They practise a budgetary austerity blind to the genuine social needs of people, deliberately reduce the state's tax base and, to top it all off, vote enthusiastically for international agreements (such as CETA) which limit their own investment and regulatory capacities.

Response 3: The welfare state

The COVID-19 crisis will be politically useful if it takes us back to the foundations of this alternative model of managing capitalism. The welfare state is not a liberal state with a small dose of generosity. Liberalism sees in society only a set of individuals who are united by contracts. Such a vision had an undeniably liberating power in the holistic, hierarchical realm of the *ancien régime*, which assigned to every individual a place and a status. But it's an insufficient vision for guiding and governing industrial societies. It can, however, be rectified by what the social sciences revealed during the 19th and 20th centuries, which can be summed up in a fairly simple idea: interdependencies bind together individuals. Organized into systems, these interdependencies constitute an autonomous level of reality, which can't be regulated by our individual wills, or even by contracts between individuals.

If there is one area in which the importance of this systemic approach to the social is borne out, it's public health. A pandemic like the one we're experiencing shows that health can't be fully privatized. Health does, of course, have an individual aspect, which is unique to each person: one person's risks differ from another's. But it also has a social aspect, whether local or broad based: my health depends on the hygiene of those around me. It depends on every other person with whom I happen, even sporadically, to be in physical contact with. Everyone's hygiene is a condition for my personal health. Since a virus can circulate and thrive via surfaces no less than fleeting interactions, everyone's health also depends on the physical infrastructure that connects us, and the quality of the water, air and food that flows between us. Hence the reality of interdependencies, which eludes the simple aggregate of individual behaviours. This is what sociologists call the 'system', whose structures and functions are irreducible to individual behaviour (although that doesn't mean the latter is insignificant).

The interdependencies that COVID-19 reminds us of also apply, *mutatis mutandis*, to work accidents, unemployment risks, financial systems, global migration and climate change. This dimension of social reality wasn't readily apparent to political philosophy. It only became salient with industrialization, which continually generates new interconnected, material and social systems. The systems emerge or decline, change or evolve, and are unpredictable. They can be identified and understood only by the natural and social sciences – not by political philosophy, whose reasoning is based only on normative concepts, themselves essential but insufficient for managing a society.

Since the Enlightenment, modern democracies have been guided by building a rational, or at the very least reasonable, society that expands individual freedom and social equality. The new systemic social theory doesn't break with this, but it does give an essential role to the state. As the expression and instrument of the collective will, the state is a system which has the responsibility to regulate other systems as much as possible. To do so effectively, the state must have three characteristics: it must be sovereign, democratic and interventionist.

State and health sovereignty

First, as to being a sovereign state, the current pandemic shows the crucial importance of *spatial* control over interactions, which is essential to stopping the pandemic and distributing aid. The modern state is a systemic protection device for a given territory. This sovereignty is never fully acquired, but it's an ideal regulator, which is repeatedly challenged by previously unnoticed interdependencies.

The current crisis demands a new concept: health sovereignty. In the health field, it would be the direct counterpart of the 'food sovereignty' (De Schutter, 2018) demanded by farmer global-justice movements. Indeed, it's absurd for Europeans to import protective masks from China or rely heavily on drugs produced in the United States. The state must strive to localize production of basic public health equipment. The deregulated world market disseminates production capacities according to the law of specialization, which is bound by comparative advantage. This is why no community can rely on free trade for its survival.

However, it's also clear that new interdependencies in terms of sickness and health are emerging. They result from the circulation of goods, people and equipment. These systems know no borders. The causes of medical problems lie both outside and within countries. New drugs are invented all over the world, products must be exchanged. Thus we must not misconstrue health sovereignty as health self-sufficiency. Health sovereignty presupposes the state's inclusion in a transnational framework that can produce and distribute worldwide equipment paramount to the health of all. Hence it has nothing to do with narrow-minded nationalism or dogmatic protectionism. Co-operation in transnational institutions is as essential as local basic infrastructure.

Democracy: a condition for efficiency

Thus we are not going to restore a 'Leviathan state', which would destroy freedom in order to guarantee security. The second condition for an effective welfare state is the existence of an open, attentive and deliberative public space.

The current pandemic provides striking proof: the greatest threats to collective effectiveness are concealment of information and lack of debate. Amartya Sen (1983) demonstrated this in the case of famine. The state must ensure that information flows completely and freely in order to allow continuous policy deliberation. Only through open debate can uncertainty and complexity be tackled. Muzzling certain members of society limits the public space as well as the choices required to address the magnitude and multidimensionality of health problems. At the same time, open discussion is essential if citizens are going to apply binding government measures. Citizens deprived of the opportunity to discuss the purpose of such measures react with suspicion and free-riding. Thus the measures fail and the state, thanks to its baffling high-handedness, loses legitimacy.

Moderate socialism

Building democracy isn't just about building a free public space. It's also about levelling the field. Without adequate infrastructure, 'right to life' and 'right to health' are empty words. Infrastructure can be partially supplied by the market, but unfortunately only at the expense of equality and with adverse effects. Indeed, we know how free-market healthcare can become 'iatrogenic', as Ivan Illich (1976) pointed out in *Medical Nemesis: The Expropriation of Health*. We know the terrible inequalities that come with it. Hence the state, assigned a dual mission of healthcare production and distribution, must introduce corrective measures. On the supply side the state must guide the economy to produce healthcare goods and services, and, on the demand side, make them universally accessible in accordance with principles of justice.

Unlike countries with a hyperliberal tendency, the welfare state offers permanent, tax-funded public health infrastructure. In addition, various social insurance and regulatory control schemes provide for affordable care, moderately priced drugs, and public hospitals. In the midst of the COVID-19 crisis, the importance of these schemes is tragically proven. Tackling health inequality is a measure of a healthcare system's legitimacy, and even of its effectiveness: the great inequalities between individuals and groups increase the risks to both the healthcare and political systems.

The collectivist structure of some public healthcare systems doesn't completely exclude the market mechanism from the healthcare sector. The market has certain advantages: it promotes innovation and productivity, and makes it possible to combat rent-seeking. Hence a state-market institutional mix must be established, as was the case in all West European countries after 1945. Certainly, we must constantly review and transform the recipe for this institutional compromise to adjust it to the economy's new constraints (digital, services and so forth). But a balance between collective and private ownership of the means of production is mandatory. Thus a certain dose of socialism is recommended in the health field, as in other fields.

Revive the welfare state

Sovereign, democratic, interventionist and redistributive: only the successor to the 20th-century welfare state can ensure the democratic resilience of our societies in the 21st. In the midst of the COVID-19 crisis, after two decades of criticism and attack, many voices are giving it new life.

Nothing is simple, however. Today's welfare state is in mortal danger, undermined by four structural challenges. The first is financial: treating it with debt and austerity has left it on life support; its tax base has to be entirely redefined (for example via a Tobin tax on financial transactions, GAFA tax, property tax). Second, the relationship between the welfare state and economic growth must be rethought. Growth isn't an end in itself but a means. If our societies' resilience (ecological, financial, health, social) is everyone's goal, the growth must touch certain sectors and not others. In any case, the umbilical cord between the welfare state and productivism deserves to be cut. Third, the welfare state's integration into transnational channels would allow it to confront long-term interdependencies, which extend (well) beyond its territory. Finally, the welfare state must reduce its bureaucracy. Hierarchical, standardized and purely managerial relationships undermine its legitimacy in the eyes of the public it claims to serve.

The COVID-19 crisis reminds us of the urgency of meeting these challenges. It forces Europe to revive the welfare state. Without new consensus in favour of the Welfare State, crises will deepen and upheavals will become increasingly violent. If that happens, then on the Old Continent, too, the way will be clear for the two state models already ravaging the planet.

Notes

[1]　Laurent, E. (2020) 'Gare à l'épidémie de solitude', *Le Monde*, 25 March, p 27.
[2]　Bieber, F. (2020) 'Authoritarianism in the Time of the Coronavirus', *Foreign Policy*, [online] 30 March, available from: https://foreignpolicy.com/2020/03/30/authoritarianism-coronavirus-lockdown-pandemic-populism/
[3]　Milman, O. and Holden, E. (2020) 'Trump administration allows companies to break pollution laws during coronavirus pandemic', *The Guardian*, [online] 27 March, available from: https://www.theguardian.com/environment/2020/mar/27/trump-pollution-laws-epa-allows-companies-pollute-without-penalty-during-coronavirus

References

De Munck, J. (2018) 'La tentación liberal-populista de los europeos', *Open Democracy/Open Movements*, 23 October, ISA RC-47.

De Schutter, O. (2018) 'Democracia alimentaria en el Sur y en el Norte', in B. Bringel and G. Pleyers (eds) *Protestas e indignación global*, Buenos Aires: CLACSO, 219–26.

Illich, I. (1976) *Medical Nemesis: The Expropriation of Health*, New York: Pantheon Books.

Klein, N. (2007) *The Shock Doctrine: The Rise of Disaster Capitalism*, Toronto: Knopf Canada.

Sen, A. (1983) *Poverty and Famines: An Essay on Entitlement and Deprivation.* Oxford: Oxford University Press.

3

Universal Social Protection Floors: A Joint Responsibility

Michelle Bachelet, Olivier De Schutter and Guy Ryder

Limited political responses to the COVID-19 crisis

The COVID-19 pandemic and related economic shutdowns have already caused wave upon wave of suffering across the world. To respond to this unprecedented crisis, governments have set up a variety of ad hoc schemes for furloughs, cash transfers or family support. But though commendable, these responses share two limitations.

First, many are short term. They are temporary fixes, put in place for the duration of lockdowns – or, at best, until the economy starts recovering. Yet in 2012, ILO member states, together with representatives of workers and employers, unanimously adopted a pledge to 'establish and maintain … social protection floors as a fundamental element of their national social security systems': in other words, permanent, human rights–based social protection floors to facilitate access to healthcare, protect people against poverty, promote gender equality and ensure the satisfaction of basic rights, including food, water, housing, health and education.

Short-term, altruistic social protection measures, including cash transfer programs, can be vital in times of crisis. But they are not a substitute for permanent social protection floors that ensure access to healthcare, guarantee basic income security for children, protect people from the risks of unemployment, sickness, maternity or disability and ensure older persons receive an old-age pension guaranteeing an adequate standard of living.

Secondly, many of the world's worst-hit communities have literally vital needs that are simply not being addressed by current measures. Although governments worldwide have dedicated at least 11 trillion US dollars to the global COVID-19 response – including by investing in social protection – by far the most important reactions, whether in absolute terms or as a percentage of their GDP, have come from rich countries. The European Union recently adopted a 750 billion euro recovery plan (equivalent to 6 percent of its GDP). Japan adopted an economic recovery plan for 1.1 trillion USD (22 percent of its GDP). But the fiscal response of low-income developing countries has remained at 1.2 percent of GDP on average (IMF, 2020).

Developing countries, and particularly low-income countries, have limited capacity to mobilize domestic resources, and are currently impacted by the low prices of commodities on which their export revenues often depend. They lack the fiscal space required to put in place social protection floors to effectively prevent their population from falling into poverty.

Furthermore, many of the 47 least developed countries face an additional constraint: their small and poorly diversified economies are highly vulnerable to outside shocks – whether economic, climatic or pandemic – that swamp entire communities and regions, resulting in overwhelming burdens on their social protection systems.

As a result, even before the pandemic, 71 percent of the global population was either not covered or only partially covered by social security systems. Almost two-thirds of children globally received no social protection coverage. Only 22 per cent of unemployed persons received unemployment cash benefits. Only 41 per cent of women giving birth received maternity cash benefits, and only 28 percent of persons with severe disabilities received disability cash benefits (UNESC, 2019).

Towards a robust social protection floor

We need to support efforts by all countries to put in place robust social protection floors now, for greater resilience to future shocks and more effective recovery. The current approach – scrambling to adopt emergency cash transfers and other makeshift mechanisms as the crisis unfolds – is like starting to recruit firefighters after the fire has broken out, and then sending them out to manage only specific sections of the blaze. Permanent, human rights – based social protection floors need to be a universal reality: we need well-trained and well-equipped fire brigades ready to intervene at all times.

International solidarity is essential to this objective – and as such, it is in everyone's interest. International human-rights law recognizes a duty of wealthy states to help fulfil social rights in other states with limited resources. Indeed, in 2011 an expert advisory group (Bachelet et al, 2020) recommended donors provide predictable, multi-year financing to strengthen social protection in developing countries, and a year later, two independent UN human rights experts proposed a Global Fund for Social Protection (De Schutter and Sepulveda, 2012), to support efforts of low-income countries seeking to guarantee social protection floors for their people.

An affordable proposal and a joint responsibility

Social protection floors are affordable. The financing gap for all 134 developing countries – the difference between what these countries already are investing in social protection and what it would take to guarantee the full range of entitlements associated with social protection floors – represents about 527 billion USD per year, or the equivalent of 1.6 percent of the GDP of these countries. But the gap for low-income countries alone is just 27 billion USD, equivalent to 5.6 percent of their GDP. This amount represents less than 18 percent of the total official development assistance provided in 2019 by OECD countries (OECD, 2020), and ILO experts rightly describe it as 'negligible' in comparison to the total wealth of donor countries (Durán et al, 2020).

Throughout the current crisis, and beyond it, there is an urgent need to enhance efforts at the national and international levels to ensure that all people, especially the most marginalized, receive the support they need. 'Building back better' means building a universal system in which everyone is protected without discrimination of any kind. This would require an improved balance between contributory and non-contributory schemes, to ensure everybody is protected against risks and contingencies, including the most marginalized who might have not been in a position to contribute formally to the social protection system.

States must deploy their maximum available resources to make social protection a reality for all, which requires progressive taxation measures, strengthening the capacity to collect taxes, fighting tax evasion and other forms of abuse and tackling corruption. These measures would contribute to effectively redistributing resources and start creating the necessary fiscal space to protect the most marginalized, curbing inequality and discrimination in the short and long term. Building back better also means deploying international solidarity to strengthen the resilience of social protection systems across the world and deliver on the 2030 Agenda's promise of 'leaving no one behind'.

This crisis is unprecedented, and its human impacts huge: we must learn its lessons and commit to work towards resolving them. If not, we risk condemning future generations to endure once more the immense suffering we see around us today.

References

Bachelet, M., ILO and WHO (2020) *Social Protection Floor for a Fair and Inclusive Globalization*, Geneva: ILO.

De Schutter, O. and Sepúlveda, M. (2012) 'Underwriting the poor: A global fund for social protection', Briefing Note 7, New York: OHCHR.

Durán Valverde, F., Pacheco-Jiménez, J., Muzaffar, T. and Elizondo-Barboza, H. (2020) *Measuring Financing Gaps in Social Protection for Achieving SDG Target 1.3* (ILO Extension of Social Security Working Paper 73), Geneva: ILO.

IMF (2020) *Policies to Support People during the COVID-19 Pandemic* (IMF Fiscal Monitor Report), Washington, DC: IMF.

OECD (2020) *Aid by DAC Members Increases in 2019 with More Aid to the Poorest Countries*, Paris: OECD.

UNESC (2019) *Progress towards the Sustainable Development Goals Report of the Secretary-General*, New York: United Nations Economic and Social Council.

4

Labour Activism and State Repression in Indonesia

Michele Ford

For the last thirty or so years, Indonesia's small and divided, but dynamic union movement has relied primarily on its mobilizational capacity in key industrial centres to wrest concessions from employers and government. It would have been no surprise if the COVID-19 pandemic, having robbed them of this weapon, had erased all evidence of the labour movement from the public domain. Instead, unions rose to the occasion, using other strategies in their repertoire to push for better containment measures and stay attempts to use the pandemic to pass a new anti-worker law. Ultimately their efforts to stay Law No.11/2020 on Job Creation were unsuccessful, but they demonstrated the movements continuing dynamism in the face of state repression.

A country in deep denial

Indonesia spent a long time in deep denial – denial of the extent to which COVID-19 had spread through the community, denial that stronger public health measures were required to contain it and denial of the risk it posed to the wellbeing of its 270 million citizens. Indeed, the depth of this denial was clearest in the initial responses of the minister for health and other senior government officials, who brushed off the threat, suggesting that Indonesia's location on the equator and the genetic specificities of its people – even divine intervention – would protect the country from harm.

COVID-19 was not officially recognized as a potential epidemic until 28 January 2020, when a month-long 'specific' state of emergency was initially declared. Flights from Hubei province were immediately cancelled, followed by flights from the rest of China from 5 February. At this time, no infection had been detected, though a few hundred people subsequently repatriated from Wuhan were quarantined on the island of Natuna. Restrictions quickly followed on travellers from Iran, Italy and South Korea. It was not until 20 March that travel ceased for certain visa classes and for all travellers from Spain, France, Germany, Switzerland and the United Kingdom. In fact, in mid-February, when other governments were considering closing their borders, Indonesia announced a series of incentives for international tourists. A taskforce was not formed until 13 March.

Although further measures were later taken, Indonesia's COVID-19 statistics continued to be suppressed by low levels of testing and by haphazard recording. The first COVID-19 case was not officially confirmed until 2 March. On 19 March, President Joko Widodo announced that massive rapid testing would take place, but by early May only 400 tests per million people had been conducted. By this time, more than double this number had been conducted in the Philippines, Southeast Asia's second-largest country, at over 1,000 tests per million. Vietnam and Thailand, the third- and fourth-largest countries in the region, had each conducted over 2,500 tests per million. By 1 September, the number of tests conducted in Indonesia had risen to over 2.2 million. However, testing rates remained low, at just 8,118 per million people.

These low testing rates were reflected in the recorded incidence of the disease. As of 1 May, Indonesia had recorded only 10,551 cases and 800 deaths. Four months later, the number of cases recorded had risen to 174,796 and the number of deaths to 7,417. The geographical distribution of cases tells a more concerning story. Cases were initially concentrated primarily on Java, Indonesia's most populous island. However, by early April the virus had already spread throughout the archipelago, with cases confirmed in all 34 provinces. Even government officials acknowledged that official reporting has been at best inadequate. At worst, it has been consciously deceptive. As the president himself acknowledged, at times data had been purposefully concealed to avoid sparking widespread panic.

The government's public health response

The government's public health response has left many scratching their heads. On 15 March, the president called on Indonesians to work and pray at home. But specific measures for schools and workplaces, and limitations on public worship and other public activities, were not announced until the end of that month. An important element of the new policy was large-scale social distancing measures. Regional governments were left to implement these in their respective localities, but they could only act *after* receiving approval from the Ministry of Health.

The resulting patchwork of containment measures was woefully inadequate. Restrictions introduced under this protocol included limits on the size of public gatherings and the use of motorcycle taxis, and religious activities. The central government also baulked at halting interregional travel despite the looming spectre of *mudik,* the annual exodus from major cities towards the end of the Muslim fasting month. After much prevarication, Widodo finally announced on 21 April that travel would be prevented from the 'red zone' surrounding Jakarta from 24 April until 31 May, the period between the second day of the fasting month and the end of the first week of the Eid celebrations.

Residents of Jakarta rushed to leave the city in the three days between the announcement of the mudik travel ban and when it came into effect. Attempts continued even after 24 April, with 25,728 vehicles turned back by police in the first ten days of the shutdown. The expected bump from travel associated with the Eid celebrations did not eventuate, but the risk of infection remained. In some towns, whole neighbourhoods were drenched in disinfectant but messages about social distancing largely fell on deaf ears. Public transport remained crowded and residents still congregated in markets and other public places. In some cases, officials' attempts to enforce social distancing were met with strong resistance. In Sulawesi, for example, a district head was reported to police for blasphemy after he attempted to follow central government policy and disperse Friday prayers.

In late May, the central government introduced a new policy, called 'the new normal', intended to help Indonesians 'live alongside' the virus. This policy imposed mandatory use of masks and social distancing while lifting restrictions on travel and allowing public buildings to open at 50 percent capacity. It required that people over 45 remain at home. Responses to this policy within Indonesia were mixed. Some lauded it as a way of protecting the economy–and, as a consequence, livelihoods–while others pointed to patchiness in enforcement and continued growth in the number of cases. Internationally, many experts remained sceptical about the Indonesian government's claims to have COVID-19 under control.

Economic and political concerns

One of the reasons the government has been slow to act, as in other countries, has been out of concern about the economic, social and political effects of strict public health measures. Although Indonesia was relatively unscathed by the global financial crisis in 2008, memories of the Asian financial crisis of 1997–8 are still raw. The currency crashed and growth in GDP dropped from an average 7.2 percent per annum for the period 1983–96 to 6.4 percent for the period 1997–9. The crisis resulted in widespread social unrest, violence and ultimately the fall of the Suharto regime, which had been in power for 32 long years.

Indonesia's economy has clawed its way back from the devastating losses of that time, with GDP growth averaging around 5 percent the last several years. But it remains fragile, and COVID-19 hit hard. Although much of the economy remains operational, worst-case scenarios in early May predicted that growth in GDP would drop to effectively zero. Government figures suggested that close to three million people had already lost their jobs by mid-April. At that time, the finance minister believed that some 70 million informal sector workers were at risk. It is not surprising, then, that there were murmurings about the possibility of social unrest. Nor is it surprising that the government made the decision to concentrate primarily on saving the economy. Its attempts to do so included making an allocation of USD 26.36 billion – about 2.5 percent of the country's GDP – for stimulus packages targeting healthcare, social protection and economic recovery. Measures targeting the vulnerable include the distribution of staples and direct cash aid, as well as free electricity for customers on the lowest available electricity supply and in some low-cost housing. A raft of subsidies and loans have been put in place for micro-, small and medium enterprises.

The stimulus package included tax incentives for manufacturers and a six-month tax exemption for manufacturing workers with an annual income of up to USD 12,500. In addition, it made credit available to labour-intensive enterprises with over 300 employees in the tourism, electronics, automotive, textiles and footwear, furniture and paper-product industries. Other programs targeted state-owned enterprises and SMEs. The minister for manpower also urged provincial governors to actively manage the risks of workplace transmission and direct employers to pay the wages of workers forced into isolation or furloughed as a result of the virus. In addition, the government expanded its labour insurance programme to cover COVID-19-related job losses, under which affected workers are entitled to USD 62.50 per month (or around a quarter of the minimum wage in the capital) for up to three months. With such generous measures in place, it would seem that workers – and, by extension, the labour movement – should have had relatively few concerns. But in Indonesia, as in many comparable countries, there is a big gap between policy and practice, which has left formal-sector workers deeply exposed.

Organized labour responds

Indonesia's labour movement was already under pressure when COVID-19 hit. It had done surprisingly well carving out space for itself since the Suharto regime fell in 1998, re-establishing independent unions that, though not strong on conventional measures, punched above their weight. In just two decades, these unions went from being politically invisible to being wooed by governors and presidential candidates. They also had some serious economic wins, leveraging their mobilizational power to convince government officials to side with them in local wage councils to achieve stunning increases in minimum wages. In 2013, the minimum wage increased by an *average* of 45 percent in metro areas. In one industrial district, it increased by a massive 57.6 percent.

But unions soon became the victims of their own success. After a massive surge in organized labour's economic and political influence in the period between 2009 and 2014, the government hit back, introducing a formula for minimum wage rises that effectively obliterated the function of the local wage councils as a bargaining arena. This, in turn, undermined unions' political clout, which had been closely tied to their ability to turn members out to demonstrate during the annual cycle of minimum wage negotiations. The government took further steps to tame the unions in February 2020, when it introduced its Omnibus Law on Job Creation to the legislature. The draft law, which promised to improve the ease of doing business and attract foreign investment, was set to amend 73 existing laws dealing with everything from environmental protection to tax provisions. But, as the chair of the employers' association noted, 'labour reform' was its 'main spirit'. Of particular concern to unions was the proposed reduction of severance payments, long a target of the business lobby. In the absence of unemployment benefits, these provisions provide vital support for retrenched workers trying to find a new job. If passed, the law would also remove provisions for paid leave for family reasons, relax controls on outsourcing and further adjust the minimum wage–setting process. In addition, dismissals could no longer be appealed in the industrial relations court.

Unions were already worried about the risk of factory closures due to COVID-19, as well as the health risks to members who could not work at home. But they were even more deeply concerned about the fact that the legislature was continuing to discuss the draft law. Unions and NGOs had begun mobilizing before the pandemic hit Indonesia, but social distancing regulations eliminated space for lawful protest. The unions had cancelled a planned demonstration to maintain social distancing on 23 March. Eleven days later, when the legislature made the decision to go ahead with its deliberations, they announced plans to mount a large-scale but socially distanced demonstration to stop the legislature in its tracks. Driving the process was Said Iqbal, the leader of the Confederation of Indonesian Trade Unions, who warned that he would bring 50,000 workers together in protest outside the legislature. Responding to journalists' questions about his plan to flout social distancing regulations, he responded by saying, "We feel threatened. First, the threat to our lives because we are still working during the pandemic. Second, the threat to our future due to the Omnibus Bill deliberation."

The leaders of all three main confederations subsequently announced that a joint protest involving hundreds of thousands of workers would be staged on 30 April. Perhaps concerned about the social contagion effect–instructions had been issued directing police to take action against anyone who criticized officials for the way that they were handling the pandemic – Widodo responded with alacrity, summoning the confederations' leaders to the Presidential Palace on 22 April to hammer out a compromise. Two days later, he announced that he had done a deal with the legislature to postpone discussion of the section of the draft law dealing with industrial relations. The postponement, he said, would provide an opportunity for stakeholder input. The confederations called off the 30 April demonstration. They also instructed their affiliates to mark May Day, not by descending on the streets as they habitually did, but by donating medical equipment to hospitals and clinics and masks to retrenched workers and to members of the community.

True to the president's word, union officials were subsequently invited to participate in tripartite discussions about the bill, which took place for the first time in early July. However, a number of confederations and unions subsequently withdrew, alleging that the Employers' Association was not prepared to negotiate in good faith. Unions large and small again threatened to take to the streets if their concerns were not taken seriously. After a series of smaller demonstrations, workers in major cities across the archipelago mounted a protest on 25 August. They also continued their print and social media campaigns, which highlighted both health concerns and job losses during the pandemic, and the ongoing risks to workers associated with the Omnibus Law. But the government stayed its course; the legislature passed the bill in October and it was signed into law on 2 November 2020. The battle is set to continue if unions are to have any chance of staving off further cuts to labour rights once the threat of COVID-19 has passed.

5

Harmoniously Denied: China's Censorship on COVID-19

Joy Y. Zhang

China's initial denials of a new SARS-like flu at the end of 2019 has been widely criticized as a significant factor that allowed the early spread of COVID-19. For people who are familiar with Chinese politics, few would be surprised by the authorities' attempted cover-up. Censorship in the name of preserving a 'harmonious society' has been an overriding sociopolitical priority in China since 2004 (Barr, 2011).[1] With the advent of Western and Chinese New Year celebrations, and with municipal and provincial congresses underway, it seemed only 'logical' that the local health authority decided to ignore the national direct-reporting system which China invested 1.1 billion RMB in after the SARS epidemic in 2003. Instead, authorities focused on suppressing whistle blowers such as Dr Wenliang Li, accusing them of 'disrupting social order' (Zhao 2020).

Yet the impact of government censorship is hugely understated (if not misunderstood) if one only sees its damage in terms of political transparency. In so doing, we miss how China, or other societies with similar censorship practices, could enhance social resilience for the next public crisis.

What the COVID-19 pandemic made visible is a much more sinister side of censorship. That is, once top-down censorship has been progressively normalized in a society (as in the case of China over the past 16 years), it is no longer just a facet of the political culture but also seeps into the collective mentality that, in Foucauldian terms, 'conducts the conduct'. As my observations of COVID-19 demonstrate, chronic censorship bends society into acquiescing to a harmonious denial of individual, social and scientific prospects.

Living with censorship

At the end of December 2019, my husband and I flew to Beijing to conduct fieldwork. On our fifth day in Beijing, we both developed symptoms of catarrh followed by a fever. Such respiratory reactions were common for non-locals when adapting to Beijing's dry winter and air pollution. At the time, a number of our Chinese friends working in the health system were already aware of a rumour that a mysterious pneumonia was spreading in Wuhan. They bantered about how 'trendy' we were, as what we had could be part of the latest health mystery. But of course, we only had a normal cold, and we recuperated quickly.

It is almost unimaginable now for anyone to joke about having COVID-19, and this is precisely what makes this lighthearted tease from our friends extremely illustrative of the general sentiment at the beginning of the outbreak in China. Our friends were acutely aware of censorship and that the truth of the (then) speculated epidemic may be whitewashed. But they calculated that the worst-case scenario would be another SARS, which China has repeatedly proven its capacity to handle.

It is difficult to say if it was our friends that miscalculated the scope of the censorship or if it was the Chinese government that miscalculated the scope of the new epidemic. For the reality quickly got lost, perhaps to everyone, under close surveillance of domestic reporting of the virus. After returning to the UK in January, a large part of my daily routine has been saving Chinese news reports and key commentaries on the virus through clusters of screenshots rather than simply saving the links. This was because 'disharmonious' web content would be soon deleted without a trace, and during January articles related to the epidemic were censorship targets. In fact, due to the eight-hour time difference between China and the UK, it was not uncommon for me to wake up in the morning only to find that half of the articles passed on by friends had already been removed or their access denied. To be sure, some of the censored content may have been fake news, but it was also evident that what remained in circulation adhered to the party line.

More importantly, COVID-19 exposed an often ignored character of how censorship works when it is effectively 'constitutionalized' in the political system. Its ubiquity in governing rationales means that censorship is not necessarily centrally coordinated but is a layered practice. That is, censorship becomes a tool wielded at the discretion of multiple authorities and can be discriminately applied in accordance with local needs. For example, compared to many other less affected cities, in the early phase, Wuhan's local media was subject to stringent censorship. According to a corpus study of Chinese official newspapers carried out by a media studies' scholar at Hong Kong University, between 1 and 20 January 2020, COVID-19 was only reported on four times by Wuhan local newspaper *Chutian Dushi Bao*, of which two instances were rebuking 'rumours' and two were press releases by the local health bureau (Qian, 2020). On 20 January, the day before President Xi Jinping publicly acknowledged the seriousness of the outbreak and three days before the Wuhan lockdown, local news was still celebrating that 20,000 free tickets to key tourist sites been handed out to the public with the expectation of a tourist surge during the Spring Festival holiday.

This localized disinformation has led to a seemingly paradoxical public reaction: Towards the end of January, when most major cities around China started to get anxious about the virus, Wuhan residents were generally still relaxed. During a late-January online meeting with a UK-trained professor in Wuhan, he dismissed my concern over the epidemic as an overreaction due to media speculations. A classic example of "risk amplification", he exclaimed on the other side of the screen. Sure, Wuhan had most of the 200 confirmed cases, but that was out of 11 million people in the city. He assured me that the "actual situation" was really not *that* serious. This professor's reaction echoes a doggerel widely circulated on WeChat, China's leading social media app, just days before the lockdown: 'People in Hankou [the district where COVID-19 was first found] are happily doing their Spring Festival shopping, rushing to dinners and parties … The whole world knows that Wuhan is cordoned off, only Wuhan doesn't know it yet'.

In fact, it was a Beijing newspaper rather than Wuhan media that first questioned Wuhan authorities' insistence on 'social harmony' at the cost of public ignorance. With the headline, 'Wuhan's calmness makes it impossible for the rest to remain calm', the article compared the authorities' attempts at harmonizing a virus into political compliance to the absurdity of 'running naked' amid dangers. A couple of days after I spoke with the aforementioned professor, Wuhan went into lockdown.

I wonder in retrospect how many ordinary citizens in Wuhan felt they were misled into 'running naked' before the lockdown when they went about the town with their daily routines. I also wonder, for those Wuhan bureaucrats, did they also feel they were 'running naked' when they knew the data reported to them by hospitals and health authorities were airbrushed with their acquiescence if not direct support? When censorship is institutionalized, or rather effectively 'constitutionalized', in a governing system, *facts* quickly become *artefacts* when passed on through multiple layers of censoring and self-censoring.

Censorship and societal resilience

A key difference between democratic and non-democratic states in the response to COVID-19 does not hinge on lockdowns but on what has been discussed and done to mitigate the various knock-on effects of lockdowns.

For example, in the days following the UK's lockdown in late March, discussion on, and sometimes protests about, the welfare of different social groups filled mainstream news outlets: discussions about the impact the lockdown would have on children with special needs and individuals in care homes, as well as on domestic violence, mental health and concerns for safety nets for the self-employed. Of course many of these issues remain unresolved or only partially resolved, but this 'explosion' of public expression of concerns made many underlying social issues visible from the start.

In contrast, few such (pre-emptive) discussions on the social consequences of lockdown could be found in Chinese media. If one types 'domestic violence' (家庭暴力) and 'coronavirus pneumonia' (新冠肺炎, the common way for Chinese media to refer to the COVID-19 pandemic) into China's search engine Baidu, the results are predominately news reports on the increase of domestic violence in the UK, US, Japan and other countries. Reports on domestic violence in China in the context of the pandemic are scarce. Of course, Baidu, as the main Chinese search engine, has long been criticized for manipulating research results, bowing to political and commercial pressure. Thus this might not be a fair representation of what has been discussed or done about domestic violence in China during the lockdown. But this perhaps further underlines my point. That is, social controversies within China are censored out of public sight, and thus out of public mind.

The true danger of political censorship, however, lies not simply in the absence of certain discussions but in the nurturing of social acquiescence to this silence. For example, similar to in other countries, medical staff were soon heralded as contemporary 'heroes' in China. Images of medical professionals on posters paying tribute to them were predominantly male, yet published lists of medical staff volunteering to join the front line were largely female. I wrote a post on Chinese social media questioning this aspect of gender inequality. The response was mixed. While some commented that this was an 'interesting point', others disapproved of my 'making a fuss'. One such criticism came from my own cousin, who, along with his wife, was a front-line doctor. He believed that everyone was or should be preoccupied with fighting the disease. So why should I 'distract' this concentration with 'the trivial matter of gender equality'?

My cousin's rationale echoes China's development strategy over the last 40 years. That is, China has been exceptionally good at identifying one goal (for example, fighting COVID-19) and concentrating the whole nation's resources on achieving that goal (for example, speedy reallocation of financial and human resources into the health system). Wider social discussions are considered as but a distraction. In fact, there is almost a 'pragmatic' argument for there being no discussion: even if issues were raised, given limited government resource and underdeveloped societal services, there is no capacity to address these problems anyway. So what's the point of discussion?

But how can a civil society grow if the social issues it may address are not allowed to be made visible or to be articulated in public in the first place? Among the COVID-19 tragedies that made world news from China were a 17-year-old boy with cerebral palsy who died at home when he was left without a carer after his relatives were put under quarantine, and a six-year-old boy who was locked in with his deceased grandfather for several days due to a gap in community support (Standaert, 2020; Kuo, 2020). If the disabled were no longer living as the 'invisible millions' in China (Campell and Uren, 2011), and if civil society were free to examine and critique the shortfall of social support for left-behind children and the elderly, could things have resulted differently?

What COVID-19 exposed is not so much the weakness of China's civil society but rather how important it is for China to encourage a strong civil society and public reflection so as to recognize and address its diverse needs. But when a society gets used to a norm according to which certain facts mustn't be true and certain discussions shouldn't be permitted, then silence may turn into indifference. The sinister side of censorship is that it shrinks social recognition of which community interests require respect and which values are worth protecting. As such, it precludes a society's civil potential through a 'harmonious denial' of community needs and their importance.

Censorship and (global) science

Global concerns over China's censorship of the pandemic have largely focused on its scientific consequences and can be grouped into two categories. They seem to be opposed but are related: On the one hand, there is scepticism over accepting China's COVID-19 statistics due to concerns that they are doctored to 'save face'. On the other hand, the international community is simultaneously agonizing over missed opportunities for engaging with Chinese data. That is, there are concerns that in a time when global research collaboration is most needed, China, the country that accounts for 36 percent of the world's scientific papers in the life sciences, and which has the largest volume of data on COVID-19, would turn into a secretive operation. This latter worry seemed to be further confirmed by a 13 April CNN report which exposed that China had tightened its censorship over the publication of COVID-19 research (Gan et al, 2020). In short, these two seemingly paradoxical concerns can be summarized in one sentence: *Do we really know what China knows?*

These are legitimate concerns, although I have discussed elsewhere why, despite the perceived secrecy, the mainstream of China's scientific community are advocates of transparency and openness (Zhang, 2017). This is also reflected by the fact that during the first two months of the outbreak, more than 60 percent of the research papers were contributed by Chinese labs (Lei et al, 2020). But there is a need to highlight another commonly overlooked but equally important question on the relationship between China's censorship and science: *Does China really know what it needs to know?*

Wuhan authorities' initial decision to bypass the national reporting system, cited at the beginning of this piece, for fear of political admonishment upon bringing up 'bad news' is just one example of how China may be the primary victim of its censorship. Censorship's potential curtailing effect on its research capacity can be seen in the aforementioned tightening of governmental scrutiny of COVID-19-related research. This new Ministry of Education directive reported by CNN includes three items that can be summarized as follows:

1. Any paper that traces the origin of the virus is subject to extra-stringent regulation and can only be submitted to journals after acquiring approval from the ministry.
2. Any other academic research related to the virus can be submitted for publication after its academic value, timing of publication, and appropriateness for domestic or foreign journals have been agreed on by respective university academic committees.
3. Research should adhere to biosecurity regulations and publication on vaccine research should avoid exaggeration.

The nationalist considerations are blatant in this censorship directive. Amid the ongoing blame game between the US and China as to who should be 'responsible' for the virus, the first item of the directive sends a strong signal to discourage the scientific community in China from conducting origin research. While there is an evident intention of 'quality control' so as to avoid national embarrassment like the recent faulty-mask and test-kit scandals (BBC, 2020), this directive also imposes political oversight which ensures scientific projects are in harmony with government narratives. But it is not far-fetched to say it has implications for domestic scientific trajectories. Given the necessity for ministerial-level approval, to what extent will this divert competent researchers into politically less sensitive topics or at least towards politically less sensitive questions? To what extent will the additional bureaucracy and institutional responsibilities discourage provincial-, municipal- and university-level support for COVID-19 research?

When censorship starts to impact scientists' decisions about what types of questions can be asked, when they can be asked and what should be avoided, the resulting scientific compliance may be at the cost of a lost realm of knowledge.

Concluding words

Censorship plays a key role in the development of the COVID-19 pandemic. Some of the more profound damage of censorship perhaps lies not so much in what has been altered or removed but in what has been 'harmoniously denied' in the first place. That is, facts not acknowledged, risks not calculated, problems not discussed and questions not asked. By the term 'harmonious', I refer both to the original censorship incentive of managing a 'harmonious society' and to more sinister effects of the collective mentality and the unconscious societal acquiescence to an authoritarian agenda.

On 1 September 2020, the aforementioned Wuhan professor sent me his class photo. It was the first day of the academic year across China and normal teaching was resumed. In the photo, despite the face masks, one can sense from the eyes of the two dozen students the same excitement and joviality that typically fills any campus at the beginning of a semester. The students all sat next to each other, with no social distancing in place. In fact, there was no need, as China has largely kept daily infections to single digits since late April.

The professor was overjoyed and said that, despite the immense stress, the 'important' thing was that China had restored normality expediently. It was difficult to disagree and I was delighted to see my friend safe and happy again. But it also reminded me of the old Chinese proverb, 'The pain is forgotten once the wound heals' (好了伤疤忘了疼). I guess a true harmonious society does require some pain to be forgotten, but it should never deny the lessons about how the pains were inflicted in the first place.

Note

[1] This is not to say that censorship has only occurred in China since 2004. But the new direction of Chinese leadership proposed by then president Hu Jintao to achieve political unity and societal harmony has further legitimized and incentivized the practice of censorship at various levels of social life.

References

Barr, M. (2011) *Who's Afraid of China? The Challenge of Chinese Soft Power*, London: Zed Books.

BBC (2020) 'Countries reject Chinese-made equipment', *BBC News*, [online] 30 March, available from: https://www.bbc.co.uk/news/world-europe-52092395

Campbell, A. and Uren, M. (2011) '"The invisibles" ... disability in China in the 21st century', *International Journal of Special Education*, 26(1): 12–24.

Gan, N., Hu, C. and Watson, I. (2020) 'Beijing tightens grip over coronavirus research, amid US–China row on virus origin', *CNN*, [online] 16 April, available from: https://edition.cnn.com/2020/04/12/asia/china-coronavirus-research-restrictions-intl-hnk/index.html

Kuo, L. (2020) 'China: Child found home alone with dead grandfather amid coronavirus lockdown', *The Guardian*, [online] 26 February, available from: https://www.theguardian.com/world/2020/feb/26/china-child-found-home-alone-with-dead-grandfather-amid-coronavirus-lockdown

Lei, D., Fan, J., JianWei, S., Yong, C., XinXin, Z., JianQing, D., GuoQiang, C., Wei, C., LuFa, Z., LiZhen, S. and QiMing, L. (2020) 'An interim review of lessons from the novel coronavirus (SARS-CoV-2) outbreak in China', *SCIENTIA SINICA Vitae*, 50(3): 247–57.

Qian, G. (2020) 'What the Party media were up to when the virus spread', *Radio Television Hong Kong*, [online] 10 February, available from: https://app3.rthk.hk/mediadigest/content.php?aid=2192

Standaert, M. (2020) 'Disabled teenager in China dies at home alone after relatives quarantined', *The Guardian*, [online] 30 January, available from: https://www.theguardian.com/world/2020/jan/30/disabled-teenager-in-china-dies-at-home-alone-after-relatives-quarantined

Zhang, J.Y. (2017) 'Transparency is a growth industry', *Nature*, 545(S65).

Zhao, K. (2020) 'The coronavirus story is too big for China to spin', *The New York Times*, [online] 14 February, available from: https://www.nytimes.com/2020/02/14/opinion/china-coronavirus-social-media.html

6

State Repression in the Philippines during COVID-19 and Beyond

Leanne Sajor

As COVID-19 continued to spread in the Philippines, the pandemic was not the only serious threat the country faced. In July 2020, President Rodrigo Duterte signed a harsh antiterrorism bill into law. The Philippines' human rights defenders, activists, scholars, journalists, lawyers and organizers now face a formidable battle to defend civil and democratic rights in the wake of legislation intended to silence any and all voices critical of the government. This chapter will discuss the implications of the Anti-Terrorism Act as part of wider state repression and movements' resistance during the pandemic.

The Anti-Terrorism Act: An attack on democratic principles

Republic Act No 11479, which became law despite 'strong cautionary comments' from within President Rodrigo Duterte's own cabinet and intense opposition from civil society organizations, is an amendment to the Philippines' Human Security Act of 2007 (Ranada, 2020). The Senate passed a version of the bill in February 2020, apparently with no consultation with human rights advocates or the broader public. Despite the opposition it attracted, the bill was approved by the country's House of Representatives on June, after being certified urgent by President Duterte, who then had 30 days either to veto it or approve it. To no one's surprise, on 3 July 2020, he did the latter. Plainly put, the law has the potential to criminalize anyone in the country's rich civil society ecosystem who is working to address the root causes of inequalities, to speak up for and protect human rights and to defend democracy.

Long before this new law came into being, Duterte's government had drawn criticism at home and abroad for its repressive, militaristic 'War on Drugs' and its neglect of Filipinos' fundamental social and economic rights. Popularly described as the 'terror law', it is seen by critics as the institutionalization of the hallmarks of Duterte's reign: a state-led, systemic attack on dissent and democratic rights and freedoms. Moreover, lawyers, legislators and human rights advocates have called attention to elements of the act that are unconstitutional.

Its broad definition of 'terrorism' will allow draconian interpretations by a government intent on silencing any criticism or dissent. Section 9 of the act states that 'inciting terrorism' can be committed 'by means of speeches, proclamations, writings, emblems, banners, or other representations of the same', and is punishable by 12 years in prison. Human Rights Watch has called attention to this section of the law, which notably leaves 'incitement' undefined, as posing 'a danger to freedom of the media and freedom of expression by providing an open-ended basis for prosecuting speech' (2020b). This is especially important in the context of the Philippines, which has ranked among the world's five worst countries on the Global Impunity Index, a report that looks at the data on journalists murdered with complete impunity, nearly every year since the index began in 2008 (Committee to Protect Journalists, 2019).

Devoid of accountability or any checks or balances via the nation's justice system, the law ushered in a new 'Anti-Terrorism Council (ATC)', comprised of unelected officials appointed by the executive. Critics warn that the ATC will become an unfettered, unaccountable arbiter of justice given its power to designate people and organizations as 'terrorists', to make arrests without judicial warrant and to detain people without charge for up to 24 days. This is eight times longer than what had been allowed under the previous law.

Section 4 of the act includes language that exempts advocacy, work stoppages, protests, industrial or mass action 'and other similar exercises of civil and political rights', provided that these activities are 'not intended to cause death or serious physical harm to a person, to endanger a person's life, or to create a serious risk to public safety'. But as it is left to the ATC to determine what constitutes 'serious risk', it is susceptible to the abuse of authority, especially as safeguards and oversight have been reduced. Furthermore, Section 10 of the act states that 'recruitment, propaganda or providing material support to 'terrorists' can all be charged to Filipinos living abroad', thereby extending surveillance and monitoring to Filipinos living overseas and to those who are members of the diaspora community. This salient aspect of the law compounds the vulnerabilities experienced by migrants and diaspora communities that make up the vibrant, transnational advocacy networks that have long been crucial in democratization efforts in the Philippines (Zarsadiaz, 2017; Quinsaat, 2019).

In the immediate aftermath of the passing of the law, the Armed Forces of the Philippines advocated to include provisions to regulate the use of social media in the Implementing Rules and Regulations (IRR) document drafted by the Department of Justice (DOJ) (Talabong, 2020). Civil society, human rights defenders and journalists warn that such provisions will further erode freedom of speech and freedom of the press. The administration has targeted media, journalists and social media users to silence criticisms of extrajudicial killings related to the 'War on Drugs' and the mishandling of the COVID-19 pandemic. The most recent examples of such silencing came when top broadcasting network ABS-CBN was forced off air in May 2020, thereby eliminating a vital news source for millions of Filipinos during a pandemic, and with the conviction of prominent reporters Reynaldo Santos Jr. and Maria Ressa in June 2020 for cyber-libel on a landmark case that has been seen as a litmus test for the country's press freedom (CIVICUS, 2020). As of writing, the text of the IRR document has not been made public by the DOJ.

Inequalities and human rights in the Philippines: the context

This unprecedented legislative move must also be seen in the context of the Philippines' status as one of Southeast Asia's most socioeconomically unequal countries. The most recent World Bank Gini index shows that it ranks highest in the region, at 44.4, while available data for neighbouring countries put Malaysia at 41 and Indonesia at 39 (ASEAN Trade Union Council, 2011). In 2009, the net worth of the 25 richest Filipinos was equivalent to the combined annual income of the poorest half of the country, 55 million Filipinos (Africa, 2013, p 131).

Inequalities in the Philippines are not confined to income disparities but extend to other critical areas including land distribution, welfare and human development. World Bank (2018) data indicate that in 2015, 6.6 percent of the country's population were 'extremely poor' (living below US$1.90 a day) and only 34.7 percent were 'economically secure' (between US$5.50 and US$15 a day). Bearing in mind the obscenely low levels at which the World Bank sets its poverty measurement, this dire situation is compounded by inadequacies in public services. The failing if the healthcare, education and social safety nets are exacerbated by debt encumbrance, chronic elite corruption, entrenched political oligarchies and reforms prescribed by adherence to the tenets of neoliberal globalization. Even segments of the population deemed 'economically secure' by the World Bank are now living in relative precarity as inequality deepens throughout the country, with the Philippines having one of the highest rates of inequality in the world (World Bank, 2018).

The Philippines' rampant poverty is a gross violation of human rights; it is a kind of economic violence visited on thousands of people. During the COVID-19 pandemic, this violence has only intensified: the criminalization of people seeking to fulfil their economic and social rights, including access to food, water and work, and especially amongst urban poor citizens, has been a daily occurrence. 'As of June 8, the police have arrested a total of 193,779 people for quarantine violations since 17 March. Of this number, it had charged 58,848 and detained 15,307', many of whom remain in congested prisons (Buan, 2020). Quarantine protocols instituted as public health measures during the pandemic have disproportionately affected poor communities, who have not received adequate provisions from the government. Duterte's administration has taken a militarized approach to enforcing public health protocols, with high numbers of arrests in poor communities for breaking lockdown measures as people look for work to pay for food, housing and utilities. In the Philippines, state repression targets not only human rights defenders and activists but also poor and marginalized communities who are criminalized simply for attempting to survive.

A people's movement that persists

The new law has pushed economic and social rights violations and violence further still: it is the most unrelenting attack yet on democratic rights and the civil society spaces where advocates, movements and activists are working to amplify and address the issues of marginalized, poor and working-class Filipinos. A report by the United Nations Office of the High Commissioner on Human Rights (2020) on the Philippines states that 'human rights defenders have been subject to verbal and physical attacks, threats and legal harassment for nearly 20 years ... The vilification of dissent and attacks against perceived critics ... are being increasingly institutionalized and normalized in ways that will be very difficult to reverse'. The degradation of the democratic environment in the Philippines over the years can be seen in the rampant violence against human rights defenders and peace advocates; several were murdered just months after passing the 'Anti-Terrorism Act, and there is pervasive use of 'red-tagging', a form of political harassment of activists through smear campaigns and by discrediting them by labelling them as members of 'rebel fronts'. The Philippines has an enduring movement of armed struggle and militant insurrection for genuine sovereignty and national democracy, developed through a history of multiple colonizations, occupations, authoritarian rule and endemic elite corruption over different regimes. The government of the Philippines has long waged a war against all forms of armed movement that seek to provide a 'counterpoint to neocolonialism and capitalism in the country' (Africa, 2013, p 6). This hostility has been indiscriminately extended to legal democratic struggles as civil society calls into question the state's neoliberal agenda in conflating them with 'rebel fronts'. This convenient homogenization and reduction has created a repressive environment that vilifies and delegitimizes dissent. Republic Act No 11479 has extended and enshrined in law what was already a widespread practice under previous administrations and Duterte's government: the outright criminalization of rights defenders.

Karapatan (2020), an NGO alliance and human rights watchdog in the Philippines, has documented the charging of nearly 1,000 activists and political dissenters with common crimes, including 619 people widely thought to be unjustly imprisoned, in stark confirmation of fears over how the Anti-Terrorism Act would be implemented. Karapatan statement reads, 'We believe terrorism can be addressed, not through a defective militarist approach that our State forces employ, but through the pursuit of just & lasting peace, through tackling the roots of social injustice and inequality, and through genuine respect for people's rights' (Malaya Movement, 2020). Arguments such as these have consistently been ignored.

Despite the systemic state repression compounded by militarized lockdown measures, the Philippines' social movements, people's organizations and civil society persist in their struggle for their rights and democracy. They have adapted their tactics to the unexpected and unprecedented circumstances of COVID-19. Activists continue to hold protests and rallies while practising social distancing and wearing masks and face shields. In June 2020, 20 people were arrested in a peaceful pride protest led by Bahaghari, a progressive LGBTQIA+ group, to condemn the Anti-Terrorism Act and discrimination and violence against the LGBTQ community. While the protest did not violate quarantine rules and safety protocols were followed, it was met with violent dispersal by police and widespread arrests. Bahaghari spokesperson Rey Valmores-Salinas' statement encapsulates the spirit of Filipino resistance during the pandemic: 'We may have been arrested now but no pandemic, lockdown, or fascist pigs could stop us from making Bahaghari shine' (dela Pena and Asido, 2020). Meanwhile, Filipino lawyers, lawmakers, retired justices and human rights defenders are pressing the Supreme Court to strike down the Anti-Terrorism Act. As of October 2020, 37 petitions have been filed against the new law. The High Court have yet to schedule oral arguments, citing COVID-19 health risks (Lagrimas, 2020), further underscoring the political dimensions of the pandemic.

What has been happening in the Philippines – and the even darker days this law will usher in – has not gone unnoticed internationally. As the country's civil society space shrinks, members of the Filipino diaspora have organized to raise awareness and campaign against the Anti-Terrorism Act. United States-based Filipino transnational activist networks have organized in-person and online rallies and petitions, increasing international support and mobilizing diverse groups amid the COVID-19 lockdown. A coalition of organizations in the United States led by the Malaya Movement, the United Methodist Church and the International Coalition for Human Rights in the Philippines, among others, initiated a legislative campaign for the Philippine Human Rights Act. It was formally introduced in September 2020 in the US House of Representatives. The act seeks to 'suspend US security assistance to the Philippines until such time as human rights violations by Philippine security forces cease and the responsible state forces are held accountable' (Philippine Human Rights Act, 2020). If passed, it would severely curtail the Duterte administration's ability to carry out its campaign of state repression, facilitated in part by $554 million in US military aid between 2016 and 2019, making the Philippines the largest recipient of such funding in Southeast Asia (de Castro, 2020). Diaspora mobilization in support of homeland activism has a deep history in the 'tactical repertoires' and traditions of progressive movements in the Philippines (Quinsaat, 2019), and the current pandemic serves to underscore the importance of international solidarity for opening and redefining the realms of engagements that redistribute power.

COVID-19 and control: when a pandemic becomes a tool of repression

The intensifying political repression in the Philippines is just one example of a global wave in which COVID-19 is being used as a pretext to criminalize and delegitimize dissent, often through militarization, heightened policing or the disruption of democratic processes. In Hungary, Prime Minister Viktor Orbán suspended elections and gained the authority to rule by decree. Suspensions of fundamental rights took place in Cambodia when the state claimed emergency powers to address COVID-19 (Human Rights Watch, 2020a). In the US, President Donald Trump called for the 'domination' of protesters through militarized responses to uprisings demanding justice for the killings of Black citizens as part of a larger struggle for racial justice for Black lives. China also passed a wide-ranging security law for Hong Kong that could criminalize protesters and will limit the city's autonomy.

As the global pandemic continues, the deepening crisis of socioeconomic inequalities has become more and more impossible to ignore. But particular attention must also be paid to the ways in which political inequalities are being exacerbated. The Philippines' new anti-terrorism law, and all other state responses that aim to shrink civil society space when it is most needed, must be loudly condemned and fought against. As uprisings around the world from the Philippines to Hong Kong and the US have shown, we are living through a crucial and unprecedented moment when we have the opportunity to move the needle in larger increments towards a more just and equitable world.

This achievement will only come through the defeat of new and potentially permanent measures by governments bent on institutionalizing repression. Human rights defenders, activists and organizers have been serving on a multiplicity of frontlines – including the fights against neoliberal economic policies and shrinking civil society space – so that all of us can access fundamental rights to healthcare, education, work and safe working conditions, housing and other social services and protections.

The fight is not over, but the battle lines drawn by repressive states are closing in. How do we hold governments accountable when responses to the current, unprecedented crisis fail – and even punish – the most vulnerable and marginalized? If draconian measures such as the Philippines' Republic Act No 11479 are left unchallenged and unchecked, who will be left to fight inequalities as the pandemic continues? Who will be left to fight for human rights when it ends?

References

Africa, S. (2013) 'Philippine NGOs: Defusing dissent, spurring change', in A. Choudry and D. Kapoor (eds) *NGO-Ization: Complicity, Contradictions and Prospects*, London: Zed Books, 118–43.

ASEAN Trade Union Council (2011) 'Philippines has highest income inequality rate in ASEAN: Manila', *ATUC*, [online] 6 August, available from: http://aseantuc.org/2011/08/study-phl-has-highest-income-inequality-rate-in-asean/

Buan, L. (2020) 'Court clears activists in quarantine case, use of "broad" law improper', *Rappler*, [online] 10 June, available from: https://www.rappler.com/nation/court-clears-activists-quarantine-case-notifiable-disease-law-improper

CIVICUS (2020) 'Attacks on the press and critic persist as UN report on the Philippines finds widespread violations', *Monitor*, [online] 25 June, available from: https://monitor.civicus.org/updates/2020/06/25/attacks-press-and-critics-persist-un-report-philippines-finds-widespread-violations/

Committee to Protect Journalist (2019) 'Getting away with murder,' CPJ, [online] 29 October, available from: https://cpj.org/reports/2019/10/getting-away-with-murder-killed-justice/

De Castro, R. (2020) 'Duterte admin (finally) acknowledges value of Philippine-US alliance', Stratbase ADR Institute for Strategic and International Studies, [online] September, available from: https://adrinstitute.org/2020/09/19/duterte-admin-finally-acknowledges-value-of-philippine-us-alliance/

dela Pena, K.A. and Asido, D. (2020) 'At least 20 arrested at Pride March in Manila', *Rappler*, [online] 26 June, available from: https://www.rappler.com/nation/cops-arrest-individuals-pride-month-protest-manila-june-2020

Human Rights Watch (2020a) 'Cambodia: Emergency bill recipe for dictatorship', HRW, [online] 2 April, available from: https://www.hrw.org/news/2020/04/02/cambodia-emergency-bill-recipe-dictatorship#

Human Rights Watch (2020b) 'Philippines: New Anti-Terrorism Act endangers rights', HRW, [online] 5 June, available from: https://www.hrw.org/news/2020/06/05/philippines-new-anti-terrorism-act-endangers-rights#

Karapatan (2020) 'Karapatan calls for release of political prisoners amid COVID-19 in online campaign', Karapatan, [online] 31 March, available from: https://www.karapatan.org/Karapatan+calls+for+release+of+political+prisoners+amid+COVID-19+pandemic+in+online+campaign

Lagrimas, N.-A. (2020) '37 petitions in, Supreme Court yet to schedule oral arguments on anti-terror law', *GMA News*, [online] 8 October, available from: https://www.gmanetwork.com/news/news/nation/759044/37-petitions-in-supreme-court-yet-to-schedule-oral-arguments-on-anti-terror-law/story/

Malaya Movement (2020) *Junk the Real Terror: An Online Forum on the Anti-Terrorism Act*, video, [online] 11 June, available at: https://www.facebook.com/MalayaMovement/videos/728484037978098/

Philippine Human Rights Act (2020) 'What is the Philippine Human Rights Act?', humanrights.org, [online], available at: https://humanrightsph.org/

Quinsaat, S.M. (2019) 'Linkages and strategies in Filipino diaspora mobilization for regime change', *Mobilization*, 24(2): 221–39.

Ranada, P. (2020) 'Duterte signs "dangerous" anti-terror bill into law', *Rappler*, [online] 3 July, available from: https://www.rappler.com/nation/duterte-signs-dangerous-anti-terror-bill-into-law

Talabong, R. (2020) 'Social media use should be regulated by anti-terror law – AFP', *Rappler*, [online] 3 August, available from: https://www.rappler.com/nation/afp-chief-gapay-says-social-media-use-should-be-regulated-by-anti-terror-law

United Nations Office of the High Commissioner for Human Rights (2020) *Situation of Human Rights in the Philippines*, Human Rights Council, [online] 29 June, available from: https://www.ohchr.org/Documents/Countries/PH/Philippines-HRC44-AEV.pdf

World Bank (2018) *Making Growth Work for the Poor: A Poverty Assessment for the Philippines*, Open Knowledge Repository, [online] June, available from: https://openknowledge.worldbank.org/handle/10986/29960

Zarsadiaz, J. (2017) 'Raising hell in the heartland: Filipino Chicago and the Anti-Martial Law Movement, 1972–1986', *American Studies*, 56(1): 141–62.

7

Normality Was the Problem

Ilán Bizberg

It has been said that crises allow us to see what is not evident even though it lies before our eyes. Hannah Arendt wrote that only when an instrument breaks down are we able to perceive it, and so we can repair it, we are concerned in how it is made, its structure and functions. The present health crisis displays what is not working, not only in our health systems, but in the societies in which we live and in our relationship with nature and with our fellow human beings. It highlights the failures of our health systems, which have been forsaken by the austerity policies applied in almost all the countries of the world as our governments give primacy to the interest of international finance over the well-being of their citizens. It exhibits the social effects of an economic system that accentuates inequalities and that implies higher health risks for the poor and migrants. All of this has already been widely discussed, and it is hoped that, in the face of the current health crisis, the governments of our countries will mend their course, as Alain Touraine has written.[1]

Human arrogance

Nonetheless, there is an even more significant aspect that concerns our attitude towards nature and which can be defined as *arrogance*. In the last decades, the most optimistic have believed that technology will deliver the solutions needed to heal the damages that our lifestyles are causing in the environment. A scientific/magical thinking similar to that of the economists who stated categorically, shortly before the 2007–08 global crisis that almost destroyed capitalism and deeply damaged the economy of various countries, that the financial mechanisms that had been created to safeguard risky investments promised that there would never again be a financial crisis; we know too well the result of these predictions. For its part, the lack of preparation of almost all countries for the current pandemic contrasts with the expectations that artificial intelligence has generated and with the promise of biogenetics to 'defeat death', as transhumanism claims.

What an impressive failure against the attack of a microscopic entity! And what terrible consequences for thousands of people directly affected by the virus, and for the millions who will suffer from the economic crisis! What an excess of what the ancient Greeks called hubris, an attitude that was portrayed by Aeschylus in his *Agamemnon*, when the king of Argos returns home after having destroyed Troy and accepts the purple carpet displayed for the great warriors, without considering that he had been helped by the gods. As we know, he was murdered by his wife Clytemnestra and her lover.

The philosopher Emmanuelle Coccia[2] suggests that the epidemic is awakening a feeling of liberation from our arrogance as a result of the helplessness we are experiencing in dealing with it. He proposes that we are not what we thought we were: the beginning and end of the planet, the only ones capable of destroying humanity. If intelligence, power and overconfidence have been the source of spectacular inventions and advances, they have also led to disasters and to our present vulnerability; perhaps we can learn from modesty how to save our ecosystems. As many analysts and social activists have claimed, climate change will have much more catastrophic consequences than the already terrible human, social and economic drama we are undergoing, since it will threaten all of humanity. Our rulers, supported by some (fewer and fewer) scientists, are betting on new technologies to come up with a solution or find an alternative planet we can all (or rather some) move to before the moment the threat Greta Thunberg has been warning us about–when she claims that 'our world is on fire'–becomes a reality.

The first epidemic of the ecological crisis

Some specialists have said that the current pandemic is a consequence of the pressure of our civilization on the environment and that it can be considered as the first epidemic of the ecological crisis. It is argued that the collapse of the diversity of species has wiped out the buffer zones between us and wild animals. The same occurs when urban zones and agricultural or livestock areas approach jungle spaces, destroying natural habitats.[3] Although not everybody accepts that this health crisis is effectively the result of the destruction of the biosphere, there is no doubt that it is so in intersubjective terms. In the past decade, we have been warned by numerous scientists that we were approaching an ecological crisis that may cause a pandemic. In this sense, the epidemic is the first crisis of a new era as it comes at a time when a significant part of the world population is convinced that our destruction of nature is putting humanity at risk.

What is absolutely certain is that, just as we were not prepared for the current health crisis, we are even less prepared for the ecological one, and although the consequences of the health crisis are still unknown, the climatic one will surely be much worse. Given our inability to cope with the present epidemic, it is derisory to think that humanity will be able to invent something to prevent the deterioration of the biosphere.

International co-operation and political responses

To face both crises, many of us believe that international co-operation is required, and that a global pact or even a world government are necessary to stop the deterioration of the environment. Although this is unlikely to materialize in the short or even medium term, we have been seeing attitudes of solidarity between countries: Germany has accepted patients from France and Italy; Portugal has legalized migrants and refugees so they can have access to healthcare; China has sent masks and respirators to several affected countries, as well as doctors; and so has Cuba. Scientists from all countries are collaborating to find a vaccine and a cure for the disease. On the other hand, we have also seen how the government of the United States tried to secure for itself a German company that was advancing in the production of the vaccine and diverted a shipment of masks destined for France. We have also witnessed the closure of almost all national borders. Several governments have been more interested in saving the economy than preserving the life of their inhabitants, especially the elderly and the poor, and it is manifest that capitalism is insensitive to ecology, as its sole purpose is economic growth.

That is why it is unlikely that the deterioration of the biosphere will be tackled directly and seriously by national governments, although some, like that of New Zealand[4] and those of Finland are Norway, are doing it; curiously, most of them are governed by women who seem to prioritize both the health of their countries' citizens and of the environment. The solution, then, will have to come from each one of us individually and from the social movements we will support or join. And, in this sense, the current crisis may harbour some hope. During the confinement, we have recognized what is truly important in life and have been forced to restrict our consumption. Some have become aware of the social gap: of the precariousness, poverty and poor working and living conditions of many of our fellow citizens. We have also become conscious of how much our lives depend on doctors and nurses and on the people who produce the most essential foodstuffs, and of the fact that they work risking their lives for us who are privileged to be confined in our houses.

Individual and social dimensions

We have also realized that each of us can infect or be infected by others. This can lead to a defensive attitude and to rejection, but it can also make us conscious that we all depend on each other and that every individual's behaviour impacts other fellow human beings. Whether this translates into empathy depends on each of us. It may awaken in every human being the idea that it is necessary to open our eyes to the challenges that we would face if we do not heed the warning that the current epidemic contains for the future of humanity, that we must begin to act and consume in a different way. One could expect that this awareness could be the source of greater solidarity.

In fact, we have already been acting differently, something that may offer a projection of the future. Those of us who have been lucky enough to be spared the experience of wars, famines and poverty and who, additionally, are able to work from home, are already travelling and using our cars less (or not at all), reducing our consumption and buying locally. We are thus learning that we can live more frugally than before and that we can communicate with others through the internet, have meetings without leaving our homes and so forth. This may have durable consequences, limiting air travel, hiking local production and reducing consumption.

The health crisis has also had an impact on our subjectivity, and especially on our rapport with time, which many philosophers, such as Bergson and Heidegger, consider to be the essence of man. In the first place, the pace of our lives has slowed down considerably, What the sociologist Hartmut Rosa considers to be the fundamental characteristic of our contemporary relationship to time, acceleration, has been detained with the confinement of half of the world population. Subjectively, it has slowed down the rhythm of the lives of millions of people. On the other hand, Kim Stanley Robinson writes that, with the pandemic, older people have seen their time horizon reduced due to the fact that they have become aware that they may face death immediately[5]. Although it is true, as Heidegger wrote, that our essence is defined by death, we usually do not think of this prospect. The pandemic has imposed this possibility in very real and close terms. If somebody who is 60 years old thought his life horizon was 20 or 30 years, the present situation has abruptly shortened its scope.

Back to normality?

It is possible, as some analysts have said, that the lockdown and the pandemic has given rise to a purely subjective and conjectural awareness, that once the emergency is over everything will return to 'normal'. The experience of the last forty years that began with the governments of Thatcher and Reagan, who considered who considered there to be no such thing as society, only individual men, women and families', can lead us to come to such a conclusion. We may think the same if we think with Foucault that power in the contemporary world is no longer imposed upon us from the centrality of the state, but that it is diffused in such a manner that it controls us, so to speak, from within ourselves, that power has been internalized. A perspective that leads us to consider, wrongly according to Wieviorka,[6] that structures are too strong to allow for any change.

The transformation of older people's conception of time may bring them closer to the preoccupations of the youth movement that was so active in different parts of the world just before the epidemic, concerns that are linked to the way in which the young experience temporality nowadays. From the demands of their movements, one can observe that young people feel that their future is closed and that time is, so to speak, slipping between their fingers. This is well exemplified by Greta Thunberg, who Eliane Brum considers to be a representative of the first generation without hope.[7] In 2018, Greta Thunberg organized a school strike, arguing it is worthless to go to school if there is no future, if 'time is running out'. She has said "I don't want your hope, I don't want you to have hope. I want you to panic, I want you to feel the fear I feel every day. I want you to act, to act like your house is on fire, because it is." This girl is the representative of young people who, according to psychologists in many parts of the world, are seeking aid for their deep concern and anguish about the future. In demonstrations and school strikes, banners have exhibited this distress: 'Later, I want to be alive'; 'I will do my homework when you will do yours'. In Santiago, Chile, I saw tags on the walls that point in the same direction: 'For a future without fear'; 'We shout because we hope it could be otherwise'.

While in the past social movements were based on Christian temporality, as they struggled for a better future based on the idea that an earthly utopia was possible through revolution, and on the faith of progress, of improvement (of the working class, of humanity), today they arise from despair, from concern for the future. Paul Mutuku, a young Kenyan activist, considers that 'Young people are the only generation that has grown up in this age of climate change. They have not seen the best of nature that other generations have had the privilege of seeing.'[8] A 27-year-old militant of the Hong Kong movement declared, 'There is less and less hope for Hong Kong now. It doesn't really matter what we try to do about it. There isn't much hope for the future, which means that there isn't much hope for us, either. That's why we have to come out and resist.'[9] Another Hong Kong activist came to the same conclusion: 'What really makes me get up and do something? I'm not that sure. Maybe because it's now a bad future, or no future at all.'[10]

Once we transcend the sanitary crisis, we may see the re-emergence of the social movements that were budding all over the world: from France with the *gilets jaunes*, to Chile with the student movement, and from Hong Kong to Beirut. These movements carried demands that were political, economic and social, but also ecological. And as the feminist turn of all of them showed, in their centre they had subjective claims. It is possible that when these movements resurface, they will receive a new impetus from the growing awareness that many individuals gained during the pandemic. And in this manner, when we overcome the current health crisis, we may become aware that, as was tagged on a wall in Santiago, Chile, during the mobilizations at the end of 2019, 'Normality is the problem'.

Notes

[1] Touraine, A. (2020) 'Esta crisis va a empujar hacia arriba a los cuidadores', *El País*, [online] 28 March, available from: https://elpais.com/ideas/2020-03-28/alain-touraine-esta-crisis-va-a-empujar-hacia-arriba-a-los-cuidadores.html

[2] Coccia, E (2020) 'La Terre peut se débarrasser de nous avec la plus petite de ses créatures', *Le Monde*, [online] 3 April, available from: https://www.lemonde.fr/idees/article/2020/04/03/emanuele-coccia-la-terre-peut-se-debarrasser-de-nous-avec-la-plus-petite-de-ses-creatures_6035354_3232.html.

[3] Einhorn, C. (2020) 'Animal Viruses Are Jumping to Humans. Forest Loss Makes It Easier', *New York Times*, [online] 9 April, available from: https://www.nytimes.com/2020/04/09/climate/animals-humans-virus-covid.html

[4] McCarthy, J. (2019) 'Jacinda Ardern Says Economic Growth Is Pointless If People Aren't Thriving', *Global Citizen*, [online] 25 September, available from: https://www.globalcitizen.org/en/content/jacinda-ardern-goalkeepers-unga-2019/

[5] Kim Stanley Robinson. (2020, May 1). The Coronavirus Is Rewriting Our Imaginations. *The New Yorker*.

[6] Wieviorka, M. (2020) 'En este momento, el poder está desbordado', *Página 12*, [online] 3 May, available from: https://www.pagina12.com.ar/263433-michel-wieviorka-en-este-momento-el-poder-esta-desbordado

[7] Brum, E. (2020) 'Los niños se hacen cargo del mundo', *El País*, [online] 1 March, available from: https://elpais.com/internacional/2019/03/01/america/1551470611_066535.html

[8] Omedes, E. (2019) 'De la protesta personal al grito colectivo: Cinco jóvenes del mundo que luchan contra el cambio climático', *20 Minutos*, [online] 5 December, available from: https://www.20minutos.es/noticia/4029723/0/cinco-jovenes-mundo-luchan-cambio-climatico/

[9] Anon. (2019) 'There has never been any talk of independence for Hong Kong', Interviewed by RFA, *RFA*, [online] 8 September, available from: https://www.rfa.org/english/news/china/hongkong-protester-09082019170611.html

[10] Lau, L. (2020) 'INTERVIEW: Solo School Striker & Hong Kong Climate Activist Lance Lau "I Want My Future"', interviewed by Sally Ho, *Green Queen*, [online] 28 November, available from: https://www.greenqueen.com.hk/lance-lau-interview-hong-kongs-student-climate-activist-i-want-my-future/

PART II

Crisis, Inequalities and Solidarities

8

Divided We Stand: What the Pandemic Tells Us about the Contemporary US

Bandana Purkayastha

By mid–December 2020, COVID-19 cases in the United States had reached 16,185,000, while almost 300,000 people had died. Unemployment claims hovered at around 850,000.[1] The pandemic has touched every part of the country, from astronomical numbers of infections and deaths in New York City and the North East earlier this year, to an increasing spread throughout the North Central parts of the US currently, including the rural counties. Earlier, there were continuing accounts detailing the lack of essential supplies and personnel to help those who are sick. In many regions, women took it upon themselves to sew masks and donate them to essential workers. Racial minorities, especially African Americans, are affected in disproportionate numbers, which is evident in rates of infections, deaths, and continuing unemployment.[2]

The political rhetoric in the US ranges from sombre assessment and advice about continuing to follow good health practices, including the use of masks as civic duty, to strident assertions about *the right* to be 'mask-free' and claims of success in managing the pandemic.[3] This period has also brought to greater public attention several patterns that had been the reality for some time. A key pattern is the trajectory of contemporary attempts to undermine the country's democratic processes. Another key pattern is the unacceptable level of police and vigilante violence against Black Americans that occurs regularly and with impunity.

The public also became conscious of the continuing investment in military-style training and weaponry for the police for use in civilian matters, including against non-violent protesters. Hate crimes against Asian Americans, as supposed super-spreaders of the virus, have escalated, including attacks with racial slurs and physical assaults. The account of this pandemic, in essence, can equally be labelled as an account of the current politics, economics and unequal social structures in the US.

As the virus moves through the United States, it has continued to revealing *persistent inequalities* that have been well documented by social scientists. Ratcliff (2017) has highlighted social determinants of health, and the political battles impeding social-environmental conditions that lead to health equalities. Access to universal healthcare has been a political battle for over a decade now. Decades of research have documented the sources of racial health disparities, including the impact of segregated housing (for example, Massey and Denton, 1993; Defina and Hannon, 2009), deep structural inequalities in jobs (among others, Ray, 2018; Stoll and Covington, 2012),[4] persistent poverty (including food insecurity), high levels of stress due to structural and everyday racism (for example, Sewell, 2016), experiences of violence (Cazenave, 2018) and lack of access to healthcare, especially among those in contingent work.

Both overcrowding and substandard housing, typical in poorer areas of cities and suburbs, exacerbate the conditions that lead to higher rates of infection. In New York City, African Americans and Latinos have died at twice the rate of the rest of the population (Maya and Newman, 2020). In an account of the rapid spread of the virus within the mostly rural Navajo territory, Romero (2020) points out that multiple people within small houses, as well as the lack of clean water—which often has to be carried to the houses—increased the vulnerability of a group with high rates of diabetes, high blood pressure and related ailments.

The 'pre-existing condition' is that, despite formal agreements with the federal government, the Navajos have not gotten the resources to build substantive—easily accessible and widely available—access to healthcare facilities. Older people living age-segregated housing (with varying facilities by class-based purchasing power) experienced significant interruptions to care services, as poorly paid, immigrant and racial minority service workers have died or have been furloughed during pandemic. Further, decisions by administrators to confine the elderly to their rooms or flats created conditions of severe social isolation and stress. Differently abled people are similarly confined and, as a result, have been infected disproportionately (Hakim, 2020). In a wealthy country like the US, unequal access, tied to structures of capitalism, stratify substantive rights to social, economic, and political resources. These patterns are starkly evident as people succumb to this pandemic.

Deepened inequalities

Social scientists have documented the impacts of the rise in contingent labour, the increasing number of people who work in the gig economy, and the patchwork of laws and policies that safeguard labour rights in the US. These labour conditions are tied to the disparate outcomes that people face during the pandemic. The development of tiered labour forces, with the ever-expanding lowest tier having little guarantee of work, wages and social benefits (for example, see Fullerton and Robertson, 2009), is intersecting with health vulnerabilities, as the lowest-paid workers are forced to work while they lack the ability – paid time off and proximity to healthcare facilities even if they have insurance – to access healthcare or sufficient protection.

The earlier images of New York City with empty landscapes actually indicate the absence of large numbers of people who cooked, cleaned, provided eldercare, childcare, personal care (cutting hair, doing nails, providing massages, running laundries), sold newspapers, provided quick lunches and dinners from carts, drove taxis, buses and other transportation and conducted a host of other such activities to support all those who can afford such services. At the other end, many are sufficiently privileged to work from home or get a fairly high-quality education through online learning initiatives. While the personal service workers suffer, families continue to require care work.

As a result, a gendered hierarchy has re-emerged, as women work multiple shifts within homes (Hochschild, 1997). While gendered hierarchies re-establish themselves in requiring mostly women to take on the burden of completing all that is needed to be done in order for themselves and others to be ready to work and learn,[5] the rhetoric of online work or learning continues to erase the time, effort and energy required to perform these tasks at home. Relatedly, a right that was acquired through sustained fights, the US government's help in addressing violence against women (Purkayastha, 2020), is perforce in abeyance; even as rates of violence appear to be increasing, women and children have few options to go to shelters or seek alternative housing to avoid abuse.

On the work and education front, the large-scale shift to online platforms has been achieved 'successfully', if one studies the question at the level of college shutdowns, and the mixed picture of some reopenings and come conversion of classes to some form of distance education.

Yet, as sociologists have been writing for years, the intersection of race, gender, class and sexuality structures inevitably added new inequalities to these forms of work and learning. Casey (2020) describes the unequal environment in which students try to learn from home: those who are in big homes with sufficient private and quiet spaces for work, robust bandwidth and up-to-date multiple computers are far better poised than their peers who move back to crowded homes (as other siblings return) and have inadequate space and varying responsibilities to attend to home-based tasks. A vast number of international students are stuck in places without access to public transportation, trying to shop for food, get to health clinics or pharmacies and to convince private landlords to extend their end-of-the-semester leases. Like the experience of many immigrants on guest worker visas, it is not clear if international students are eligible for debt or rental relief.

Data colonization amid the pandemic

Social scientists have also begun to warn us of another process: data colonization. It is transforming our lives as human beings around the world. As we rely more and more on technologies to work and socialize during the pandemic, we are further entrenched in what Safiya Noble has described as 'algorithms of oppressions' (Noble, 2018). Couldry and Mejias (2018), among others, have argued that in the contemporary phase of colonization, we, as human beings, provide the mine from which data are extracted by companies whose profits are based on both trading on our data and, concurrently, controlling the knowledge (including the range of political and sales messages) that can be generated and distributed.

Part of these complex arguments indicate that we are 'owned' by those who own our data because our privacy safeguards are insufficient to address the larger structural changes associated with data extraction and mining. The worlds of science and the caveats about validity and generalizability are interruptions to the seemingly simple messaging. Histories are altered, dissident voices are silenced, especially through increasing surveillance in digital and tangible spaces, and knowledge for profit–including fake news–is distributed (Kumar, 2018).

Equally important, due to the reach of these companies, there are few political processes in place to assert controls over their activities, globally, across multiple political systems. Irrespective of the exact details of these arguments, what is pertinent right now is that most of us are providing more and more data on our work, our social lives, our buying patterns and about our relationships as we live through this period of lockdown. The racist interruptions of zoom meetings that have been reported also showcase how fragile some of these systems are in terms of privacy assurances. Thus, along with the pains of experiencing this pandemic, we are providing more and more data, most likely for profit, to entities with whom we may not have had any previous dealing. And these data are generating algorithms of oppression, which feed very questionable information to destabilize expectations about norms and rules of democratic political systems and our lives.

From intersecting oppressions to voter suppression

These patterns of intersecting precarities are centrally implicated in the political reckoning–protests, mobilization and discursive battles–underway in the US currently. Strident political rhetoric from the White House blaming others—the previous administration, the states with Democratic governments—*and* taking credit for successes that are yet to materialize sets the larger stage. This rhetoric has significant consequences. The repeated emphasis on the 'Chinese virus' has resulted in a spike in hate crimes against Asian Americans who 'look Chinese' (Boboltz, 2020). Advocacy groups and scholars have pushed governments to investigate these incidents—including a knife attack against an adult, a two-year-old and a six-year-old—as hate crimes (Jeung, 2020).

As social movement scholars have documented, discursive frames do not simply lead to protests and movements, they are assertions of power to define, reflect and alter political reality. In the age of social media, trolls, data colonization and the production and distributions of messages to control populations, the intersections of discourse and what social scientists saw as traditional forms of protest and mobilization have been expanded to new worlds.

This point is particularly important for understanding how the calls by Donald Trump to White vigilante groups to open up states or to stand by for action, as well as his consistent support for the actions of White domestic terrorist groups,[6] are associated with vigilante shootings[7] and plans to kidnap a democratically elected governor for supposedly violating constitutional rights when she ordered temporary closures of business and the wearing masks in public spaces to flatten the pandemic curve.[8]

At the same time, however, the ruling party's agenda has continued, including severely negating immigrants' rights (Romero, 2018), aggressive restrictions on labour rights including unions' ability to function (McNicholas, 2020) and rapid dismantling of environmental standards (Roberts, 2020); the exact structures that create and ensure conditions of human security, including the freedom to survive, to be free of fears of want and violence, to be able to create and live lives of human dignity (Purkayastha, 2018).

A stark operation of undermining the US's democratic process has been under way as exemplified through active attempts at voter suppression. Two examples illustrate these trends which have been imposed upon earlier attempts to undermine democratic processes through redistricting.[9] Krugman (2020) has described the situation in Wisconsin: The state elected a Democratic governor, and 53 percent supported Democratic candidates; yet the state's rules, set by a Republican government, allocated only 36 percent of the assembly seats to Democratic candidates. The state's elections (primaries) ignored calls to extend the data and allow mail-in ballots during the pandemic.

A particularly important point of this argument is that many voting centres in the mostly Democratic strongholds had been shut down by the Republican lawmakers, and the denial of mail-in ballots was more likely to affect Democratic areas. As a result, there were very long lines and frustrations over the challenges voters faced as they broke their quarantines to vote in these elections. In a series of reports, the *New York Times* revealed that thousands of mailed-in ballots were disqualified as having been mailed late, or were not delivered. At the same time, the White House was actively dismantling the US Postal Service. In Texas, realizing people were pivoting to early voting, the governor restricted drop-off centres to one per county. In counties with very few people (Loving County, for example, has only 150 registered voters) this might appear to be reasonable, but one drop-off box for 2.4 million registered voters in Harris county is less reasonable.[10]

Just like in other times, there have been significant attempts to fight back (see Silva's contribution to this book on the Black Lives Matter movement in Chapter 24). It is important to repeat the intersections of larger disparities in health, access to economic, social and political resources, and experiences of routine violence (Purkayastha and Ratcliff, 2014) that the current phase of Black Lives Matter protests and movements have brought back into public consciousness. The horrific incidents of violence that galvanized protests across urban and rural parts of the country are a reflection of the growing insistence by a wider swath of the population that Black lives ought be treated with the same respect as White lives, and that the government – and the police as a unit of the government – need to ensure protection from violence instead of killing Black Americans (Cazenave, 2018).

Remarkably in the midst of pandemic, thousands of people organized through loose, decentralized networks, overwhelmingly maintaining good health protocols,[11] have marched peacefully, facing police in military-style armor using tear gas and tasers,[12] to demand justice. Along with multiple and sustained protests demanding much-needed action against excessive force and violence used against Black Americans for many years, there is a reckoning underway, state by state, and locality by locality, concerning police practices and budgets.[13] At the same time, these marches for Black lives highlight a wider responsibility of citizens to act – to ensure every American's ability to build *secure lives* free of threats to their survival and well-being – and to hold governments accountable especially as they ossify practices that entrench inequalities.[14] The social, political and economic factors that promote the health of any society, including laws, policies, practices and consistently available resources to dismantle inequalities, as social scientists and activists have documented for decades, are being brought more forcefully to public attention during this pandemic.

Oppressions unveiled, again

In sum, the problems of the US's political, economic and social systems, which often remained less visible or were explained through political rhetoric as individual or cultural failures, are, again, revealed starkly through this pandemic. The BLM movement, by drawing attention to routinized violence, galvanized discourse and some action in many, but not all, regions of the country; the pushback against the issues brought forth by this movement are strident, powered by the president and his supporters. The tragedies unfolding right now are the consequence of earlier and current decisions not to travel on the path to ensure widespread human rights and human securities.

Notes

[1] See: https://www.dol.gov/ui/data.pdf

[2] See: https://www.brookings.edu/blog/up-front/2020/06/16/race-gaps-in-covid-19-deaths-are-even-bigger-than-they-appear/

[3] Along with attempts to circulate conspiracy theories about the pandemic being a hoax: https://www.splcenter.org/hatewatch/2020/04/17/hate-groups-and-racist-pundits-spew-covid-19-misinformation-social-media-despite-companies

[4] While the Department of Labour's bulletin indicates that the total figures for unemployment have decreased, it remains the same or higher for African Americans and Latinx groups.

[5] See: https://www.nytimes.com/2020/10/06/science/covid-universities-women.html

[6] See: https://www.nytimes.com/2020/09/29/us/trump-proud-boys-biden.html

[7] See: https://www.npr.org/sections/live-updates-protests-for-racial-justice/2020/08/31/908137377/trump-defends-kenosha-shooting-suspect

[8] See: https://www.nbcnews.com/news/us-news/six-men-charged-alleged-plot-kidnap-michigan-gov-gretchen-whitmer-n1242622?fbclid=IwAR37PnZiZi6qzLPWPMW8ummXzPClW9vuJxhFBj8d_C6zPKw0KM3Ys4l15lA

[9] https://www.nytimes.com/2019/08/15/us/gerrymandering-redistricting-wisconsin.html

[10] See: https://www.statesman.com/news/20201008/judge-urged-to-void-abbott-order-limiting-ballot-drop-off-sites

[11] See: https://www.vox.com/2020/6/26/21300636/coronavirus-pandemic-black-lives-matter-protests

[12] See: https://www.wired.co.uk/article/police-brutality-minneapolis-floyd-blm-trump

[13] See: https://www.washingtonpost.com/graphics/2020/national/police-use-of-force-chokehold-carotid-ban/

[14] The larger point, not developed in this paper, is that BLM mobilization is also creating a much more widespread awareness about the ways in which violence has been routinized and how the ability of many other marginalized people—for instance, other racial minorities, sexual minorities, immigrants and indigenous groups—to build lives free of threats to their survival and well-being, that is, lives that reflect human security, continues to depend on repeated mobilizations. The BLM movement is also the current fulcrum leveraging synergies between activists from other movements and protests *against* gun violence, against violence against women and against processes of slow killing such as through contamination of water, location of toxic wastes, pollution and so forth.

References

Boboltz, S. (2020) 'The stabbing of Asian American toddler and family deemed a hate crime: Report', *HuffPost*, [online] 1 April, available from: https://www.huffpost.com/entry/stabbing-of-asian-american-toddler-and-family-deemed-a-hate-crime-report_n_5e84b65fc5b6871702a84c0b

Casey, N. (2020) 'College made them feel equal: The virus exposed how unequal their lives are', *New York Times*, [online] 4 April, available from: https://nyti.ms/39CsszO

Cazenave, N. (2018) *Killing African Americans: Police and Vigilante Violence as a Racial Control Mechanism*, Abingdon: Routledge.

Couldry, N. and Mejias, U.A. (2018) 'Data colonialism: Rethinking big data's relation to the contemporary subject', *Television & New Media*, 20(4): 336–49.

Defina, R. and Hannon, L. (2009) 'Diversity, racial threat and metropolitan housing', *Social Forces*, 88: 373–94.

Fullerton, A. and Dwana, R. (2011) 'Labor rights after the flexible turn', in W. Armaline, D. Glasberg and B. Purkayastha (eds) *Human Rights in Our Own Backyard*, Philadelphia: University of Pennsylvania Press.

Hakim, D. (2020) '"It's hit our front door": Homes for the disabled see a surge of COVID-19', *New York Times*, [online] 8 April, available from: https://nyti.ms/2JMC6p0

Hochschild, A. (1997) *The Time Bind: When Work Becomes Home and Home Becomes Work*, New York: Metropolitan Books.

Jeung, R. (2020) *Incidents of Coronavirus Discrimination March 26–April 1, 2020: A Report for A3PCON and CAA*, Los Angeles: Asian Pacific Policy and Planning Council available from: http://www.asianpacificpolicyand planningcouncil.org/wp-content/uploads/Stop_AAPI_Hate_Weekly_ Report_4_3_20.pdf

Krugman, P. (2020) 'American democracy might be dying', *New York Times*, 9 April, available from: https://nyti.ms/2VewZDm

Massey, D. and Denton, N. (1993) *American Apartheid: Segregation and the Making of the Underclass*, Cambridge: Cambridge University Press.

Maya, J. and Newman, A. (2020) 'Virus is twice as deadly for Black and Latino People than Whites in NYC', *New York Times*, [online] 10 April, available from: https://nyti.ms/34kO6rr

McKenzie, L. (2020) 'Zoombies take over online classrooms', *Inside Higher Ed*, [online] 3 April, available from: https://insidehighered.com/ news/2020/04/03/zoombombing-isn't-going-away-and-it-could-get- worse?fbclid=IwAR2LOVaVvXqJLFkQLD-w1VSw1heJCife2s5-OPj

McNicholas, C. (2020) 'Labor in the midst of a pandemic, Trump's NLRB nearly makes it impossible for workers to organize unions', *Portside* [online], available from: https://portside.org/2020–04-01/midst-pandemic-trumps- nlrb-makes-it-nearly-impossible-workers-organize- union?fbclid=IwAR 389SuIHUmgHPkxgLwtqxO9bCTMx

Noble, S. (2018) *Algorithms of Oppression: How Search Engines Reinforce Racism*, New York: New York University Press.

Purkayastha, B. (2018) 'Migration, migrants, and human security', *Current Sociology Monograph*, 66(2): 167–91.

Purkayastha, B. (2020) 'From suffrage to substantive human rights: The unfinished journey for racial minority women', *Western New England Law Journal*, 42(3): 119–38.

Purkayastha, B. and Ratcliff, K. (2014) 'Routine violence: Intersectionality at the interstices', in M. Segal and V. Demos (eds) *Advances in Gender Research*, London: Emerald Publications.

Ratcliff, K. (2017) *Social Determinants of Health: Looking Upstream*, London: Polity Press.

Ravish, K. (2018) *The Free Voice: On Democracy, Culture and the Nation*, New Delhi: Speaking Tiger Books.

Ray, R. (2018) *The Making of a Teenage Service Underclass: Poverty and Mobility in an American City*, Berkeley, CA: University of Berkeley Press.

Roberts, D. (2020) 'Gutting fuel economy standards during a pandemic is peak Trump', *Vox*, [online] 2 April, available from: https://www.vox.com/energy-and-environment/2020/4/2/21202509/trump-climate-change-fuel-economy-standards-coronavirus-pandemic-peak

Romero, M. (2018) 'Trump's immigration attacks, in brief', *Contexts*, 17: 34–41.

Romero, S. (2020) 'Checkpoints, curfews, airlifts: virus rips through Navajo Nation', *New York Times*, [online] 9 April, available from: https://nyti.ms/2VaK14O

Sewell, A. (2016) 'The racism-race reification process: A meso-level political economic framework for understanding racial health disparities', *Sociology of Race and Ethnicity*, 2: 402–32.

Stoll M. and Covington K. (2012) 'Explaining racial/ethnic gaps in spatial mismatch in the US: The primacy of racial segregation', *Urban Studies*, 49(11): 2501–21.

9

The Data Gaps of the Pandemic: Data Poverty and Forms of Invisibility

Stefania Milan and Emiliano Treré

Since the COVID-19 virus was first identified in mainland China at the end of 2019, the pandemic has affected an exceptionally high portion of the world population. Not surprisingly, numbers are at the very core of the narration of the pandemic. Figures of various kinds fill the news, accounting for the death toll, the progress of population testing, the growth of individuals who tested positive for the virus and the saturation of intensive care units, among others. These numbers contribute to making the problem 'amenable to thought', and thus serve as 'both representation and intervention' (Osborne and Rose, 2004). As such, they shape both governmental action and the popular response to it.

Although they are not neutral or absolute, they are attributed a sort of 'mechanical objectivity' (Porter, 1995) that positions the exercise of enumerating and comparing above other forms of knowing and feeling (see also Bowker and Star, 2000). In a nutshell, numbers determine the existence of the problem, and they determine which countries and social groups ought to elicit our concern. They affect our ability to care, to empathize and to abide by the oftentimes draconian measures adopted in the effort to curb the pandemic. Yet many communities at the margins, including many areas of the so-called Global South, are virtually absent from this number-based narration of the pandemic.

Communities that remain in the shadows include but are not limited to: undocumented migrants, refugees and people on the move, members of labour forces operating in submerged markets and/or under precarious conditions such as sex workers, gig workers and farmhands, impoverished families, victims of domestic violence, but also developing countries with a suboptimal statistical and testing capacity.

This has two main implications. First, the pandemic might exacerbate existing inequalities, aggravating the difficulties of populations at risk who are made even more invisible by mediocre monitoring and by exclusion from healthcare or welfare subsidies. Second, in the absence of reliable data, institutions, including governments in the South, might be tempted to 'import' predictions and models from other socioeconomic realities and base domestic measures on these, further ignoring invisible sectors of the population. The urge to 'universalize' both problem and solutions – basing local policy on policy responses meant to address different contexts – overlooks the fact that numbers are deeply ingrained in specific socioeconomic and political geographies.

In this chapter, we build on critical data studies (Dalton et al, 2016) to warn against the universalization of problems, narratives and responses (Milan and Treré, 2019), and encourage scholars to reflect on the challenges of COVID-19, specifically when observed from the margins. 'The margin,' argues Rodríguez, is 'a shortcut to speak of complex dynamics of power inequality. Processes of asymmetrical access to material and symbolic resources shape differentiated and unequal access to the public sphere' (Rodríguez, 2017, p 49). We argue that this asymmetrical access is particularly virulent in the *datafied society*, which grounds the so-called public sphere in data generation, trade and processing.

More specifically, this chapter explores the widening data gaps of this pandemic, which largely map onto known, historical gaps in the economic and digital realms, and exposes how, even during the pandemic, the disempowered manage to create innovative forms of solidarity from below that partially mitigate the negative effects of their invisibility.

Two types of data gaps

If numbers are at the core of the COVID-19 problem, we ought to pay attention to who is represented in these numbers and who is (deliberately or not) left out. These data gaps concern both data generation and data quality, which even in ordinary times can jeopardize 'evidence-based policy making, tracking progress and development, and increasing government accountability' (Chen et al, 2013, p 1).

Data gaps are a known weakness of the datafied society. Among others, Boyd and Crawford (2012) warned against the 'big data divide' in matters of ownership and access, while Manovich (2011) exposed the 'data analysis divide', highlighting disparities in data usage and related skills. Reinterpreting the somewhat forgotten literature on the digital divide, which at the turn of the millennium provided a word of caution concerning the optimistic narratives associated with the 'digital revolution' (Norris, 2001), McCarthy (2016) explains how this divide perpetuates severe 'digital inequalities', which affect a number of areas of human activity, including identity, self-determination, visibility and agency.

The data gaps exacerbated by the pandemic, however, assume also another dramatic connotation. Rather than solely revealing 'the asymmetric relationship between those who collect, store, and mine large quantities of data, and those whom data collection targets' (Andrejevic, 2014, p 1673), these data gaps expose a new type of 'data poverty' (to paraphrase Boyd and Crawford) – one that is essentially a *sine qua non* condition of existence. It is no longer solely a matter of data exploitation (Zuboff, 2019) or data colonialism (Couldry and Mejias, 2018), but rather it gets to the bottom of what it means to be human. That is, data is tied to peoples' visibility, survival and care. Today's 'data poor' are not in opposition to the 'Big Data rich' evoked by Boyd and Crawford (2012). Rather, their concerns have to do with very fundamental types of inequality that predate the emergence of the datafied society but are possibly worsened by policymakers' over-reliance on 'calculative publics' (Gillespie, 2014, p 188), brought into existence by omnipresent data infrastructures.

We can identify at least two problematic situations related to this data poverty. The first concerns developing countries, while the second has to do with invisible populations within a variety of geopolitical and sociopolitical contexts.

Data poverty in low-income countries

Facing an outbreak that knows no borders, the problems of developing countries vis-à-vis the pandemic are manifold (see, for example, Masiero, 2020). One of the worst-case scenarios on the large scale relates to the (in) ability of many countries in the South, on the one hand, to produce reliable population statistics, and on the other, to test their population for the virus, due to the scarce availability of testing kits as well as adequate medical facilities (Diallo, 2020). The consequences of this data poverty are particularly harsh when lack of monitoring capabilities meets the absence of a nationwide health system, like in the sub-Saharan region (Quaglio et al, 2020).

To be sure, progress in population monitoring followed the revision of the United Nations' Millennium Development Goals in 2005, when countries in the Global South received support to devise National Strategies for the Development of Statistics (Chen et al, 2013). The urgency of the pandemic seems to have had the positive effect of accelerating the response: the Regional Office for Africa of the World Health Organization (2020) reports that as of mid-May 2020, 44 countries in the region can test for COVID-19. There were only two countries on this list at the start of the outbreak.

Lack of reliable numbers to accurately portray the COVID-19 pandemic as it spreads to the Southern hemisphere might result in the dangerous equation 'no data = no problem'–with consequences that transcend epidemiological considerations to affect society at its core. Most notably, it offers fertile ground for the spread of misinformation (or what has been termed an 'infodemic'; see United Nations Department of Global Communications, 2020) as well as distorted narratives mobilized at the service of populist agendas.

For example, Mexican left-wing populist president Andrés Manuel López Obrador responded to the COVID-19 emergency insisting that Mexicans should 'keep living life as usual', and went as far as declaring that the pandemic is a plot to derail his presidency (Agren, 2020). On the opposite side of the political spectrum, Brazil's far-right president Jair Bolsonaro dismissed the pandemic as a collective 'hysteria', notwithstanding the rising death toll (Phillips, 2020). The 'fake news' that individuals of African origin are 'immune' to the disease swept social media in both Western countries and the African continent itself (Maclean, 2020). In Italy, the fact that most hospitalized patients are White while undocumented migrants have no access to healthcare has unleashed a plethora of racist comments and anti-migrant calls for action (Huffington Post, 2020), which leads us to discuss a second form of data poverty.

Data poverty as a form of invisibility

A distinct instance of data poverty concerns many of the populations at the margins identified, most notably undocumented foreign nationals, workers of informal economies and vulnerable populations in general, including those who are homeless and gig workers. These segments of society suffer invisibility in ordinary times as well. Oftentimes, this invisibility is a blessing for those living at the margins, who might, for example, put food on the table by engaging in informal or illegal activities. This is the case for some sex workers, who are often part of groups who are already marginalized, like people of colour, or lesbian, gay, bisexual or transgender (LGBT) individuals, for whom sex work might represent 'one option among bad ones' (Wheeler, 2020).

During the pandemic, this invisibility translates into the virtual absence of 'official' data about these groups–with two main consequences. On one hand, it means augmented risks for these people but also for their surrounding communities (Milan et al, 2020). On the other hand, it results in the absence of specific support measures also within resource-rich countries. For example, sex workers are typically excluded from pandemic-triggered recovery plans; operators of the shadow economy unable to work are often not part of the count for unemployment subsidies.

Furthermore, a mix of fear, social stigma, criminalization and short-sighted legislation prevents individuals and social groups at the margins from coming forward when in need of care. In many such cases, invisibility might equal death—for example, in the case of victims of domestic violence (Villaseñor, 2020)—or might trap people in the conditions that make them vulnerable in the first place.

Countering data poverty: collective solidarities from below

While institutional responses to these forms of invisibility have been varied and largely absent, the COVID-19 pandemic has exposed how vulnerable and marginalized groups have nonetheless managed to construct innovative forms of solidarity from below, which serve to soften the negative impact of their invisibility.

This is part of a counter-hegemonic emotional culture (see Gravante and Poma, Chapter 20 of this book) of collective solidarity, care and grassroots activism that signals 'the desperate yearning of the population for some sense of solidarity amid the crisis' (Gerbaudo, 2020). Trying to overcome the absence or slowness of state action, grassroots groups have mobilized to support neighbours, elderly people, individuals with disability and long-term health conditions, precarious workers, indigenous communities and counting. Mobilizations and activist groups have been spurred on in the Global South and high-income countries alike, ramping up the creation of mutual aid groups, strike actions and solidarity networks to make visible the data poor and improve the conditions of marginalized groups during the pandemic. For instance, women's collectives have expanded their reach within the community by distributing food, medicine and essential products across Mexico (Ventura Alfaro, 2020) and China (Bao, 2020). Kenya is witnessing a resurgence of social movement activities, which provide alternative narratives of the crisis (Chukunzira, 2020). In China, activists have sought to bypass governmental censorship about the pandemic by documenting the spread of the virus on the software repository GitHub (Anon, 2020).

New repertoires of action emerge to counter the effects of the lockdown imposed in many countries that prevent people from taking the streets, with several actions going digital. Along the so-called Balkan route, solidarity with people on the move resulted in a 48-hour campaign called 'A soap for IOM (International Organization for Migration)', denouncing the mismanagement of the refugee centres run by IOM in the region, which deprive migrants of basic rights (Milan, 2020).

Chenoweth and colleagues (2020) have documented over 140 strategies of dissent and collective action specifically related to COVID-19. Their preliminary mapping displays the incredible richness of these novel online, offline and hybrid repertoires of contention, which include grassroots tactics of 'data making' (Pybus et al, 2015) at the margins, where vulnerable groups and their allies become active producers and consumers of alternative narratives to reclaim their visibility amid the pandemic. Together, these forms of solidarity, protest and resistance warn us against turning a blind eye to the impending forms of data poverty.

References

Agren, D. (2020) 'Coronavirus advice from Mexico's president: "Live life as usual"', *The Guardian*, [online] 25 March, available from: https://www.theguardian.com/world/2020/mar/25/coronavirus-advice-from-mexicos-president-live-life-as-usual

Andrejevic, M. (2014) 'Big data, big questions: The big data divide', *International Journal of Communication*, 8: 1673–89.

Anon (2020) 'In memory of COVID-19 in China: Various forms of digital resistance towards censorship', Datactive, [online] 22 May, available from: https://data-activism.net/2020/05/bigdatasur-covid-in-memory-of-covid-19-in-china-various-forms-of-digital-resistance-towards-censorship/

Bao, H. (2020) '"Anti-domestic violence little vaccine": A Wuhan-based feminist activist campaign during COVID-19', *Interface: A Journal for and About Social Movements*, 12(1): 55–63.

Bowker, G.C. and Star, S.L. (2000) *Sorting Things Out*, Cambridge, MA: MIT Press.

Chen, S., Fonteneau, F., Jütting, J. and Klasen, S. (2013) *Towards a Post-2015 Framework That Counts: Developing National Statistical Capacity*, Paris: Partnership in Statistics for Development in the 21st Century.

Chenoweth, E., Choi-Fitzpatrick, A., Pressman, J., Santos, F.G., Ulfelder, J. (2020) 'Methods of dissent and collective action under COVID: A crowdsourced list', Crowd Counting Consortium, [online], available from: https://sites.google.com/view/crowdcountingconsortium/view-download-the-data

Chukunzira, A. (2020) 'Organising under curfew: Perspectives from Kenya', *Interface: A Journal for and about Social Movements*, 12(1): 39–42.

Couldry, N. and Mejias, U.A. (2018). 'Data colonialism: Rethinking big data's relation to the contemporary subject', *Television & New Media*, 20(4): 336–49.

Dalton, C.M., Taylor, L. and Thatcher, J. (2016) 'Critical data studies: A dialog on data and space', Big *Data & Society*, 3(1).

Diallo, M.C. (2020) 'Africa: A virus without borders – is Africa fully prepared to embrace the fight against the pandemic of the 21st century?' *Daily Observer*, 1 May.

Garden, D. (2020) 'The British government has abandoned the Global South to coronavirus', *Open Democracy*, [online] 25 March, available from: https://www.opendemocracy.net/en/opendemocracyuk/british-government-has-abandoned-global-south-coronavirus/

Gerbaudo, P. (2020) '#Clapforcarers: Why grassroots solidarity against coronavirus matters', *Open Democracy*, [online] 27 March, available from: https://www.opendemocracy.net/en/can-europe-make-it/clapforcarers-why-grassroots-solidarity-against-coronavirus-matters/

Gillespie, T. (2014) 'The relevance of algorithms', in T. Gillespie, P. Boczkowski and K. Foot (eds) *Media Technologies: Essays on Communication, Materiality, and Society*, Cambridge, MA: MIT Press, 167–94.

Huffington Post (2020) '"Africani immuni? È una ipotesi" : Ma Galli precisa: "La tubercolosi non c'entra"', *Huffington Post*, [online] 24 March, available from: https://www.huffingtonpost.it/entry/extra-comunitari-immuni-e-una-ipotesi_it_5e79d2c4c5b63c3b6496e69f

Maclean, R. (2020) 'Africa braces for coronavirus, but slowly', *New York Times*, [online] 17 March, available from: https://www.nytimes.com/2020/03/17/world/africa/coronavirus-africa-burkina-faso.html

Manovich, L. (2011) *Trending: The Promises and the Challenges of Big Social Data*, Minneapolis: University of Minnesota Press.

Masiero, S. (2020) 'Beyond touchscreens: The perils of biometric social welfare in lockdown', *Datactive*, [online] 23 April, available from: https://data-activism.net/2020/04/bigdatasur-beyond-touchscreens-the-perils-of-biometric-social-welfare-in-lockdown/

McCarthy, M.T. (2016) 'The big data divide and its consequences', *Sociology Compass*, 10: 1131–40.

Milan, C. (2020) 'Refugee solidarity along the western Balkans route: New challenges and a change of strategy in times of COVID-19', *Interface: A Journal for and about Social Movements*, 12(1): 208–12.

Milan, S. and Treré, E. (2019) 'Big data from the South(s): Beyond data universalism', *Television & New Media*, 20(4): 319–35.

Milan, S., Pelizza, A. and Lausberg, Y. (2020) 'Making migrants visible to COVID-19 counting: The dilemma', *Open Democracy*, [online] 28 April, available from: https://www.opendemocracy.net/en/can-europe-make-it/making-migrants-visible-covid-19-counting-dilemma/

Norris, P. (2001) *Digital Divide? Civic Engagement, Information Poverty and the Internet in Democratic Societies*, Cambridge: Cambridge University Press.

Osborne, T. and Rose, N. (2004) 'Spatial phenomenotechnics: Making space with Charles Booth and Patrick Geddes', *Environment and Planning D: Society and Space*, 22(2): 209–28.

Phillips, T. (2020) 'Bolsonaro faces calls to change tack on COVID-19 as Rio heads for "great hardship"', *The Guardian*, [online] 30 April, available from: https://www.theguardian.com/world/2020/apr/30/brazil-rio-coronavirus-great-hardship-bolsonaro

Porter, T.M. (1995) *Trust in Numbers: The Pursuit of Objectivity in Science and Public Life*, Princeton, NJ: Princeton University Press.

Pybus, J., Coté, M. and Blanke, T. (2015) 'Hacking the social life of big data', *Big Data & Society*, 2(2).

Quaglio, G., Putoto, G., Brand, H. and Preiser, W. (2020) 'COVID-19 in Africa: What is at stake?', *European Science-Media Hub*, [online] 22 May, available from: https://sciencemediahub.eu/2020/05/22/covid-19-in-africa-what-is-at-stake/

Rodríguez, C. (2017) 'Studying media at the margins: Learning from the field', in V. Pickard and G. Yang (eds) *Media Activism in the Digital Age*, Abingdon: Routledge, 49–60.

Tutton, R. (2007) 'Opening the white box: Exploring the study of whiteness in contemporary genetics research', *Ethnic and Racial Studies*, 30(4): 557–69.

United Nations Department of Global Communications. (2020) '5 ways the UN is fighting "infodemic" of misinformation', United Nations, [online] 30 April, available from: https://www.un.org/en/un-coronavirus-communications-team/five-ways-united-nations-fighting-'infodemic'-misinformation

Ventura Alfaro, M.J. (2020) 'Feminist solidarity networks have multiplied since the COVID-19 outbreak in Mexico', *Interface: A Journal for and About Social Movements*, 12(2): 82–7.

Villaseñor, T. (2020) 'La otra epidemia: Los feminicidios que no se cuentan', *Datactive*, [online] 12 May, available from: https://data-activism.net/2020/05/bigdatasur-covid-la-otra-epidemia-los-feminicidios-que-no-se-cuentan/

Wheeler, S. (2020) 'Sex workers struggle to survive COVID-19 pandemic', *Human Rights Watch*, [online] 4 May, available from: https://www.hrw.org/news/2020/05/04/sex-workers-struggle-survive-covid-19-pandemic

World Health Organization (2020) 'African countries move from COVID-19 readiness to response as many confirm cases', *WHO*, [online] 22 May, available from: https://www.afro.who.int/health-topics/coronavirus-covid-19

Zuboff, S. (2019) *The Age of Surveillance Capitalism*, London: Profile Books.

10

Necropolitics and Biopower in the Pandemic: Death, Social Control or Well-Being

Montserrat Sagot

Every crisis creates its own ways to experience life, and, in some cases, death. The crisis generated by COVID-19 allows us to see the worst of times and the best of times to live and die, but it has also opened up the possibility to imagine better times. The crisis is transforming our ways of envisioning the world and how we live in the it. This is why this is not a health crisis, as some have called it. The COVID-19 pandemic has the potential to become a *civilizational crisis* that could disrupt social relations, the organization of production, the role of states, the path of neoliberal globalization and even the place of humans in history and nature. This chapter will explore these deeper aspects of the crisis of contemporary capitalism, especially how the pandemic made contemporary necropolitics and biopower even more visible.

Necropolitics and the killer phase of capitalism

This crisis has exposed some facets of capitalism that are sometimes hidden behind colonial, racist, sexist or efficiency-driven discourses associated with the ideologies that seek to reduce the size of the state. Firstly, the crisis allows us to clearly see what I define as the *killer phase of capitalism*. This has always been a key characteristic of capitalism, whose techniques of extreme devaluation of life produce bodies vulnerable to marginalization, exploitation and even death. However, things look different when dead bodies fill an ice rink in Madrid or a mass grave is opened in a New York park compared to when the dead are African migrants crossing the Mediterranean or people from Central America whose remains are scattered on the deadly road to the

United States. The level of alarm and awareness of death and vulnerability are heightened when the victims are closer to the centres of power. The 70 military trucks carrying corpses out of Bergamo, a small city in the alpine Lombardy region in Italy, contributed more to the visibility of the lethal phase of capitalism than the burnt bodies in the streets of Guayaquil, the largest city of Ecuador.

These new manifestations of the mortality produced by capitalism have even led to a redefinition of certain public and private spaces. Spaces such as ice rinks or parks, once places for recreation, became mortuaries or cemeteries. Extreme forms of privatization have also started to appear, reflected in the recent expansion of the market for the purchase of private islands, castles, bunkers or large yachts, as a result of the interest of the most privileged in isolating themselves and removing themselves as far from the dead bodies as possible. Dead bodies that are produced by how their companies organize, produce and exploit, and by their ways of doing business and making excessive profits.

Another problematic redefinition of the public brought about by this crisis has to do with the work of criminal organizations (whether they are Mafia, Camorra, maras, cartels or others). In countries like Italy, Mexico, El Salvador or Brazil they have a key role distributing food, medicine, soap and even disinfecting communities abandoned to their fate by governments. These organizations, which play an important role in the contemporary necropolitics, have begun to occupy parts of the public space that states have left empty, especially in vulnerable and impoverished territories, and to solidify their status as de facto powers. This could have serious consequences for democratic governance in the future.

The lethal aspects of capitalism have also been evident in the quasi-eugenic policies of some countries, such as Sweden, for example, which denies access to intensive care to people over 80 years old who are ill with COVID-19 and to those between 60 and 80 years of age with underlying health conditions. Similarly, this phase of capitalism can be seen in the practice of some municipalities in Spain of not taking ill people who live in care homes to hospitals, a policy which has been repeatedly denounced by the families of the deceased.

In the case of Central America, we have the government of Nicaragua, which has decided to adopt a denial position, quite similar to that of Trump or Bolsonaro despite supposedly being the ideological opposite of those governments. Nicaragua has decided to do nothing to resist the pandemic such that whoever has to die just dies.

An important element in these deadly policies is that many of those who were first infected belong to the privileged sectors, with the capacity to travel and take holidays in other countries. However, the virus later spread to those who always suffer the most: the old and weak, the Blacks and Latinos in the Unites States, the indigenous population and the working people from the most exploited sectors who have now become 'essential workers'.

Recognition for these workers during the pandemic was mainly symbolic. In other words, they have been given a new adjective on the scale of social value and they were applauded in some cities for five minutes every night. But, in general terms, they didn't receive better salaries that reflect the risks they take and the service they provide in keeping civilization going, nor have they received minimum levels of safety equipment in order to do their job under pandemic conditions. They were, and continue to be, still the same 'unworthy' lives that capitalism uses and discards, except that they were elevated in rhetorical terms to the category of 'essential'.

Health systems and biopower

The crisis caused by COVID-19 also reveals decades of neglect in public health systems, the privatization of these systems, the precarization of work and the erosion of labour rights. In fact, the dismantling of public health, privatization and outsourcing of services are some of the main reasons for the high mortality rate.

This is the context for the emergence of a utilitarian discourse of crisis and public institutions management. What needs to be protected, most governments say, is the health system so it doesn't collapse. And some of us were naïve enough to think that it was *life* that had to be protected. It is obvious that to protect life you have to protect the health systems, but the order in and emphasis with which this is spoken about are very striking. This discourse, as outlined in most countries, actually suggests that lockdown measures are not being set up to protect life but to avoid having to treat many people in hospitals and through public health services. The order is to stay at home, and if possible, recover or die there or in a care home, so as not to spend resources on people who are already considered disposable.

The lockdown measures also revealed a homogenizing policy that doesn't take into account inequalities and different types of vulnerability. It is a policy of surveillance and micromanagement of bodies, assuming the existence of a population with equal opportunities, life chances and access to resources. Such a policy will only increase precariousness, hunger and even increase the risk of contagion unless it is introduced alongside redistributive measures that offer a basic income for all of those who cannot afford to go into quarantine or who cannot meet the supposedly altruistic rhetoric of protecting the common good and public health that accompanies the slogan *#StayAtHome*. After the first months of the pandemic, when many countries began to relax their lockdown measures, it was clear that these policies should also recognize that there are groups more prone to contagion and death because of their material conditions of existence, the ways they move around cities and the types of jobs they perform.

The pressing need for access to healthcare and for competent public services and redistributive policies, which the pandemic has made evident, has generated a renewed demand for welfare states that respond to the different needs of the population and allow for social and economic redistribution (as several chapters in the first section of this book suggest). While these claims are being put on the public agenda, at the same time, the most authoritarian and controlling features of the state are also being reinforced. This means that the crisis is giving new justifications for the implementation of repressive measures and new forms of political and social coercion.

Central America is an example of this. El Salvador's, Honduras's and Guatemala's governments are reviving the repressive repertoire of the past and imposing states of exception. There is a radicalization of the apparatus of biopolitical control, no longer in the name of national security, as in the past, but in the name of public health. The arbitrary arrests of women in El Salvador out getting food simply because they don't have shopping lists or the arrest of a mother accompanying her child to use an outside latrine are examples of the increasing coercion.

The novelty of these situations during the pandemic is that the fear of death or disease makes many people accept these extreme conditions of biocontrol without protest. And they are not only accepting them but also demanding them from their governments. There is even an explicit willingness by some to become an active part of the control mechanisms by reporting people who do not conform to the rules of lockdown. In the case of Central America, people who lived under dictatorships and who were exposed to the repressive powers of the state now submit because of fear to the unprecedented mechanisms of social control. The fear of becoming just a biological entity, bare life, at the mercy of an invisible enemy – a virus – which can be anywhere, seems to unleash more fear and willingness to surrender than the repressive political apparatuses.

Some possibilities for the future

There is justified fear that this crisis could produce more repressive societies, with ultrasophisticated mechanisms of biopower through the use of new technologies, and that we will continue to act as if we were still in 1990, believing in the virtue of neoliberal policies and denying global warming. But the crisis also opens up the possibility of imagining a different future.

In addition to uncovering the lethal phases of capitalism and the potential of neoliberal recipes to set off humanitarian disasters, the pandemic has also exposed other complexities and risks. Firstly, the lockdown measures have created a fairly widespread debate about the nature of the domestic space. Feminists have been talking about this for centuries, but now, with a large percentage of the population confined to their homes, conversations about the unequal distribution of reproductive work and domestic tasks, family violence against women and the importance of care have entered the mainstream (see Batthyány, Chapter 34 of this volume).

In this sense, the pandemic has helped to undermine the conservative notion of the family and home as spaces of peace, security and harmony, and exposed the persistent sexual division of labour and the centrality of women in life-sustaining care work. This 'discovery' and the visibility of the issue can become the first step in initiating processes of change. The renewed appreciation of care work and other neglected jobs is another unintended consequence of the crisis. Although much of the valorization of these tasks is only symbolic, the crisis could be an opportunity to reaffirm the importance of the objects and resources with use value. In addition, this could be an opportunity to increase our understanding of the importance of the work that allows for social reproduction and of the people who perform this kind of work.

In addition, the crisis could also create opportunities to reindustrialize locally and to promote domestic production, especially since many international trade links have been broken. It is, therefore, an opportunity for policies to disengage from the market logic of neoliberal globalization towards a promotion of national industries and local food production, which would help guarantee food security especially in the Global South (see also Bringel, Chapter 35 of this book).

This crisis has generated renewed demands for welfare states that take care of the commons, implement measures for the protection of the entire population and become agents of redistributive justice, taking into consideration the different manifestations of inequality. This point is fundamental since, until now, many people have considered this discussion to be over. Ever since Margaret Thatcher said, more than 40 years ago, that "there is no society", and Ronald Reagan said that "government is not the solution to our problems, government is the problem", the ideologies of neoliberalism have done everything possible to obscure the importance of states being at the service of the common good. However, the COVID-19 crisis has highlighted the need not only for a type of state that exercises the monopoly on violence and promotes a good business environment but also for a state and society that operate under the principle of solidarity.

COVID-19 has also allowed for a revaluation of science as a service to humanity. After the recent growth of anti-science and anti-vaccine organizations, flat-earth conspiracies, and religious fundamentalist groups that question basic scientific principles, this pandemic has restored the privileged position of science. It seems clear that the pandemic cannot be solved just with vaccines or drugs. It will require policies that promote the universalization of public health coverage and the reparation of inequalities. However, it is extremely important to reclaim the production of scientific knowledge that is not instrumental in the development of new modes of life.

Finally, the crisis could serve to help us recognize our own vulnerability and fragility and the interdependence of human life with nature and with the life of other species. Perhaps fear will not only lead us to submissively accept the biocontrol measures deployed by many governments but also to question a process of capital accumulation that has become deadly and left in its wake the disappearance of species, territories, cultures and peoples. In sum, this crisis allows us to see that the tragedy is not on the horizon but is here now. Perhaps this diagnosis can also allow us to imagine and generate changes for the construction of a new world.

11

COVID-19 in the Urban Peripheries: Perspectives from the Favelas of Rio de Janeiro

Aercio Barbosa de Oliveira, Bruno França, Caroline Rodrigues, Emanuelle Anastasoupoulos, Milla Gabrieli dos Santos Faria, Monica Oliveira and Rachel Barros (FASE Team Rio de Janeiro)

The characteristics of the formation of Brazilian society, built under the aegis of slavery, land ownership and patrimonial and authoritarian traditions, are adopting dramatic shapes in the context of the COVID-19 pandemic. The virus can reach an entire population, given its extremely high contagiousness, but its most harmful consequences will continue to reinforce the inequality and structural racism that characterize Brazil's society. Nevertheless, this cannot be considered as something new.

As a result of this structure, the *favelas* (slums) and the urban peripheries remain a living testimony of the struggle for the right to exist and to live in urban spaces. Since the rise of the favelas in Rio de Janeiro, these housing spaces, occupied by impoverished segments, have been fundamentally related to the process of exclusionary modernization that takes shape in the urban space, given Brazil's urgency to enter into the industrialized world, eschewing its 'backward' characteristic.

The first favela in Rio de Janeiro, Morro da Favela, currently named Morro da Providência, dating from the end of the 19th century, was initially occupied by soldiers returning from the War of Canudos along with residents of the adjacent tenement, Cabeça de Porco[1], which was demolished in 1893. During Pereira Passos's renovation programme,[2] which took place at the beginning of the 20th century, most of the tenements existing in the city centre were demolished without any alternatives offered for the displaced occupants. Since then, the favela has become a housing possibility for the strata that could not afford the needed costs of inhabiting the 'formal' city

(Valladares, 2005). The strength of this unequal structure, with public housing provision policies that were inconsistent and selective, always benefiting wealthy social classes, is reflected in numbers. The 2010 Census, performed by the Brazilian Institute of Geography and Statistics (IBGE), recorded that 19.1 percent of the population of the city of Rio de Janeiro live in favelas.

Therefore, removal of the poorest segments of the formal city was related to the search for a new way of life, which was accompanied by the stigmatization of the favelas and peripheral communities' inhabitants. Since then, there has been one theoretical perspective that sees poverty, slums and peripheries as 'social problems' and another that overcomes this stigmatizing view and sees them as the result of the way cities are produced under capitalism. According to this last perspective, there is no doubt that Brazilian urbanization has historically produced the formation of uneven cities, where there is a systematic denial of the right to access urban goods and services for large portions of the population.

Dealing with social injustices resulting from the COVID-19 pandemic in a country with these roots is always delicate, especially at times when the structural racism of Brazilian social formation is taking on new dimensions. Data from the IBGE's survey of 2018 concerning social inequalities by colour or race in Brazil show that, in Rio de Janeiro, 30.5 percent of Black and mixed-race people live in favelas, against 14.3 percent of White people. In terms of basic health coverage, it is the same story. Also in 2018, Black and mixed-race people constituted the majority of the population living in places with inadequate infrastructure and increased exposure to diseases: 12.5 percent of Black and mixed-race people live in places without garbage collection, against only 6 percent among the White population; in places without general water supply, Black and mixed-race people represented 17.9 percent and White people 11.5 percent; in places with sanitary drainage through sewage collection or rain networks, Black and mixed-race people represented 42.8 percent of the population, against 26.5 percent for White people.

Between desertion of the state and solidarity

At the beginning of the pandemic, the population in the favelas and urban peripheries of Rio de Janeiro had seen the state governor Wilson Witzel (of the conservative Social Christian Party) emerge on the national political scene with some degree of common sense concerning the pandemic of COVID-19, if compared to the position taken by Jair Bolsonaro. Contrary to the recommendations of the World Health Organization (WHO), the Brazilian president has been attending public events without any protection and downplaying the risks of COVID-19, saying, "it's nothing but a little flu" (Bringel, 2020).

The importance of the measures taken by the governor when the pandemic spread and uncertainties were huge is undeniable. He communicated to the population the health risks associated with COVID-19, and then took legal measures to limit the traffic between the state's countryside and metropolitan region. However, when we look at the cuts in the state's public budget, his disregard for the most vulnerable people who need social and basic income policies, particularly in the face of the health emergency, becomes clear.

Witzel considerably restricted the budget amid the pandemic,[3] which directly affected social spending linked to housing and education. It is also worth noting the contingency plan of R$7.6 billion made in the budget under the justification of the drop in oil prices and of the need to shift the budget to face COVID-19. The State Welfare Housing Fund, for example, also lost 29 percent of its budget, which could have been used to improve conditions in the slums. What is striking is that with the exception of health, the only sector not subject to budget cuts is public security (military and civil police, civil defence, the fire brigade and the '*policía presente*' programme). The decision of where to cut and where to invest is another example of the genocidal policies of Brazil's government.

For people living in the favelas and the peripheries, such measures have already had direct consequences. The actions to contain the virus have already had a drastic impact on the livelihoods of communities composed mainly of Black people with limited access to formal employment and surviving through work in the service industry – which is generally precarious, intermittent and informal. One example is access to public transport. Using trains and travelling between cities now requires proof of formal employment. There have also been a number of rights violations, as the train and bus stations have become crowded and long lines form, further exposing workers to the risk of infection. Another negative impact is the decrease in family income for residents of these areas that have been forced into quarantine because of state and municipal regulation, who have been forced into situations of extreme need. The pandemic, therefore, has made the cruellest aspects of living in a city as unequal as Rio de Janeiro visible: those who are left with the worst effects of COVID-19 are those who no longer have access to their rights.

In addition, political turmoil has only deepened. An impeachment process was opened against Witzel on 11 June 2020 due to corruption charges regarding misappropriating COVID-19 funds. Two months later, the Brazilian Court of Justice suspended Witzel from his duties due to an investigation involving fraud in the acquisition of supplies destined for the pandemic crisis. This only worsened the instability in Rio de Janeiro, which, in recent years, seems to be a place in ruins.

No health, no water and 'social isolation'

Long before the COVID-19 pandemic reached the favelas and peripheries, the health services in these areas were already in a precarious position. The neoliberal logic, which guides the management of public services, has dismantled Rio de Janeiro's public health services over the last few years. Instead, the so-called social health organizations (SHOs) have emerged, which operate through a public-private partnership. The poor quality of the healthcare offered by the Emergency Care Units (*Unidades de Pronto Atendimento*) leaves no room for doubt.

Another example of the denial of rights to the population of the favelas and peripheries occurred in 2019, when the city's mayor, Marcelo Crivella, drastically reduced the staff working at Family Health Support Centres (NASF) and delayed the salaries of employees linked to these institutions. As a result, health professionals called a strike, which, despite functioning at 30 percent capacity, directly affected the Black and poor population, who have in the Universal Healthcare System (SUS) their only possibility for accessing the right to health. In the same way, at the federal level, the Proposed Amendment to the Constitution (PEC) 95/2017 froze public investment for the next 20 years. Therefore, the slowness and the lack of response by the authorities to the poor populations regarding the COVID-19 add to the feeling of helplessness that has already been experienced by the population of the favelas and peripheries.

The reality of imposing social distancing and basic sanitation as preventive measures in slums, peripheries and occupied buildings represents a huge challenge. How would that be possible in houses with only one room, without ventilation and where the single common space is often used by many people, including old people? In practical terms, social distancing in the favelas is almost impossible from the point of view of housing and the associated way of life, which is completely different from that of the middle class. Washing hands is also a critical issue because the right to water is not a reality for many people who live in the favelas. In fact, houses usually have more than one water tank as a measure to try to live with the intermittent and precarious supply. There, storing water is a matter of survival.

Alternatives from inside

Since the government has failed to implement actions aimed at the population of the favelas, the residents themselves are mobilizing and creating alternatives to combat the spread of COVID-19. These measures are based on four main ideas: sharing and compiling information on prevention and symptoms; collecting donations for the purchase of food and cleaning materials; educating people about the importance of water rationing; monitoring people belonging to at-risk groups.

In the favelas of Complexo do Alemão, for example, efforts are being made to collect food donations, hand sanitizers, soap and so forth. There are also several measures being taken to raise the inhabitants' awareness of the importance of social isolation and hand hygiene. These actions are carried out using cars with loudspeakers and through posters displayed in the neighbourhood. Due to the lack of basic resources, this favela is suffering from a precarious water supply. As a result, a large part of the population has not only taken steps to save water but also to share it. This solidarity stands out in times of chaos.[4]

According to Raul Santiago,[5] a journalist living in the Complexo do Alemão, a "community crisis office" was created with the aim of developing health awareness in the population, finding resources to deal with the pandemic and pressuring governments to act in the favelas to ensure basic conditions for the prevention of COVID-19. At the same time, in Complexo da Maré, the residents used local radios to spread information about prevention. As a way of reaching the most people possible, funk has even been used as a tool to raise awareness.[6] The inhabitants are also recording videos that promote community information campaigns on COVID-19, as well as WhatsApp groups and channels to respond to questions and provide mutual support.

In another favela called Manguinhos, two popular social movements, the Social Forum of Manguinhos and the Mothers of Manguinhos, launched a campaign on their social media accounts to receive food and cleaning kits as a way to help the residents who are unemployed or in more vulnerable situations.

In all of these favelas, the residents are collectively caring for the elderly and monitoring their needs so they don't have to leave their homes. Volunteers and organizations are in constant contact with the health units so they can provide up-to-date information and ensure measures are taken to help with prevention. And, despite the difficulties in accessing the internet, their social media accounts have been an important tool to spread information and tackle fake news, which is so widespread in Brazil at the moment.

Finally, in the Baixada Fluminense region, a densely populated region in the state of Rio de Janeiro, the initiative #CoronaNaBaixada took place, which brought together around a hundred social leaders and organizations to combat the spread of COVID-19 and to build collective proposals to confront the crisis. In their manifesto,[7] signed by more than 50 groups, collectives and civil organizations, they condemn the fact that there were no coordinated actions between the municipalities of Baixada and the state government and urge the testing of all patients with symptoms of COVID-19.

Besides the struggle for survival, people are also living with a constant feeling of uncertainty. For those who live in the favelas and peripheries, beyond the uncertainty caused by the pandemic, there is a fear that, in the name of COVID-19, anything could be used as a justification for the suppression of their rights. This situation may result in deaths that have no connections with the virus. The violent acts committed by the security forces, as well as the deaths caused by the precariousness of health and sanitary services, are significant concerns.

Once more the population in the favelas is suffering the overlap of different types of violence that, in our view, must be made visible and contested. At a time when there is an ideological dispute between 'saving lives' versus 'saving the economy', it is essential to defend life but also the social principles that guided the construction of the welfare state. Although this is far from being a reality in Brazil, the defence of rights is an important strategy in disputing the current political status quo.

Notes

[1] The tenement eradication programme led by Mayor Barata Ribeiro (1892–1893) devastated several mansions and inns and, in 1893, demolished the largest and most famous tenement in Rio de Janeiro, Cabeça de Porco, where more than 4000 people lived. The fight against tenements continued for the rest of the decade in Brazil's major cities, aggravating the housing crisis and leading to the emergence of new forms of precarious housing, such as the favelas (Santucci, 2008).

[2] In 1903, Mayor Pereira Passos (1902–1906), inspired by Haussmann's model for Paris, implemented the first major state intervention in the urban environment in the city of Rio de Janeiro. Known as the 'boot down' policy, due to the large demolitions in the downtown areas, this reform aimed to 'sanitize' the city, which meant demolishing most of the precarious housing in the city centre. As a result, the poor population was forced to move to the peripheries or occupy the city's hills, especially those in the city centre, due to their proximity to the workplaces. Therefore, in an attempt to 'clean up' the most valued areas of the city, Pereira Passos's renovation programme contributed to the growth of the favelas.

[3] This action represented, for example, a 29 percent reduction in the budget of Brazil's National Fund of Social Housing, a 19 percent reduction in the budget of the Rio de Janeiro State University and a 15 percent reduction in the budget of the Ministry of Education.

[4] Miranda, E. (2020) 'Favelas do Rio sofrem com falta d'água e população fica mais vulnerável a coronavírus', *Brasil de Fato*, 23 March, available from: https://www.brasildef ato.com.br/2020/03/23/favelas-do-rio-sofrem-com-falta-d-agua-e-populacao-fica-mais-vulneravel-a-coronavirus

[5] Stabile, A. (2020) 'Na pandemia, descaso do governo impacta mais a favela', *Ponte*, 25 March, available from: https://ponte.org/raull-santiago-na-pandemia-descaso-do-governo-impacta-mais-a-favela/

[6] Ribeiro, G. (2020) 'Coronavírus: Comunidades criam gabinetes de crise e usam funk para ajudar na prevenção', *Extra Globo*, 22 March, available at: https://extra.globo.com/noticias/rio/coronavirus-comunidades-criam-gabinetes-de-crise-usam-funk-para-ajudar-na-prevencao-24321336.html

[7] For more info, see: https://drive.google.com/file/d/1LzEDMM98lgMFLWD98Svdh GrTD8qhu663/view

References

Bringel, B. (2020) 'Mucho más que un cacerolazo: resistencias sociales en tiempos de pandemia'. In: B. Bringel and G. Pleyers (Eds) *Alerta Global: Políticas, Movimientos Sociales y Futuros en Disputa en Tiempos de Pandemia*, Buenos Aires/Lima: CLACSO/ALAS, 181–7.

Santucci, J. (2008) *Cidade Rebelde: as revoltas populares no Rio de Janeiro no início do século XX*, Rio de Janeiro: Casa da Palavra.

12

Generational Inequalities in Argentina's Working-Class Neighbourhoods

Pablo Vommaro

The COVID-19 pandemic produced a generalized crisis that made visible pre-existing social dynamics. This chapter will focus on the multidimensional social inequalities, taking an intersectional approach, including the generational, gender, territorial and labour dimensions. I will shed light on young people from the *barrios populares*[1] of Latin America's urban centres. For this, I will mobilize some specialized literature available in a multidimensional and situated perspective (Vommaro, 2017b), considering the inequalities in the living conditions and the generational inequalities as constitutive features of contemporary Latin American youths (Vommaro, 2017a and 2019).

Before the pandemic, the living conditions of young people in Latin American were shaped by multiple intertwined inequalities. According to data from the Economic Commission for Latin America and the Caribbean (ECLAC) and the World Bank, young people between 15 and 29 years of age living in Latin America and the Caribbean represent 20 percent of the total population. That is approximately 150 million people. Almost two-thirds of them live in poor households, a percentage that is even higher among young women (ECLAC, 2019). In Argentina, approximately 10 percent of young people live in slums and precarious settlements (approximately 850,000 young people), according to data from the Observatory of Argentina's Social Debt (Observatorio de la Deuda Social Argentina, 2020). The data shows that, in the first semester of 2020, 38 percent of the population between 18 and 29 years of age were considered to be poor.

Young people from the barrios populares

Since the beginning of the pandemic, lockdown measures have been implemented in Latin American and the Caribbean. What used to happen in the public space started happening at home. The processes by which the private space of the household in the barrios populares becomes public by being appropriated and reinvented by the community intensified. The households of representatives of the barrios populares had already been transformed into headquarters for territorial and community organizations.

In times of a pandemic, the retraction of social life towards the domestic space reinforces the precariousness of living conditions, jeopardizing, for instance, the possibility of carrying out schoolwork and of following remote learning. On the other hand, the restriction in the use and appropriation of public spaces reinforces the spatial and territorial segregation processes that characterize most large cities in different forms.

These processes are experienced particularly by young people who were restricted, even before the pandemic, from moving freely through various cities. The symbolic and geographical separations between neighbourhoods produce invisible borders that are difficult to cross, especially for young people from the barrios populares. These borders and separations weave networks of inequality (Reygadas, 2004) that are experienced and configured differently depending on age, and they have deepened during the pandemic.

The closure of public space and the increased control over its use has reduced the possibilities for young people to meet together. Young people from the barrios populares are particularly affected as they have lost the corners, parks and squares as their places of socialization. Surveys (Facultad de Psicología, 2020; Fundación SES, 2020) conducted in the first months of the lockdown and the young people I interviewed clearly show that the possibilities for socializing, supporting each other and having a sense of belonging provided by the public space cannot be entirely replaced by the virtual space.

The segregation experienced by young people from the barrios populares coexists with a second dynamic: stigmatization. The stigmatization produces 'discredited social identities' (Goffman, quoted in Valenzuela, 2015) that deny, make invisible or criminalize ways of being and of presenting themselves as young people to others. Likewise, the stigmatization denies the recognition of different youth lifestyles and attributes all social ills to one of these lifestyles. Thus, young people representing a particular lifestyle are negatively labelled as responsible for a specific social problem (increased crime, spread of COVID-19), and are disqualified and persecuted for their practices and bodies.

Spatial segregation and subjective stigmatization constitute two features of generational inequalities expressed and produced in the territory. Both dimensions converge in police harassment and institutional violence against youth, which have increased in the recent months in various countries of Latin America and the Caribbean. Persecutions, criminalization, arbitrary detentions, harassment, humiliation, torture and cases of disappearance and murder of young people have grown with the pandemic, especially in the barrios populares (but also in rural areas), and hand in hand with the greater powers that security forces have received to enforce lockdown measures.

In Argentina, 40 percent of the population of the barrios populares said that, between April and May 2020, there were no more conflicts with the police (understood as police harassment and criminalization of stigmatized youth) than before the lockdown, but there wasn't an increased police presence either; 20 percent described various types of harassment by the security forces (National University of General Sarmiento, UNGS, 2020).

Strengthening community organization

The crisis fuelled by the pandemic has also fostered the strengthening of the way in which the barrios populares organize. Representatives of different municipalities of the Buenos Aires Metropolitan Area report that since mandatory social and preventive isolation was decreed, there has been a significant reactivation of community- and neighbourhood-based organizations (clubs, local support groups, mutual companies, food banks, soup kitchens, cultural centres), as well as more support and commitment from neighbours (UNGS, 2020).

The strengthening of the territory and community's organizational fabric in the barrios populares (mainly led by women and young people) provides a possible answer to the following frequent questions: In economies with a large informal sector (40 or 50 percent), is it possible to implement mandatory social isolation? Is isolation or quarantine really enforced in the barrios populares? Does the call to stay home imply class privilege?

Undoubtedly, these questions will be answered in practice and by experience. Social and economic policies to support people working in the informal sector and the inhabitants of the barrios populares should be implemented, such as a universal basic income.

Is lockdown a class privilege?

It is important to challenge the idea that isolation applies only to the middle or upper-middle classes and that prevention measures are not followed in the barrios populares because poverty generates chaos or anomie.

First of all, the resistance to comply with social isolation grows as the population's income increases according to reports and opinion surveys (see Kollman, 2020). The authors' experience with the inhabitants of the barrios populares allows us to affirm that neighbourhoods, communities and territories deploy support strategies in other ways, with other modalities. We haven't found an empirical basis to sustain the notion that isolation and prevention measures against the pandemic are only implemented by the middle or upper-middle classes.

Of course, the overcrowding makes social distancing difficult, and informal and precarious workers need to earn income every day. However, the communal social organization's persistence and power should not be underestimated when it comes to ensuring prevention, when necessary, through isolation or distancing. The inhabitants of the barrios populares comply with it by creating other forms of support and prevention. For instance, they implement distancing and community healthcare strategies in shared spaces, such as schools, clubs and soup kitchens. They collectively control circulation within the neighbourhood and care for individuals at higher risk as a community. Likewise, in many instances, the social representatives of the barrios populares carry out contact and case tracing with a capillarity and management capacity that the state rarely achieves.

The patterns and intersections of inequality experienced by young people from the barrios populares in major Latin American cities include work and labour relations. During the lockdown, homeworking appears as a solution for carrying on with activities and ensuring basic productivity for companies. Nevertheless, can all workers homework? Obviously not, and that depends on the type of activity, as well as on the individual's working and living conditions. Remote work can increase precariousness and social and labour inequalities, and can weaken young people's employment opportunities in the barrios populares.

Inequalities are reinforced and reproduced for precarious workers (for instance those employed in home delivery, supermarkets or platform economies), who tend to be young people and often continue to work during quarantines without the possibility of adequate precautions or protection. These job opportunities have grown at the same time that job insecurity has increased. In this way, the paradox is that, during the pandemic, youth unemployment may decrease – it is currently between two-and-a-half and three times higher than adult unemployment, according to various reports, such as one from the ECLAC (2019) – but the jobs will become increasingly precarious, with fewer rights and degraded working conditions.

David Harvey (2020) suggests that there is a 'new working class' that is bearing the brunt of the crisis, both because it is the workforce that bears the most significant risk of exposure to the virus at work, and also because these workers can be fired without compensation due to the economic downturn and the precariousness of their rights. Who are the workers that can actually work from home? Who can afford to self-isolate or to quarantine (with or without pay) in the event of contact with a confirmed case or of contagion? These multidimensional inequalities intensify and intersect with gender, territory, class, race/ethnicity and generation. It is thus a 'class, gendered and racialized pandemic' (Harvey, 2020).

The emergence and persistence of generational inequality

How can the majority of young people's lives not become more precarious in a situation such as this? How to prevent the policies implemented in the face of the pandemic from becoming an engine that accelerates the production and reproduction processes of multidimensional social inequalities? How to counteract persistent and emerging inequalities in times of a pandemic? The resolution of these dilemmas and crossroads will depend on social and political disputes, many of which young people are already developing.

On this point, Judith Butler (2020) argues that the pandemic shows the speed with which radical inequality and capitalist exploitation find ways to reproduce and strengthen themselves. Butler points out that the deepening of inequalities will also manifest in the disputes over vaccines and medicinal products. In an unequal world, where competition, commodification, racism, xenophobia, segregation and stigmatization dominate, the distribution of vaccines and medicinal products will follow the prevailing logics. Those living in the barrios populares could be deprived of their rights to health and to a decent life. The closure of borders, segregation and reinforced control of circulation would help achieve the exacerbation of what Foucault and Deleuze have discussed as the dynamics of biopolitical control and domination societies: the politics of 'making live and letting die'.

Youth resistance, expansion of the public sector and equality policies

Young people's realities in the barrios populares of Latin America are marked by multidimensional and intersectional social inequalities that have been deepened by the pandemic. However, young people also resist, dispute meanings, deploy alternative practices every day and reaffirm their ways of being and producing themselves daily. We can distinguish five forms of resistance and youth activism in times of pandemic:

1. Occupation of public space using mobilization techniques that allow maintaining care and distancing measures. For example, in Chile the protestors used floor markings to identify the distancing requirements, and in Uruguay they protested in cars or on bicycles.
2. Appropriation of public space using modalities that already existed before the pandemic, even if wearing masks and avoiding close contact

is difficult, particularly in the face of police repression, as has been the case in Colombia, Ecuador, Bolivia and Chile.

3. Use of balconies or house doors to protest and for enhancing the expressive, aesthetic and communicative dimension of youth collective action and transformation of the domestic space into a public space (as has been the case in most of the cities in Latin America and the world).

4. Use of digital social networks, such as TikTok and Instagram, the politicization of which intensified with the pandemic and the impossibility of on-site mobilization.

5. Densification of social organization networks at the territorial and local levels and a search for ways to strengthen the communities' or neighbourhoods' resistance based on pre-existing and emerging affections and affinities.

Conclusion

The educational inequalities have deepened with the digitalization of learning at all levels (see Chapter 13 of this book by Nicolás Arata). Some governments have reinforced their control over the occupation and use of public space, especially by young people, through repressive measures supposedly aimed at fighting the pandemic. The changes in young people's social lives and disputes over public space show that this conjuncture has reopened and fuelled the discussion and conflict over the commons in Latin America.

Youth resistances and activism demonstrate that the public cannot be viewed only as of the state; it is necessary to consider the communal and social as part of the public. Will these disputes over the commons, strengthened by the youth's collective actions, signify a revitalized place for the state? Or will the social eagerness to defend and expand what is public overwhelm the state and drive back capital, reducing the commodification of different spheres of life? Will these disputes over the meaning of public and collective space include an understanding that market forces weaken and narrow the commons? According to our analysis of youth initiatives during the pandemic, persevering in the public and common and putting life at the centre is a path forward for today and for tomorrow.

Assuming that prevention is fundamental at this time and perhaps in the years to come, it seems that social responsibility and solidarity, together with comprehensive, situated, territorialized, unique and effective public policies (not only state ones), are a possible path towards constructing alternatives. We require different public policies in order to counteract the social devices of production and reproduction of multidimensional social inequalities and advance towards producing diverse equality, which recognizes and is configured by the difference. We need equality-based policies focused on listening, recognizing and making visible the diversities and the different ways of life of the youth living in the barrios populares in order to counteract stigmas and segregation. It seems that equality has returned to centre stage. Let us imagine that it is just a starting point.

Note

1   *Barrios populares* is a Spanish term that covers 'slums', 'working-class neighbourhoods' and 'informal settlements'.

References

Butler, J. (2020) 'La pandemia, el futuro y una duda: ¿qué es lo que hace que la vida sea vivible?', La Vaca, [online] 2 June, available from: https://www.lavaca.org/notas/judith-butler-la-pandemia-el-futuro-y-una-duda-que-es-lo-que-hace-que-la-vida-sea-vivible/

CEPAL (2019) *Social Panorama of Latin America 2019*, Santiago de Chile: ECLAC.

Etchevers, M.J., Garay, C.J., Putrino, N., Grasso, J., Natalí, V. and Helmich, N. (2020) *Mental Health in Quarantine. Survey of the Psychological Impact at 7–11 and 50–55 Days of Quarantine in the Argentine Population*, Buenos Aires: Applied Social Psychology Observatory, University of Buenos Aires.

Facultad de Psicología (2020) *Salud Mental en Cuarentena. Relevamiento del impacto psicológico a los 7–11 y 50–55 días de cuarentena en población argentina*, Buenos Aires: Universidad de Buenos Aires.

Fundación SES (2020) *Sumar nos suma*, Survey.

Harvey, D. (2020) 'Anti-capitalist politics in the time of COVID-19', *Jacobin*, [online], available from: https://jacobinmag.com/2020/03/david-harvey-coronavirus-political-economy-disruptions

Kollmann R. (2020) *Encuesta: ¿Cuánto apoyo tiene la cuarentena?*, Buenos Aires, August 3.

Nuñez, P. (2020) 'Educational inequalities in times of coronavirus', *La Vanguardia*, [online] 14 April, available from: http://www.lavanguardiadigital.com.ar/index.php/2020/04/14/desigualdades-educativas-en-tiempos-de-coronavirus/

Observatorio de la Deuda Social de la Argentina (2020) *Poverty beyond Income: New Report on Multidimensional Poverty 2010–2019: Data Presentation Based on a Human Rights-Based Approach*, Buenos Aires: Pontificia Universidad Católica Argentina, [online] available from: http://wadmin.uca.edu.ar/public/ckeditor/Observatorio%20Deuda%20Social/Documentos/2020/2020-OBSERVATORIO-DOCUMENTO-TRABAJO-NUEVO-INFORME-PM-ENFOQUE-DERECHOS.pdf

Reygadas, L. (2004) *The Networks of Inequality: A Multidimensional Approach*, Mexico City: UAM.

Sociedad Argentina de Pediatría (2020) *The Emotional State of Children and Adolescents a Month after the Beginning of the Social, Preventive, and Compulsory Isolation*, Buenos Aires: Sociedad Argentina de Pediatría.

Universidad Nacional de General Sarmiento (2020) *The Greater Buenos Aires in Quarantine I and II*, Buenos Aires: Los Polvorines.

Valenzuela, A. and Manuel, J. (eds) (2015) *The System Is Anti-Us. Youth Cultures, Movements and Resistance*, Mexico City: UNAM/COLEF/GEDISA.

Virno, P. (2005) *Creativity and Innovative Action: Towards a Logic of Change*, Buenos Aires: Editorial Tinta Limón.

Vommaro, P. (2017a) 'Territories and resistance: Generational configurations and politicization processes in Argentina with a Latin American perspective', *Iztapalapa. Revista de Ciencias Sociales y Humanidades*, UAM-I: 101–33.

Vommaro, P. (2017b) 'Latin American youth: Diversities and inequalities', *Revista Temas*, 87–8: 4–11.

Vommaro, P. (2019) 'Inequalities, rights and youth participation in Latin America: Generational processes approaches', *Revista Direito e Praxis*, 10(2): 1192–213.

13

Pandemic Pedagogical Lessons and Educational Inequalities

Nicolás Arata

Latin America is going through an unprecedented moment marked by the exacerbation of the inequalities already suffered by large social sectors before the outbreak of the pandemic.[1] In the face of the complexity and uncertainty of the historical present, the state and society must establish a new social contract to relocate the place of the school as a space that strengthens and builds *educational networks*, promoting other *ways of being together* and emphasizing that *nobody is unnecessary*, sustaining an unwavering *defence of the public sector* and guaranteeing *equality of care* as an indispensable condition for life in democracy. In times of growing intolerance, the school must be seen as the place where awareness is raised and thought is given to the *common good* in a space destined to *awaken an interest in the world through its discovery, interpretation and transformation*.

I identify three major groups that have emerged around the crisis unleashed by the pandemic: those that have placed the emphasis on technocratic responses (delegating the management of the crisis to technological devices aimed at video surveillance or facial recognition, trusting that controlling the behaviour of citizens will solve the crisis *per se*); those that embraced a neo-Malthusian stance (assuming that the population-flock will contract the virus and that lives will necessarily be lost, but that those who will survive will be strengthened and immunized); and those that approached the epidemic as a health-political problem (appealing to a series of measures based on scientific arguments and social policies that strengthen and articulate the knowledge of the state and its capacity to face the crisis). The first two are derived from the neoliberal paradigm combined with reinforced doses of neo-fascism, while the third is a vision that highlights the centrality of collective ties, solidarity and care for others inscribed in the tradition of the social state that makes itself present through an ensemble of public policies (not exempt from contradiction).

The course and effects of these narratives are, in some cases, painfully palpable: the political leaders who underestimated the virus have paid the price for their arrogance with countless lives (the most resounding cases: England, Brazil and the dictatorship of Bolivia). Other narratives raise questions that cannot be answered simply: what effect will the installation of a type of algorithmic governance through compulsory position-tracking or immunity passports have on such basic rights as privacy or human mobility? What will happen when these initiatives land in the educational spheres? What will happen after? How far are we from acquiring canned goods from multinational companies? From orienting training proposals in line with the interests of the centres of power and with our backs turned to local and community, national and regional needs?

Such a programme involves a key issue: abdicating sovereignty. With the exceptions of its policies regarding COVID-19, Argentina is no longer walking along that path. The country had already been walking it during the four years of the Cambiemos government,[2] which we can summarize in three important metaphors to remember: when the state spoke with false affliction of 'falling into public school', or when they affirmed with a burlesque smile that 'nobody who is born in poverty today reaches university', or when they said, displaying a historical memory that makes one shiver for its banal vindication of one of the worst atrocities committed by the state, that 'this is the new Conquest of the Desert, but with education instead of swords'.[3] The statements were made by President Macri, the governor of Buenos Aires Province Vidal, and the minister of education Esteban Bullrich, and condense a conception of education, school and culture.

The place of schools in the political-health crisis: the Argentinean case

The case of the current State of Argentina is undoubtedly one that fits into the political-sanitary narrative. The government has taken a stand against the false dichotomy between the preservation of society and the economy, putting collective life and health before any other factor (see the Introduction of this book by Bringel and Pleyers and Sagot, Chapter 10). This was done without ignoring the responsibilities that the state must assume in the context of a crisis of unprecedented proportions.

I wish to emphasize 'unprecedented', because there is no previous knowledge of how to manage the multiplicity of problems that a pandemic with these characteristics unleashes. There is, of course, specialized scientific knowledge that is indispensable but insufficient for managing the social effects that a crisis of this magnitude triggers. There is also knowledge of the current situation generated in the territory and through collective strategies that allows us to overcome this time of enormous difficulty as a community. And finally, there are a handful of political definitions on which lie the basis of a prospective view under construction for a post-pandemic temporality marked, without doubt, by the numerous debates that will be opened on the present and future of life on earth.

The State of Argentina, through its minister of education, has maintained that schools are irreplaceable. This is a modest but fundamental definition, since it allows the set of actions undertaken to be included in a narrative that understands the school as the institution that guarantees – together with the right to education – a set of basic rights, and that recognizes the school as the place where teachers work, as a meeting place between subjects, where people with different knowledge and ways of knowing, with different experiences of socialization, with different paths and knowledge, interact and learn to live together. Moreover, the school is irreplaceable because an infinite number of unique relationships are produced there. In other words, without schools, without the opportunities they provide to have moments of simultaneity, to meet, to share, to feel and to think, to share an interest in the world and to learn to be among equals, our societies would be infinitely more unequal than they already are.

Beyond Argentina: the school under threat

The school is under threat. In many countries, the voices that have been calling for the end of schooling for decades have been raised again. Large companies producing school software and content have offered their services to the state in exchange for large sums of money or access to the data of the users of educational services. There is an aspect of Big Data active in education that segments and questions pedagogical individuals on the basis of their consumption capacities or their political sympathies, which is on a planetary scale and which has had and may have very powerful effects on the formation of the perception and manipulation of public opinion.

The crisis has offered a new opportunity to the merchants of education, who are rubbing their hands together and displaying their voracity for business. Precisely because of this, the educational representatives of progressive governments have the possibility of leading a defence of the school, combining the greatest political efforts to preserve its pedagogical mission associated with the public good while working to transform it into a more democratic space than the one we have. I refer to educational authorities, since this initiative must be promoted by the state. However, the state alone is not enough. It is essential to release the teaching capacities, to strengthen teaching positions as well as those of researchers and intellectuals in the public science system, in order to build multiple nodes of collaboration with organized civil society.

Learning from history to build a new political-pedagogical imagination

The history of Latin American education is full of experiences and projects that give historical density to a new democratizing and inclusive narrative. Among the teaching memories and in the pedagogical traditions of the region there are traces of discourses and practices that consign the school as the axis of life in common. One only has to stop and archive times, connecting them with stories, pedagogical readings with political concerns.

Each period has the mission of reassembling traditions and organically connecting the past with the present. In other words, we have the responsibility *to read in tradition* with the purpose of recreating, through political-pedagogical imagination, the public education that the future of a country like the one led by President Alberto Fernández needs. In a conversation held with Marcelo Caruso and Elsie Rockwell carried out by the National Institute of Teacher Education (IFOD),[4] a challenge was foreseen: to recalibrate the relationship of pedagogical alternatives with the defence of the state educational systems.

There is currently a co-optation of the meaning of 'alternative' by right and far-right forces, which challenges us. For years, I have claimed in courses, seminars and workshops the need to rethink Sarmiento[5] beyond prejudices and evaluations, convinced as I am myself that we must not give away the name or the legacy of Sarmiento to the conservative right (which, by the way, has no qualms about appropriating it). And this is not an uncritical or nostalgic claim but an effort to release our capacity to think critically and without prejudice about the ambivalences and contradictions of a key figure in Argentina's history of education. This is certainly true in other countries as well, but in our case, if we are willing to do this with Sarmiento, how can we not be willing to do it with the fertile notion of alternatives?

The school in a pandemic context

School is irreplaceable. The experience of living without schools during the pandemic reinforces the need for proactive state policies. The more unequal the society where it is located, the more important the role of the school will be. This is a key question for tackling educational inequalities and hence also other forms of social inequalities.

The enormous efforts made to continue teaching do not replace the complex processes of transmission and exchange that take place in school, but they do mitigate their absence. Moreover, they stem from a political decision emerging from a greater responsibility: to continue to guarantee the right to education. To affirm the centrality of the school in a pandemic context is to place the focus of efforts on *strengthening pedagogical ties* even before the completion of a teaching programme or its evaluation.

Providing the means to ensure connectivity is essential but not an end in itself. It is a right that is guaranteed when there is pedagogical sovereignty, that is to say, when there is a state that guarantees effective access to a set of experiences, knowledge and know-how that allows for the integral development of citizens through its own platforms whose free connection is guaranteed, where access to all information is free and where users' data is protected both from commercial interests and from those linked to security paradigms.

Likewise, the transition from face-to-face to digital education is neither linear nor direct but rather crossed by partial substitutions, displacements and overlaps: in a hybrid or bimodal system, would a school calendar designed from and for face-to-face education be maintained? Is a recess equivalent to a day of disconnection? There is a need not only for curatorial work in relation to the educational content that will circulate digitally but also for weighing the challenges of the face-to-face/digital equation around the construction of knowledge, and not taking it for granted.

An indicative list of topics to think about in this hybrid format would include the formation of critical intellectual capacities on the same footing as the promotion of convivial sensibilities, co-operation skills and socially productive knowledge; learning through dialogue and the search for consensus around the idea of life in common; a sensitivity and commitment to caring for the environment and the people who live in it; comprehensive sexual education and respect for dissidences; and thinking historically and situating ourselves regionally both from a federal perspective and from that of our insertion in local, national or regional traditions.

The democratization of science and the defence of public school

Little or nothing of what we have discussed is possible or feasible if the teaching position is not strengthened as a central tool of an education policy based on the defence of public school. The strengthening that I imagine begins in three directions: First, the claim for the specificity of teaching work as responsible for the selection and transmission of fundamental elements of a cultural legacy (a profession that is very much a craft and not like any other). Second, the development of new and challenging training proposals that put in dialogue the knowledge learned with the new contemporary pedagogical problems (that do not aim at deepening what is already known but at immersing oneself in other readings, at searching for other approaches, at generating perplexities that invite us to review our learned knowledge without disqualifying it). And lastly, the generation of adequate working conditions to deploy them. Along with this, we must listen to teachers and find out which training proposals are most valued by them. In sum, in this new 'risk era' (see Domingues, Chapter 29 of this book); we must take risks and try out new training proposals, bearing in mind and recognizing the heterogeneity of populations, teachers and schools that exist, while ensuring that training proposals reach everyone equally.

There is an open opportunity to promote the democratization of science and to rethink the relationship between science and democracy. There are many possible ways (and some of them have probably already been explored), from encouragement of scientific vocations to dissemination and teaching of scientific knowledge and its relationship with the ecosystem of knowledge that is produced and which circulates in society, among others. Once again, the position adopted by the government of Argentina, which places scientific knowledge in a prominent position when making decisions that affect the public agenda, opens up an opportunity to rethink the place, teaching and dissemination of science in schools.

Educational institutions can be a space to promote and generate reflection on what scientists are saying and to think, through the tools provided by the humanities, about how what they say affects us or influences the definition of public policies. The science journalists Sonia Shah (2020) recalls during the pandemic the importance of democratizing science rather than influencing science to become even more elitist and authoritarian than it is. Indeed, what is the point of advocating living in the society of knowledge if it is hijacked by elites for their own benefit?

Rethinking the teaching of social sciences from a regional perspective is another ongoing challenge. Political responses cannot be limited to local and national scales, as Bringel points out in Chapter 35. The pandemic's character as a global event can serve to situate problems that are affecting our countries in similar ways and make them comparable in order to address them from regional perspectives. This is visible in the crisis in health systems, the chain of gender inequities faced by women in the region, the enormous challenges linked to food sovereignty (a fact that is as relevant as it is painful: more than 85 million children and young people in Latin America eat lunch at school), the vulnerabilities to which migrants are subjected, human rights violations and the seriousness of the ecological crisis on a global scale, among other issues.

As a result, manuals, documents and courses that contribute to thinking about these problems in a connected and comparative way (questioning the hegemonic comparative form proposed by the institutions behind the ranking system) could be developed. Universities, academic centres and regional institutions (such as the Latin American Council of Social

Sciences–CLACSO–and others) could create a commission to think about common problems and possible didactic approaches to working on these issues from regional perspectives, making the results of this research available in open access, in what would undoubtedly be a significant and very well-received contribution among Latin American teachers.

What about the day after?

Archiving this experience will be vital in order to treat the multiple traumas that this pandemic will leave behind. Preserving the memory of all times, but especially of difficult times, is a responsibility of the state that cannot be delegated. Rather than a repository or archive, I understand the archive as a social bond that is built in a context of conviviality in which, under a diversity of unequal configurations, textual, audiovisual and sound objects coexist. The question of who compiles and under what criteria is as pressing as the concern over where the infinite number of experiences and initiatives carried out by hundreds of thousands of teachers will end up.

In the history of education, we always hear the voices of those who regret not having an archive to be able to report on an experience or to deal with a fragment of the past for lack of sources. States must lead the task of systematizing documents, experiences, voices and testimonies that can–in critical times like this–become a valuable archive of school memories that are significant for the study of the development of the education system in our recent history of education.

'New Normality' is the hegemonic label that was given to the day after the pandemic. It is unlikely that the effects it triggered can be quickly absorbed and incorporated into a liveable everyday life, especially when all the forecasts indicate that the pandemic will leave societies more unequal than those we knew before these months of confinement and the fight against the virus. The unfolding of this crisis has unforeseeable edges and unexpected twists and is far from over.

It would be risky or irresponsible to say how and when we will get out of it. In school terms, Dussel, Ferrante and Pulfer mention that what this pandemic leaves behind 'will not be a simple restoration of the previous situation nor something radically different from the configuration we left before the pandemic' (Dussel et al, 2020: 1). For this reason, and before talking about a new normality, it is essential to begin by systematizing the lessons that it leaves behind. Among many others, the absolute priority that a present state must assume is to make a greater investment in public policies aimed at strengthening public health, science and education systems, which are undoubtedly the most attacked by neoliberal policies. These investments must have a strategic plan to first attend to those who are in a situation of greater social vulnerability. I would like to imagine that such a plan should emerge as the result of a great social consensus in which all the voices of society are represented, but such consensus can only emerge from the generation of a space in which to think collectively about the bases of a new social contract around education and school that we want in order to build a pedagogical sovereignty that is equal to the challenges we face.

Notes

[1] This chapter was written originally in December 2020, at a time when the return to school had not yet taken place anywhere in my country, Argentina, but when measures had already been announced and protocols had been established to organize the return to school. These ideas seek to build a bridge with other readings and aspirations of a longer term. They are based on a recognition of the multiplicity of efforts and initiatives that hundreds of thousands of teachers, professors, union leaders and social movements as well as teams from the National Ministry of Education and provincial ministries are developing, each with their own impressions and styles.

[2] The Cambiemos coalition governed the country from 2015 to 2019. During Mauricio Macri's presidency, the foreign debt grew from 52 to 81 percent of GDP, the interests of concentrated capital were shamelessly favoured and opponents and social leaders were persecuted through illegal espionage and the establishment of a judicial panel (see Desojo, 2020).

[3] The self-styled 'Conquest of the Desert' military campaign took place from 1878 to 1885 and consisted of the extermination of the native peoples who inhabited Argentina's pampas and Patagonia regions. As a result of this repressive process, 56,000 square kilometres were annexed and 14.000 indigenous people were completely decimated and reduced to servitude.

[4] The conversation took place within the framework of the National Teacher Education Days: Ministerio de Educación (2020) 'Jornadas Nacionales de Formación Docente. Apertura y primera mesa', 21 May, available from: https://www.youtube.com/watch?v=b-ar2w23QU4&t=196s&ab_channel=MinisteriodeEducaci%C3%B3n

[5] Domingo Faustino Sarmiento (1811–1888) is considered the founder of the education system of Argentina and a key figure in the construction of Argentina's modern state. His controversial role has been the subject of constant debate about his figure and his political and educational positions, mainly his open contempt for the native peoples and the claim of European culture as the only viable model.

References

Desojo, E. (ed) (2020) *Justicia a la carta. El poder judicial en la era macrista*, Buenos Aires: CLACSO.

Dussel, I., Ferrante, P. and Pulfer, D. (2020) 'La educación de pasado mañana. Notas sobre la marcha', *Fundación Carolina*, 41, [online], available from: https://www.fundacioncarolina.es/wp-content/uploads/2020/06/AC-41.-2020.pdf

Shah, S., Hernandez, L.O., Kuruvilla, B., Jara, M. and Ahmad, U. (2020) 'Building an internationalist response to Coronavirus', Panel discussion, Transnacional Institute, [online] 2 April, available from: https://www.youtube.com/watch?v=t5qN35qeB1w

14

Social Work with Homeless People in Belgium

Stéphanie Cassilde

Belgium decided to implement a lockdown on 18 March 2020. While most citizens were busy reorganizing their lives, schooling their children and rushing to the supermarket to stock food and hygiene products, the situation of homeless people suffered a quick and strong deterioration.

Social workers in the homeless sector are frontline professionals in this COVID-19 time. The crisis implies an enormous work overload, in addition to the usual challenges of social work. It also implies sanitary risks for them and their family. However, they remain invisible and are almost never mentioned in the fight against COVID-19. They remain invisible and are forgotten by the population and policymakers when it comes to acknowledging the contributions of those who help us struggle against the pandemic and maintain some humanity in a crisis that has challenged solidarity outside of reduced family circles.

In this chapter I will shed light on social workers and volunteers who helped homeless people at the beginning of the pandemic, on their work and the challenges they face, drawing on my long-term fieldwork experience and my active participation in a social centre during the COVID-19 pandemic in Charleroi, a former industrial town with a high unemployment rate in the French-speaking part of Belgium.

Social work with homeless people in Charleroi

The social centre Comme Chez Nous (which means 'just like home', hereafter CCN) provides food and shelter, on average, to some fifty homeless people a day in Charleroi. In 2019, 1088 individual persons found their way to this day-care centre. CCN is open 365 days a year, unlike any other social work services, and is one of the very few places that is still open for homeless people in Wallonia (Belgium's southern French-speaking region) during the COVID-19 pandemic. The centre belongs to those exemplary associations supported and distinguished by the European Union because of its practice of a holistic, person-based approach – though rarely chosen, this approach is the most efficient regarding homelessness.

On the evening of 12 March, the Belgian federal government required all public gatherings to be cancelled, and closed schools and restaurants on 13 March. On 14 March , there were still no instructions regarding social distancing at work, let alone in the day-care centres for the homeless. The physical distance required to avoid virus propagation raised questions about the social work conditions at CCN, as the central room regularly welcomes as many as 70 individuals sitting close to each other. On 16 March, in the afternoon, a man started coughing, and became lethargic on the spot. The team suspected a case of COVID-19 and immediately decided to close down the centre. For the second time since its foundation in 1995, CCN was confronted with a two-day closure – a very long period of time considering that it acts as a last-chance institution for homeless people.

On 18 March, homeless people in Charleroi no longer had access to basic-needs facilities. They had no food, no access to drinking water, no sanitary equipment. Their usual survival routines were shattered; begging (or being offered coffee or some food) is impossible when no one passes by. The town was empty. At this stage, a whole group of citizens was thus forgotten and excluded from all protective (individual and collective) measures linked to the COVID-19 pandemic. On 19 March, CCN reopened after a two-day closure in order to provide basic-need services for homeless and people living in precarious conditions.

On 18 March, CCN itself had taken the lead to maintain its services for the homeless. It asked the city council to be relocated. On 20 March, however, the city crisis plan for homeless people was announced in news coverage. The health crisis does not put institutional issues on hold.

On 19 March, while Belgium entered lockdown, the CCN social workers, newly recruited volunteers replaced the older ones that had to isolate themselves. They reopened the day-care centre to distribute very basic cheese sandwiches and glasses of water in front of the main door. This reopening was made possible thanks to a local solidarity initiative launched by a textile designer and one of her students, who began to sew cloth masks based on the tutorial given by the Grenoble University Hospital in France. That day, thanks to these cloth masks, some 80 persons – among whom some were skinny children – could at least fulfil one basic need. For some of them, it was the only meal of the day. On 20 March, one of the city food charities reopened, but as of 21 and 22 March, CCN was again the only food distribution point, as is usually the case during the weekends.

On 23 March, CCN operated in a new location provided by the municipal authorities. Thanks to local solidarity initiatives, about one hundred cloth masks were available for the 50 social workers and volunteers. Should the day-care centre have waited for the public authorities' support to receive protective material, it would probably not have opened yet. Indeed, the surgical masks promised by the public authorities were made available on 25 March, and only ten masks per week were going to the day-care centre. The homeless social work sector in Charleroi had received 500 masks for eight weeks, which was far below the numbers needed. CCN was still dependent on cloth masks and social workers kept asking for better equipment.

On the one hand, CCN continues to fulfil its mission as far as social work is concerned. In the temporary day-care centre, access to sanitary facilities is provided under strict precautions (systematic disinfection of the showers and toilets between each use, mandatory handwashing), and food, water and coffee are available all day long, as well as a lunch (mostly a sandwich and soup). On the other hand, a fundraising action has had to be launched in order to cope with additional expenses.

What do homeless people think about this? On 21 March, a silent queue formed down the street: people were waiting, respecting the required physical distance, to receive a piece of bread and a piece of cheese – some had not eaten anything for a day. On 4 April, I met a man in the city centre asking for food and describing the new location to be too far away to be worth it (a one-hour walk, 20 minutes on public transportation, but with a limitation on the number of persons in each bus and a lot of tension among passengers). On 27 March, a man showing all the COVID-19 symptoms had put his hands together in prayer and looked up to the sky when he was told he would be confined.

The challenges of doing social work in times of sanitary crisis

Some homeless people almost wish to have COVID-19 symptoms in order to have their own room. They ask for a temperature check several times a day. Others first seem reluctant to be confined. For example, an elderly woman with a persistent cough was offered housing: being homeless for years, her first reaction was: "Then, I cannot go out." She needed about ten days to accept the proposal.

As social workers are able to target the most at-risk persons among the homeless, they also try finding housing for them – this goes beyond their current primary mission, which 'just' consists in assisting the homeless in satisfying basic requirements, but forms part of the their regular goals. As homelessness is a multidimensional issue linked to various factors, getting out of homelessness is a complex process too. The widespread view that finding housing is the only – and the 'easiest' – solution is by far too simplistic. Housing may rather be considered the starting point for another kind of social work, aiming to bring about long-term improvement in the life trajectory of the person. And this is all the more the case when this person also has mental health issues.

The enforcement of sanitary rules is another challenge. One day, a man entered the centre and started shaking hands with everyone, which is against one of the key sanitary instructions. Providing unconditional basic-needs access implies welcoming some people who question or infringe upon the rules. In order to protect the majority of the homeless people attending the day-care centre, as well as the social workers and the volunteers, those who do not respect the fundamental rules are denied entry. However, they still benefit from 'service at the door', that is, social workers bring them food and drink in front of the day-care centre. As they are not allowed to enter, they can no longer access the sanitary facilities.

It is difficult to find the right balance between providing access to basic-needs facilities for everyone and enforcing the rules. The most usual infringements include threats and aggression, but also, in COVID-19 times, the ignoring of the sanitary precautions. Social work does not stop during the COVID-19 pandemic. The crisis requires redesigning the organizational framework of the day-care centre.

For now, social workers are focusing on the urgency of coping with the impact of COVID-19 as it affects basic-needs access, and have no more time to help the homeless to change their life trajectories. However, the usual concerns and questions remain. The challenge is how to coordinate basic-needs access in COVID-19 times while dealing sometimes with uncontrollable and dangerous situations. As the pandemic continues, another challenge is how to restart regular social work during a sanitary emergency.

Perspectives

Analysing the reality of the most vulnerable people during the COVID-19 crisis sheds light on what is essential to human beings but also on the reality of people taking care of them. How we take care of our most vulnerable citizens in times of COVID-19 speaks a lot about who we are and reveals the societal representations associated with these vulnerable citizens. I would like to draw three lessons from this experience at a social centre in Charleroi.

First, policymakers take homeless people rather quickly into account, including the municipal and regional authorities which aim to eradicate homelessness according to the current regional policy statement. Second, the crisis acts as an opportunity to identify good practices and major issues in the city plan to help homeless people. The result of this experience should be shared with other cities, policymakers and national governments in order to improve social work for the most vulnerable citizens. Third, the continuation of social work during the pandemic clearly indicates that taking care of the most vulnerable people is a fundamental and absolutely essential aspect of upholding human dignity in a society – a subject that goes far beyond the mere survival issue of the homeless.

In the meantime, and in spite of the importance of their work, social workers in the homeless sector remain invisible and are almost never mentioned as frontline professionals, whereas they should be more visible during the pandemic. They are still absent from the growing list of people to whom we express our thanks – cashiers in supermarkets, garbage collectors, medical professionals. The fact is that, just like homeless people, *social workers are invisible*: though their work provides a precious 'safety net' and is a benchmark for what our society calls dignity, it is hardly acknowledged.

15

Community Spaces in India: Constructing Solidarity during the Pandemic

Supurna Banerjee

In 2019 a wave of protests broke out in various parts of the world against inequality, authoritarianism and violence. India too saw its share of such protests. The enactment of the undemocratic Citizenship Amendment Act (CAA) and the National Register of Citizens which sought to fundamentally redefine the criterion of citizenship, making it contingent on religious identity and the possession of legacy documents, was met with protests in all parts of the country (Deka, 2019). The protesting masses made themselves visible everywhere, walking together in rallies, creating barricades and being present in large number on the streets. In a country like India, with very limited reach of digital activism, such resistance continues to be built on the physicality of presence at sites of protests. The materiality of the protesting bodies emerges as central to enacting and/or visibilizing the protest.

Coming in the wake of such heightened protest movements, COVID-19, with the essential requirement of physical distancing, preventing access to and crowding of public places, poses an unprecedented challenge to future of activism across the country. The suspension of the street, emblematic of the infrastructure of substantive democracy, is a dissolution of a public political culture that thrives on gatherings, crowd formations, graffiti, barricades, traffic suspension, territorial battles, theatrical performances and speeches (Bandopadhyay, 2020).

This then threatens to be a moment of critical disjuncture and obstruction of solidarity building. Can we rethink traditional movements beyond the materiality of their sites, beyond the public political culture of the street and gathering? Further, the pandemic and its handling exacerbates existing socioeconomic inequalities whereby people belonging to marginal groups face a greater crisis both in terms of access to public health and in terms of protection against an authoritarian state. The need for constant resistance against anti-humanitarian stances and demand for policies that place the most vulnerable at their core is acute. Solidarity needs to be forged on intersectional lines where questions around caste, class, gender and religion need to be constantly articulated.

This chapter situates itself in the present context of India where the pandemic-induced crisis has been progressively worsened by the anti-poor, anti-democratic measures of the government. Looking at instances from across India, I map also the ways in which solidarity practices are being reimagined. The shift of site and mode is evident from the street to the neighbourhood, from the eventual to the everyday. While being a discrete tract of time, it is hoped that the lessons inherent in the pandemic have implications for a longer period. Even though the tendency in the very first rush of reading the pandemic was to look at it in terms of disjuncture, it is also important to understand the continuities in terms of the lives of the marginalized and nuanced solidarity practices through both notions of continuity and change.

Context: challenges to solidarity

As the pictures of migrant workers walking for hundreds of kilometres, children eating grass, road accidents and resultant deaths began to circulate at the very early stages of the outbreak, it became increasingly clear that the effects of this pandemic had escalated into a humanitarian crisis. With no physical distancing, high comorbidity and less or no access to healthcare and testing centres, the poor have been severely affected (Das, 2020).

This is especially true in an economy where informal labour consists of 92.8 percent of the total workforce. Added to this is the loss of livelihood, which for the daily wage earner means lack of access to food, shelter and basic necessities as well as an uncertain future ahead. Nor can the crisis and the response to it be evaluated outside the realities of migrant workers, locked out in different regions, jobless but unable to return home or returning home at great human cost. With an unprecedented shrinkage in India's economy there does not seem to be immediate relief in sight.[1]

With a relentless rise in infections, the relief measures offered by the central government, with insufficient budget allocation, lack of clarity and reassurance, have ignored such realities. In fact, the central government has used this pandemic-induced withdrawal of public protests to relentlessly push forward its agenda of privatization and *Hindutva*.[2]

In fact, following Naomi Klein's concept of disaster capitalism, economist Jayati Ghosh (Sampath, 2020) argues that the state in India is pursuing disaster authoritarianism whereby the government is not just pushing through a slew of neoliberal policies, so far resisted by the people, but also using the pandemic to suppress dissent of any kind against it. This has been evident in the use of the undemocratic and draconian Unlawful Activities Prevention Act (UAPA) which has been used to arrest and incarcerate numerous students, activists, academics and politicians who have criticized the state.

Both the need of and obstacles to activism at this juncture are critical. The anti-people stance of the ruling constellation has to be opposed while negotiating with the distancing measures. The reality of the pandemic has given rise globally to creative forms of showing solidarity through the use of balconies as spaces of communion and through digital means. But co-option by the Indian state of such creative use of spaces to turn these into blind allegiance to a personality cult, in combination with the limited reach of digital activism in India, poses unique challenges for the country's social movement actors.

Digital activism in India has to a very large degree remained the preserve of the privileged. With a reported 560 million internet users in India in 2019 (Keelery, 2020), this might be a moment to rethink how solidarities can be digitized democratically across the vast user base of the internet. The key to overcoming crisis in this period of distancing lies in the creation of social solidarity among communities and groups so that resistance can continue in this period of physical alienation.

This chapter is based on news reports and the author's personal interaction with activist groups and organizations. Rather than providing deep ethnographic insights, this chapter offers a glimpse of the general trends, especially in relation to community-level solidarity and activism in urban sites, and tries to rethink how solidarity can look in pandemic times and beyond.

Earlier plagues

COVID-19, deadly as it is, is not the first pandemic to have affected this country. The plague outbreak in 1898 illustrated how disease and policies around it are never just medical but are embedded within the politics of the socioeconomic fabric of the country. Sarkar (2013) shows how the entire governance of that disease was based on zeroing in on working-class areas as 'plague suspect' areas. This in turn built resistance and led citizens to devise various subversive ways to contest the demonization that saw Hindus and Muslims making common cause against intrusive police searches, abusive colonial state policies that violated their religious customs and social norms, the humiliation women and the destruction of property. There was a critical questioning of the state underlying the resistance, which rather than building itself on the negation of scientific methods, pointed out the state's inaction in this direction.

In 1918, the 'Spanish' flu, locally called the Bombay Fever, broke out, claiming 4 percent of the total population of the country, accounting for a fifth of the global death toll. Spinney (2017) argues that the pandemic was instrumental in uniting India against the British as it became clear that the medical infrastructure in India was in a shambles due to the systematic way in which it had been ignored by the British. At great human cost, the pandemic provided momentum to rebuild solidarity, to re-evaluate alliances.

Of course, these were different diseases and different eras from the present pandemic facing us, but the ways these periods of crisis facilitated creative solidarities contain lessons. Learning from the ways in which the state response during that pandemic crafted new dimensions in the critique of colonialism and imperialism, this moment of failure of a neoliberal, unending consumption-led world might lead us to question the tenets of the economic organization of such capitalist growth and its minimal attention to health and education.

Rethinking solidarity through community spaces

Postcolonial cities produce an urbanism that entails a spatial and material embodiment of marginal lives, requiring constant negotiation, challenge and subversion of the intended use of the spaces of built-in inequality. Bhan et al (2020) note that the pandemic and its induced responses have not created but exacerbated the vulnerability of the urban precariat by eroding the arrangements through which they create and recreate ways of getting by. Such a concept of urban sites as exclusively middle/upper-class spaces, allowing for logistics of distancing norms to be followed, deepens existing inequality and also reveals the complete absence of a 'community infrastructure' (Singh, 2020). The responses to Ebola in 2014–16 highlighted the centrality of community participation not just to consciousness building but also to questions of social mobilization (Lavareck and Manocourt, 2015).

On the other hand, the pandemic-induced crisis requires mass movements in streets and squares to rescale themselves. Transforming and locating activism in neighbourhood spaces allows for resistance to their abandonment by national governments while at the same time creating or reiterating community spaces as sites of solidarity. Such community networks, facilitated through social media or through grassroots networks of political parties and other organizations, have sprung up all over the country to distribute food, medicine and essentials to the elderly and working-class families living in their neighbourhoods, people often left without resources to feed themselves. These acts of social solidarity also constitute resistance to xenophobia, the demonization of Muslims and the antipathy evident in many such middle-class neighbourhoods. Such initiatives re-establish the empowering potential of the radical politics of care.

Civil society organizations, grassroots networks of political parties/groups and groups of citizens coming together have creatively used social media, telephones and digital payment to create network of support such as for rations, shelter and immediate necessities for stranded migrant workers or their families in villages. It is these networks of solidarity, rather than the state, that provided a semblance of support for the most vulnerable. While networked across the country through activist groups and organizations, the entire logistics of such relief operations were based on local infrastructures, providing rations from local shops, medicines from local pharmacies and the like.

It was the side street, the square, the community kitchen that became the sites of new practices, sites which were able to repurpose themselves to become what Bhan et al (2020) call the 'multifaceted nodes of intervention'. Drawing upon commitment to social justice and shared histories of coping makes possible the imagination of a new form of collective life which is organic but also located in a larger network of solidarity. Hock (2020) holds that this pandemic might be a moment in which collective action could demonstrate alternatives to the urbanization so far normalized and built on embedding and invisibilizing inequalities.

Similarly, students and faculties of many of the universities and colleges across the country have engaged in producing hand sanitizers and soaps which can be distributed at a low cost or free to those who cannot afford to buy these items at regular prices. Surprisingly, these are exceptional actions in a neoliberal world of constant motion. In their individualness they are small acts of kindness, but when taken together, and especially in a context where the state has not shown any initiative towards supplying such essentials to the poor, these are acts of resistance, acts of building solidarities against the inherent inequality of the neoliberal order. Such acts of organized or spontaneous solidarity create communities able to exert themselves as enfranchised. One of the most prominent sites in which communitarian practices have expressed themselves has been community kitchens.

Community kitchen

One of the focal points that the pandemic brought to the fore among large sections of people is the dearth of food and resultant hunger. While some policies were put in place for distributing rations to the urban poor, most of these efforts were inadequate in the face of the scale of the crisis. Moreover, many of the labouring poor felt humiliated to stand in queues for hours waiting for inadequate food. Conversely, community-run kitchens provided a site of food provision without making people feel invisible and disenfranchised. Community kitchens still running in different parts of the country, in Lucknow, in various cities in Kerala, in Kolkata and Delhi among others, are critical sites of organic solidarity. Kundu (2020) observes that each self-organized kitchen provided new scope for building networks and alliances as well as for strengthening resilience.

Cooking together has been rediscovered as one of the oldest forms of showing solidarity. Following all the requirements of hygiene and distancing, these kitchens have seen strangers banding together to prepare meals to be then distributed among those suffering from food shortage. In a caste society like India, with deep anxieties around touch and stigma around washing dishes and cooking together, community kitchens are of a special importance in combating this grammar of difference. Embedded in local dynamics there is of course the likelihood of unevenness in decision-making about food distribution, shaped by extant inequalities and prejudices (Kundu, 2020).

While acknowledging these possibilities, community-run kitchens have, like after the Delhi pogroms in February and March 2020,[3] become sites of caring. Following Hayden's (1981) notion about soup kitchens in the USA, community kitchens can also be seen as feminist sites based on a reimagining of women's labour, divorcing it from the private kitchen of the household and placing it as a constituent of community-level infrastructure. Through different modalities, cooking 'protest food' defies the anti-poor, anti-democratic hierarchical sociopolitical order. The community created around the act of preparing food also poses a challenge to the atomist neoliberal society, and provides an alternative way of living and sharing, not just in times of crisis but as a way of reorganizing social life at all times.

Of course, these are nebulous moments, uncertain as yet, and spontaneous, often dependent on the initiative of disparate groups, and it remains to be seen whether such moments, such initiatives, can actually pave the way for a more organic basis, not just for community organization, but in fact for the exercise of participatory democracy, of solidarity as a way of everyday living.

Conclusion

With physical distancing as a need of the day, society can only function through a reimagination of social solidarity. This is a moment of waiting, but it cannot be allowed to become an empty moment. Crises such as this, with anxieties, lockdowns and global panic, are perfect moments for authoritarian governments to increase their power, as is evident in India. Here the state has used the pandemic to push for greater privatization, to disband relief and rehabilitation efforts and to gag, witch-hunt and try to wipe away from public memory the powerful protests against it.

At the same time, the crisis has exposed the fragility of neoliberal capitalism and its inability to deliver services to people. In this increasingly globalized, networked world, COVID-19 is the first pandemic. The extreme crisis, however, also allows for the possibility of a radical reimagining of the normal – the normalcy of competitive economy, of relentless urbanization, of atomist living. The heart of such resistance lies in creating communities in the local context. The solidarity networks built across such communities need to acknowledge the local communities and their organic leadership as owners of their own lives – activism lies in comradeship, in collaboration, and not in a top-down charity model. Following the trajectory of the anti-CAA movement, resistance needs to invoke the categories of rights and citizenship.

The slippers left by the protesting women in Shaheen Bagh at the start of the lockdown, to remind the state of their presence in their absence, became powerful expressions of resistance.[4] In such times, acts of remembering and remembering together, reevaluating and reimagining communitarian spaces, become central to creating spaces of solidarity and to visualizing a future which is discontinuous with the present socioeconomic order in which we live. It is in the radical act of caring and caring together that we can build up the basis of resilience to such a predatory socioeconomic and political order.

Notes

[1] In the first quarter of 2020, India's economy shrunk by 23.9 percent, the worst ever slump since the government started recording GDP. Coming in the wake of a four-decade-high unemployment rate, this forecasts a shrinking of the economy and widespread hardship. See more: https://www.financialexpress.com/economy/q1-gdp-live-india-economy-growth-rate-coronavirus-lockdown-first-quarter-agricult ure-manufacturing-services/2070263/ and https://www.indiatoday.in/business/story/india-unemployment-rate-6–1-per-cent-45-year-high-nsso-report-1539580–2019-05–31

[2] Nationalist ideology from the Hindu far right, supported and diffused by the Bharatiya Janata Party and the current president of India Narendra Modi.

[3] See: https://www.thehindu.com/topic/delhi-violence-2020/

[4] Editors note: Shaheen Bagh is a neighbourhood in the South Delhi district of Delhi. Shaheen Bagh's protests started in late 2019 and lasted until March 2020, when Delhi police contained the initiative after the beginning of the pandemic. Led by women, they rose up against the approval of the Citizenship Law by the parliament, but also against police brutality, unemployment and poverty, and for women's security.

References

Bandyopadhyay, R. (2020) 'Why do empty streets threaten democracy?', *Antipode Online*, [online] 25 June, available from: https://antipodeonline.org/2020/06/25/empty-streets/

Bhan, G., Caldeira, T., Gillespie, K. and AbdouMaliq, S. (2020) 'The Pandemic, Southern urbanism and collective life', *Society Space*, 38(4).

Das, K. (2020) 'Hunger, poverty and jobs: India's poor pay heavy price in fight against Coronavirus', *India Today*, [online] 28 May, available from: https://www.indiatoday.in/business/story/coronavirus-impact-india-poor-population-poverty-unemployment-hunger-economic-crisis-recession-1682890–2020-05–28

Deka, K. (2019) 'Everything you wanted to know about the CAA and NRC', *India Today*, [online] 23 December, available from: https://www.indiatoday.in/india-today-insight/story/everything-you-wanted-to-know-about-the-caa-and-nrc-1630771–2019-12–23

Hayden, D. (1981) *The Grand Domestic Revolution*, Cambridge, MA: MIT Press.

Hock, S.S. (2020) 'Questioning normalcy: Rethinking urbanisation, development and collective action through COVID-19 movement', *Medium*, [online] 20 June, available from: https://medium.com/@lseseac/questioning-normalcy-rethinking-urbanisation-development-and-collective-action-through-the-3a3fc1a873f0

Keelery, S. (2020) 'Internet usage in India: Statistics and fact', *Stastita*, [online] 7 July, available from: https://www.statista.com/topics/2157/internet-usage-in-india/

Kundu, R. (2020) 'As hunger grows, Mumbai's community kitchens may hold lessons on ensuring nutrition for the poor', *Scroll*, [online] 27 July, available online: https://scroll.in/article/968612/as-hunger-grows-mumbais-community-kitchens-may-hold-lessons-for-ensuring-nutrition-for-the-poor

Laverack, G. and Manocourt, E. (2016) 'Key experiences of community engagement and social mobilization in Ebola response', *Global Health Response*, 23(1): 79–82.

Sampath, G. (2020) 'The "shock doctrine" in India's response to COVID-19', *The Hindu*, [online] 15 June, available from: https://www.thehindu.com/podcast/comment-the-shock-doctrine-in-indias-response-to-covid-19/article31831402.ece

Sarkar, A. (2013) 'The city, its streets, and its workers: The plague crisis in Bombay', in R. Ahuja (ed) *Working Lives and Worker Militancy: The Politics of Labour in Colonial India*, Delhi: Tulika.

Singh, V. (2020) 'Community infrastructure: The missing piece in the COVID-19 puzzle', *Hyderabad Urban Lab*, [online] 22 May, available from: https://hydlab.in/blogposts/community-infrastructure-the-missing-piece-in-the-covid-19-puzzle?fbclid=IwAR0aq8wg9f4KE2FVq0OUwd UbarQCyGrz0a_Cy2m6FmAYVlAsOZ68h0iT1qg

Spinney, L. (2017) *Pale Rider: Spanish Flu of 1918 and How It Changed the World*, New York: Public Affairs.

PART III

Social Movements, Mutual Aid and Self-Reliance during COVID-19

16

Social Movements in the Emergence of a Global Pandemic

Donatella della Porta

Times of pandemic bring big challenges for the activists of progressive social movements. Initially, it was thought that they were not a time for street activism or politics in the squares. Freedoms were restricted, and physical distancing made the typical forms of protest impossible to carry out. Mobilization was not only difficult in public places but also in our places of work, given the very strict limitation on the right to meet and the reduced opportunity for face-to-face encounters.

The continuous emergency also constrains our mental spaces, challenging our creativity. Individual and collective resources are focused mainly on everyday survival. Hope, that stimulant for collective action, is difficult to sustain, while fear, which so discourages it, spreads. Crises might trigger selfish defensive choices, turning the other into an enemy. We depend on governmental efficiency and expert opinions.

Nevertheless, social movements have also shown, since the beginning of the pandemic, that they often do emerge in moments of high emergency, of calamity and of strong repression of individual and collective freedoms. Wars have triggered waves of contention in the past. Not only is it the case that states make wars and wars make states, but portentous contestations have accompanied military conflicts—before, after, at times even during. Such revolutions testify to the strength of engagement in moments of deep crisis. This article seeks to reflect on social movements during the initial moment of emergence of the global pandemic, based on some lessons from social movements studies.

Crisis and alternative forms of protest

Times of deep crisis can (even if not automatically) generate the invention of alternative forms of protest. The broad spread of new technologies allows for online protests—including, but not limited to, e-petitions that have multiplied in this period (ranging from the quest for Eurobonds to the request for a suspension of rents for students). Car marches have been called for in Israel. Workers have claimed more security through flash mobs, implemented by participants keeping a safe distance from one another. In Finland, public transport drivers have refused to monitor tickets. In Italy and Spain, collective messages of contestation or solidarity are sent from balconies and windows. Through these innovative forms, protests puts pressure on those in government and control their actions.

Faced with the glaring need for radical and complex transformation, social movements also act in various ways that differ from protests. First of all, social movements create and recreate ties: they build upon existing networks, but also, in action, they connect and multiply them. Faced with the manifest inadequacies of the state and, even more, of the market, social movement organizations form—as is happening in every country hit by the pandemic—into mutual support groups, promoting direct social action by helping those most in need. Thus, they produce resilience by responding to the need for solidarity.

Movements also act as channels for the elaboration of proposals. They make use of alternative specialist knowledge, but they also add to this the practical knowledge arising from the direct experiences of citizens. Constructing alternative public spheres, social movement organizations help us to imagine future scenarios. The multiplication of public space allows for cross-fertilization, contrasting with the overspecialization of academic knowledge and facilitating the connection between abstract knowledge and concrete practices. From this cross-fertilization comes also the capacity to connect the various crises—to prise out the connection between the spread and lethality of COVID-19 and climate change, wars, violence against women and the expropriations of rights (first of all the right to health). In this way, reflection in and of social movements increases our capacity to understand the economic, social and political causes of the pandemic, which is neither a natural phenomenon nor a divine punishment.

Uncertainty and new spaces for innovation

In this way, social movements can exploit the spaces for innovation that open up in moments of uncertainty. In the most dramatic way, the crisis demonstrates that change is needed, a radical change that breaks with the past, and a complex change that goes from politics to the economy, from society to culture. If, in normal times, social movements grow with the opportunities for gradual transformation, in times of deep crisis movements are spread instead by the perception of a drastic and deep threat, contributing to cognitive openings. While everyday life changes drastically, spaces for reflection about a future that cannot be thought of as being in continuity with the past also open up.

Crisis also opens up opportunities for change by making evident the need for public responsibility and civic sense, for rules and solidarity. If crises have the immediate effect of concentrating power, up to and including its militarization, they also demonstrate the incapacity of governments to act merely through force. The need for sharing and widespread support in order to address the pandemic might bring with it the recognition of the richness of civil society mobilization. The presence of social movements might thereby provide a contrast with the risks taken by an authoritarian response to the crisis.

What is more, crises show the value of fundamental public goods and their complex management through institutional networks but also through the participation of the citizens, the workers and users. They demonstrate that the management of the commons needs regulation and participation from below. In any mobilization during a pandemic, the value of a universal system of public health emerges as not only just but also vital. If claims for health in workplaces and the universal protection of health as a public good are traditionally the demands of trade unions and of the left, the pandemic demonstrates the need to reaffirm these rights and expand them to include the least protected. In its global dimension, the pandemic triggers reflection on the need for global protection of the right to health protection, as often explained by civil society organizations such as Doctors without Borders or Emergency.

Of course, all this does not happen automatically. These crises are also give occasion for the accumulation of profit by dispossession, for the experimentation of authoritarian governments and for social anomie. Emergencies and shocks create rich occasions for speculators. But, if the crises increase competition for scarce resources, they also increase the perception of a shared destiny. Increasing inequalities rather than levelling them, crises also instil a deep sense of injustice, bringing with it the singling out of specific political and social responsibilities. As in wars, the exacting of terrible sacrifices from the people fuels claims over rights and participation in decision-making. As collective mobilization grows, the hope for change ensues – for another world that is still possible and all the more needed.

17

COVID-19 and the Reconfiguration of the Social Movements Landscape

Sabrina Zajak

The COVID-19 pandemic is challenging and changing social movements worldwide. Since the beginning of 2020, the crisis has been reconfiguring the social movements landscape within and across countries. This chapter discusses the changing patterns of mobilization during the crisis. Using examples from Germany and beyond, it pays particular attention to the reconfiguration of the social movements landscape as expressed in two ways. First in terms of new challenges for progressive social movements, including restraints on their protest mobilization, reduction of resources and media attention and the intensification of social inequalities based on race and class. Secondly in terms of the emergence of a new countermovement, the anti-lockdown or COVID-19-denial protests.

While at the beginning of the crisis all movements seemed equally challenged and restrained by the lockdown, it became clear that there are differences across groups and networks in their ability to deal with the situation. On the one hand, we see differences in coping capacities, in particular of those grassroots organizations mobilizing the marginalized. On the other hand, we see the rise of new conspiracy-theory-inspired mobilizations, which not only contest the existence of the virus but also mix conspiracy theories with esoteric, racist, right-wing and populist ideologies. This chapter suggests that this double development (of new challenges and restraints for progressive movements and of the rise of a new counter-mobilization) has the potential to have long-lasting effects on civil society in Germany and beyond through reconfiguring the social movement scene.

Social movements, crises and new conflict structures

Crisis situations can be important moments of change, that is, critical junctures (Collier and Collier, 2002), which alter both underlying social structures and how social movements interpret social relations in society. That social movements play an important role in crisis situations has been particularly well documented for the global financial and economic crisis of 2007–08. Movements emerged and reorganized, becoming a political force in shaping the crisis politics and its aftermath (Fominaya, 2020).

The COVID-19 pandemic is currently pushing transformations in societies at various levels: we can already observe increases in digitalization (Skulmowski and Rey, 2020), significant changes in public policy and public administration (Radin, 2020) and accelerating social-economic inequalities (Bapuji et al, 2020). Activists are not only affected by the pandemic but also by its broader political, economic and societal consequences. However, social movements do not simply react to the crisis situation. They also creatively shape and construct agency and new ideas about what to do, for example by naming and framing the problems and what can be done about them (Pleyers, 2020) or by creating new narratives and ideologies that different groups in society then embrace or oppose (see Bringel, Chapter 35 of this volume).

The challenges the COVID-19 pandemic presents for social movements are manifold. I would like to draw attention to two main developments, as they can inform the restructuring of the social movements landscape with potential medium- and long-term effects on the capacity for progressive movements to mobilize within and across different countries. On the one hand, the implications of the pandemic increase the challenges for social movements not only in terms of resources they can mobilize but also in terms of opportunities to mobilize and form collective actions. On the other hand, we see COVID-19-denial protests, which a diversity, and right-wing populists. It increasingly becomes clear that this COVID-19-denial movement, which at the beginning also included activists from the left, is now increasingly dominated by right-wing ideologies (Nachtwey at al, forthcoming). This is problematic, as we know from social- movements studies that alliance formations long ago lead to a reshaping of identities and issues (Van Dyke and McCammon, 2010). Ideologies become diffused through networks and the media, and this again can increase the regressive turn in society. Progressive forces will have to fight ever-increasing battles within the field of civil society as well as in the political sphere.

Changing dynamics: increasing inequalities, progressive mobilization and regressive counter-mobilization

In order to understand how the pandemic is reshaping social movement dynamics, we can take two theoretical insights from social movements studies into account. First, social movements operate in multi-organizational fields, which means activists groups continuously interact with multiple actors in specific settings (Rucht, 2004). Thus, social movements are directly and indirectly influenced by their opponents. Second, social movements are also impacted by the political environment (usually captured as 'political opportunities' or 'threats') and then social structure of society. In short, social movements are not isolated phenomena but are expressions and manifestations of social conflicts, rooted in cleavages and frictions between groups, together shaping broader processes of social change (Zajak and Haunss, 2020, p 2).

As I would like to sketch out here, the pandemic is now affecting both the social-movement field as well as the underlying social basis of mobilization – together reshaping the social movement landscape potentially for years to come. In the early weeks of the pandemic the lockdown affected the modus operandi of all social movements. The COVID-19 topic monopolized media coverage, and assembling bodies in the street to demonstrate was temporarily prohibited. Everyone seemed to be affected in similar ways. But it quickly became clear that this was not the case. As the first weeks and month (February, March, April) passed, it became clear that people and social movements were affected in different ways.

Some activists have to deal with their own difficult situations, loss of income, the threat of unemployment or even struggling for their own survival. This holds particularly true the more we look at the mobilization of already marginalized groups, for whom mobilization become more difficult. This resonates with literature that indicates that people affected by intersectional marginalization (racial/ethnic minorities, migrants, women) who work in low-paid jobs (for example in the healthcare system) have a much higher risk of becoming infected or even of dying (see Bringel and Pleyers' introduction to this book, and also Bowleg, 2020). Other literature gives evidence for the proliferation of discrimination of different groups. For example, studies observed the increase of anti-Asian racism as a response to the framing of the virus as the 'Chinese threat' (Gover et al, 2020). But also other forms of exclusion and devaluation have been observed to be spiralling, including racism against Black people, or anti-Roma racism (Matache and Bhabha, 2020). Others have suggested that there are additional marginalization effects brought on by the increasing reliance on digital tools. The already existing digital divide increased further, and not everyone was able to bridge the social distance via digital tools (Beaunoyer et al, 2020). In sum, the pandemic is accentuating pre-existing inequalities but also adding another layer of marginalization affecting already vulnerable peoples the most.

These developments have been affecting progressive movements in multiple ways, in particular those mobilizing with and for the marginalized. In our study of pro-migrant mobilization in Germany we found that mobilization did take place (very prominently in Germany under the Hashtag #LeaveNoOneBehind) largely online or in hybrid formats. However, marginalized groups, such as self-organized refugee groups, could hardly participate. For some, the digital infrastructure was missing or they were simply relying on face-to-face- exchange for organizing and mobilizing. Others have such severe problems they have had to rely on very local solidarity and social support work (Zajak et al, 2020).

Likewise, some movements reported new internal struggles over how to position and frame the pandemic situation. Some environmental groups had to battle (or pre-empt) racist framing within their movements. Activists from Fridays for Future and Extinction Rebellion, for example, explicitly distanced themselves from narratives that COVID-19 is a response of nature to overpopulation and environmental destruction, basically the earth's self-healing process. The environmental activist Clara Thompson warned that such framing could 'lead to the promotion of eugenics or a one-race state achieved by oppressive anti-immigration policies' (Thompson, 2020, p 3).

Despite all such challenges, mobilization has taken place. #LeaveNoOneBehind for example, tried to show solidarity with everyone confronted with racism and discrimination. They created new symbols of solidarity and new online spaces where people could exchange ideas and generate knowledge (Zajak et al, 2020). They also began to discuss the weaknesses of the current systems the pandemic so painfully revealed (for example in the healthcare systems, in the global economy, in climate, refugee or gender-equality politics, or in the imbalances within and between states). But the challenges did and still do not only come from the pandemic crisis, the lockdown restrictions and the intensification of inequality and racist discrimination. Progressive social movements are, furthermore, challenged from within the sphere of (un)civil society by the rise of the COVID-19-denial movement.

COVID-19-denial movement

COVID-19 and the political responses to the pandemic have not only significantly affected existing movements but have also led to the emergence of new forms of protest around the globe which are largely used against the lockdown and pandemic restrictions. These protest events are given different labels across countries, including 'anti-lockdown' or 'anti-mask protest', 'coronavirus-denial movement', 'corona-conspiracy movement' or 'hygienic demonstration'. Although we know relatively little about the composition of this emerging movement in different countries, we can deduce their issues, demands and motivations from observing their calls for action, posters and social media posts (Nachtwey et al, forthcoming).

Leading figures for these protests include populist politicians like Donald Trump or Jair Bolsonaro, who downplay the effect and consequences of the virus to stabilize their far-right populist nationalism. They use misinformation and denial of scientific and evidence-based recommendations, present their own pseudo-information about symptoms, risks and cures and delegitimize and discredit everyone in support of social isolation measures (for the Brazilian case, see Ricard and Medeiros, 2020; for the US, Dyer, 2020). The underlying conspiracy theories are fuelled by websites such as StopWorldControl.com, NoMoreFakeNews.com or Rense.com and by message boards like QAnon.

We can observe such protests in many countries in the world, including countries with relatively low death tolls and comparatively moderate lockdown regulations such as in Germany. With some variations, they share the belief that the virus is either harmless or introduced by powerful elites or a 'deep state' to control, suppress and lock up the people. Such conspiracy theories are mixed with racist and far-right ideologies, and get diffused within online networks and through offline demonstrations. As Ulrike Vieten pointed out in an analysis of the German COVID-19-denial initiatives Querdenken 711 and Widerstand 2020, the real danger lies in the 'blurring boundaries between legitimate democratic political protest and racist far-right populist positions' which are 'linked to wider battles over entitlements and (White) supremacist claims of who belongs to the people' (Vieten, 2020).

Such broad alliances between vaccination opponents, conspiracy theorists and activists with drastically different political views seem to be relatively unique to Germany – and the US.[1] The broadness of the alliance structures is particularly dangerous as it facilitates the diffusion of racists and right-wing beliefs. This could push the regressive turn in society and the move of radical ideologies towards the middle. Moreover, it could also have lasting effects on progressive mobilization through the shrinking of the civic sphere and supportive (discursive) opportunity spaces.

Progressive movements quickly began to respond to these mobilizations, for example through their hashtags such as #StayAtHome or #FlattenTheCurve, but also through the organization of counter-protest events. However, the organization of physical protests in the streets following social distancing rules remains challenging for progressive movements during the pandemic. It remains to be seen if progressive movements lose ground in the years to come or if they are able to forge new broad alliances against the regressive turn in society.

Conclusion

This chapter suggests that the COVID-19 pandemic is affecting progressive social movements in two ways. First, through the broad changes the pandemic is accelerating or even driving in societies around the globe. These include changes in public politics, reduction of financial resources, job losses, increasing inequalities and racial discrimination – to name a few. Progressive social movements need to formulate, frame and fight these problems even while they are themselves struggling with marginalization, loss of resources and new conflict lines within single movements and activist groups.

Furthermore, I suggested that the COVID-19-denial protests are an additional threat to progressive movements, as these protest could contribute to the 'normalization' of right-wing ideologies and might support the regressive turn in society long after the demonstrations are gone. This reconfiguration of the social movements field seems to be taking place in many countries around the globe. However, resistance and new modes of progressive mobilization are already forming, and there is hope that, in the medium and long term, progressive movements will play an important role in shaping the post-COVID-19 order and may be able to channel the frustrations and experiences of rupture in individual lives in progressive ways.

Note

1   This of course needs comparative academic analysis. For public reports on that see: https://www.dw.com/en/how-are-germanys-coronavirus-protests-different/a-53443502

References

Bapuji, H., Patel, C., Ertug, G., and Allen, D.G. (2020) 'Corona crisis and inequality: Why management research needs a societal turn', *Journal of Management*, 46(7), available from: https://doi.org/10.1177/0149206320925881

Beaunoyer, E., Dupéré, S., and Guitton, M.J. (2020) 'COVID-19 and digital inequalities: Reciprocal impacts and mitigation strategies', *Computers in Human Behavior*, 111, 106424.

Bowleg, L. (2020) 'We're not all in this together: On COVID-19, intersectionality, and structural inequality', *American Journal of Public Health*, 110(7): 917.

Collier, R.B. and Collier, D. (2002) *Shaping the Political Arena: Critical Junctures, the Labor Movement, and Regime Dynamics in Latin America*, Notre Dame, IN: University of Notre Dame Press.

Dyer, O. (2020) 'COVID-19: Trump stokes protests against social distancing measures', *BMJ*, 369, doi: https://doi.org/10.1136/bmj.m1596

Gover, A.R., Harper, S.B. and Langton, L. (2020) 'Anti-Asian hate crime during the COVID-19 pandemic: Exploring the reproduction of inequality', *American Journal of Criminal Justice*, 45(4): 647–67.

Matache, M. and Bhabha, J. (2020) 'Anti-Roma racism is spiraling during COVID-19 pandemic', *Health and Human Rights*, 22(1): 379.

Nachtwey et al (forthcoming) *Politische Soziologie der Corona-Proteste*.

Pleyers, G. (2020) 'The pandemic is a battlefield: Social movements in the COVID-19 lockdown', *Journal of Civil Society*: 1–18.

Radin, B.A. (2020) 'What have we learned in the fields of public policy and public administration that might be relevant to the coronavirus pandemic?', *American Review of Public Administration*, 50(6–7): 743–5.

Ricard, J. and Medeiros, J. (2020) 'Using misinformation as a political weapon: COVID-19 and Bolsonaro in Brazil', *Harvard Kennedy School Misinformation Review*, 1(2): 1–6.

Rucht, D. (2004) 'Movement allies, adversaries, and third parties', in S.A. Soule, D.A. Snow and H. Kriesi (eds) *The Blackwell Companion to Social Movements*, Hoboken, NJ: Wiley, 197–216.

Skulmowski, A. and Rey, G.D. (2020) 'COVID-19 as an accelerator for digitalization at a German university: Establishing hybrid campuses in times of crisis', *Human Behavior and Emerging Technologies*, 2(3): 212–16.

Thompson, C. (2020) '#FightEveryCrisis: Re-framing the climate movement in times of a pandemic', *Interface: A Journal for and about Social Movements*, 12(1): 225–31.

Van Dyke, N. and McCammon, H.J. (2010) *Strategic Alliances: Coalition Building and Social Movements*, Minneapolis: University of Minnesota Press.

Vieten, Ulrike M. (2020) 'The "new normal" and "pandemic populism": The COVID-19 crisis and anti-hygienic mobilisation of the far-right', *Social Sciences*, 9(9): 165.

Zajak, S. and Haunss, S. (eds) (2020) *Social Stratification and Social Movements: Theoretical and Empirical Perspectives on an Ambivalent Relationship*, Abingdon: Routledge.

Zajak, S., Stjepandić, K. and Steinhilper, E. (2020) 'Pro-migrant protest in times of COVID-19: Intersectional boundary spanning and hybrid protest practices', *European Societies*: 1–12.

18

Social Movements as Essential Services in Toronto

Lesley Wood

In an unjust pandemic world, social movements are essential services. But the question of how to transform a system under pressure is a delicate one. The scale of the need, the poverty, the lack of housing, the immune-compromised, the children and elders pushes us towards the state. Like social movements over the last few hundred years, movements demand more benefits, more space and more resources. Such demands may paradoxically strengthen a system that helped to create racial, class and other inequalities. Without our usual repertoire, how can we ensure that the most vulnerable are included, while continuing our efforts to nurture the seeds of a more just, fruitful world?

In February 2020, visible and vibrant protests filled the streets and the news. In Canada, indigenous communities and allies blocked roads and railways in support of the hereditary chiefs of the Wet'suwet'en, reaffirming their sovereignty and challenging the legality of a natural gas pipeline across their territories. The legitimacy of the settler state and its extractivist economy was called into question. These movements held space, and reaffirmed connection to the land in ways that imagined a society beyond the state. Internationally, pro-democracy protesters in Hong Kong, Chile and Turkey filled the streets, went on strike and clashed with police. In India, women held hands in widespread protests challenging the right-wing citizenship laws that targeted and excluded Muslims.

As news of the virus spread, activists were faced with a difficult question. Should we cancel our plans? If we did, were we stepping back? But veterans, particularly those connected to homeless, undocumented, prisoner and immune-compromised populations argued that social solidarity required both physical distancing and mutual aid. We shifted. In early March, at a meeting planning a prison abolitionist conference, anti-racist activists explained it was unethical for movements building another world to ask people to travel and physically converge at this time, that doing so would most likely harm indigenous and Black communities, particularly prisoners or recently released folks. So, we turned away from the streets and towards one another, arguing that those who are most vulnerable must be at the centre. The cancellations flooded in. Following the lead of the World Health Organization, the local, provincial and federal governments announced closings, cancellations and shutdowns.

COVID-19-era movements in Toronto: four models

By the end of March, the streets were empty, nor could we have physical meetings, but social movement organizing continued in four modes. This organizing defends the needs of workers, it demands more from the state for the most marginalized, it disrupts exploitation and it provides direct support for vulnerable communities. Each mode holds contradictions within it – choices that can either reinforce inequalities or build another world in the shell of the old. We know that how we organize now will matter in the future. This COVID-era movement work varies by location and by history, as pre-existing movements, organizations and networks lean in.

Essential workers

The first mode is led by workers deemed essential. Both formal unions and informal workers movements are demanding increased access to personal protective equipment. These include healthcare workers, truck drivers, first responders and grocery store workers. The importance of these workers to the functioning of society has never been more apparent. Some have used this moment to flex their power – striking and holding work stoppages. On 2 April, Canadian Union of Public Employees workers wore stickers 'to protest a decision by the government to give registered nurses a different level of protection than other professions, such as respiratory therapists, personal support workers and registered practical nurses.' These efforts, amid the desire by power holders to maintain control and legitimacy, are likely to be successful. We see broad public support for these workers – from the nightly banging of pots to the crafty folks sewing masks and the signs in people's windows supporting letter carriers.

Workers have also been fighting layoffs and for compensation and financial support. More than 2 million Canadians filed for employment insurance in the last two weeks of March because of company shutdowns. The government has rolled out the Canada Emergency Response Benefit (CERB) that supports some contract and self-employed workers who have been affected, offering them $2000 a month for four months. Although these programs are intended to maintain the functioning of an exploitative economy, they are important victories that reflect the longstanding efforts of movements to expand the recognition and value of workers, and include gig and other precarious workers. They build on struggles to defend the public sector, gutted by years of neoliberal austerity. The recognition and resources given to these sectors right now are long overdue. However, inequalities still exist, and these programs and funds can end up further abandoning those most marginalized. Some are excluded from these benefits; those who had no job to begin with, migrant workers, student workers or those who had no status. *La lucha continua*.

Defending the most vulnerable

Ensuring that the most vulnerable people are not abandoned is the second mode of movement activity. This includes prisoners, people in long-term care facilities, non-status people, those on welfare and the homeless. Veteran anti-poverty activists who have fought for years for more, more affordable and better housing, shelter beds and supports for the homeless have, in the context of widespread public fear, succeeded in getting the city to open up beds in community centres and hotels. They work to get more money into the hands of poor people, with emergency assistance to those on welfare. These movements organize online and drive phone and email campaigns that are making a difference to people's lives.

Immigrant justice and health activists have succeeded in pressuring the Ontario healthcare system so that hospitals will now see non-status people with any healthcare emergency without charge. This change has spread to other provinces. The Migrant Rights Network has succeeded in getting some financial support to some workers with temporary immigration status affected by the shutdowns. In the wake of a hunger strike led by immigrant detainees in the holding facility in Laval, No One Is Illegal, the End Immigrant Detention Network, Solidarity Across Borders and the Migrant Rights Network have continued their push to end immigrant detention, and indeed, they are succeeding in undermining the argument that these people must be detained, as many have been released in the past few weeks.

In the midst of COVID-19 fears, prison justice activists like those of the Prison Justice Society and the coalition Contain COVID Not People have reiterated demands to improve conditions and release prisoners. They have succeeded in pushing phone companies to stop charging exorbitant rates to prisoners, and joined by more mainstream allies like the Ontario Lawyers Association, have succeeded in getting the prison system to release many non-violent prisoners.

Disruption against exploitation

The third mode of social movement organizing disrupts exploitation. Toronto's housing prices are some of the highest in the world, and there is an active tenant-rights movement which succeeded in getting a sign-on letter from many organizations and achieving a moratorium on evictions right now, and then turned to campaign for a rent strike. The tactic raises fundamental questions about the right to housing, and became front-page news. One landlord-advocacy spokesperson noted, 'We have the concept that no one should worry about paying the rent. This has caused chaos.' While it is unclear how many people refused to pay rent, the *idea* of challenging such exploitative housing relations is circulating and building momentum. This will aid longer-term struggles against exploitative housing.

Mutual aid, direct action and immediate support

The last way that movement activists have been operating is through direct action and mutual aid to support those most vulnerable through food, care and supply runs. Sometimes called Caremongering (vs fearmongering), horizontalist movements have a long history of such efforts. One can think of how activists became central in Hurricane Katrina and Hurricane Sandy efforts. However, the effectiveness of such initiatives attracts those who understand it as charity for the needy rather than as part of a longer-term effort to build a more just society. Helping one's neighbours is a wonderful thing, but when one neighbourhood is homogenous and well resourced, and another is not, that charity may simply reinforce durable inequalities through opportunity hoarding. These tensions can erupt: when the Toronto Caremongering Facebook group that had been started by social justice activists with a strong anti-racist, anti-capitalist analysis grew over 15,000 strong, they did.

On 18 March 2020, an administrator on the site posted:

> caremongering is not about 'nice canadians' helping each other out
>> caremongering is fighting injustice and moving with love for our people
>> caremongering is solidarity with Wet'suwet'en[1] online week of action
>> caremongering is seeking justice for missing and murdered indigenous women, girls, trans and two spirit people
>> caremongering is building alternatives to capitalism
>> caremongering is recognizing the failures of the state and doing it ourselves
>> caremongering is recognizing that the system isn't just broken, it was built this way
>> caremongering is pushing for structural change not band-aid solutions

caremongering is solidarity with marginalized people not wealth hoarders

caremongering is building local power to push for a liveable planet for all of us

caremongering is knowing our struggles are interconnected

caremongering is people before profit

caremongering is part of a lineage of care networks built by indigenous, Black, poc, sick, disabled, queer, trans, and communities abandoned and oppressed by the canadian state. (https://www.instagram.com/p/b9xe1hyfz7w/)

Mutual aid projects have flourished in this moment—in some, but not all, activists are working to ensure that these efforts avoid building relationships that further marginalize and exploit.

Social movements in times of pandemic and beyond

We know that social movements are most likely to emerge and succeed at particular moments, when regimes are more open to challengers. Pandemics, like economic instability, war or social unrest, create such moments because power holders are uncertain, making them pressurable by outside actors, including social movements that aim for more just social relations, but also by those who seek to close borders, exclude, criminalize and arrest.

Those voices of top-down enforcement seem attractive to many when the numbers of sick and dead continue to rise. But such emergency orders will inevitably be used most frequently against those who law enforcement see as risky—people of colour and youth. They will condemn those without safe shelter, identification and resources—undocumented or homeless people, the sick, the old, the vulnerable.

But in a pandemic, no one should be left behind. Transformative, anti-authoritarian social movements play an essential role in building trust with each other, incorporating the most vulnerable, multiplying the possible ways of relating and making us less dependent on centralized power that has a historical tendency to abandon and exploit. As my colleague Cary Wu notes, 'Public health crises stress public trust in at least four ways. Trust in fellow citizens, trust in politicians, trust in healthcare and trust in perceived outsiders.' Anti-authoritarian social movements can help to build trust. Because of the way movements can redistribute and reorganize resources and create the spaces and relationships that we need, we can challenge the dominant, top-down mode of organizing social life.

With fear, anxiety and rage, people look for things they can rely on. If anti-authoritarian social movements retreat, state approaches to social order gain more power, with dangerous consequences for creating just social relationships for the short and the long term. As James C. Scott (1999) warns, social order is not 'brought about by such professionals as policemen, nightwatchmen, and public officials.' He reminds us that such state logics encourage us to trust top-down authority, logics of control and criminalization. And they don't work. Instead, working for the long haul, social movements recognize how society can work best for ordinary people, through building relationships among the people.

At their best, social movements play this essential role, building voluntary and trusting relations among one another–pushing the state to distribute its resources to the most vulnerable, so that we can build together. Social movements save lives, now and in the future. We must, as thinker Chris Dixon (2014) reminds us, work within, against and beyond the existing system to ensure that when the pandemic recedes, we all flourish.

Note

[1] Wet'suwet'en are a First Nation who live in British Columbia, Canada.

References

Dixon, C. (2014) *Another Politics: Talking across Today's Transformative Movements*, Berkeley, CA: University of California Press Books.

Scott, J.C. (1999) *Seeing Like a State: How Certain Schemes to Improve the Human Condition Have Failed*, New Haven, CT: Yale University Press.

Creating a Hyperlocal Infrastructure of Care: COVID-19 Mutual Aid Groups in the UK

Anastasia Kavada

The COVID-19 crisis brought an upsurge of local and neighbourhood organizing in the UK. At the beginning of March, when COVID-19 cases started climbing and lockdown was looming, COVID-19 mutual aid groups started cropping up in different parts of the country. At the time of writing in November 2020, there are 4,260 such groups across the UK that are registered on the national COVID-19 Mutual Aid UK website (2020a), covering both rural and urban areas.

The groups are formed by neighbours coming together to help those self-isolating in their area due to COVID-19. Neighbours run errands for those who cannot leave their homes, including dog walking, picking up shopping and prescriptions, posting mail or paying bills at the post office. They also make friendly phone calls to those who may be feeling lonely and anxious in self-isolation.

The political power of mutual aid

This type of community organizing is often considered apolitical as it aims at offering relief of people's immediate needs rather than at changing government or corporate policy. Of course, the reality is much more complex than that as caring for the community can build alternative social relationships and change dominant ideas about how society works.

Groups that subscribe to the notion of mutual aid have this potential, as mutual aid operates outside formal frameworks and places the emphasis on horizontality and equality. As the COVID-19 Mutal Aid website notes:

Mutual aid is where a group of people organise to meet their own needs, outside of the formal frameworks of charities, NGOs and government. It is, by definition, a horizontal mode of organising, in which all individuals are equally powerful. There are no 'leaders' or unelected 'steering committees' in mutual aid projects; there is only a group of people who work together as equals. Mutual aid isn't about 'saving' anyone; it's about people coming together, in a spirit of solidarity, to support and look out for one another. (COVID-19 Mutual Aid UK, 2020a)

This has the potential to transform social relations and lead to deep shifts in political culture.

Of course, this more political understanding of mutual aid is not necessarily embraced by all the community groups that have registered themselves on the platform. For some, this may simply be a way to help vulnerable neighbours in a spirit of charity, which implies a more hierarchical relationship, where the 'helpers' are more powerful than the people they help.

Mutual aid groups and hyperlocal digital organizing

It is difficult to identify the exact date when the first COVID-19 mutual aid group was created in the UK, but many of them were established around 10 to 15 March 2020. In the beginning – and as is common with such bottom-up organizing – there were overlapping efforts by different organizations to facilitate this process.

Call-outs were circulated on Facebook and Twitter for people to launch a group in their locality by setting up a Facebook page or a WhatsApp group. People could then register the links to their Facebook or WhatsApp groups on a list initially compiled by Freedom Press, which runs Britain's oldest anarchist press and magazine and its largest bookshop. Common Knowledge, a co-operative that designs digital tools for radical change, soon incorporated this list into one using Airtable. They then collaborated with volunteers from the UK national website, who had also been doing their own data gathering, to create one unified list of all registered groups. These volunteers also produced new software that allowed visitors to the UK mutual aid website an easy way to find the group operating in their area. Multiple efforts were thus streamlined into a single process of creating, registering and finding mutual aid groups.

But how were these localities defined? How did participants decide on the boundaries of their neighbourhood, particularly in large cities such as London? The maps of electoral wards were very useful in this respect, as they allowed participants to use a ready-made framework for designating localities: the definition of mutual aid groups was therefore based on the electoral geography of the UK.

Still, many groups servicing large electoral wards decided to break into 'micro-groups', focused on smaller neighbourhoods of the ward or even on specific streets. This is because, as the organizing of mutual aid groups took off, participants realized that smaller is better: micro-groups could get to know the needs of their specific area in granular detail and facilitate relationships between close neighbours. In areas where people did not know their immediate neighbours, this helped to establish trust, as admitting your vulnerability and requesting help from strangers can be very challenging. Geographical closeness helped to moderate this fear.

The digital infrastructure of mutual aid groups

The move to micro-groups was also dictated by the technology employed for organizing. WhatsApp was one of the main organizing platforms. Neighbours used it to create specific WhatsApp groups for those requesting help, for volunteers, for organizers and for a host of activities, such as coordinating the phone line or dispatching volunteers. However, with WhatsApp groups being limited to 256 members, it was impossible for large wards to use WhatsApp for incoming requests in a way that covered most of the ward. Micro-groups were a solution to this problem.

WhatsApp provided many benefits for organizing. Employed by 73 percent of internet users in the UK (Burcher, 2019), it is a widely accessible application. WhatsApp also allows the quick exchange and forwarding of information, and messages have end-to-end encryption. Groups can be public, and people can join simply by clicking on a link or by scanning a QR code.

However, WhatsApp is not a platform built for organizing. New members of the group do not have access to previous discussions, obliging admins to post a 'welcome message' with useful information about the group every time a new member joined. The speed of posting led to information overload, which meant that useful information could be lost in the flow. Information overload can also increase the risk of burnout, as members become overwhelmed by the volume of messages and are constantly interrupted by notifications. The WhatsApp chats also included information that was not relevant to organizing. Members were often reprimanded for engaging in small talk, while, in some areas, groups created WhatsApp spaces for general discussion to direct the chatter away from the groups used for practical tasks.

Participants began to employ other platforms that are more suitable for organizing, such as Slack, built specifically for project coordination. The digital infrastructure of mutual aid groups also included Zoom for calls involving organizers and volunteers, Skype for operating help-request phone lines, and various Google apps: Gmail for the email address of the group, Docs for the minutes of meetings, statements and guidelines, as well as Sheets and Forms for compiling databases of volunteers and requesters and for recording information about pharmacies and shops in the area. In other words, the digital infrastructure comprised some of the most widely used applications for project work.

Despite the use of such proprietary applications by some local groups, it is worth noting that all of the software behind the efforts of the national coordination, including the website, is open source (Common Knowledge, 2020). The team involved has also been coordinating internationally to create the necessary resources for mutual aid groups. This international coordination has generated the initiative Mutual Aid Wiki (available at https://mutualaid. wiki), which, according to its website, enables 'mutual aid communities to find each other, share approaches and support one another'.

The groups also had to use physical media, such as leaflets and posters, for reaching people with low internet connectivity or digital literacy. They undertook mass leafleting to people's homes and put up posters in shops and in the street. There were of course concerns about the risks of spreading the virus through such physical media. Thus, groups developed detailed guidelines about leafleting to ensure the safety of both volunteers and those self-isolating.

National coordination occurred through the COVID-19 Mutual Aid UK website that was set up to gather information and resources about these groups. One administrator per group could also participate in a closed Facebook group to exchange ideas and tactics. Yet, despite these more organized efforts at national coordination, the learning and diffusion of information mainly occurred in a more organic manner, as members would follow neighbouring groups on WhatsApp and cross-post useful content. Information diffusion was quick, but having some basic resources on the national website as early as possible would have speeded up this learning process even further.

Two models of organizing: mutual aid groups and the NHS Volunteer Responders service

The decentralized organizing model employed by mutual aid groups becomes clearer if we compare it with the more centralized NHS Volunteer Responders scheme. The latter was set up by the UK government and the National Health Service (NHS) to help those registered as vulnerable by facilitating volunteers to undertake similar activities to those assumed by mutual aid groups. The NHS stressed that this service was not meant to rival what local groups and charities were already doing. Indeed, while some of their activities did overlap, the two models were also complementary, as they were not servicing precisely the same users.

This is because the NHS scheme was launched to help the 1.5 million UK inhabitants who are registered as vulnerable (NHS, 2020). For people to request help they needed to have this formal registration or to be referred to the service by their doctor. This excluded people who were unwilling to register formally, for instance, because of their immigration status. By contrast, mutual aid groups cover everyone who is self-isolating, whether they are formally registered as vulnerable or not.

One of the key differences between the two models is speed. The NHS scheme was announced by the government on 24 March 2020, a full two to three weeks after the launch of mutual aid groups. The scheme had an initial target of 250,000 volunteers, but, within a few days, 750,000 people had registered, so the service stopped accepting new applications as it could not process them quickly enough. Volunteers also complained about delays in getting assigned to tasks, sometimes having to wait for more than two weeks after they applied to the service (Marsh and Sabbagh, 2020). As a centralized and formalized system, the personal details and identities of volunteers had to be carefully checked. Conversely, the informal nature of mutual aid groups, which are not a legal entity, meant that they did not engage in the verification of personal details, a feature that enhanced their speed but potentially decreased their safety. The NHS scheme also had to handle a very large number of volunteers in comparison to the local mutual aid groups which are much smaller, and thus nimble and agile.

The NHS has partnered with the GoodSAM application to deliver the service. Volunteers need to register with the application, and they receive requests for help through the app. Here a key difference arises between the centralized and decentralized approach to the handling of personal data. While both work in accordance with GDPR rules, the mutual aid groups were advised by the national coordination website not to keep any personal data. Some of them do temporarily retain some information on requests for help and on volunteers, with guidelines about deleting data when they are no longer necessary. Data are accessible only to a few volunteers – in the Shacklewell ward group that I am involved in, it is only those who run the dispatching service who have access to this data.

By contrast, the GoodSAM app has access as 'joint controller' to the names and email address of all volunteers registered on the service. Users also submit data directly to GoodSAM when they use the app, of which GoodSAM is the 'sole controller' and agrees to use the information according to its own privacy notices (NHS, nd). This points to two different logics of data management: one that decentralizes the information among informal groups that have access to the data of only a small portion of the total population; and another, in the case of the NHS volunteers, that centralizes the information in formal groups, both state and corporate actors, who retain access to all or some of the data pertaining to the whole population.

With the current development of track and trace applications, thorny questions are arising with regards to the second model, particularly around the increasing capacity of corporate actors to utilize the large-scale information compiled by the state.

A final difference refers to how care is viewed. As mentioned earlier, although not all COVID-19 groups embrace this ideology, mutual aid refers to equal and horizontal relationships of solidarity. Conversely, the NHS Volunteer Responders scheme follows the more hierarchical model of charity as it makes a clearer distinction between those who are vulnerable – and registered formally as such by the state – and the volunteers who help them.

Conclusion: community resilience and political implications

Mutual aid groups have created a hyperlocal infrastructure of care that includes diverse digital platforms and applications as well as physical media such as leaflets and posters. Members of these groups have also developed common organizing practices and social norms. The interpersonal relationships fostered between neighbours who need and receive help can go across generational, racial, gender and political divides, depending of course on the diversity of each locality.

With the gradual exit from lockdown in the summer of 2020, groups saw the demand for their services wane. People's capacity to volunteer also declined, as some furloughed workers went back to work, while other volunteers had less time to devote to mutual aid activities. Some groups started operating only a skeleton service, while others focused on addressing more infrastructural and long-term needs of local communities, such as supporting food banks. A key question that arises here is whether, with time, some groups shift from tending to the immediate needs raised by self-isolation to more enduring projects of community resilience around COVID-19. At the time of writing in October 2020, the UK is undergoing a second wave of the pandemic, which is expected to revitalize mutual aid groups. Whether and to what extent their way of functioning will be different from the first wave is another interesting question that can be answered by further research on the topic.

As the COVID-19 crisis is becoming politicized, these groups may also get more involved in political campaigns that address the broader impact of the pandemic. The economic fallout of this crisis is expected to generate a wide range of campaigns on unemployment, homelessness and housing. It also highlights class, gender and race inequalities, as COVID-19 is disproportionately affecting minority ethnic groups and those living in deprived areas.

As the multiple aspects of this crisis unfold in the months and years to come, it would be interesting to study whether this hyperlocal infrastructure is used for mobilizing around these different campaigns. Elements of this are already visible. For instance, on 24 May 2020, activists associated with COVID-19 mutual aid groups staged a die-in outside the house of Dominic Cummings, a senior advisor to the prime minister who has been accused of breaching COVID-19 regulations around social distancing (Braddick, 2020). At the time of writing, when Black Lives Matter protests are taking place all over the world, information about how to support BLM is circulating in COVID-19 WhatsApp groups. There is also the question of how these mutual aid groups can influence local elections and local government.

As a hyperlocal infrastructure of care, COVID-19 mutual aid groups revolve around caring for neighbours. This care may take many forms as needs change, but one thing is for sure: by strengthening the relationships of people living in geographical proximity, the problems of health, isolation, discrimination, unemployment or housing are no longer experienced as abstract societal issues but as local realities that are affecting someone you know personally. This can have a powerful impact on political mobilization and social transformation.

References

Braddick, I. (2020) 'Activists stage "die in" protest outside Dominic Cummings' home in stand against Government's coronavirus response', *Evening Standard*, [online] 4 June, available from: https://www.standard.co.uk/news/politics/protest-dominic-cummings-home-coronavirus-response-a4460371.html

Burcher, B. (2019) 'WhatsApp has grown its user base by 20% in UK', *Messenger People*, [online] 4 February, available from: https://www.messengerpeople.com/whatsapp-user-base-uk/

Common Knowledge (2020) 'COVID-19-mutual-aid-list-sync', [online], available from: https://github.com/commonknowledge/covid-19-mutual-aid-list-sync

Covid-19 Mutual Aid UK (2020a) 'Find your local group', [online], available from: https://covidmutualaid.org/local-groups/

Covid-19 Mutual Aid UK (2020b) 'Frequently asked questions', [online], available from: https://covidmutualaid.org/faq/

Marsh, N. and Sabbagh, N. (2020) 'NHS says coronavirus volunteer scheme taking time to get up to speed', *The Guardian*, [online] 10 April, available from: https://www.theguardian.com/society/2020/apr/10/nhs-coronavirus-volunteer-ionger-than-expected

National Health Service (NHS) (2020) '"Your NHS needs you"– NHS call for volunteer army', [online] 24 March, available from: https://www.england. nhs.uk/2020/03/your-nhs-needs-you-nhs-call-for-volunteer-army/
National Health Service (NHS) (nd) 'Privacy information', [online], available from: https://nhsvolunteerresponders.org.uk/privacy-policy

'Solidarity, Not Charity': Emotions as Cultural Challenge for Grassroots Activism

Tommaso Gravante and Alice Poma

The COVID-19 pandemic that is afflicting the world is not only a public health problem. The different responses of states to the millions of infected people, dead people and people in isolation demonstrate and exponentially magnify the consequences of the social, cultural and economic model that has guided public policy over the last decades: the neoliberal model. Like all domination systems, the neoliberal model is a cultural and economic model, and is characterized by its adherence to the principles of social Darwinism. It is a model in which the natural order of things is control of some living things over others and over nature, in addition to hierarchies, extreme individualism, egoism and lack of empathy, among other aspects. Egoist values, rather than altruistic or biospheric values, dominate, and they must be aspired to if one wishes to climb the social ladder.

The emotional culture of neoliberalism: between fear and narcissism

As Arlie Hochschild (1979) points out, all of society is characterized by a series of structural norms and rules regarding social, legal and economic discipline, but also by a series of 'feeling rules' that are needed to entrench that system. The neoliberal system has therefore educated us and has imposed its own emotional culture, characterized by feeling rules such as mandate expressing loyalty to capitalism and private companies (Hochschild, 2016), respect and admiration for people who have achieved economic success, belittling lower social groups, blaming other individuals and governments for things that do not work, being afraid of expressing our discontent or being ashamed of feeling sad. These feeling rules are revealed in everyday practices, such as intolerance towards others, denial of social problems like poverty, inequality, racism, domestic violence and so forth—for which victims are blamed—or consumerism as a way to buy happiness. The message that is constantly repeated is that we live in the best possible system.

The cultural model encouraged by the neoliberal system that is being revealed in this COVID-19 pandemic enables us to understand the response to this crisis by some governments at the early stage of the pandemic: the denial of the virus or the associated risks, and a desire to continue as if nothing has changed. Denial of the seriousness of the pandemic clearly reflects an ideology in which economic growth is worth more than human life and whereby human life is arranged by importance, where lower social classes and older people can be sacrificed, the latter because they are no longer productive. An analysis of the emotional dimension shows how narcissism— which is due to an extreme lack of empathy (Baron-Cohen, 2011)—egoism and cynicism are at the heart of this response. But, furthermore, we have seen other emotional strategies, including demonizing fear of the disease and devaluing caring and worrying about others; for example, the Brazilian president's accusations of cowardice[1] against those who stay at home and request measures to avoid the virus spreading. Neoliberal emotional culture is so deeply rooted that many people have surely been more afraid and anxious about losing privileges that until now they believed to be untouchable or at least safe than about losing their lives or their loved ones. This is also influenced by what psychologists call the myth of invulnerability; in other words, it will affect others but it will never affect me.

However, after the rise in the number of infections, denial became a politically incorrect narrative in several countries. Other feeling rules have been revealed. By not admitting that the neoliberal system has made us more vulnerable, because that may generate a moral shock among those who feel they are supported by it, inevitably leading blame to fall at the door of those who feed and promote this system, emotions such as anger and blame have been channelled towards other individuals.

There are many examples of this: from blaming the people who brought the virus because they travelled (which in Mexico's case is fed by resentment towards the middle and upper classes generated by social inequality) to blaming those who do not follow 'social distancing' or self-isolation rules. This is joined by hatred towards communities we believe to be inferior and culpable for this pandemic, resentment towards the most vulnerable who could not stop their productive activities, admiration for those who are most able to benefit from this situation and so forth. These rules have caused and legitimate: violent attacks on Asian communities;[2] social control and denouncements carried out by neighbours who report people breaking quarantine in Europe; attacks by communities on buses transporting residents from old people's homes so they cannot enter their areas;[3] roadblocks set up by area residents who don't want 'outsiders' in their communities;[4] demands for and acceptance of authoritarian measures implemented by different governments, which will very likely take advantage of this crisis to clamp down on individual and collective freedoms.

Why grassroots activism matters

In this Orwellian landscape of authoritarianism, individualism and despair, social movements continue to play a fundamental role in building social alternatives since, as collective mobilization grows, the hope for change also ensues – for another world that is still possible and all the more needed (see della Porta's contribution in Chapter 16 of this volume).

On the one hand, we can observe how social movements at the national and transnational levels have cancelled and suspended their public actions and have quickly adapted to the new social circumstances we are living in. One example is the organization of webinars, conferences, teach-ins, assemblies and other online initiatives, as well as digital protests. These activities, from an emotional point of view, allow participants to connect with other people from all around the world and feel united and stronger instead of alone and powerless. On the other hand, at the local level, many grassroots groups are organizing themselves to deal with the social costs of this pandemic and to cope with the needs that the most underprivileged communities are experiencing. We are not talking about associations of social workers, NGOs or other bodies paid for using public and/or private funds to resolve the needs created by the system by way of support from the system itself.

The grassroots activism we mean is born of autonomous, self-organized groups that carry out direct action not only at protest events but also in everyday practices. In this case, direct action is aimed at producing improvements in the human condition within a certain oppressed community, and is able to develop self-organization methods to weaken the links of dependence and blackmail relationships existing between the state and communities, such as, for example, illegal immigrant communities, homeless people, nomadic communities, prisoners and the many different marginalized communities in cities.

Groups that were already working on matters of health and care among marginalized communities are proposing guides for self-care, prevention of COVID-19 and support for ill people, who are often illegal or in a situation of vulnerability and who cannot go to hospitals or consult a doctor to request their medication. In Milan, a city located in the most affected area of the contagion in Italy, the anarcho-syndicalist organization USI Sanitá (the health sector of base organization USI, the Italian Syndicalist Union) has opened a help point for residents of the Torricelli neighbourhood[5] where they issue medical prescriptions, deliver free medicines and provide medical, psychological and labour-related consultations that are specialized in this topic and always free of charge.

These practices can also be observed in other countries, such as the USA, where different groups are trying to provide access to medication, cures and first aid to those marginalized by the current social model.[6] Grassroots and autonomous unions, such as the USI[7] and Spain's CNT (Confederación Nacional del Trabajo),[8] have also opened help points to support workers whose rights are being flouted in this crisis, and have supported strikes in non-essential sectors where production has not been stopped. Another important category that can be observed in this context is that of groups that collect and distribute food and essential supplies. One example in Newcastle upon Tyne (in the United Kingdom) is the community soup-kitchen project The Magic Hat Café,[9] which reuses food products thrown away by supermarkets and is now distributing food parcels to families most in need. This group alone is able to distribute 800 food parcels to more than 200 families in Newcastle every day. Other anarchist groups in Latin America and the USA are redistributing food among poor people that they steal from department stores (which is a different practice to the one deployed by criminal groups who are stealing goods and reselling them in the black market).

A third, broad category of grassroots activism comprises the many groups that were involved in local and/or highly specific topics such as support for migrants, the fight against evictions, defence of labour rights, anti-racism and support for people in prisons, among others. These groups are reorganizing their work in light of this social crisis. Some are producing information about the pandemic, explaining how to organize as a group to cope with the problems that are emerging and how to create affinity groups. This material is exchanged by groups in different countries, translated into different languages on a voluntary basis and adapted to local needs. One example is *Surviving the Virus: An Anarchist Guide*,[10] currently translated on a self-organized basis into nine languages. Other groups, due to the loss of millions of jobs, are demanding a suspension of rent payments, such as the Station 40 collective in San Francisco, who are among the organizers of the 1 April global rent strike.[11]

Groups that manage independent media are trying to produce news stories free from the manipulation of official channels dedicated to the current social crisis and its drift towards authoritarianism, and are organizing open-mic programmes to exchange first-hand experiences. One example is the public radio assembly organized by Radio Blackout in Turin, Italy, with the programme *Rompi l'isolamento, parliamone insieme* ('Break isolation, let's talk about it together').[12] Other groups are producing and gathering open-access audio and video material for children. These are joined by experienced purchasing groups to sustain autonomous, self-organized farming projects, such as Campi Aperti – Associazione per la Sovranità Alimentare.[13] Yet others, such as have occupied social spaces in Italy, are transforming themselves into mutual support centres for the neighbourhoods where they are located, providing support to those most in need and to people most at risk of the virus, such as older people and the immunocompromised. One example is CSOA Askatasuna in Turin, with the Solidarietá di Quartiere (neighbourhood solidarity) project which involves neighbours in mutual support actions.[14]

The responses that these grassroots activists are producing to cope with the health, social and economic crisis can be summarized in two slogans that circulate within these groups: *Collective Care Is Our Best Weapon against COVID-19* and *Solidarity Not Charity*. These slogans reflect the values behind the groups, such as mutual support, self-managed solidarity, anti-authoritarianism and so forth. The call made by these groups is to overcome the powerlessness that can be felt when facing the pandemic by taking part in different activities.

Unlike the individual actions that we can all do (going shopping for a neighbour who can't go out, sharing information on social networks and so on), this activism, by developing and putting into practise community proposals, has disruptive potential because it reveals the failure of a system founded on individualism and competence, generating a response based on compassion and solidarity. This process is extremely important to create mobilization, as it makes it possible to transform fear and pain into anger, feeding discontent and encouraging identification of those responsible. Similarly, a new narrative can also be observed that is spreading in several countries, including Mexico, which reveals how the 'true' virus is capitalism. These arguments are strengthened by literature that shows the links between pandemics, damaged ecosystems and the livestock industry(Quammen, 2012; Wallace, 2016).

Returning to direct action by grassroots movements, we can also say that, as well as mitigating social problems created by the system, it makes it possible to tie certain practices and values to specific collective emotions. Mutual support and self-managed solidarity make it possible to feed hopes that we humans are able to get past this crisis, as well as those to come, such as climate collapse. This is relevant in particular for young people who feel powerless with regard to what is happening (pandemics, climate collapse, more precarious lifestyles and so forth) and feel unhopeful about the future.

An emotional impact of grassroots activism can be observed on the most vulnerable people these groups support, such as older people and undocumented migrants, who can feel less alone and vulnerable and more beloved in the community where they live.

Furthermore, these experiences are able to channel moral emotions (Jasper, 2018) such as indignation and outrage about being considered 'disposable' or 'expendable' citizens, anger and mistrust towards the authorities that cynically show the number of deaths (a small number, in their view) as an achievement of their administration,[15] respect and moral pain for those who are suffering and admiration towards those who keep working in order to maintain the basic services during the pandemic (from doctors and nurses to street cleaners, garbage collectors and those who provide us food), making it possible to break away from a state of narcissism.

The aspects described show a type of activism that promotes and puts into practise collective practices that break individualism and social distancing (which is different from physical distancing). Furthermore, these groups are characterized by the feeling rule of compassion towards the most vulnerable, which also counters hegemonic responses based on individualism and cynicism. These mutual support networks, as well as mitigating social problems generated by the crisis at local level, make it possible to collectively work past a series of emotions, such as powerlessness, despair, shame or sadness, and encourage the emergence of other collective 'resistance' emotions (Whittier, 2001), such as hope in collective action and moral anger, indignation, and outrage towards capitalism. Moreover, grassroots activism strengthens reciprocal emotions such as love and respect, which help people, among other things, to cope with trauma emotions, recover from grief and overcome powerlessness and despair (Champagne, 1996; Whittier, 2001).

Emergence of a counter-hegemonic emotional culture

Grassroots activism questions – with its practices, values and feeling rules – the dominant social and cultural model. Channelling and legitimizing emotions such as moral pain and anger, indignation and compassion, among others, can turn into cultural and political achievements.

Returning to Hochschild (1979), our reading of these grassroots activism experiences is that, as well as helping people, they feed a counter-hegemonic emotional culture, which will be needed not only to overcome this pandemic but also the other crises that we will have to face, such as the climate emergency. In order to overcome the neoliberal system, social movements and actors have to undermine its cultural dimension based on suspicion and fear of people who are different from us, in which blame is always directed at other individuals and where human and non-human life are devalued and happiness is measured by consumer goods and social visibility and so on. The cultural basis of an alternative world needs alternative feeling rules, such as love and compassion towards all human and non-human living things, or blame, anger and indignation towards those who prioritize wealth and economic growth over life.

We are still only at the beginning of a much wider and more painful crisis, and we don't yet know the consequences of it, although we can forecast them because we know the systems that are causing them. Despite this, all is not lost, because thousands of people are mobilizing together around the world to open up cracks that can weaken a system whose intentions are clearer than ever. We don't yet know if grassroots activism will be able to strengthen counter-hegemonic feeling rules to weaken the cultural component of neoliberalism, and even less if they will be able to slow down or offer an alternative to the economic and political crises that are on their way. What we know is that every effort everyone is making in this way is needed. It is very likely that there will be no normality to which to return, because the crisis will leave very deep social wounds and fractures, but we also know that normality is what has brought us to where we are, and we still have time to create another reality.

Notes

1 See: https://global.ilmanifesto.it/bolsonaro-a-danger-to-brazil-staying-home-is-for-cowards/

2 See: https://www.theguardian.com/world/2020/mar/24/coronavirus-us-asian-americans-racism

3 See: https://www.elperiodico.com/es/sociedad/20200325/coronavirus-cocteles-molotov-autobus-ancianos-7904371

4 See: https://www.jornada.com.mx/ultimas/estados/2020/03/29/se-atrincheran-11-municipios-por-temor-al-coronavirus-2801.html

5 See: https://www.facebook.com/permalink.php?story_fbid=3036838223032629&id=814318405284633

6 See: https://itsgoingdown.org/autonomous-groups-are-mobilizing-mutual-aid-initiatives-to-combat-the-coronavirus/

7 See: http://www.usiait.it/

8 See: https://cntmadrid.org/coronavirus-informacion-laboral/

9 See: https://www.facebook.com/themagichatcafe/

10 See: https://es.crimethinc.com/2020/03/18/sobreviviendo-al-virus-una-guia-anarquista-capitalismo-en-crisis-totalitarismo-en-ascenso-estrategias-para-la-resistencia

11 See: https://crimethinc.com/2020/03/19/on-rent-strike-against-gentrification-and-the-pandemic-an-interview-with-residents-of-station-40-in-san-francisco

12 See: https://radioblackout.org/2020/03/assemblea-pubblica-radiofonica-28-marzo-2020/

13 See: https://www.campiaperti.org/

14 See: http://www.ansa.it/sito/videogallery/italia/2020/03/28/coronavirus-i-centri-sociali-di-torino-in-aiuto-di-chi-ha-bisogno-per-emergenza_b8cfabf8-58eb-49f1-aeee-f6cd5a4a9531.html?fbclid=IwAR39EUBDFaqn-6tXxbE2oMWL9UJBZz2fx7ejAik_YQVOsLlxBXoA6qlEV34

15 https://www.indy100.com/article/coronavirus-trump-white-house-death-toll-goals-9440281

References

Baron-Cohen, S. (2011) *The Science of Evil: On Empathy and the Origins of Cruelty*, New York: Basic Books.

Champagne, R. (1996) *The Politics of Survivorship*, New York: New York University Press.

Collins, R. (2001) 'Social movement and focus of emotional attention', in J. Goodwin, J.M. Jasper and F. Polletta (eds) *Passionate Politics: Emotions in Social Movements*, Chicago: University of Chicago Press, 27–44.

Hochschild, A.R. (1979) 'Emotion work, feeling rules, and social structure', *American Journal of Sociology*, 85: 551–75.

Hochschild, A.R. (2016) *Strangers in Their Own Land: Anger and Mourning on the America Right*, New York: The New Press.

Jasper, J.M. (2018) *The Emotions of Protest*, Chicago: University of Chicago Press.

Quammen, D. (2012) *Spillover: Animal Infections and the Next Human Pandemic*, New York: W.W. Norton & Co.

Wallace, B. (2016) *Big Farms Make Big Flu: Dispatches on Influenza, Agribusiness, and the Nature of Science*, New York: Monthly Review Press.

Whittier, N. (2001) 'Emotional strategies: The collective reconstruction and display of oppositional emotions in the movement against child sexual abuse', in J. Goodwin, J.M. Jasper and F. Polletta (2001) *Passionate Politics: Emotions and Social Movements*, Chicago: University of Chicago Press, 233–50.

21

Self-Reliance as an Answer to the Pandemic: Hopes from India's Margins

Ashish Kothari

Can you imagine Dalit women farmers in Telangana, once facing hunger and deprivation, contributing 20,000 kgs of food grains for COVID-19-related relief? Farmers on the Tamil Nadu-Karnataka border continuing to send organic food to Bengaluru consumers even during the lockdown? Villages in Kachchh and Tamil Nadu handling anti-COVID-19 health measures, with minimal outside help? And Adivasis (indigenous people) in Central India with community funds able to take care of migrant workers who have had to come back to their villages?

These and many other stories across India show the potential of empowered rural communities to cope with crisis. And they expose the tragedy of a path of 'development' and governance that has not recognized, or worse, has taken away, the extraordinary agency of ordinary people to manage their own lives. COVID-19 has pointed sharply to our horribly unequal society, in which hundreds of millions of people do not have food, livelihood and basic-needs security, even as 1 percent of the richest own or control most of the country's wealth. It has also brought into focus the utter chasm between the nation's rulers and its poor. It has highlighted how safeguarding nature, not only for its own sake but for human survival, is so crucial.

Women farmers and community-supported agriculture

"I grow 40 kinds of crops on my rain-fed land and don't use chemicals; I have enough food to last my family in the lockdown period and beyond", said Chandramma, one of Telangana's Dalit women farmers. She was participating in a webinar organized in April 2020 by the network 'Vikalp Sangam', a process bringing together people's initiatives in alternative pathways of well-being. She is part of the Deccan Development Society, whose women's *sanghas* are active in 75 villages.

Through these, several thousand women who were on the margins of casteist, patriarchal society have revived their dryland, millet-centred agriculture, and increased overall production while retaining control over land, seeds, water and knowledge. Having achieved *anna swaraj* (food sovereignty) and self-sufficiency, in COVID-19 times these women are feeding landless families in their villages, contributing 10 kgs of food grains per family to the district relief measures, and daily feeding one thousand glasses of nutritious millet porridge to health, municipality and police workers in nearby Zaheerabad town.

The second story is from a village self-help group (SHG) in the Krishnagiri district of Tamil Nadu. In 2017, the SHG launched a Community Supported Agriculture (CSA) initiative with help from Navadarshanam, a community founded in 1990 to live ecologically sustainable and simple lives.

The initiative helps local organic farmers plan their operations based on commitments from urban subscribers for a weekly box of vegetables, fruits and groceries. All revenues are passed on to farmers, due to which incomes have risen between 10 and 20 times for some of them.

Remarkably, during the lockdown, CSA deliveries are continuing without interruption. This has helped farmers avoid a problem millions of their counterparts elsewhere have faced: making distress sales to whoever buys at very low prices. And consumers in Bengaluru, even in the zones where COVID-19 infection rates have been highest and the lockdown most intense, continue getting fresh, organic produce. Of course, all norms for physical distancing are being followed.

Communities safeguarding themselves against COVID-19

In Kachchh, the village of Kunariya set up a crisis management team, used social media to raise awareness about COVID-19 and facilitated a full health survey. Three hundred and sixteen needy families, including those of visually impaired and differently abled individuals, single-women and other marginalized people, were assured all basic necessities using panchayat (village council) funds or local donations.

All this happened because over the last few years, dynamic facilitation by its sarpanch (elected village head) Suresh Chhanga has enabled Kunariya to move towards greater public participation in governance of local affairs. It has also been able to build effective bridges with the government authorities, implement schemes and laws like MNREGA and the Food Security Act, create transparency in the use of budgets and strengthen women's voices in decision-making.

When I phoned Suresh Chhanga, he excitedly recounted what they did with children in the lockdown period. Recognizing that they are stuck at home, bored or even in some cases facing aggression of equally bored or worried adults, the panchayat encouraged elders to teach them whatever special skills they had—music, crafts, cooking, traditional technologies, gardening—or engage them in environmental activities like caring for trees.

Then there is the Sittilingi Panchayat in Tamil Nadu, which mobilized itself as soon as Kerala announced the first COVID-19 case in January. Panchayat president Ms Madheswari called for an urgent meeting with relevant government departments and a civil society institution called Tribal Health Initiative (THI), and went into disaster control mode. This included mass awareness campaigns, enforcing physical distancing in all places of public gathering and isolation of returning migrants. As an income generation initiative, local tailors were asked to stitch masks in bulk. This panchayat has had many years of inputs by THI, an initiative by Drs Regi George and Lalitha Regi to create an Adivasi-oriented health facility along with organic cultivation, education, empowerment, crafts and other livelihood activities.

Self-reliance in tribal communities

Other stories of resilience from tribal and other forest-dwelling communities come from many parts of India, where they have been able to restore their collective rights to govern and use the forests under the Forest Rights Act 2006. For instance, several villages in eastern Maharashtra, after two centuries of centralized control by the Forest Department through which revenues from the sale of forest produce like bamboo were mostly cornered by contractors and the government, have been able to do their own harvesting. This has been crucial to securing availability of nutritional forest foods, medicinal plants and culturally and spiritually important sites. Sustainable harvesting of forest produce has earned villages substantial income, part of which has gone into community funds. In settlements like Rahu in Amravati district and Kukdale and Salhe in Gadchiroli district, these funds are being used to help returning migrant labour or landless people obtain basic relief materials. Civil society organizations Khoj and Amhi Amchya Arogyasathi have been active in these areas, but in Gadchiroli there is also the remarkable mobilization of 90 villages into a Maha Gramsabha (federation of village assemblies), towards greater self-rule, resisting mining and economic self-reliance.

Small-scale manufacturing

Many communities have also shown the enormous livelihood potential of rural, small-scale industries. The India's crafts sector has involved 150 to 200 million people, second only to agriculture. Government policies have severely disabled them, but in places like Kachchh, innovation in local supply and production chains and in design has revived handloom weaving, such that youth are coming back into it—a form of reverse migration.

Kuthambakkam village near Chennai has demonstrated how small-scale manufacturing (for instance of solar fan-bulb kits) and grain processing have helped families avoid having to migrate out for work. Its ex-sarpanch Elango Rangaswamy has come up with a solar-powered way of making disinfectant as a response to COVID-19, which he says can be set up cheaply in any village for both employment and disease prevention.

From other parts of the country come inspiring stories at a larger scale. Groups under Kerala's state-supported Kudumbashree programme, which has provided dignified livelihoods for thousands of women, worked with panchayats and urban ward sabhas to spread awareness about COVID-19, set up community kitchens to cater to those needing food aid and mass-produce sanitizers and masks. Goonj, a civil society initiative working in 20 states, is bringing relief to over 40,000 families and using its *Vaapsi* programme of restoring livelihoods to create or re-establish localized barter-and-exchange systems that enable dignified livelihood generation. In Madhya Pradesh, Samaj Pragati Sahayog is working in several hundred villages to revitalize the rural economy and substantially reduce outmigration, and has reached over 13,000 families with relief packages. For this, it procured wheat from a local farmer-producer company, so that cultivators did not have to resort to distress sale.

Lessons from the margins

What can we learn from these and many other such stories of COVID-19-time resilience? Are they in our prime minister's mind when he seems to realize the need for self-reliance and waxes eloquent on it in addresses to the nation in the middle of the pandemic? Perhaps not, for his government simultaneously pursues memoranda of understanding (MoUs) with dozens of foreign companies, dilutes laws protecting the environment and labour rights, puts heavy tax burdens on handicrafts and continues to forcibly acquire land, forest and other resources so vital to the rural economy only to hand them over to corporations. His government's stimulus plan to move out of the COVID-19 lockdown is ecologically illiterate and dangerous.

What these initiatives are demonstrating is the opposite of this. Self-reliance is about the revitalization of rural livelihoods (leaving aside cities for the moment). Note that I am talking here about *livelihoods*, not jobs; these are occupations linked to everyday life, social relations and culture, providing the body and soul with satisfaction. For the vast majority of people in our industrializing economy, jobs are *deadlihoods*, soul-deadening mass-production places where one desperately waits for the weekend to 'enjoy' oneself (if you happen to be one of the lucky ones in IT or government or banking), or worse, where you go to sleep wondering if you will have work and an income the next day (if you are part of the labouring class).

Hundreds of initiatives for local self-reliance or self-sufficiency in food, livelihoods, water, energy, sanitation, housing and other basic needs around India tell us of the urgent need to move towards *localization* instead of economic *globalization,* which has left hundreds of millions of people across the world in a precarious situation. They tell us that clusters of settlements can be self-reliant in basic needs, significantly reducing distress migration to cities and industrial zones as well as widespread trade and travel. They tell us that communities can govern themselves, while making the state accountable. They tell us that achieving all this also requires struggles to remove patriarchy, casteism and other forms of discrimination that traditional occupations can be mired in. They show us the power of using hybrid knowledge systems and respecting cultural diversity (while rejecting religious identity politics), as well as the need to reconnect with nature while respecting all of life. They also point to many transformations that need to happen in India's cities, but that is a subject for a future article.

If the Indian state is really interested in rural self-reliance, it needs to support a rainbow New Deal, supporting dignified livelihoods through agriculture, pastoralism, forestry, fisheries, crafts and small manufacturing in each village; to help set up producer-consumer links eliminating exploitative corporate middlemen and retailers; to reserve most production in labour-intensive small- and medium-scale workshops; to stop pandering to large corporations (Indian or foreign); to eliminate goods and services tax and other burdens on hand production; to ensure minimum support prices for primary sector products, and so on. Its current policies are, by and large, the complete opposite, and there is little in the COVID-19 recovery or stimulus packages that points to any fundamental shift. The packages are also socioecologically bankrupt. Given this, it is left to communities themselves, with help from civil society (and some sensitive state governments), to use the COVID-19 crisis as an opportunity for moving towards justice, equity and sustainability.

22

Social Movements and Self-Reliance: Community Mobilization in South Africa

Kate Alexander

This chapter foregrounds the Community Organizing Working Group, specifically the multiple meanings of its call for *Asivikelane*, an isiZulu term meaning, roughly, 'I protect you, you protect me'. It is a companion to an earlier piece published in Spanish and English, extending the narrative and deepening the analysis.[1] That piece was completed on 18 May 2020 and this one takes the story up to 9 September and was updated on 10 December 2020.

Context

Just under half of all COVID-19 infections and deaths in Africa have occurred in South Africa. When new infections and total active cases peaked at the end of July, the hospital system was on the brink of collapse. At that point, the country ranked fifth in the world for total cases, and those above it had much larger populations (the USA, Brazil, India and Russia); even now it is eighth, with over 640,000 cases. 'At least we haven't had too many deaths', some say, but actually, the country currently ranks 11th for new deaths and 13th for total deaths (over 15,000), and none of those higher on the list has an average age of population that is greater (South Africa's is 28 years, the same as India's).

Economically, the country is in a parlous state. Already in recession before lockdown began on 27 March, the second-quarter figure for GDP was 17.1 percent lower than a year before. Publication of Q2 figures for unemployment has been delayed, but it is estimated these will show about

3 million extra people without jobs. Including discouraged work-seekers, the unemployment rate will have risen from just under 40 percent to about 50 percent. Under pressure from business, levels of lockdown and levels of infection moved in opposite directions, from Level 5 lockdown to Level 4 on 1 May, and to Level 3 on 1 June. This sent mixed messages and it became difficult to maintain compliance with regulations requiring mask-wearing and distancing. With Level 2, introduced on 18 August, there was rapid worsening of the situation in the townships (urban areas demarcated for Black residents under apartheid and now home to most of the country's working class). Given trends elsewhere, there is likely to be a second wave of infection, and this will probably hit the townships worse than suburban areas, where most better-off people reside.

No country in the world with a larger population than South Africa has a higher level of inequality. The impact is ubiquitous. One example must suffice. In early July, schools were reopening, starting with just two year groups and then expanding. It was clear that a high proportion of schools in the townships could not cope. Teachers' unions opposed further reopening, parents and students voted with their feet and school governing bodies began shutting their schools. In a survey conducted by researchers from the University of Johannesburg and the Human Sciences Research Council, it was found that 60 percent of adults were *opposed to re-opening for the rest of the year*. The government backed down and rescheduled its plan. There was outrage from many suburban parents, elite intellectuals and the main opposition party. This was a class issue: only 41 percent of those earning more than R20,000 per month (approximately US$1200) wanted the schools closed, but for those on lower incomes the figure was 61 percent. In the suburbs, people felt fairly safe, and parents were worried about losing a year's fees, about R45,000 even for public schools; in townships, infections were rising sharply, and fees are minimal, so there was dread about death rather than fear about finance.[2]

The 'schools argument' was relatively polite, but there is also growing chaos, much of it a carry-over from pre-pandemic days and exacerbated by lockdown (see Chapter 35 for a global perspective). Support for President Cyril Ramaphosa soon plummeted, and backing for social solidarity – *ubuntu* in South African parlance – declined rapidly. Among poorer people in particular, economic distress swelled discontent; among a core of the middle classes, alcohol and tobacco bans stoked rage; and among everybody, a new orgy of corruption was met by anger and dissatisfaction (though little surprise). Distribution of food by councillors intent on buying votes diminished their credibility, already low. Further down the pecking order, long-haul drivers are killed because they are foreign, food trucks are hijacked because people are hungry, and crooks strip wires from lamp posts in broad daylight. The parastatal electricity company regularly cuts power because it lacks generating capacity, a consequence of its own misjudgements and corruption, and then, to pay back debt, it disconnects individuals, neighbourhoods and, now, whole municipalities, and it does this in the cold of winter to people who cannot pay their bills because they have lost their jobs.

A moratorium on evictions is widely ignored, and police use rubber bullets and sometimes live ammunition in support of landowners. Then they use their guns again in response to misdemeanours or perceived disrespect, recently killing an adolescent who could not speak because he had Down's syndrome. In the townships, lockdown regulations are ignored, and people crowd into taverns until late at night, get drunk, and then some, nearly always men, return home and attack their partners. The police either cannot or will not intervene, the politicians lack the credibility and the confidence to respond and, as we will see, people sometimes take the law into their own hands.

Protest and movement: the bigger picture

How has the populace responded? What has happened to the level of protest action, one of the highest in the world? Figures from the ACLED (Armed Conflict Location and Event Database) are drawn from media reports, so massively undercount the true number of protests, but nevertheless, used carefully they give the most reliable indication of trends there is. For South Africa, February 2020 was a record month, with hundreds of community protests, a high level of student action and some strikes. However, with lockdown, there was a sudden collapse in the number of protests.[3]

The ACLED recorded no protests at all in the last five days of March and very few in April. Universities were emptied, so there were no students to protest, and even now, while gradually returning, they are loath to take action, despite complaints about the disadvantages of online teaching. Under Level 5, only essential employees were at work, and movement for union organizers was limited, so protest action was minimal. It has gradually risen but is still at a low level. There were protests at hospitals and elsewhere about lack of personal protective equipment. Some drivers of minibus taxis refused to work until limits on carrying capacity were relaxed, and some workers in the hospitality industry also protested. In both these cases, workers had support from their employers. Recently, the National Education, Health and Allied Workers Union (NEHAWU), which represents manual workers in the education and health sectors, has held limited protest strikes, mainly over pay, but it remains to be seen how far they will push their demands.

Numbers for community protests tell a different story. Many of the old complaints remain: no water, power cuts (which increased as industry picked up, and increased again when the weather turned cold and heating was required), boundary issues and corrupt or useless councillors and council officials. Other issues have also attracted prominence. There were demands that police take action against criminals, including murderers, and when people have become disillusioned with lacklustre and possibly corrupt policing, they sometimes take action themselves. With few sanctions available, popular justice can have a bloody outcome. As a consequence of hunger and evictions, people have occupied land in increasing numbers. They start food gardens (a process reminiscent of Zimbabwe when hunger was widespread), and they erect shacks on vacant land (which the authorities, and now some homeless people, call 'land grabbing'). Some actions resonate with Asef Bayet's notion of 'quiet encroachment', but the government is weakened by health and economic crises not revolutionary upheaval, and when the state intervenes, sometimes with assistance from private militias, it acts with great brutality, and the scenario resembles 'bold encroachment'.[4]

But what about the sleeping giant of South Africa's working class, its labour movement? There are signs that it is beginning to wake up – not yet out of bed, but it can hear the alarm and its eyelids have opened. The largest federation, the Congress of South African Trade Unions (COSATU), is held back by its allegiance to the governing African National Congress, with which it is negotiating a social compact. At the same time though, NEHAWU, one of its largest affiliates, is in conflict with the government, which must limit wage increases to stave off economic meltdown. The more militant federation, the South African Federation of Trade Unions (SAFTU), is reportedly divided, and its dominant affiliate, the National Union of Metalworkers, has been weakened by its blunder in creating a revolutionary party to contest the 2019 general election. But there is pressure from below, and COSATU and SAFTU jointly called for a general strike on 7 October. Both federations focus on corruption, an issue the Ahmed Kathrada Foundation (named after Mandela's close comrade) and the South African Council of Churches are also voluble about.[5]

Earlier, on 18 March, a large number of civil society organizations and prominent individuals founded the C19 People's Coalition (C19PC). Sectoral, thematic and geographical working groups (WGs) were rapidly formed, and, at first, the coalition appeared to have considerable potential. However, lack of resources and a decentralized structure produced a diffuse and sometimes factional organization that lacked mobilizing capacity. There are still about ten functional working groups, many active in their own domains, and it is possible the current political situation will radicalize its WG Conveners' Forum and constituent groups, but at present, it makes little impact on national debate. In terms of protest mobilization, the coalition's one successful activity was on 1 August, a 'Day of Working-Class Action' coordinated by the Simunye Workers' Forum, which was outside the coalition, as well as the Workers' Rights WG and COWG, which were affiliated. The event was remarkable for inspiring protests in rural areas, many organized by low-paid farm labourers, community health workers and participants in the government's Extended Public Works Programme. There were about 40 protests in total.

Community Organizing Working Group

The COWG organizes in townships and informal settlements located in and around Johannesburg, South Africa's largest city.[6] I am an 'insider', with the benefits and drawbacks this brings, but my role is that of a 'support person' rather than a leader. COWG is the most dynamic part of the C19PC, and its creativity makes it worthy of discussion. Had there been more organizations of similar kind, the ecology of South Africa's C19 social movement would have been quite different, and more lives would have been saved.

In the early days, two activities were central: popular education and food distribution. These were regarded as complementary and as part of strengthening community organization, which, we reasoned, would become especially important once concern to claw back treasury revenue came to the fore. Going door to door with leaflets helped activists identify households that were especially vulnerable and in need of food; distribution of food added credibility that was valuable in demonstrating protective measures; both activities raised the standing of COWG's leaders and activists in their respective communities. Unlike some organizations, COWG always delivered food directly to an allocated household, rather than distributing resources to a queue. This reduced the risk of stampedes and a breakdown of physical distancing, and it demonstrated that COWG helped the most vulnerable rather than the most favoured (unlike ANC councillors).

In raising funds for purchasing food and paying for its distribution, COWG was assisted by the C19PC Food Security WG. Funders wanted accountability, and on the COWG side, this developed alongside a network for supplying leaflets, which was especially tricky under Level 5, when printing and physical movement were highly restricted. In addition to the leaflets (produced in increasing numbers and in three languages), we distributed masks, gloves, sanitizer, lists of vulnerable people, delivery slips, receipts and reports. Over time, food distribution fell away as a major activity. Support from the government's Solidarity Fund dried up (probably, we now know, because of corruption, at least in part), assistance from major private donors dwindled (partly through fatigue and partly through obstacles imposed by government), and the Food Security WG reprioritized its work to focus on food sovereignty and food gardens. It is likely, too, that hunger declined a little (though it is still widespread). This was a consequence of some workers being paid again, some benefits being increased and distribution of the government's temporary Social Relief of Distress grant (a measly R350 per month, about US$21).

COWG's first and most enduring campaign has been around popular education. From the beginning, comrades were busy explaining how the virus worked, marshalling queues and persuading people to practise physical distancing and make frequent use of soap and sanitizer. These activities were even conducted in densely packed, informal settlements where water supply and sanitation were rudimentary (if present at all). On one occasion, the argument was dramatized by a well-organized 'walk-through' with about 30 physically distanced activists bearing homemade placards. As early as 31 March, we published an op-ed in a local paper offering to work with the government by mobilizing community auxiliaries; but rather than co-operation, activists were often obstructed by police demanding permits.[7] Some comrades noted that if there was an election there would be party placards, canvassers, loudspeakers, rallies and T-shirts all over the place, but with COVID-19 there was none of this.

The earliest collective action was on 16 June, the anniversary of the 1976 Soweto Uprising. For this, comrades distributed posters and leaflets and displayed banners and placards (sometimes on the sides of roads, and sometimes in the middle of the road, or 'down the line' as it was termed), and they stood in silence for George Floyd and South African victims of state repression. Activity took place in the 17 locations where COWG had teams, and there was a presence at the grave of Hector Pieterson, the iconic victim of the 1976 repression, and also at the site where he was killed. Street action was followed by a rally held on Zoom. The operation was repeated on 18 July, International Mandela Day. This time, street activity and a protest outside the Mandela House in Soweto were accompanied by an online presence through WhatsApp, Twitter, Instagram and Facebook. Decentralized protest, made necessary by lockdown, was a new phenomenon in South Africa. It had the benefit of bringing widespread contact with working-class people, and in addition, social media allowed activists to watch each other's actions, and permitted those who could not be on the street—due to comorbidities or age—to promote messages internationally.

The group was well prepared for the 1 August action, when it protested in the city centre alongside Simunye and others, as well as in local communities. For South African Women's Day, 9 August, local activity was followed by a rally and speeches outside the Women's Jail on Johannesburg's Constitution Hill. Then there was a walk—a march really. Demands about gender-based violence (GBV) were prominent. Most of the 200+ activists were meeting each other for the first time, and it was a jubilant occasion. Throughout all these mobilizations, physical distancing was practised and taught.

Funds are drying up, but COWG's leaders—there are 15 of them—and support personnel—four of them—continue to meet weekly, as does the smaller organizing committee. At the beginning there were 16 leaders, but one was suspended following a claim of sexual harassment and a formal disciplinary procedure. In earlier days, each leader had a team, which varied in size but averaged about 15. After complaints from some volunteers, we provided them with a small amount of food when they were on active duty distributing food or undertaking popular education. That money no longer exists, but many volunteers are still involved.

Activities are reported at the weekly meeting and in written accounts. The activities have broadened, and reflect the multiple roles of active community leaders in this period. Some examples: assisting a dying women refused a hospital bed; helping somebody whose house burnt down; caring for a baby deserted by its mother; advising about COVID-19 symptoms and what action to take; supplying soap; maintaining good relations with a shopkeeper willing to provide food; maintaining good relations with a police commander willing to tolerate a protest and check conditions in the local prison; monitoring a school for implementation of safety protocols; attending a school governing body; picketing a school; helping people who had been shot (with live ammunition) and detained (and beaten), allegedly for occupying land; finding legal assistance for people forcefully evicted from houses they had lived in for many years; organizing community solidarity for shopworkers ill-treated by their bosses; consoling a family whose daughter had been murdered in appalling circumstances, and later protesting outside the court to make sure the killer was detained; holding a candlelight vigil for a young woman who had been raped and shot; mobilizing a mass funeral for the young man killed by police; organizing music and cultural events around COVID-19, and now climate change; starting food gardens; assisting with land occupations; sanitizing hands and organizing distancing at a large mall, thus pressuring the manager to accept responsibility for this; and much more. All this while dealing with a multitude of family crises and COVID-19 deaths and infections. The COWG meetings provide an opportunity for explaining, learning, advising and mobilizing solidarity.

Throughout all this, two issues standout. The first is use of Zoom for meetings. This can be challenging because connectivity is poor in some areas, electricity gets cut, phones are stolen and, initially, it was a new technology for most activists. But it has worked, and not a single meeting has been cancelled. Because of Zoom, COWG has operated in a democratic manner, with everybody using their blue hands and respectfully addressing their comments through the Chair. If somebody misses a meeting, they nearly always send an apology. Without Zoom, meetings would have been far more time consuming, far more expensive to organize and much less frequent. It has also enabled poor working-class people to participate in the C19PC, other networks and organizations, and in the occasional webinar. Zoom has been linked with a WhatsApp group, which provides scope for further sharing of information, especially photographs, and for forwarding notifications from outside the group. Discussions on both platforms are nearly always comradely. I am reminded of the impact of older technologies on working-class organization: the role of railways and the postal service in developing national unions in Britain; motor cars helping organizers with union recruitment in mining areas of the USA and South Africa; and mobile phones used for mobilizing flying pickets in Britain and mass demonstrations in Egypt. Certainly Zoom and WhatsApp can also be undemocratic and they can demobilize activity, but for COWG they have been overwhelmingly positive. Indeed, COWG would not have been possible without them. This should not be conflated with digital activism. Even where Zoom and WhatsApp have involved a wider audience, the use of these platforms has been linked to on-the-ground activism.

The second issue is mobilization around the theme of *Asivikelane*! This is a concept and a slogan that fits the moment, and COWG has linked it widely to wearing masks. While masks have some limited benefit in protecting the wearer, their main purpose is to protect uninfected people from those who are infected. For this reason, it is necessary that a high proportion of the population—maybe 80 percent—wear them, to be fully effective. The notion of 'I protect you, you protect me', is one of mutual solidarity, where we all protect each other to stop suffering and possible death. But it can be used in many other contexts. For instance, the 16 June leaflet included: 'We must not starve! Asivikelane!' 'GBV. Asivikelane!' 'Close schools if they are unsafe. Asivikelane!' 'Black Lives Matter. Asivikelane!' 'We must fight for equality. Asivikelane!' *Ubuntu,* meaning 'I am, because you are', can also convey social solidarity, but in contemporary South Africa this is solidarity without struggle, a notion that almost anybody can accept, just like the Kenyan *harambee,* 'All pull together'. Perhaps asivikelane can also be hijacked in time, but for now it conveys a working-class 'we'. 'I' and 'you' imply close proximity, not the distance of class difference. Further, COWG has promoted asivikelane in a context where *we* must protect each other, because the state is failing to do so. *It is about self-reliance.*

Despite these achievements and despite the need for an organization that can coordinate poor communities in the face of continuing onslaughts, COWG faces challenges. The first of these is simple: finance. At a minimum COWG requires funds for data for Zoom meetings. COWG will probably need to develop a formal structure, which has implications for 'NGO-ization' that may follow. The second is a tension between solidarity for the 17 aligned communities and 'expansion', mobilizing widely, which makes sense if COWG is to be taken seriously by the unions or win battles with the state.

Conclusion

In the sense that COWG mobilizes working-class people for social action it is a 'social movement', but it does not conform neatly to northern definitions. While not averse to making collective claims, this is done in piecemeal fashion rather than as part of an overarching campaign. Much day-to-day activity is about self-reliance. COWG offers education and distributes food because the government fails to undertake these critical tasks. Elsewhere, people encroach on land, and also on the policing and judicial responsibilities of the state. As with many protests, people are less interested in reform and more in reinvention of responsibilities. This is not an argument for libertarianism. The state remains a powerful force – it is the hospitals, schools and social grants, as well as the police and army. But it is beginning to retreat from crucial aspects of social life, a process becoming clearer under the COVID-19 lockdown. For academics, 'self-reliance' figures more prominently in development studies than in social movements studies, and the time is ripe for dialogue, not just a discussion within the Global South but one that challenges assumptions within northern studies. The early unions gained much from the self-reliance of friendly societies, and 21st-century northern movements may find there is much to learn from the travails of community organizations pitted against a failing state.

Notes

[1] Alexander, K. (2020) 'Hambre, ira y un nuevo movimiento social en Sudáfrica', in B. Bringel and G. Pleyers (eds) *Alerta global: Politicas, movimientos sociales y futuros en disputa en tiempos de pandemia*. Buenos Aires: CLASCO; Alexander, K. (2020) 'Hunger, Anger and a New Social Movement in South Africa', *Review of African Political Economy* [online], 8 September, available from: http://roape.net/2020/09/08/hunger-anger-and-a-new-social-movement-in-south-africa/

[2] Alexander, K. (2020) 'The Great Schools Argument: A Response to Stephen Grootes and Nic Spaull', *Daily Maverick,* 27 July, available from https://www.dailymaverick.co.za/article/2020–07-27-the-great-schools-argument-a-response-to-stephen-grootes-and-nic-spaull/

[3] Alexander, K. and Lenka, L. (2020) 'Skirmishes on the South African battlefield', *Open Democracy*, 11 September, available from: https://www.opendemocracy.net/en/skirmishes-south-african-battlefield/

[4] Bayat, A. (1997) *Street Politics: Poor People's Movements in Iran*, New York: Columbia University Press; Gillespie, T. (2017) 'From quiet to bold encroachment: contesting dispossession in Accra'a informal sector', *Urban Geography* 38(7): 974–92.

[5] Almost no workers participated in strikes or joined demonstrations on 7 October. Despite this, unity between COSATU and SAFTU was novel and generally welcomed in the labour movement.

[6] There are teams in Orange Farm, Eldorado Park, Pimville, Klipsruit, Thembelihle, Diepkloof, Meadowlands, two parts of Orlando, Nomzamo Park, Protea South, Braamfischerville, Bekkersdal, Ivory Park, Alexandra, Tsakane and Makause.

[7] Xezwi, B. and Alexander, K. (2020) 'State must enlist community activists in the war against COVID-19', *Daily Maverick*, 31 March, available from: https://www.dailymaverick.co.za/article/2020-03-31-state-must-enlist-community-activists-in-the-war-against-covid-19/

23

Resilience, Reworking and Resistance in New York City

John Krinsky and Hillary Caldwell

We finished a first version of this article on 14 April 2020 (updated in November 2020).[1] In the space of one month, the number of people who had died from COVID-19 in New York City—our city—had just surpassed 10,000. Each day brought news of loss, borne by the internet or by the incessant ambulance sirens heard across the city. New Yorkers like to think of themselves as being at the centre of the world, an idea facilitated by the city's being a centre of global capitalism. At the same time, it became clearer by the day that not only is COVID-19 leading to significant failures in capitalism but also capitalism is failing a world beset by COVID-19.

On one hand, the social distancing measures meant that most business—and certainly the tourism that is one of New York City's economic backbones—ground to a halt, throwing millions out of work, decimating their incomes and government tax receipts alike. On the other hand, the predatory quality of American capitalism—from the systematic exclusion from social benefits of many low-wage workers, to unliveable wages, lack of healthcare, disproportionately polluted neighbourhoods and finance-fuelled asset-stripping of communities of colour—has virtually guaranteed that the COVID-19 crisis would hit working-class communities and communities of colour in vast disproportion to white middle- and upper- class communities. Further, as the federal government passed relief bills, many in these very communities were neglected. Even in the public hospitals at the epicentre of the city's COVID-19 epidemic, the distribution of personal protective equipment lagged, with nurses and other hospital staff required to reuse masks in ways that would have gotten them dismissed months earlier.

In New York City and New York State, both Mayor Bill de Blasio and Governor Andrew Cuomo, helped set the stage for this crisis through status-quo neoliberal policy and practice, in addition to which they were slow to respond to the crisis and seemed incapable of putting aside their rivalry to provide consistent leadership, each giving conflicting accounts of measures to be taken to stop the spread of the virus. With regard to New Yorkers' housing, for example, the result has been a 'sudden shock to an overburdened system' (Mironova and Waters, 2020), a system that *already* had nearly 80,000 homeless people in shelters on a given night, including one in ten students in public schools. Worse still, it took them months to deconcentrate homeless people and people in jails from congregated living situations, despite having 100,000 empty hotel rooms in the tourist-bereft city and the resources to do it.

As a result, to take one example, Rikers Island jail had more than *three times* the infection rate of the city overall. When the virus subsided by the summer, and when, by early fall, the city had some of the lowest – rather than the highest – rates of spread and incidence in the country, the city's moves to use hotel rooms for homeless men ran into an organized 'not-in-my-backyard' campaign, whereby wealthy neighbours of hotels in neighbourhoods across Manhattan organized to reject homeless people. Though there was some pushback from other neighbours, the mayor decided to move homeless people from place to place like chess pieces, while the governor expressed the desire to reopen more congregate shelters (even as cases began to rise again in September).

Disaster budgeting

To make matters worse, Governor Cuomo – who gained national prominence through daily press conferences that appeared as a rational counterpoint to President Trump's increasingly unhinged press briefings – pushed through a state budget in early April that is a model of neoliberal austerity. The budget cut funds to hospitals, including the very public hospitals in the hardest-hit communities in the city, where shortages of personal protective equipment put staff at extreme risk in the spring. The budget cut education – at all levels, including public universities – on which working-class New Yorkers depend. It added nothing to the public housing budget, even as public housing in New York housed people at the highest risk, and where long-standing cuts had led to situations in which tenants had no water to wash their hands and were forced to crowd into the few working elevators. In the budget, as well, were provisions that have no clear economic justification or link to falling tax receipts, like rolling back recent reforms to the bail system that will now send more people into jails before trial, or provisions that will make it more difficult for candidates from third parties to appear on the ballot.

In 'normal' times, New York City grassroots movements – around housing and homelessness, police reform, immigrant rights, low-wage workers' rights and higher education at a minimum – would have mobilized days of occupations at the State Capitol against the budget. They would have pushed for the state legislature to insist on raising taxes on the wealthy in order to redress the imbalances in the most unequal state in the country. But in April 2020, large gatherings were banned and dangerous, and the governor, citing the possible loss of billionaires who might move to other states if taxed, convinced a compliant legislature to ignore revenue-raising strategies and cut the budget to the bone.

Though stung by their inability to block the governor's austerity budget, New York's movements would not stay out of the street for long. Just six weeks after the budget passed, video of the police murder of George Floyd in Minneapolis circulated, as did news of the police killing of Breonna Taylor in Louisville, Kentucky. In spite of the still-raging epidemic in New York, the movements in the city galvanized anew. As cases and deaths declined rapidly, New Yorkers hit the streets in protest, as did people across the United States. Protests would continue throughout the summer and into the fall. The protests drew many to the streets who were unaffiliated with existing organizations, and many of the protests were organized by relatively new, ad hoc groups of activists. At the same time, established organizations were also critical to planning, strategizing, putting out calls and mobilizing their members, meaning that existing movement groups were at the centre of the action. Nevertheless, understanding how New York's working-class-movement organizations worked March through May – weathering real emergencies among their members and punishment and disorganization at all levels of government – and then mobilized afterwards can suggest ways in which crises like the COVID-19 pandemic and triggering events like publicized police murders can shift and even strengthen a movement field.

Working-class movements in the city

New York City's social movements are rooted, as many movements in the United States are, in issue-specific and neighbourhood-based nonprofit organizations, rather than in groups affiliated, for example, with political parties or labour unions. This has certainly been the case since the 1970s due to reductions in federal support and increasing reliance on voluntary organizations for social reproduction, as well as corresponding changes in federal tax law that allowed tax-exempt donor support for community-based organizations and advocacy groups. Many nonprofits that still do community organizing and base-building among New York's working-class communities began as projects or affiliates of radical groupings of different sorts in the more general 'movement' of the late 1960s and 1970s, and converted into nonprofit organizations in order to more stably and formally raise resources.

Today, and for the last ten years or so, issue-specific movement groups around housing, homelessness, environmental justice, healthcare, low-wage workers' rights, immigrant rights, public education, financial justice and police reform – among others – and have worked more closely with neighbourhood-based groups. Adam Reich (2017) has shown that Occupy Wall Street helped to make the networks of movement groups in New York City denser as they scrambled to contribute to, and even helped to steer, a suddenly visible and long-lasting mass protest. We analysed the membership and supporters of seven coalitions in New York City around housing (3), criminal justice (1), immigration (1), public higher education (1) and public banks (1).

These coalitions were chosen both for the breadth of issues they cover and for the fact that the issues they cover have cohesive coalitions working on them. We found that 66 of 170 groups overlap with at least one other group in at least two coalitions, and 28 of these with more than that. By and large, the groups that overlap the most are base-building groups that respond to their members' multifaceted needs: working-class New Yorkers are not just fighting their landlords to stave off eviction, or fighting the city to keep their neighbourhoods affordable, they are also fighting banks for fair credit, the police for harassing their young people, employers for stealing their wages and threatening undocumented workers with immigration enforcement, industries for polluting their neighbourhoods and the state government for cutting public education funds. Nevertheless, the largest coalitions are around housing, immigrant rights and police reform. These form the basis of network clusters, with the first two more distinct from each other, and the police-reform coalition providing significant links between them.

Prior to COVID-19, the central coalitions of New York City's movement organizations were gaining strength. On the heels of Occupy in 2011, and before the emergence of Black Lives Matter in 2013, a just-policing coalition called Communities United for Police Reform mobilized groups from across the city – and the general public – to win several pivotal legal cases and significant legislative reforms. Since then, many of the same groups have worked together on many other issues. Moreover, the presence and combination of progressive political parties in the networks – the Working Families Party and the Democratic Socialists of America – meant that these networks mobilized around several state senate candidates and, for the first time in several generations, put the State Senate under Democratic Party control in 2019.

Also, many groups have broadened their base beyond New York City, opening chapters in low-income communities across the state and working with ally groups in other cities. In the past year, criminal justice activist groups have pushed forward bail reform (the laws that Governor Cuomo partially rolled back in the budget); immigrant rights groups successfully pushed the state legislature to pass a New York State Dream Act, which offers state-funded financial aid and scholarships to attend university to undocumented youth who arrived in the United States before the age of 18, and a law allowing undocumented immigrants to get driver's licenses. One of the housing coalitions, the Right to Counsel Coalition, won low-income tenants a right to a lawyer in housing court in 2018; and the Housing Justice for All campaign, based in a coalition uniting New York City and upstate New York tenant groups, won an epochal victory by getting the state legislature to overturn two decades' worth of landlord-friendly loopholes that had been added to New York State's rent regulation statutes.

Fresh off these victories, movement networks were poised to win more changes in housing policy, and to extend these victories to other, overlapping issues. COVID-19 prevented the groups from pushing their advantage in state government, and the communities in which the organizations that compose these networks are based have borne the brunt of the COVID-19 crisis. As the Association for Neighbourhood and Housing Development has shown, the incidence of COVID-19 closely tracks the geography of neighbourhoods with majorities of people of colour, with renters paying more than 30 percent of their incomes on housing, and with a high proportion of residents being employed in service work (Afridi and Walters, 2020).

In response, the networks have mobilized in ways that combine what geographer Cindi Katz (2001) has called the 'three R's'– resilience, reworking and resistance. Resilience speaks to the basics of social reproduction, the ability of people to survive and live up to socially recognized standards, despite structural disadvantages and in the face of threats like COVID-19. Reworking refers to the efforts people make to rearrange and refashion aspects of local conditions and institutions in ways that suit their projects either of resilience or of deeper social transformation. And resistance refers to more overt, collective demands for change and direct actions that push these demands forward.

Many community-based organizations have addressed the resilience of New York's working-class communities by setting up mutual aid projects alongside those of industry-based groups (for example restaurant workers, street vendors, domestic workers) and political groups (for instance Democratic Socialists of America, various anarchist groupings). Mutual aid involves getting people food and medicine that they need, delivering personal protective equipment to hospitals and to other essential workers and raising funds for workers who have been thrown out of work, many of whom are ineligible for unemployment benefits or federal relief checks because of their immigration status or job category (for example, sex work). An effort to coordinate among mutual aid projects occurred quickly, spurred in part by veterans of Occupy Sandy – the mutual aid efforts that responded to the destruction wreaked by Hurricane Sandy a year after Occupy Wall

Street—who were involved in groups in the city's movement networks. Mutual Aid NY brings together more than 85 such projects; other projects exist beyond its orbit.

These efforts are quite different from charity work: mutual aid both comes from the resources mustered by groups rooted in the communities they are otherwise organizing politically and, at least in these times, feeds into this work. To be sure, this involves community-based nonprofits reworking their own institutions in order both to meet the immediate needs of their members and even just to show support to their members. But it also involves reworking relations more broadly, at least in some cases. For example, a subset of the housing networks demanded that the city and state move homeless and incarcerated people out of congregate living situations and into empty hotel rooms. Seeing continued inaction and misinformation coming out of the city government, they resorted to a petition and funding campaign that raised enough money in two days to put up 20 people in hotels—a mainly symbolic accomplishment (except, importantly, for those people moved out of danger) that nevertheless prompted much-belated city action that followed in the summer.

But these same networks have pushed for more radical reworking and resistance as well. The overlapping housing groups pushed early for a moratorium on evictions. They won it. It was clear, of course, that with record numbers of people with no savings to speak of suddenly thrown out of work, April rent would be difficult if not impossible to meet. Mass evictions during the week projected to be the worst of the pandemic in New York were simply untenable. But as it became clear that the effects of the pandemic would stretch at least into 2021, the same groups have mobilized across their online networks to demand *cancelling rent* and mortgage payments altogether, so that tenants paying 30 or 50 percent of their incomes on rent when they *had* work, will not face the end of the eviction moratorium still out of work and owing months of back rent. If landlords and banks need money, *they* can demonstrate their need and apply for help. The tenant activists know the likelihood is that banks and the private-equity firms that increasingly back landlords will be bailed out before anyone else, in any case.

The centrality of police reform and Black Lives Matter

The uprisings that began after the police murder of George Floyd in Minneapolis spread quickly to New York City. Protesters—masked to prevent the spread of COVID-19—faced off nightly with police, who seemed determined to prove right the protesters' accusations of police brutality. After a few early nights of rioting and property destruction, mainly in the city's posher business districts, the mayor declared a week-long curfew. But because 'essential workers'—hospital workers, transit workers, restaurant and food-service workers, core building maintenance staff and many others – had permission to be out past the early hours set for the curfew (8pm in the summer!), policing of the curfew was selective and discriminatory. Already in May, more than four-fifths of all social-distancing violation summonses had been issued to Black or Latinx New Yorkers. Policing growing protests against police violence became more violent. Frequently unmasked police faced off against masked demonstrators, culminating in an episode in the South Bronx, one of the areas hardest hit by COVID-19, in which police prevented a crowd of several hundred from dispersing before the curfew and then moved in to arrest them for curfew violations, beating and gassing them.

The demonstrations for Black lives and against police violence quickly took on a policy-specific cast as the City's fiscal year wound down at the end of June and as negotiations over the 2021 fiscal-year budget wound down. A demand to 'Defund the NYPD' or cut $1 billion from its $6 billion budget became a rallying cry for protesters. For two weeks before the budget passed, Black Lives Matter groups and VOCAL-NY, a multi-issue base-building organization with roots in AIDS and housing activism, called for people to 'Occupy City Hall'. The large and diverse encampment on a plaza outside City Hall echoed Occupy Wall Street in September 2011 and the 'Bloombergville' encampment protesting the city budget that June (named for the New York City mayor at the time). The budget ended up including only a symbolic cut in the police budget, even amid enormous austerity-driven cuts to many social services and public agencies.

Nevertheless, the spirit of direct confrontation – of resistance – symbolized by the call to defund the NYPD became even more apparent across the movement field. The fact that Communities United for Police Reform – the police-reform coalition – connected the immigration and immigrant-worker and housing parts of the movement field, meant that defunding the police became a means for diverse groups to link their own issues to the imbalances in the city budget. The calls, after all, were not simply to take money from the police but rather to redistribute it to Black and brown communities in targeted ways.

Therefore, amid the housing justice groups' organizing of tenants to go on rent strike and to convert an inability to pay rent into a refusal to do so in service of the demand to cancel rent, these groups *also* articulated more publicly a critique of the racial capitalism that has structured a chronic housing emergency for Black and brown communities during the entire post-World War II period. While this critique had been building within the movement alongside criticism of the more recent global trends towards the financialization of housing, the protests centring Black lives helped to solidify these more systematic claims throughout the movement field, and not just in housing activism. Behind this, as well, was the 'abolition' movement within justice-reform work, which seeks to abolish policing – and the conditions that give rise to modern policing – by investing in Black and brown lives and communities.

Accordingly, the demand to defund the NYPD was present at marches around housing justice, cancelling rent, and keeping housing courts closed, as well as for funding for the City University of New York and for workers who were excluded from federal relief (often because of immigration status).

COVID-19 and policing: twinned crises

Increasingly, the organizations involved in New York's movement networks are holding joint Zoom forums, often with sympathetic politicians, and circulating online petitions for their demands. They are also figuring out new ways of reaching out to community members who live in their neighbourhoods but who may not be reliably connected to the internet. In some cases, outreach is done jointly with mutual aid. But as the incidence of the virus has reduced citywide and restrictions have loosened, New Yorkers are turning out to demonstrate—even with caution—in large numbers. The complex interweaving of resilience, reworking and resistance across an increasingly integrated network of groups means that these networks will emerge from the crisis with new campaigns and deeper relationships. They will have new capacities to help communities be resilient and perhaps also less dependent on the structures that oppress them in normal times and consign them to vastly unequal burdens in times of crisis.

If anything, the twinned COVID-19 and policing crises have heightened the contradictions of neoliberal New York. Dissatisfaction with the mayor and governor are at a peak as eviction moratoria loosen and as the New York Police Department and its unions have fought every effort at holding the police accountable (the unions even came out to support Trump's reelection as Trump withholds federal funding to the city). Rich people in 'liberal' areas of the city have organized to keep homeless people out of their neighbourhoods. And yet, the activity of working-class and immigrant community groups has made the dissatisfaction of a great portion of the city—often lauded otherwise as 'essential workers'—increasingly clear. Having gone into the COVID-19 crisis relatively stronger than they had been in a long time, and having been provoked by another wave of police murders and violence, New York's movements have only grown together in the nine months between March and the end of 2020. They may now be positioned to support more radical action and demands in the face of the inevitable neoliberal austerity and disaster capitalism that is still the default of an ever-more-visibly decadent system.

Note

[1] We would like to dedicate this chapter to the memory of Thomas J. Waters, housing researcher and great friend to the New York City housing movement, who died of complications from COVID-19 on 4 April.

References

Afridi, L. and Walters, C. (2020) 'Land use decisions have life and death consequences', *Association for Neighborhood and Housing Development*, [online] 10 April, available from: https://anhd.org/blog/land-use-decisions-have-life-and-death-consequences

Katz, C. (2001) 'On the grounds of globalization: A topography for feminist political engagement', *Signs*, 26(4): 1213–34.

Mironova, O. and Waters, T.J. (2020) 'A sudden shock to an overburdened system: NYC housing and COVID-19', *Community Service Society NY*, [online] 6 April, available from: https://www.cssny.org/news/entry/nyc-housing-covid-19

Reich, A.D. (2017) 'The organizational trace of an insurgent moment: Occupy Wall Street and New York City's social movement field, 2004 to 2015', *Socius: Sociological Research for a Dynamic World*, 3: 1–21.

PART IV

'The COVID Will Not Kill the Revolution': Protest Movements in the Pandemic

24

'Defund the Police': Strategy and Struggle for Racial Justice in the US

Nara Roberta Silva

The killing of George Floyd, an African American man, by a White officer in late May 2020 inspired the most massive uprising in the US since the 1960s. Floyd's death set out a wave of protests against racialized police brutality for around six months—in a continuous steady pace after the incredible level of mobilization in the initial one and a half months. Protests brought to the public's attention the names of deceased Black people whose deaths at the police's hands had fallen under the radar—Elijah McClain, Daniel Prude, Dijon Kizzee. Protests also pushed back against relentless excessive violence witnessed in some recent cases—such as those of Rayshard Brooks and Jacob Blake. What explains the latest struggle for racial justice in the US and its path? Social movements—here freely defined as collective action to promote change—should be considered, as the noun suggests, *in movement*. The latest struggle for racial justice in the US can illustrate valuable lessons in social movement development and demonstrate the importance of a strategic, long-term vision.

Grievances are commonly pointed out as great protest and movement sparkers. When protests erupted after George Floyd's death, it was common to hear in news analyses and protesters' testimonials that Floyd's fate was 'the last straw'—or some form of it. The video of Ahmaud Arbery's murder surfaced a few weeks prior, and the renewed attention to the death of Breonna Taylor, shot in March of that year, fuelled the outrage. The 'last straw' explanation seems even more plausible once Floyd's killing is considered in light of two additional factors.

First, Minneapolis diligently adopted the Obama-era reform playbook following other high-profile police killings, including that of Jamar Clark in 2015 and Philando Castile in 2016.[1] For five years, the city has implemented measures to enhance procedural justice, reduce implicit bias and foster reconciliation through training, mindfulness and de-escalation practices, crisis intervention guidelines, the hiring of more Black cops, the use of body cameras, the review of use-of-force standards and the promotion of police-community dialogues along with early-warning systems to identify problem officers.[2] But none of that prevented a White officer with a record of complaints from placing his knee on Floyd's neck for almost nine minutes.

Second, by late May, it was evident that the toll of the COVID-19 pandemic was distributed unequally in the US. Blacks and Latinos have gotten sick and died at higher rates, even in areas where they make up a smaller portion of the population.[3] Blacks and Latinos are more exposed to the virus for they are often employed in frontline activities – such as in grocery, convenience and drug stores; in public transit; in trucking, warehousing and the and postal service; in healthcare, childcare and homeless, food, and family services; and in building and cleaning services. Furthermore, several studies attest to the intersections between poverty, race and underlying health conditions and comorbidities making people of colour more vulnerable to COVID-19. In this context, the death of George Floyd was a strong symbolic representation of the scandalous disposal of racialized bodies in the current United States.

What made the spark become a fire?

While blatant racism certainly inspired the acts to which protests were responding, it is crucial to consider other elements for a more accurate picture of their rise. The latest struggle for racial justice does not mean or imply that racism has gotten worse – even in light of the horrifying scenario described. Floyd's murder and the country's racialized COVID-19 deaths could be considered sparkers, but what other mobilization processes have allowed the movement's formation? In other words, what made the spark become a fire? The COVID-19 pandemic is also relevant to the answer.

Mutual aid networks

With the spread of the new virus, mutual aid networks flourished across the country, especially in large cities and metropolitan areas. These networks offered immediate relief when lockdown measures and a rapid surge in COVID-19 cases led to job losses, forced isolation and, consequently, an increased inability to provide for oneself.

A distinguishing feature of the early summer demonstrations was its occurrence in thousands of US locations – both small towns and large cities, both rural and urban areas.[4] This is indicative of hyperlocal presence and connections – a result of the infrastructure of care built over the previous months. By addressing communities' needs, mutual aid networks' high local density – a mix of online and offline communication – facilitated the work needed for and in the protests. Pre-existing networks routinely accelerate the conceiving and conducting of protests – for example, a targeted audience to invite to the demonstrations, knowledge of the relevant available resources to take to the streets (from microphones and bullhorns to signs and banners) and potential in-street support (like first-aid and de-escalation teams) are practically granted when individuals and groups have been working together prior. When demonstrations broke out in cities across the US, several Slack channels, social media groups and email lists started to share information about safety guidelines, coordinate to gather and distribute supplies for protesters, spread the word about bail fund initiatives and launch calls to provide shelter/bathroom stops for those on the streets, among others.

The rapidness in putting a demonstration together was also inspirational – it is not a coincidence that numerous US teenage groups without protest experience or activist backgrounds have organized local actions independently. Furthermore, in places such as New York City, the pre-existing mutual aid networks helped overcome the challenges imposed by both the hesitation or inability to commute brought by the pandemic and the one-week curfew enacted when protests grew in numbers. Rather than concentrating in a few traditional locations, marches, rallies, vigils and so forth turned to the neighbourhoods and, in consequence, ignited impressive liveliness. By engaging with each neighbourhood's geographical references and identity, protests drew in even more people.

To summarize, mutual aid created connections, promoted regular participation and fostered the importance of it in the eyes of people. The mutual aid networks' capacity to mobilize was, therefore, the gasoline to the spark represented by Mr Floyd's killing.

A long-term horizon

In addition to considering the capacity to mobilize, a proper assessment of the latest struggle for racial justice must consider what caused the movement's longevity. In other words, this movement has not only taken people to the streets but also opened paths for organization. The most important contributor to the enhanced capacity to organize was the demand to *defund the police* – and its embracement by a larger number of movement participants and supporters. Defunding the police has always been a central idea to contemporary abolitionist thinkers, circles and organizations. But until the protests following Floyd's death, this was a fringe proposal often sidelined by calls for police reform or broad criticism of racism. Police reforms' constant failed promises of hindering racial disparities slowly undermined arguments for incremental change and paved the way for those who have repeatedly highlighted reformism's weaknesses – or even naiveté. But the formerly outlying demand's rise into mainstream conversations and the change in the narrative should also be understood in light of the COVID-19 pandemic. With cities scrambling to guarantee proper equipment for medical personnel and fighting numerous simultaneous crises, the disproportionate sum of dollars allocated to police departments across the country – in comparison to other services – appears even more unjust and irrational.

The calls to defund the police came together with a precise, concrete target while still signing towards profound consequences in the short and long term. Across the US, police departments consume a sizeable portion of municipal budgets – money to be potentially diverted to services such as physical and mental healthcare, housing development and preservation, and youth and workforce development. Therefore, defunding the police is a promising door to alleviating inequality and undermining the pillars of neoliberal cities – where social matters are inevitably turned into police matters. People of colour would see not only their communities improve and thrive but also the aggressive approach applied to them diminish since the extensive funding and, hence, vast resources available to the police are in intimate connection with their militaristic mentality and practice.

Defunding the police means eroding the institution that oppresses and kills people of colour regularly in the US for centuries – and, of course, in other countries – and which has been extremely efficient as the prison industrial complex's everyday arm in the present. Finally, defunding the police offers a better position from which to contemplate restorative justice practices and deeply embrace abolitionism for centuries a huge cultural shift away from the predominant framework focused on retribution and punishment.

The uniqueness of these last protests for racial equality in the US is, thus, found not merely in their size, the impressive number of participants and the spread of supporters. What is unique is the emergence of a particular strategic path provided by the calls to defund the police – a vision towards the future that places organizers in a better position to plan their work, make decisions and assess potential alliances. While the Movement for Black Lives has had a comprehensive policy agenda since 2016,[5] the restructuring of the conversations around *defunding* fine-tunes the argument about racism's structural, institutional dimension – solidifying the position that goes beyond the 'bad apples' explanation.

A new phase of the struggle for racial justice?

While city and state governments promptly responded to the first protests with reforms, the fight for racial justice, just recently in the spotlight, pressed for more profound structural transformations. Having a strategic vision is valuable to figuring out the next steps of the struggle since protests inevitably suffer from internally and externally motivated constraints. First, while demonstrations are potentially more effective when held in great numbers, it is difficult to sustain high turnout for an extended period overall. Maintaining attendance beyond seasoned participants is increasingly difficult as weeks pass by, and, in the specific case at stake, protest-goers became less available as cities moved towards reopening phases. Second, city and state legislatures' refusal to cut money from police departments while still pushing for austerity in other areas frustrated expectations of immediate victories and led activists to reassess their efforts and the amount of time and energy spent on displaying discontent on the streets. Finally, the extension of demonstrations for several weeks expectedly triggered opposing reactions that affected the demonstrations' pace – in fact, situated in a larger social and political landscape, movements' moves and impacts can never be dissociated from other actors. Initially, 'Blue Lives Matter' rallies started to be hosted in some cities, but the backlash went further, and two protesters were shot dead by a vigilante following the Jacob Blake riots late in the summer in Kenosha, a Midwestern town in the state of Wisconsin. The federal intervention in cities such as Portland and Chicago in the same period is also worth noting – since it was an escalation of the regular state tactics to break down dissent.

While some remain visible on the streets and will probably opt for keeping the grievances constantly visible to a broader public, a fast reconfiguration of activist circles is happening as groups and organizations resettle, adjust their campaigns and focus on carrying them out. The demand to defund the police is pertinent to all of those promoting a racial justice agenda and can connect a plethora of relevant issues to communities of colour in the US – immigrant communities included, whose calls to 'abolish ICE' is just another side of the same coin for it also denounces the racist nature of policing in the US. This demand also fits a mix of approaches and organizing models – something different from the Movement for Black Lives' policy agenda released a few years ago. While such a policy agenda presumes institutional negotiation on multiple fronts, the calls to defund the police are also appealing to groups operating under autonomy-inspired frameworks. Consequently, the loosely assembled movement has the ability to keep up the pressure through the hybridization of organizing models. This ability is crucial since the elections in 2020 hurt the debate on social and political matters to some extent by reducing the protests for racial justice to misrepresentations of the confrontational tactics (for example, property destruction) sometimes deployed. The calls to defund the police have been swiftly mobilized to promote 'red scare' among voters and even fracture Black communities, but the demand can still be a vehicle for mobilization as well as radical cultural and policy change.

Public support or opposition to a certain demand does not follow a straight line and can, thus, increase or retract as the debate continues, policies are advanced (or stalled) and other issues get to the spotlight. But by having an eye towards the future, the movement can guarantee a smoother coordination of actions and bet on some meaningful transformation ahead.

Notes

[1] Minneapolis was one of the six cities that served as pilot sites for the National Initiative for Building Community Trust and Justice. For more info, see: https://trustandjustice. org/pilot-sites

[2] A report on the Minneapolis' experience under the National Initiative for Building Community Trust and Justice can be found here: https://trustandjustice.org/pilot-sites/ info/minneapolis-minnesota

[3] A summary of the data available when this chapter was written can be found here: https://www.theguardian.com/world/2020/sep/08/covid-19-death-rate-african-americans-and-latinos-rising-sharply

[4] A map can be found here: https://www.nytimes.com/interactive/2020/07/03/us/george-floyd-protests-crowd-size.html

[5] The movement's platform is called 'Vision for Black Lives' and is available on the movement's website: https://m4bl.org/policy-platforms/

25

A Matter of Survival: The Lebanese Uprising in Times of Pandemic

Alexandra Kassir

A hundred years after the declaration of the State of Greater Lebanon, the country is in agony. On 4 August 2020, a massive explosion hit the Port of Beirut, killing more than two hundred people, injuring thousands, destroying half the city and leaving around three hundred thousand people homeless or displaced. Months after the explosion, seven people were still missing.

According to initial reports, the explosion was triggered by a fire igniting 2750 tonnes of ammonium nitrate stored for years in a warehouse. While the specific circumstances that led to one of the largest non-nuclear explosions in history are yet to be determined, for the people gathered during the mass funeral in Martyrs' Square few days after the disaster, there is no doubt, the Lebanese government killed its own people. 'They knew!' one could read all over social media after evidence revealed that the presence of ammonium nitrate in the port had long been an open secret among the key decision-making authorities, and after the Lebanese president admitted that he had been made aware of the security risk it posed nearly two weeks prior to the explosion.

Since the October 2019 uprising, Lebanese people have been massively and relentlessly calling for the downfall of a political class that has ruled the country for more than three decades. For them, the port tragedy is the last in a series of crimes committed by the former warlords turned politicians. It is the result of sectarianism, endemic corruption, a broken judicial system and years of poor governance and deadly negligence.

A context of multiple crises

Prior to the devastating blast, the country was already reeling from a number of overlapping crises. The COVID-19 outbreak compounded the existing economic and financial crises and painfully exposed the deep shortcomings of the Lebanese social protection system. Estimates from the Economic and Social Commission for Western Asia revealed that, as of May 2020, more than 55 percent of the country's population was living under the poverty line. Lebanon has one of the most unequal wealth distributions in the world, ranking twentieth globally (ESCWA, 2020), and for years the political economy of sectarianism trapped the population in a vicious cycle whereby the sectarian oligarchy appropriates the bulk of economic surplus and redistributes it through communal clientelism (Baumann, 2016).

In recent years, Lebanon witnessed important mobilizations against the sectarian powers, specifically in 2011, when a series of rallies echoing the Arab uprisings called for the 'Downfall of the sectarian regime', and in 2015 after the garbage crisis triggered the so called 'You stink' protests against a 'rotten system'. Yet, the October uprising marked a turning point in post-war Lebanon. On the evening of 17 October 2019, the walls of fear crumbled under the weight of the ever-growing economic crisis, and massive, peaceful and leaderless protests exploded across the country calling for a revolution to overthrow the established political order. Under the slogan 'All of them means all of them', thousands of people from different age groups and social backgrounds spontaneously took to the streets, naming and shaming politicians and sectarian leaders across the political spectrum. Unlike the typically Beirut-centric movements in post-war Lebanon, the 'October Revolution' was inherently decentralized, and from North to South, major cities and smaller towns witnessed a unique explosion of anger and hope. Youth were at the forefront of the protests, reclaiming the streets, transcending sectarian divides and embodying the unity they aspire to.

While the October uprising widened the horizon of possibilities, the COVID-19 outbreak four months later and the authorities' lethargic response to the multiple crises lead to rapidly deteriorating standards of living and offered the sectarian oligarchy a golden opportunity to tighten its grip on the country, threatening the last remnants of democracy. In Lebanon, the ruling class is more pernicious than the pandemic, and protesting is a matter of survival.

A ruling class 'more dangerous than the virus'

On 21 February 2020, Lebanon confirmed its first case of COVID-19. After downplaying, at first, the risks posed by the virus and delaying the suspension of flights from highly affected areas, authorities announced a state of 'general mobilization' in mid-march and enforced a series of extraordinary measures, which have been subsequently extended, tightened or loosened.

The spread of the pandemic gave the newly appointed government at the time a convenient reason to suppress the protests after the uprising had built momentum following months of massive street mobilizations. Lockdown measures drastically restricted the freedom of movement and assembly. For weeks, a curfew was imposed, a ministerial decree regulated the circulation of cars according to their plate numbers and military and security forces were deployed nationwide, setting up checkpoints and patrolling the streets. In these scenes reminiscent of war times, COVID-19 was not the only 'enemy' to fight. On the first night of curfew, riot police dismantled the revolution's tents in Martyrs' Square, despite the sanitary precautions taken by the few protesters watching over the camp. This was also the case in Al-Nour Square, the beating heart of the uprising in north Lebanon, and in different sites across the country occupied by protestors since October.

With the onset of the pandemic, Tripoli became the epicentre of the uprising. The rapid devaluation of the Lebanese currency, the capital controls imposed by the banking sector, the inflation in food prices and the salary cuts, along with the state's slow and inadequate response to the crises, left many families struggling for bare necessities. For the protesters in the second-largest city of the country and the most impoverished one, 'hunger is deadlier than COVID-19' and pushed many families to the streets. A few weeks into the lockdown, the festive mobilizations filled with dance and music seemed far behind. Some protestors hurled Molotov cocktails, smashed banks' facades or threw stones at security forces who responded with disproportionate violence. On 27 April 2020, as hundreds of people gathered to denounce the dire living conditions, the army fired live ammunition to disperse them. Twenty-six-year-old Fawaz Fouad Al-Samman was killed and many were seriously injured.

The use of excessive and lethal force against mostly peaceful anti-establishment protestors had worsened since October 2019. Under the guise of public safety or national security, authorities retaliated with violence every time people attempted to reclaim the streets. In the immediate aftermath of the blast, a state of emergency was announced, granting sweeping powers to the army. While the country was still in a state of 'general mobilization', it constituted a further attempt to undermine the popular uprising and quell people's growing anger in the wake of the catastrophe.

For the people protesting in Martyrs' Square on 8 August 2020, 'the establishment strived to continue what the ammonium had started', 'firing tear gas on those who had no tears left' and 'live ammunition on those who survived'. Hunting guns were used, excessive tear gas targeted first aid stations, while bullets and pellets were fired directly into the crowd including in their eyes, causing hundreds of injuries (Human Right Watch, 2020). In addition, a leaked circular issued by the Ministry of Health, attempted to 'turn doctors into informants', requiring hospitals to notify the Internal Security Forces of those injured during protests.

While public squares were being emptied, protesters were prosecuted, arbitrarily arrested and subject to torture, and attacks on freedom of expression continued to silence dissident voices. A medical doctor had his practice license withdrawn by the Ministry of Health after he criticized the government's management of the COVID-19 crisis on a television show. Activists and artists were increasingly interrogated for writing their opinions on social media, reporters were attacked, lawsuits were filed against journalists and media outlets were asked to obtain prior permission from the army to film in public spaces. Even the lyrics of a popular patriotic song were censored during a televised celebration of Lebanese Army Day and the word 'revolution' was replaced with music.

Authorities also took advantage of the heightened security measures to hold parliamentary sessions and place controversial bills on the agenda, including a general amnesty law that would further entrench impunity in the country. Rather than enacting an effective public health plan to contain the pandemic, members of parliament rejected some of the protesters' demands, such as the proposal to end the construction of a dam project in the Bisri Valley, despite the World Bank agreement to halt its funding and transfer the undisbursed amounts to respond to the more pressing needs of the population.

Addressing the devastating impact of the crises was undeniably not a priority for the political establishment. As the immediate response to the pandemic demonstrates, the sectarian oligarchy has a vested interest in maintaining the underdevelopment of public welfare. In the first parliamentary session held during lockdown, quorum was lost when the time came to vote for a bill to fund a social safety net to protect the most vulnerable households, and the distribution of emergency aid was delayed several weeks, while the sectarian leaders rushed to provide relief aid to polish their image and sustain their clientelist networks.

Likewise, the state's first lethargic response to the blast was rapidly followed by an attempt to control the relief effort organized by communities and organizations. On several occasions, authorities refused or delayed the arrival of international aid and rescue work, and a circular issued by the Lebanese army required all bodies engaged in relief work to obtain prior permission before entering the affected neighbourhoods, hindering the access of humanitarian actors, notably informal volunteer groups which were among the first assisting residents in the immediate aftermath of the blast.

Protesting is a matter of survival

With the outbreak of the pandemic, undeterred by the establishment's repressive measures, protesters immediately asserted that 'COVID-19 did not kill the Revolution'. At night the sounds of banging pots could still be heard, and on several occasions people defied the lockdown measures to reiterate the demands of the uprising. With their masks on, they gathered in front of the police stations where activists were detained, blocked roads and organized different sit-ins against the embezzlement of public funds, the commodification of education, the arbitrary dismissal of workers, the military trials of civilian protesters and the severe electricity cuts. They rallied on Workers' Day, celebrated the six-month anniversary of the uprising and, in the era of social distancing, organized car protests in many regions. Yet overall street mobilizations remained scattered during lockdown, before people's growing anger following the blast led to more intense protests under the banner 'Justice for the victims, revenge from the regime'.

To better capture the nature of the uprising and reflect on its capacity to open breaches in a social and political order that seems resistant to change, looking beyond protests and behind the scenes of conventional politics is critical. During the pandemic, the uprising did not enter a period of latency, but protesters sustained their grassroots efforts to build the country they aspire to. Attention to the unanticipated scope of street protests since October 2019 has in fact largely overlooked the long and often 'invisible' struggle of the post-war antisectarian movement that paved its way and the 'alter-activist' mode of engagement youth have been resorting to for years to challenge the sectarian oligarchy (Kassir, 2016).

On the six-month anniversary of the uprising, Lebanese citizens flooded social media with #WeWillBeBack. Since 17 October 2019 people have heavily relied on digital activism, and even more so after the lockdown, to organize, debate, live-stream protests and assert that the revolution is ongoing. For the past ten years, social media platforms, notably Facebook and Twitter, have been privileged spaces of mobilization, and digital activism largely contributed to help build and sustain a growing network of antisectarian activists. Likewise, the burgeoning of alternative media platforms played a critical role. Their independent editorial lines and rights-based approach contributed to open a more democratic space in a media landscape very much controlled by the sectarian oligarchy. Throughout the years, they succeeded in building a growing audience, facilitated the mainstreaming of an anti-establishment discourse and, since 2019, have become to a large extent 'the voice of the uprising'.

With tweets, graffiti or signs hanging on their windows, protesters didn't stop calling for their rights. Women were at the frontline of the October Revolution, reclaiming the streets, shattering stereotypes and battling the patriarchal sectarian system. From the first days of lockdown they instantly joined the fight against the surge in domestic violence and hung sheets on their balconies to share the hotline number of the nongovernmental organization that initiated the campaign.

The country's first domestic violence law was endorsed in 2014 after being watered down by sectarian authorities, and six years later people keep on calling for its amendment. Whether at home or in the streets, activists challenged the old ways and strived to embody their transformative visions in their everyday practices. As the economic crisis and surge in food prices further exposed the country's heavy reliance on imported products and the lack of a strategy to enhance food security, people increasingly began to grow their own food and gardening communities flourished on social media. In December 2019, a group of activists, planted vegetables in Al-Nour Square and founded Habaq ('basil' in Arabic) to advocate for a more sustainable food system. The success was immediate, and initiatives to encourage local production, revitalize the agriculture sector and promote food self-sufficiency are booming across the country.

After years of coercion and co-optation of labour movements and trade unions by the sectarian powers, the October uprising witnessed the birth of interest-based alliances and the revival of professional associations, but struggled to translate its demands into an alternative political and economic project. With the deepening of the crises, and even more so after the blast, activists went into survival mode and resolved to take matters into their own hands through direct social action. Several groups born during the uprising, along with well-established anti-sectarian collectives, channelled their energy to support those most affected by the crises. While protesters' massive participation in the relief effort might raise concerns about a depoliticization of the movement, it cannot be reduced to its sole humanitarian aspect.

Through these acts of solidarity, people sustained their fight for social justice and strived to challenge the political economy of sectarianism. They urged donors not to disburse emergency aid to the Lebanese government but directly to those in need through independent civil society organizations. Likewise, they fiercely rejected the donations of the sectarian parties and through different initiatives sought to liberate from their grips those who might be bound to accept their conditional offer. They cleaned the rubble, organized fundraising, distributed food baskets and found shelters for families in needs.

Justice as the first remedy

Nearly a year after the onset of the uprising, the economic grievances, the rampant corruption and the waning faith in the governing parties that drove thousands of Lebanese to the streets are as prevalent as ever, but the vibrant October protests seem like a distant memory. People are mourning their city and loved ones and searching for a ray of hope. Today, the country is on the verge of collapse, torn between sectarian divisions, regional tensions and diverging international interests, but the heart of the revolution keeps beating. In spite of the pandemic, the devastating blast and the violent repression, the October uprising strived to sustain its fight against a ruling class that 'raged a war on its people'.

The obstacles are massive, and activists are struggling to find the best way forward and to devise a roadmap to address the multilayered crisis. Yet, through daily acts of resistance and alternative practices, they are laying the foundations for a structural change. As the ruling class seized the crisis as an opportunity to expand its authority and enforce a police state, activists are striving to preserve a democratic space, and by responding to immediate needs and collecting the shattered pieces they are building new solidarities and challenging the political economy of sectarianism.

Lebanon is at a critical juncture, and if the development of an alternative political project is vital to confront the neoliberal sectarian system and address its structural inequalities, despite their fragility, these grassroots efforts remain critical to pave the way for a new kind of politics. If it's too early to anticipate how the movement will evolve and whether it will succeed in breaking the circle of impunity and shifting the balance of power, what's certain is that in Lebanon today, protesting is a matter of survival, and justice is the first remedy to revive the country.

References

Abu-Ismail, K. and Hlasny, V. (2020) *Wealth Distribution and Poverty Impact of COVID-19 in Lebanon*, Beirut: ESCWA, available from: https://www.unescwa.org/sites/www.unescwa.org/files/publications/files/wealth-distribution-poverty-impact-covid-19-lebanon-english_0.pdf

Baumann, H. (2016) 'Social protest and the political economy of sectarianism in Lebanon', *Global Discourse*, 6(4): 634–49.

Human Rights Watch (2020) 'Lebanon: Lethal Force Used against Protesters', [online] 26 August, available from: https://www.hrw.org/news/2020/08/26/lebanon-lethal-force-used-against-protesters

Kassir, A. (2016) 'Anticonfessionnalisme et alteractivistes au Liban', *Agora Débats Jeunesses*, 73(2): 77–90.

26

Hong Kong: From Democratic Protests to Medical Workers' Strikes in a Pandemic

Chris Chan and Anna Tsui

Hong Kong observed the authoritarian regime's horrible approach to COVID-19 infection control in its early stage. This included sanctioning whistle-blowing doctors who exchanged news within hospital internal communications and delaying the announcement of the discovery of human-to-human virus transmission.

Hong Kong's infectious control has been considered a good example with low infection and death rates. Yet, the government of the Hong Kong Special Administrative Region (SAR) displayed its share of complacency in infection control at the initial phase of the pandemic, despite being promised a 'high level of autonomy' from Beijing. While towns and villages in mainland China had already enforced mandatory self-isolation for personnel entering from Hubei (the province with the most confirmed cases), by the end of January, the Hong Kong government still resorted to making nonbinding appeals to Hubei visitors to self-isolate or leave the city. While Singapore, Taiwan, Macau, Malaysia and mainland China had all taken steps to provide facemasks or controlled their supply, the Hong Kong government insisted price control would negatively affect supply.

The Chief Executive of Hong Kong, Carrie Lam, refused to wear a mask at press conferences and claimed that doing so was unnecessary, despite respected local scientists advising on the importance of wearing masks, which was a lesson learnt from the outbreak of Severe Acute Respiratory Syndrome (SARS) in 2003 in this densely populated city. These signs of the government's lax emergency responses created much anxiety among Hong Kong citizens. Prominent scientists also suggested the Hong Kong government should tighten border control, a common practice across countries. But it only happened after an historical five-day strike staged by 7,000 medical workers in the city. The government was criticized for putting political reasons (not to upset Beijing) above scientific advice from experts when making decisions. In this article, we analyse the context, causes and consequences of this strike.

The political context

The former British colony had enjoyed relative autonomy since the 1997 handover to China, under the principle of 'One Country, Two Systems' established in the SAR's mini-constitution. Hong Kong is one of Asia's most important international financial centres, operating under a pro-capital, low tax rate and minimal welfare regime. Its population of 8 million struggle with the highest housing prices on earth and a Gini coefficient of 0.539. The city's civil society movement focuses on political rights of universal suffrage for the chief executive and legislative council elections, as well as the defence of the city's autonomy from the Chinese Communist Party's encroachment.

These themes were consistent throughout the city's annual Tiananmen massacre candlelight vigils, the 2003 mobilization against national security legislation and the 2014 Umbrella Movement. In the ongoing Anti-Extradition Bill Movement (AEBM) that started in June 2019, millions took to the streets to protest against plans to allow extradition to mainland China, which could endanger dissidents and undermine the city's judicial independence. An increasingly hard-handed approach by the police and the court against ongoing street protests created a strong 'Hongkonger' identity-based resistance, bringing a landslide victory for the pro-democratic camp in district council election in 2019 as well as a wave of new trade unions gathered under the banner of resistance. Hong Kong experienced a collective trauma in the 2003 SARS outbreak, which claimed over 200 lives including those of doctors and nurses. The fear of a potentially devastating COVID-19 outbreak created strong solidarity among citizens and deep collective anger and anxiety over the government's inaction.

In this context, public hospital workers who were on the frontline of the pandemic became the leaders on the frontline of civic resistance. A newly established trade union, the Hospital Authority Employees Alliance (HAEA), demanded of the government—indirectly through the Hospital Authority (HA) accountable to it—that it deploy much stricter border control policies towards visitors from mainland China, extend mandatory quarantine measures and ensure occupational safety for hospital workers. It became the representative of over 20 percent of public medical sector employees, and 7,000 eventually took part in a five-day strike from 3 to 7 February. Organized labour's show of strength reflected a paradigm shift: Hong Kong citizens began to accept union organizing as a mode of collective resistance. Following the strategies of confrontation within the legislature, street resistance and a consumer movement boycotting pro-China business, this new union movement will reshape the landscape of Hong Kong's political, social and economic struggles. In this sense, the Hong Kong medical workers' strike is epoch making.

Revitalizing the role of organized Labour

Hong Kong has always been a haven of liberal capitalism. Hong Kong's mini-constitution, the Basic Law, promised the right to strike, but the Employment Ordinance only protects union activities outside working hours or with employers' approval, leaving the strike in a legal grey area. The right to collective bargaining is nonexistent in the legal system, even though the city did ratify the ILO Convention No.98: 'Right to organize and collective bargaining'. The largest trade union federation is controlled by the Chinese Communist Party. Most workers join a union motivated by the benefits they will get. Rights-based unions in the pro-democracy camp rarely exceeded a thousand members, especially newly established ones. However, HAEA has been the exception to the rule. Even though the union organized as recently as October 2019, membership skyrocketed from 300 in December 2019 to over 18,000 applications and over 10,000 successful registrations by 30 January 2020, following its public call to strike.

Following the relocation of manufacturing industries to China, the number of strikes in Hong Kong in the 1990s had become negligible. Even in incidences that aroused public attention, such as the 2007 ironworkers' strike and 2013 dockworkers' strike, the number of strikers rarely exceeded a thousand. On 5 August 2019, the public called for a one-day symbolic 'general strike' as a new strategy to advance the AEBM. The organizers estimated that 350,000 people joined the strike assemblies across Hong Kong, though many actually took a leave of absence from work, and participants also included freelance workers, teachers and students who were free from work on that day. In comparison, 7,000 hospitals employees had already signed a pledge to strike by 31 January, far exceeding the lower limit of 4,000 (5 percent of hospital staff) set by union organizers to initiate the strike.

As medical workers, taking part in a strike despite a looming pandemic is a difficult decision. Yet HAEA members demonstrated strong determination to protect themselves and Hong Kong citizens from a man-made disaster of government inaction. Organize unions, everyone joins the three-strikes (workers' strike, shopkeepers' strike, class boycott) was a new consensus formulated during the AEBM to demand democratic reform in the city. Although the movement was abruptly cut short by the pandemic, the crisis further revealed the absurdity and danger of the authoritarian tendency of Hong Kong-China politics. This had pushed medical workers to the forefront of the new labour movement. The HAEA strike, as well as the public support behind it, will affect the future direction of Hong Kong's democratic movement, potentially bringing organized labour back as one of the main agents of the democratization movement.

Strong public backing from broken government legitimacy

Starting from 23 January, HAEA pressured the hospitals administration to publicly demand the government ban any traveller from entering the city from the Chinese mainland border and ensure safe working conditions for all employees by providing a sufficient supply of isolation wards, stopping non-emergency services and ensuring the supply of masks. A week and a half later, the strike took place. This fast development reflected not only the scale of the crisis facing the medical sector but also the crucial fact that new unions were able to inherit the public support and mobilization capacity of the AEBM. The resistance in Hong Kong had learned to adopt organized modes of collective action to break through the political deadlock.

Having experienced symbolic 'three-strikes' and countless road-blocking actions, Hong Kong citizens seemed to be accustomed to disruptions in their daily lives. This had spilt over into their support for HAEA, but the scale and type of work stopped by the medical workers' strike arguably posed a new challenge to citizens' level of tolerance of industrial action. On 23 January, HAEA began their seven-day notice of an Emergency General Meeting on 1 February. They proposed that if the HA refused to fulfil their demands, they would begin a five-day strike. The first phase (3 February) involved only non-emergency services. The second one (4–7 February) would limit work to emergency services. Despite the potentially devastating impact of the strike on hospital operations, a popular opinion survey released on 31 January revealed that 75 percent of interviewees were discontent about the government's performance in handling the outbreak, 80 percent supported a strict border closure and over 60 percent expressed support for a medical workers' strike if the government responses remained ineffective.

Arguably, this broad public support was due to the breakdown of government legitimacy since the AEBM. The government condoned police violence against protestors and indiscriminate pro-government gang violence against civilians from June 2019 onwards. Thousands of protestors were arrested, many sentenced to years of prison, and some were reportedly severely abused. This was considered a marked aberration from the earlier policy of relative restraint and tolerance towards the opposition, a culmination of scaled-up authoritarian measures since the 2014 Umbrella Movement. In addition, voluntary first-aiders at the protests were arrested unreasonably during police action, leading to widespread anger in the medical sector against the government. COVID-19, dubbed 'SARS 2.0', again fuelled public anger as the government ignored reasonable public demands as it did with the AEBM.

Strong membership and cross-sector union support

HAEA represented the public medical sector, one of the largest sectors in the city, providing a strong membership base favourable to long-term unionizing. The Hospital Authority is a statutory body managing all public hospitals and institutions in Hong Kong, governed by its board and accountable to the government. Over 90 percent of its income in the year 2018/19 came from government funding. It is the second-largest employer in the city (after the government itself) with nearly 80,000 employees. Hong Kong's medical sector had long aligned with the pan-democratic camp with a professional and liberal image. This time, employees from different ranks took part actively in signing the HAEA's pledge to strike (73 percent being nurses, 11 percent allied health professionals, 8 percent doctors, 7 percent support staff and 1 percent administration and other staff), reflecting strong solidarity within the sector. HAEA already represented 22.5 percent of the HA workforce by 30 January, while the committee and membership of HAEA consisted mainly of young and junior staff who were more ready to take militant actions. Its power to conduct collective bargaining on behalf of HA staff was solid.

The COVID-19 resistance movement had gained cross-sector support. The medical sector was well supported by unions from other sectors. On 24 January, 50 unions, including the HAEA, raised demands for prevention against the pandemic in a joint press conference. Besides border closure, these unions requested provision of masks for employees and customers, cancellation of all business trips to China and the establishment of homeworking arrangements by their employers. Many unions showed active support for the HAEA strike, including Railway Power, Hong Kong Financial Industry Employees General Union and Unions for New Civil Servants. These unions were all formed after the AEBM.

Outcomes of the strike

By the time the HAEA announced the end of the strike, following a democratic vote among members on 7 February, none of HAEA's five demands had been completely fulfilled. Worse still, the HA had not formally recognized the status of the union. Nevertheless, the strike was a historic success for democratic unionism in Hong Kong, both because it won immediate concession by the government and because it shows the establishment of a democratic decision-making process in the resistance.

Chief Executive Carrie Lam's claimed that new border-closure and quarantine measures had 'nothing to do with HA employees' strike' and that 'using extreme measures to threaten the government will never succeed'. However, we can readily observe a pattern of tactical concession from the government, aiming at dividing the strikers and sympathizers. On 28 January, after HAEA announced that they would hold an EGM to vote on the strike plan, the government announced the closure of the Express Rail Link to mainland China and halved the flights from the mainland in two days. On 3 February, when 3,000 non-emergency service staff took part in the strike and demanded open negotiation at HA headquarters, Carrie Lam announced the closure of four more ports connected to the mainland. On the third day of strike (5 February), when a number of strikers remained as high as 7,000 and several transport unions announced their intentions to call for industrial actions, Carrie Lam announced that all persons entering through mainland China would be required to self-isolate for 14 days starting from 8 February, the day when the strike was planned to end. Even though some demands of the union – that non-residents shall not enter via the mainland – were not entirely met, they won important concessions. They succeeded in maintaining a high level of participation despite step-by-step concessions thanks to the union's comprehensive strike plan. The plan's legitimacy was further established by the EGM's democratic vote and the signing of strike pledges. It took three months for Carrie Lam to revoke the Extradition Bill after mass mobilizations of up to 2 million demonstrators by the AEBM. In contrast, the strike brought solid concessions within a week, indirectly reflecting the relative effectiveness of strikes as a strategy of resistance.

The strike demonstrated the importance of internal democracy within the resistance to avoid fractioning and internal fighting. The strike began with over 3,000 medical workers voting in person at the EGM, with 99 percent of votes in support of the strike, and over 9,000 signing a pledge to strike in their real names. This established a strong endorsement for the strike among the membership. On the last day of strike (7 February), 3,000 voted for the strike to continue while 4,000 voted to resume working. 7,000 took part in the strike and in this final vote. Eventually, the union followed the majority's will and announced the end of the strike, which reflects its respect for democracy. Within the union, militant members would go as far as taking part in a mass resignation to force the government's hands. Other members were more pragmatic and possibly concerned about their livelihood and medical-ethical problems raised by an indefinite strike. The vote successfully handled this internal difference. This was especially important to social movements in Hong Kong, which had been prone to a bitter internal division between the 'militants' and 'peaceful resisters' since 2014.

Despite these achievements, the chief executive openly called the strike 'an act of extremism', while the HA issued isolated dismissal threats and remained ambiguous on whether they would retaliate against strikers. Looking back at the HAEA strike, the right to strike and collective bargaining seemed a necessary demand in order for the union movement to grow.

Future of democratic and labour movements in Hong Kong

The COVID-19 outbreak and lagging government response provided a focal point for cross-sector resistance. Resistance continued after the strike. HAEA announced on 7 February that they would establish a 'defence fund' in support of members of HAEA and other sectorial unions, in case of suspension, dismissal or demotion due to participation in industrial actions. The union kept organizing at constituent hospitals, pressuring the HA through legal means and an employees' forum, and revealed the lack of medical supplies in multiple hospitals. The activism of new unions also inspired older unions, such as the Association of Hong Kong Nursing Staff, to initiate work-to-rule action in protest of insufficient protective equipment.

Many sectors realized that they were also on the frontline of outbreak resistance alongside medical workers. During the strike, over 20 unions came to action scenes in a show of solidarity, while new unions representing occupational therapists, physiotherapists and speech therapists employed by organizations other than the HA had also taken part in the strike. The Union for New Civil Unions led ten other unions to demand a promise from the HA not to retaliate against strikers, and asked Carrie Lam to revoke the claim that strike was 'an act of extremism'.

The public sector medical workers' strike in Hong Kong has laid a strong foundation for a new wave of union movements and inspired members of society to reimagine the forms that democratic resistance and demands can take. It demonstrated that civil and socioeconomic rights are tied to political rights, from outbreak prevention policies and occupation safety to the right to strike and collective bargaining. Many struggles remain to be fought in Hong Kong's democratic labour movement, however.

27

Morocco, Algeria and Tunisia: A Return to Authoritarianism after the Revolutions?

Kamal Lahbib

Fear, isolation and control are the key words during the pandemic in the main countries of the Maghreb region (Morocco, Algeria and Tunisia). Confinement measures and other 'states of sanitary emergency' have been implemented to contain the pandemic, and rightly so. For the governments in power, this has been an opportunity for recovering a certain political legitimacy and retaking possession of the public space they had lost since the Arab Spring by restoring fear, a feeling that had been overcome by the revolutions, with the help of a double-edged sword that is virtual space and new technologies. The pandemic is a windfall for the military dictatorship in Algeria, for the Tunisian regime that has emerged out of nothing, without political identity or programme, and for authoritarianism in Morocco, which is desperately seeking to re-establish the 'Hiba', a mixture of fear and submission to the central power and its agents.

There is no question of diminishing the measures taken by the states, which were sometimes courageous, such as the closure of mosques during Ramadan, in an environment with a strong religious influence that has caused religious extremists to react on the internet and through demonstrations. However, the measures adopted by the states, the media noise aimed at frightening people, the adoption of new laws, the deployment of security forces and of the army in the streets as well as the ban on gatherings and demonstrations, created an unusual situation. This is particularly the case in Algeria, where the 'Hirak' (the protest movement) had been holding weekly demonstrations since February 2019. There were also student demonstrations and sit-ins in Morocco, and about a thousand demonstrations per month in Tunisia.

In Algeria, the authorities are taking advantage of the pandemic and the voluntary suspension of the Hirak's weekly demonstrations to speed up the prosecution and trial of activists, journalists and supporters of the movement. In Morocco, the restrictions on freedoms in the management of the COVID-19 pandemic have led to detentions for expressing opinions on social media.[1] The government believed the time was right to pass a bill increasing control over virtual communication.

A defused revolution?

Sociological studies note that 'social protest in the Maghreb region has gone from riots, characterized by the use of deadly violence by the citizens and the state ... to peaceful demonstrations, sit-ins, marches'.[2] The social nature of protests has changed. They are no longer reduced to class conflicts, as elsewhere. They have not disappeared, but new types of contradictions, mobilizations and actors have emerged that do not fit into the classical paradigms of the workers' movement. They highlight new social conflicts. While the traditional social movements seek to defend material and categorical interests and focus on economic relations of production, the new movements organize themselves around values related to citizenship, justice, gender equality, the right to be different, the fight against rape and violence and the protection of the environment. They highlight other forms of social, sexual, cultural or linguistic domination and challenge traditional forms of social conflict management and political representation.

The pandemic and the ensuing economic crisis mark a momentary halt in the demand for social justice but will exacerbate conflicts and worsen the vulnerable situation of large sections of the society. The pandemic has had the positive effect of convincing the undecided of the urgency and primacy of social protection, the right to health and the right to benefit from scientific and medical progress. Throughout the Maghreb region, global confinement has already led to protests and demonstrations by poor families and people with limited income.

If the activists seem to accept, out of duty, this 'sanitary truce', resistance has been maintained and amplified through social media. In Morocco, for example, activists forced the withdrawal of the bill on the control over social media. Movements have multiplied declarations all over the Maghreb region. They have denounced violence against women, claimed rights for migrants, called for the release of prisoners to lower the virus spread and demanded transparency in the management of financial support for businesses. Associations set up a vast solidarity movement for the most vulnerable people. All these initiatives show the vitality of civil society and augur a resurgence of protest movements after the lockdown. Will the Maghreb states have the intelligence to defuse the revolution by questioning the development model and respecting freedom and democracy?

The search for a new development model has become the leitmotiv of governments in Morocco and Tunisia. King Mohamed VI described the current development model 'unable to satisfy the pressing demands of citizens'.[3] The commission he set up to come up with alternative proposals will be heavily influenced by the pandemic. The option of privatizing sectors, such as the electricity and gas sectors, is no longer on the agenda.

However, politics no longer takes place only in conventional spaces (parliaments, political parties, and so forth) and is no longer only about electoral power. Politics also takes place in the streets, around social issues, inequalities or access to public services.

A systemic revolt against neoliberalism

The Maghreb revolts took different forms: corporatist, political, with trade unions or without them. However, they all formulate the same radical critique of neoliberal policies and the same rejection of authoritarianism, dictatorships and classic forms of delegated democracy (where it exists), rent-based economies, privatizations of public services and goods and the collusion between economic and political elites. They express the same aspiration for democracy, freedom, dignity and social justice. The slogans affirm a radical criticism of states, which have become inseparable allies of neoliberalism. Neoliberal states are challenged for abandoning their commitment to protect citizens from abuse and ensure equity and access to decent public services.

The pandemic offers an opportunity for a break with the primacy of the market and mercantilism. It confronts social movements and democrats with the dilemma of 'the stock market or life', and calls more than ever before for getting out of neoliberal capitalism. It also questions the limits of 'protest democracy', the nature of power and, therefore, our relationship and alliances with representative democracy and elections, our territorial approaches and the extension of local power.

A triple crisis

The Maghreb is experiencing a crisis of values, political structures and forms of action. How can we tackle these three interconnected crises? The crisis of values requires a break with all kinds of conservatism, with religion as a major frame of reference in the public space. We must advocate and defend values of gender equality without any reservation as well as the respect of individual and collective freedoms.

Democracy, as a value and a political system, does not benefit the opponents of democracy. The electoral victories of the conservatives in the Maghreb were mostly the result of an election boycott by young people disenchanted with party politics. Democracy is the recognition of plurality and the fair competition of the forces involved, in complete freedom and transparency for popular legitimacy. The adaptability of Islamist groups to the norms of democracy and their electoral victories confront them with the only possible choice left to them in this social and financial crisis, intensified by the pandemic: a moralizing discourse and restrictive measures wrapped in religious precepts, but within the framework of ultra-liberalism. The exercise of power by Islamist governments opened an era of fierce battles to preserve or regain public, collective and individual freedoms.

The crisis in political structures requires a break with the traditional forms and heritage of the 1970s' left, as well as a break with the idea that neoliberalism is the only option.

The multi-dimensional political crisis calls to restore hope and connect with a new generation that often feels left with only two options: risking their life as "boat peoples" to cross the Mediterean sea to Europe or religious extremism. In today's protests, contentious actions have aesthetic, theatrical and musical dimensions. Communicational physical and cognitive resources are created to enable each person to express, in her or his own way, the humiliation, impoverishment and injustice that she or he experiences every day. The movements break the boundaries between politics and aesthetics.

It must also stand clear that ballot boxes are not democracy. They are a form of expression that does not necessarily guarantee democracy or respect for the vote's results. For several decades, the social movement has set itself the goal of developing a new concept and practice of democracy, and experimenting with alternative models to parliamentary democracy.

From the health crisis to the reinvention of politics

The global health crisis highlights the failure of development policies, economic liberalization, globalization and crony capitalism, as well as the exhaustion of the ideologies (socialist, nationalist, pan-Arab) of postcolonial states.

The movements are confronted with the need to rebuild politics on the principles of nonviolence and decentralization. Therefore, they are called upon to examine the memory of previous struggles in order to invent their own future. But, above all, as Gustave Massiah explains, it is necessary to 'reposition the local and municipal levels in a multi-scale approach of action and policies' and 'redefine the place of local and municipal institutions in the strategies for transforming societies'.

In sum, it is necessary to explore the bases and alliances of a new democratic pole. This cannot be reduced to the creation of a new party or alliance between parties. It can only be a new form of organizing and a philosophy of networking, drawing on experiences, such as the World Social Forum, while overcoming the constraints that limited its actions.

Notes

[1] Human Rights Watch (2020) 'Maroc: Campagne de répression contre les utilisateurs de réseaux sociaux', [online] 5 February, available from: https://www.hrw.org/fr/news/2020/02/05/maroc-campagne-de-repression-contre-les-utilisateurs-de-reseaux-sociaux; Kabbabj, O. and Saoury, Y. (2020) 'Réseaux sociaux: #Condamnés au silence?' *Telquel*, [online] 10 January, available from: https://telquel.ma/2020/01/10/reseaux-sociaux-condamnes-au-silence_1664415; Saoury, Y. (2020) 'Face à la pandémie, le CHU Ibn Rochd confrontéà des choix difficiles'. *Telquel*, [online] 9 April, available from: https://telquel.ma/2020/04/09/face-a-la-pandemie-le-chu-ibn-rochd-abandonne-une-partie-de-ses-patients_1678661

[2] Abderrahman, R. (2018) 'Comment expliquer les multiples mouvements de protestations au Maroc', *Le Point*, [online] 12 February, available from: https://www.lepoint.fr/monde/comment-expliquer-les-multiples-mouvements-de-protestation-au-maroc-12-02-2018-2194160_24.php

[3] Mohamet VI. (2017) 'Discours à l'ouverture de la session parlementaire'. *Portail national des collectivités territoriales.*

28

The French Strike Movement: Keeping up the Struggle in Times of COVID-19

Clément Petitjean

In his 16 March 2020 TV address to announce the national lockdown, French president Emmanuel Macron repeated six times that 'we are at war'. The war metaphor implied a call to national union as a solution to the crisis, the obvious reference here being the 'sacred union' which the French government had declared on 4 August 1914, at the outbreak of World War I. By 16 March, Macron had already shut down restaurants, bars and 'non-essential businesses', closed down schools and universities and banned all gatherings of 50 or more people.

In this context, it became very difficult to engage in collective action. The combined effects of the pandemic and the lockdown seemed to bring to a sudden halt the strike movement that had started in December 2019, which had become the longest wave of continuous strikes in contemporary French history (Quijoux and Gourgues, 2020). Likewise, Macron's announcement on 16 March that the pension reform was 'suspended' might appear as a willingness on the government's side to call a political truce.

What I would like to suggest, however, is that the lockdown did not so much put an end to the contentious episode as it transformed its performance (McAdam et al, 2001). After going through a general chronology of the movement and some of its ramifications, and focusing on the immediate effects of the lockdown on mobilizations, this article will focus on the reconfiguration of contention under confinement.

Chronology of the strike

Beginning on 5 December 2019, an 'indefinite' national strike was launched by the main union confederations against a pension reform plan that promised a sharp drop in the value of workers' pensions, an increase in the legal retirement age and a shift towards private pension funds. The strike rapidly assumed mass proportions, primarily among workers in the Paris public transportation system and national railways, but also including teachers, nurses, air traffic controllers, electricians and gas fitters, oil refinery workers, lawyers and dancers at the Paris Opera. The strike brought the capital's transportation system to almost complete paralysis for several weeks and severely limited service on high-speed trains across the country. There were mass demonstrations, with around one million protesters taking to the streets of towns and cities across France on four days of action in December and January.

Support from the general population manifested itself in opinion polls, too. All polls consistently showed that a large majority of the population was opposed to the government's plan–close to 75 percent of the population, according to a poll for *Le Figaro*, France's historically right-wing newspaper.[1] And a significant majority seemed to back the strike itself, despite recurrent attempts to discredit the strikers' motivations.

Of course, the movement against pension reform did not emerge out of the blue. As Maxime Quijoux and Guillaume Gourgues (2020) argued, 'It [served] as a point of convergence for the grievances which various groups of workers have expressed' since 2016 and the national movement against a labour 'reform' bill, the so-called 'loi Travail'. In the fall of 2017, a few months after Macron was elected president, opposition to a further reform of labour law triggered large protests. But the most significant–and unexpected–outburst of discontent and revolt was undoubtedly the 'Yellow vests' movement, which erupted in November 2018.

The movement represented an upsurge in mobilization not seen since May 1968 and seemingly novel in terms of social composition and repertoires of action. Although it did not result in policy changes, its rhetoric and symbols disseminated widely within the social fabric. Starting in March 2019, hospital workers organized strikes against budget cuts and a more general neglect of public hospitals (Stangler, 2019), with the support of various collectives. Similarly, the feminist movements which came to the fore in the wake of #MeToo in 2017 reinvigorated social conflict in innovative ways, through International Women's Day protests and events, massive demonstrations against sexist and sexual violence on 23 November 2018 and 2019, but also calls for women's strikes or 'guerrilla-style street art' against femicides.

Such efforts dovetailed with the pension reform movement: in the winter of 2019, feminists emphatically and convincingly emphasized how the reform would systematically harm women and aggravate the already gendered nature of the labour market. The pension reform movement had the potential to bring together struggles under a shared umbrella: a refusal of Macron's neoliberal agenda, of widening social inequalities and of police repression and violence, and a call for stronger public services existing outside of the market logic. At the 17 December national day of action for instance, an insightful banner held by hospital workers read 'The State is counting its money, we'll be counting our dead'.

The pension movement also spurred the development of new sites of struggle. In late December 2019, a movement in academia took shape against a government plan to further 'reform' the French university system and generalize already existing competition between universities and faculty, project-based funding for research and precarity as a mode of government of students, faculty and administrative personnel alike. Contention took form, spread, and manifested itself in increasingly militant ways and in interdependence with the movement against pension reform and the feminist movement.

At the local level, dozens of statements emanated from research centres, teaching departments and/or universities. Local organizing committees were set up to debate, plan for actions and convince colleagues to join the movement. Hundreds of university instructors—the vast majority of them graduate students and precarious, underpaid, overworked adjuncts—went on strike and stopped teaching or grading papers. Several general assemblies were held in Paris, followed by two 'national coordinations' bringing together hundreds of people. On 5 March, the three-month anniversary of the strike movement which had been set as the day when French universities would 'shut down indefinitely', tens of thousands demonstrated in Paris and the rest of the country.

Aside from demonstrations, repertoires of collective action included flash mobs, teach-ins, digital blockades and shutting down various public events organized by the higher education minister. More surprising tactics included a strike by academic journals, suspending all editorial activities to highlight the role of unpaid labour in knowledge production, to publicize their opposition to the government's plan and to liberate time to mobilize.

In the early days of March, a lot of people who had played an instrumental role in shaping and structuring these movements were exhausted by the frenzy of the previous months. But it seemed that political opportunities were expanding, that a process of cognitive liberation was under way and that the ruling class had more and more difficulty producing and reproducing hegemony, as its consistent, escalating use of police coercion suggested – 'Something was definitely going on', as a popular expression in activist circles put it. In mid-March, when it dawned on a lot of people that COVID-19 was not just 'a big flu', however, movement activists and organizers realized that whatever measures the government would take would fundamentally alter the terrains of struggle.

Did the movement stop?

In terms of contentious activity, the most direct effect of the confinement measures which were announced between 12 and 16 March was to shut down mobilizations almost entirely. Numerous protests were supposed to happen during the weekend of 14–15 March in Paris, including a march against police violence and a climate march. Most events were called off by organizers for public health reasons. In the higher education movement for instance, on 13 March the 70-odd members of the Paris organizing committee exchanged thousands of messages on their main Telegram group to decide what to do. In order to prevent the virus from spreading further, the general consensus was to cancel all upcoming actions, shift to online organizing and come up with 'quarantined' ways to keep the movement going. The digital infrastructures which had been built in the previous months became the main communications channels.

This general process of demobilization should not be seen, however, as an automatic endorsement of the 'sacred union' agenda. As journalist Chloé Leprince notes,[2] the fundamental goal of Macron's sacred-union rhetoric was to produce consent, 'a durable, unyielding base for consensus which first relies on the idea that not only is the war effort indispensable, urgent, and non–negotiable, but also that it's legitimate.' If consent to confinement seems to have been secured, it does not imply that it relies on a newly found 'durable, unyielding base for consensus'.

Maintaining contention by building solidarity

The lockdown drastically limited the possibilities for collective action, but contention did not stop. In other words, the lockdown did not destroy the social ties, networks and more or less formalized collectives and institutions, or the collective frames which had been built through social movement activity during the previous months. By bringing to the fore existing class inequalities, issues of social redistribution or the effects of working conditions and wage disparities on pensions, the strike movement popularized collective frames and narratives which were reactivated by the current realization that 'we're not all in this together', as Lesley Wood puts it in Chapter 18.

Similarly, when feminist activists, journalists, writers, social workers or academics insisted on the gendered effects of the lockdown, when they called into question Macron's picturing of 'the home' as a safe and benevolent refuge, when they demanded that the government actually invest into rather than just pay lip service to the fight against sexual and sexist violence, or when they pushed for actual recognition of care work and reproductive labour, they used resources, repertoires and frames from the recent feminist movements.

Because physical interactions were limited, digital activism now occupied a more prominent place in the available repertoires of collective action. The development of social media campaigns, video clips, memes, petitions, newsletters and 'online demonstrations' showed the adaptation of traditional repertoires as well as more innovative ones. The paradox of digital organizing (van Haperen et al, 2018), however, is that the capacity of digital activism to transcend barriers depends on proximity (geographical and social), which is an essential condition for sustaining relations over time. In other words, digitally networked collective action cannot exist without the production and reproduction of real-life infrastructures. It would therefore be interesting to study the extent to which people's social ties shrunk under confinement and how such shrinking affects the sustainability of digitally networked activism.

Despite the newly found prominence of online activism, locked-down collective action cannot be reduced to its digital manifestations. 'Offline' collective action did not altogether disappear. The most visible example was probably the daily applause from doorsteps, windows and balconies to support doctors and other healthcare workers, which became routinized in France as in other countries across the globe. While it is arguable that the applause paradoxically signalled a form of 'social distancing' from healthcare workers (Juri, 2020), the moment also became a strategic site for politicization. Partly because this moment of solidarity was depoliticized and recuperated by the government and local authorities, there were numerous initiatives to politicize the applause – to attribute responsibility for the current situation to state actors, to stress social conflict and to make the case that what doctors and nurses and paramedics needed most was not moral support but more beds, more masks, ventilators that actually work, better wages and a real, ambitious plan to strengthen *public* healthcare.

Such politicization happened through various, interconnected means. In addition to handclapping, people sang songs which were often variations on the same songs that had been sung for the previous months or during past movements. People also hung banners outside their windows to publicize their anger and demands. In Normandy, where I was locked down, my friends and I hung a banner that read 'More money for public services'; in neighbouring streets, during the one-hour walks we were allowed to take, I saw banners with 'Beware of revenge. The bad days will end', 'Less cops, more money for public hospitals', or 'Money for hospitals, not for capital'. Finally, people projected slogans, memes or videos on the walls of buildings to emphasize the inconsistency and hypocrisy of the government's handling of the crisis. On 31 March, which had been set by labour leaders as a national day of action against the pension plan, one of the videos that was projected boasted: 'We'll be confined as long as we need, we'll take to the street as soon as we can'.[3]

Finally, the reality of confinement cannot be fully grasped without acknowledging its fundamental class character. A majority of White-collar workers and managers worked from home, while workers in healthcare, but also in retail, agriculture, post offices or sanitation – the 'essential sectors' of the economy – kept going to work every day, very often without necessary sanitary protections being provided to them.

The current crisis is likely to exacerbate conflicts in the workplace and shape the 'wage consciousness' (Clouet and Quijoux, 2020) of 'workers and unionists who are intent on striking a balance between their health, viable economic production and general-interest-oriented goals.' This was the case in Amazon warehouses, where protests and strikes were held right after the lockdown started, creating a national outcry and causing labour inspectors to order Amazon to address safety hazards. Class inequalities overlapped with the gendered division of domestic labour, which was reinforced by the lockdown. Several government reports highlighted that women in general spent more time than men performing domestic duties (cleaning, cooking, washing the dishes or going grocery shopping) or, when they had children, attending to their educational needs, but they also noted a significant increase in calls to report intimate partner and family violence.[4] While the 3919 national hotline received 10,000 calls or so per month in 2019, the number skyrocketed to 30,000 in April 2020 and 23,000 in May.

There were numerous workplace-based solidarity efforts, often led by union members, to protect their colleagues, but also to produce goods that are essential to fight the pandemic (masks, ventilators) or turn worksites into solidarity hubs. Other direct, community-based solidarity efforts included food collection and distribution to vulnerable individuals and families, migrants or homeless people. The meaning of these mutual aid initiatives itself was an object of struggle. While some framed it in terms of basic human decency and justice, thus escaping the scope of political conflict, others used a more contentious language to define them in opposition to the government's public health strategy, which seems to be largely determined by economic and ideological imperatives – to protect profits over people.

Contention was also fuelled by public authorities. The government's inconsistencies, contradictory injunctions, lies and generalized incompetence undermined its ability to secure people's consent. The most blatant example of this was the masks scandal: in the buildup to the lockdown, the Health Ministry and other government officials maintained not only that wearing masks was superfluous, even for COVID-19-positive people, but also that there was no mask shortage. After an in-depth investigation led by online daily *Mediapart* entitled 'Masks: proof of a government-sanctioned lie' was published in early April, revealing the lies about the shortage and the absence of adequate political reaction, Macron and Édouard Philippe's government completely reversed their positions.[5]

The lockdown turned the police into a daily presence in people's lives. Arbitrary policing was no longer a reality experienced only by racial minorities and other marginalized groups. A wealth of testimonies publicized in local, regional and national media outlets shed light on the number of fines and arrests that targeted working-class, racialized groups but also people who fell outside the scope of the traditional 'police clientele'. Those testimonies suggested that controls fuelled distrust and 'infrapolitical' behaviours to circumvent the arbitrariness of police power (writing double certificates, tweaking the time of departure to enjoy some extra minutes outside, and so on).

Such distrust did not come out of nowhere; it actually tapped into the criticisms of widespread police violence and repression that the yellow vests movement and other movements had brought to the attention of the general public and legitimized as a political grievance. Between 5 and 18 April, the police killed at least five people.[6] In late April, a woman and her roommates were arrested in Toulouse and brought to custody for hanging a banner reading 'Macronavirus, when will it end?' The arrest generated broad-based national support from individuals and left-wing organizations. As a popular slogan used on social media in the higher education movement at the beginning of the lockdown went, 'We're locked down but not beaten down.'

Notes

[1]   Maurer, P. (2020) 'Retraites: malgré un recul, le soutien des Français à la grève reste majoritaire', *Le Figaro*, 3 January. https://www.lefigaro.fr/politique/retraites-malgre-un-recul-le-soutien-des-francais-a-la-greve-reste-majoritaire-20200103

[2]   Leprince, C. (2020) ' "Chair à canon" et "soldat sans armes" face au virus: ce que vaut le détour par 14–18 sans les clichés', *France Culture*, 23 March. https://www.franceculture.fr/histoire/chair-a-canon-et-soldat-sans-armes-face-au-virus-ce-que-vaut-le-detour-par-14-18-sans-les-cliches

[3]   Massemin, E. (2020) 'Partout en France, les « manifs de confinement » prennent de l'ampleur', *Reporterre*, 1 April. https://reporterre.net/Partout-en-France-les-manifs-de-confinement-prennent-de-l-ampleur

[4]   Harris Interactive (2020) 'L'impact du confinement sur les inégalités femmes/hommes', [online] 15 April, available from: https://harris-interactive.fr/opinion_polls/limpact-du-confinement-sur-les-inegalites-femmes-hommes/

      MIPROF (2020) 'Les violences conjugales pendant le confinement: évaluation, suivi et propositions', Mission interministérielle pour la Protection des Femmes contre les Violences 15 July. https://www.vie-publique.fr/rapport/275675-violences-conjugales-pendant-le-confinement-evaluation-suivi-proposition

[5]   Philippin, Y., Rouge, A. and Turchi, M. (2020) 'Masques: les preuves d'un mensonge d'État', *Mediapart*, [online] 2 April, available from: https://www.mediapart.fr/journal/france/020420/masques-les-preuves-d-un-mensonge-d-etat?onglet=full

⁶   Le Pennec, T. (2020) '5 morts lors de contrôles de police: pas vu à la télé', *Arrêt sur Image*, [online] 24 April, available from: https://www.arretsurimages.net/articles/5-morts-lors-de-controles-de-police-pas-vu-a-la-tele

References

Clouet, H. and Quijoux, M. (2020) 'Lutte des classes pendant l'épidémie. Le pouvoir des salarié·e·s comme réponse à la crise?' *Contretemps*, [online] 19 April, available from: https://www.contretemps.eu/lutte-classes-travail-covid/

Harris Interactive (2020) 'L'impact du confinement sur les inégalités femmes/hommes', [online] 15 April, available from: https://harris-interactive.fr/opinion_polls/limpact-du-confinement-sur-les-inegalites-femmes-hommes/

Juri, C. (2020) 'Applause as a form of social distancing', *Open Democracy*, [online] 21 May, available from: https://www.opendemocracy.net/en/can-europe-make-it/applause-form-social-distancing/

McAdam, D., Tarrow, S. and Tilly, C. (2001) *Dynamics of Contention*, Cambridge: Cambridge University Press.

Philippin, Y., Rouge, A. and Turchi, M. (2020) 'Masques: les preuves d'un mensonge d'État', *Mediapart*, [online] 2 April, available from: https://www.mediapart.fr/journal/france/020420/masques-les-preuves-d-un-mensonge-d-etat?onglet=full

Quijoux, M. and Gourgues, G. (2020) 'France's strikes show the unions are alive', *Jacobin*, [online] 1 January, available from: https://jacobinmag.com/2020/1/france-strikes-trade-unions-gilets-jaunes

Stangler, C. (2019) 'A strike to keep us working', *Jacobin*, [online] 26 July, available from: https://jacobinmag.com/2019/07/france-hospital-strike-nice-gilets-jaunes-yellow-vests-emmanuel-macron

van Haperen, S., Nicholls, W. and Uitermark, J. (2018) 'Building protest online: Engagement with the digitally networked #not1more protest campaign on Twitter', *Social Movement Studies*, 17(4): 408–23.

PART V

Critical Thinking and Emerging Theoretical Challenges

29

COVID-19, Risk and Social Change

José Maurício Domingues

The world is undergoing a deep crisis, which was superimposed on the many ills that already beset it. The new coronavirus SARS-2, with its COVID-19-related disease, has turned much upside down. It brutally impacted human health, but its effects are really far reaching. I address them here with recourse to a discussion of *risks* and *threats*, as well as of *vulnerability* and *resilience*. I then move on to evaluate how state and parastate global organizations have coped with the crisis, specifically through the concept of *capabilities* as well as broader societal aspects, especially regarding the imaginary. Such changes may partly imply a true shift of modernity, though how this will develop is not as yet defined.

Political choices and issues underpin the development of my argument. How to answer to them cuts across the text and in the last paragraphs this is given a specific formulation in relation to possible further developments of modernity, within a critical theory, as broadly conceived, perspective. Not all pandemics have resulted in far-reaching social change. This looks likely now, especially since populations seem to be central to political life and discourse, even though, paradoxically, political systems have become more oligarchical and closed in the last decades. The economic effects of the pandemic are also brutal, since simply keeping the economy running (as distinct from what happened on other occasions, for instance during the Spanish flu) was hardly an option for governments.

Risks and threats, vulnerability and resilience

As is well known, Beck (1986, 1998) developed the concept of *risk society*. Although the concept lumped too many issues together, his idea clearly applies to the COVID-19 outbreak. Moreover, 'risk' became pivotal for the World Health Organization's (WHO) discourse (McInnes and Roemmer-Mahler, 2017), although, despite warnings from its joint committee with the World Bank, in practice risks were largely ignored by national governments, regarding both health and economic issues (GPMB, 2019: 7–15). In order to make such a framework productive however, conceptually we need to be very precise. Risk can thus be seen as the chance, the precisely or loosely calculable possibility, of some specific 'hazard' (that is, a potential danger) befalling us. In any case, even if risks can remain invisible, as Beck suggested, and therefore incalculable, the COVID-19 risk was highly visible if not really statistically calculable: after SARS-1, MERS and H1N1, the possibility of a new, deadly outbreak loomed large. Yet what we face now is not risk any longer. We are dealing with a *concrete and immediate threat* and the effects it produces: the COVID-19 outbreak and its related COVID-19 disease, as well as widespread economic mayhem (see Domingues, 2020).

Risks and threats have been related also to vulnerability, individual and collective, as well as mostly to system resilience (see, for instance, Hammer et al, 2019). The United Nations has been at the core of such conceptual and discursive moves. Populations and individuals can be more or less vulnerable, therefore, to risks (and their transformation into threats), and can be more or less impacted by them. Likewise, more or less vulnerable individuals and populations can react to the hazards that befall them in different ways and with greater or lesser so-called resilience (UN/ISDR, 2004). The latter is a concept that stems from engineering and is connected to complexity theory, meaning the capacity of a system to adapt to changes and particularly a 'disaster', even bouncing back stronger. It has been, along with vulnerability, ubiquitous in discussions of risk, both, again, flaunting plural and often loose meanings. Most vulnerability and resilience definitions imply a de-politicization of the issues they deal with, covered by technical perspectives. A critical view of vulnerabilities, which implies the agency of the individuals and collectives affected by risk and threat as well as a social identification of the causes and situations which make them more vulnerable, is crucial, alongside a remobilization of the modern imaginary. The same applies to the possibility for responses and concrete answers that allows for the different levels of resilience of social systems. Both issues are deeply political (Olsson et al, 2015).

State and para-state answers, individualism and solidarity

States have been the main instrument to handle epidemic crises, and responses to pandemics have been regulated by international treaties. Eventually the

1948 creation of the WHO, and its strengthening in the 2000s, produced a global entity to confront pandemics. Market mechanisms and networks of solidarity, as we see in the present crisis, have been part of national and global efforts to cope with these issues. But states and para-state organizations are absolutely central in such situations and have quickly deployed what may be called their *capabilities* (Domingues, 2019) vis-à-vis the present outbreak. They are all also at the core of 'global health governance' (Fidler, 2004).

We can link the deployment of state and global para-state capabilities to Foucault's (2004) concept of 'biopolitics', namely the management of populations, including the administration and avoidance of infectious disease risks and ensuing threats developing from the top down, in tandem with individual 'discipline' and general behavioural 'norms'. But the rights of populations can be also at the core of renewed efforts to tackle global health. The differential deployment of capabilities will move one way or another along these lines. Moreover, economic reconstruction in the aftermath – and even in the course – of the present crisis will display features that can strengthen social solidarity or return to the former pattern of austerity, neoliberal individualism, finance accumulation and the like. Thus far, the state has mostly had to take the former option. Likewise, nationalism or globalism can provide different answers to the crisis and possible others in the future. While in the past the rich had to combat the diseases of the poor in order to be safe, the possibility of containing the spread of infectious diseases on a national level, especially in such a globalized world, seems very limited.

Yet we should remember that Foucault (1984), in the third volume of his *History of Sexuality*, also spoke of one's 'care of self'. This can be seen in the present pandemic, possibly with lasting consequences (a point feminism stresses too, regarding the paramount role of women in domestic and collective care). Will this eventually strengthen social solidarity, with collective responsibility, or will it lead to radical forms of isolated individualism? Moreover, both are in tension with or even truly opposed to other views of individuality which, neoliberal or savagely liberal, mean to overrun other people's rights (to the point of making it a right to infect fellow citizens and make money no matter what). Care of self and solidarity have the upper hand now, but socially irresponsible individualism will not easily disappear.

Some present developments

Let me consider now how these capabilities have been mobilized vis-à-vis the concrete COVID-19 threat, as well as their future prospects, along with more encompassing social phenomena including individualism and more broadly the modern imaginary with its core values – freedom or liberty and equality (actually equal freedom), solidarity and responsibility. This allows me to draw, additionally, some conclusions about vulnerability and resilience.

Little has happened for now to the capacity of 'taxation' in relation to the COVID-19 crisis. Nonetheless, it will become crucial. Much of the expenditure to cope with the pandemic, its health effects and the sharp economic downturn that isolation measures entail can be paid for simply by the emission of money and debt management, but some increase in taxation is highly likely. In the last decades the rich have been spared and today pay far less, while the poor, via taxes on consumption, and the middle classes, taxed on their income, have become the main pillars of fiscal policy. This lies at the core of class power and redistribution today, as a result of the end-of-century neoliberal counterrevolution and the prominence given to the role of finance capital, whose power may be weakened.

'Materialization' as a capability has come to the fore. Lending, financing, giving social support to the weakest and workers more generally, building health facilities and financing research: the state has made a strong comeback. The economy is in tatters and will certainly be on the state ventilator for a while. Politicians have promised the strengthening of health systems and deployed an emergency sort of Keynesianism likely to produce significant changes in the regime of capital accumulation and its regulation, with the strengthening of social policies, not necessarily through social rights, more likely through social liberal arrangements. Minimal citizen-income schemes may be implemented, though labour legislation may still be enfeebled. Political conflict will decide the direction of development. How peripheral and semiperipheral countries will answer to both sanitary and economic crises is also relevant. The vulnerability of populations has had a lot to do with class, racial, ethnic, gender and global inequalities – indeed it has been partly generated by it – while the increase in their resilience depends on how this materialization capability will evolve. Politics, solidarity, individual (equal) freedom and responsibility feature centrally here too.

'Managing', within the state and as to its intervention in society, has never been dampened. The state was relatively slow regarding the COVID-19 emergency, but soon, state management stepped in strongly and swiftly, sometimes disconcertedly regarding health issues, but decisively as to the impending recession. The resilience of national states and populations will remain directly dependent on it, which depends on political decisions, never on merely technical evaluations.

What about 'moulding', what will become of our individual and collective behaviour? Will discipline, individual and collective, in the face of the virus and afterwards will change, becoming more intense? Personal responsibility and its links to solidarity have been stressed by most governments as a particular form of subjectivization, accompanied, conditioning and partly conditioned by societal moves, according to embedded views and standards related to social cohesion and solidarity, individualism and freedom. Rarely did they, such as in Brazil, dismiss the gravity of the crisis, though how they reacted was different across the world (the Americas doing particularly badly), while key elements of the modern imaginary, freedom (actually equal freedom) and solidarity (along with responsibility, individual and collective) have been played out in the course of the crisis. How this will evolve largely depends on politics: we may have a return to austerity, more social liberalism, or social-democracy may make a comeback.

Many other things have been affected by the pandemic, including relations between generations and how we experience intimacy, social media-mediated interactions, friendship and sexuality. Changes promoted from above – especially by the state – are easy to spot, but how they will entwine with bottom-up mutations will demand a subtler look. Sociologists, psychologists and anthropologists will be fundamental to developing and understanding of possible long-term changes unfolding from already developing trends or directly engendered by the pandemic.

'Surveillance' and 'coercion' have been bolstered by the crisis in a few countries, especially China, but this does not appear to have happened elsewhere – though of course lockdowns have brought them out. Surveillance and coercion tend to become especially important in countries that are already more authoritarian. More liberal ones are not likely to go down this path. Freedom – or its restriction – pops up again. The 'legal meta-capability' furnishes means by which the state can formally regulate itself internally as well as its intervention in social life, including surveillance and repression. Legal meta-capability has been very active during the crisis, through legislation and bureaucratically. Clearly, the definition of freedom is at the core of such issues, as well as its balance with solidarity. Furthermore, state authority is understood and enforced differently in different countries. Despite that aforementioned individualistic response of a number of social agents (among which the extreme-right thrives), it is interesting to see how the majority sought to defend itself and chose solidarity as value, policy and behaviour. Yet authoritarianism has also been highly visible in important countries, China above all.

In the aftermath of SARS-1, the WHO, as the main health-oriented global para-state organization, became stronger. It was transformed with the enactment of the International Health Regulation (IHR), its internal constitution. This allowed it to intervene more directly and draw upon non-state sources of information in order to carry out its mandate of outbreak surveillance. Nationalism and the Westphalian sovereignty model prevented it from going further. It has now concentrated on deploying its technical capabilities, and how this will politically develop is an open question. The WHO's approach and possibilities – including how it harnesses states' and other agents' capabilities to its ends – are at stake. Some commentators were very optimistic after the 2000 crisis and now take the opposite tack (Fidler, 2004, 2020), but 'global health governance' is likely to become more robust. Note that 'surveillance' has a particular meaning in global epidemiology and for the WHO, referring to the monitoring of possible epidemics. This has failed in the present crisis, increasing populations' vulnerability, but it is likely to be strengthened.

The COVID-19 pandemic was largely or at least partly an avoidable disaster, with people enjoying a lesser level of vulnerability as well as of resilience, nationally and globally. The destiny of globalization is partly in the balance, particularly regarding health, while relocations of industrial production and border regulations, nationally bound, will strongly interact. Solidarity may have a chance, though conflicts in other areas may deeply harm it, especially due to the tensions between the United States and China.

Conclusion

If it is true that Minerva's owl spreads its wings only at dusk, our effort to distinguish possible paths of development in the aftermath of the COVID-19 pandemic may be doomed to fail. Yet, while certainties cannot be ascertained, trends and possibilities can always be identified. I have implicitly taken a critical, ecumenical tack, offering a diagnosis of the present in relation to this specific issue. Particular political questions must be born in mind, such as the opening of the political and discursive space as well as the weakening of the extreme-right, whether permanently or temporarily—it has been shown to be savagely individualistic, despite its appeal to workers. Moreover, science has received a boost, which might help us deal also and especially with climate change, a risk fast becoming a threat. Truth and reason, inequality and justice, democracy and authoritarianism, alongside the values of equal freedom, solidarity and responsibility, within and across borders, have sprung forth, although this is far from settled.

A lot has been changing. New paths have opened up, particularly so as to cope with hazards, risks and threats, vulnerabilities and resilience, but not only these. Some changes will be reversed, others will be deepened. In the face of such changes, a far-reaching conceptualization may be necessary. Modernity could hitherto be theorized in three phases. Liberal modernity was strongly based on the market—especially as a project. The second phase was state-based, and finally we had the coupling of extreme complexity, dealt with by networks, which made a comeback, with neoliberalism. We may be entering a new phase in the development of modernity, with more direct state presence and further changes in its imaginary. How it will be newly articulated remains to be seen, if this comes to be the case. This possible fourth phase of modernity will take a while to become fully realized yet some of its contours may be emerging in the present turmoil. Things can definitely go awry and turn for the worse – with authoritarianism and savage individualism gaining the upper hand in the process; but they may turn for the better – with positive values and policies regaining part of the room they had lost lately, until we move to a really different sort of civilization, perhaps as part of this long-term process. It is true, however, that a new phase of modernity may not truly emerge. However, even if the present third phase of modernity is not overcome, important inflections are bound to happen, institutionally and regarding the imaginary.

The direction of changes will also hinge on how we mobilize to push modernity towards an emancipatory and more nature-harmonious direction, despite the tragic consequences of the COVID-19 crisis. The future is not given, though, and how things unfold will depend in part on our own capacity to move and our clarity of mind. This is a task we must not skirt.

References

Beck, U. (1986) *Risikogesellschaft: auf dem Weg in eine andere Moderne*, Frankfurt am Main: Surhkamp.

Beck, U. (1998) *Weltrisikogesellschaft: auf der Suche nach der verlorenen Sicherheit*, Frankfurt am Main: Surhkamp.

Domingues, J.M. (2019) *Critical Theory and Political Modernity*, New York: Palgrave.

Domingues, J.M. (2020) 'From global risk to global threat: State capabilities and modernity in times of coronavirus', *Current Sociology*, 68.

Fidler, D.P. (2004) *SARS, Governance and the Globalization of Disease*, Houndmills: Palgrave Macmillan.

Fidler, D.P. (2020) 'The World Health Organization and pandemic politics', Think Global Health, Council on Foreign Relations, [online], available from: https://www.thinkglobalhealth.org/article/world-health-organization-and-pandemic-politics

Foucault, M. (1984) *Histoire de la sexualité* (Vol 3), Paris: Gallimard.

Foucault, M. (2004) *Sécurité, territoire, population*, Paris: Gallimard and Seuil.

GPMB – Global Preparedness Monitoring Board (2019) *A World at Risk: Annual Report on Global Preparedness for Health Emergencies*, Geneva: World Health Organization, available from: https://www.google.com/search?q=World+at+Risk%3A+Annual+report+on+global+preparedness+for+health+emergencies.&rlz=1C1CHZL_pt-BRBR697BR697&oq=World+at+Risk%3A+Annual+report+on+global+preparedness+for+health+emergencies.&aqs=chrome..69i57.639j0j9&sourceid=chrome&ie=UTF-8

Hammer, C.C., Brainard, J., Innes, A. and Hunter, P.R. (2019) '(Re-)conceptualizing vulnerability as a part of risk in global health emergency response: Updating the pressure and release model for global health emergencies', *Emerging Themes in Epidemiology*, 16(2).

McInnes, C. and Roemer-Mahler, A. (2017) 'From security to risk: Reframing global health threats', *International Affairs*, 93.

Olsson, L., Jerneck, A., Thoren, H., Persson, J. and O'Byrne, D. (2015) 'Why resilience is unappealing to social science: Theoretical and empirical investigations of the scientific use of resilience', *Science Advances*, 1(4).

Rosenberg, C. (2003) 'What is disease? In memory of Owsei Temkin', *Bulletin of the History of Medicine*, 77.

UN/ISDR (United Nations Inter-Agency Secretariat of the International Strategy for Disaster Reduction) (2004) *Living with Risk: A Global Review of Disaster Reduction Initiatives* (Vol 1), Geneva: United Nations.

30

Challenges to Critical Thinking: Social Life and the Pandemic

Kathya Araujo

Despite the numerous ongoing interpretations about the pandemic and its nature, perhaps one of the points of agreement is the traumatic status of the COVID-19 pandemic for social life. Even if it is true that, as virologists and epidemiologists maintain, it was something that could be seen coming, this does not diminish its character of irruption and its capacity for destabilizing societies. A destabilization that advises us to address our loss of certainties. It is from this uncertain and risky place that these lines are written. It is from here that I would like to contribute to this reflection through some ideas about what this crisis (which will surely not be the only one but the beginning of a series) shows and questions regarding the social bond, and the way in which it challenges the critical thinking of our time.

In what follows, I will review three widespread conceptions in social sciences and especially in critical thinking, which in the light of what we face today seem to require serious revision. First, the idea that the national scale is not only unimportant but deserves our mistrust. Second, the conception that the individual is a threat. Third, the equivalence often established between social regulation and domination. Each of these notions is linked to what are considered major components in studies on the social bond: the production of 'the common'; the relationship between the individual and the collective; and social regulation, respectively.

The construction of 'the common': the nation and the national level

Much of the discussion in social sciences in recent decades highlighted the globalized dimension of the world. It suggested that the understandings of phenomena, threats and conflicts should take on this scale. Furthermore, it trusted that this scale would provide new forms of solidarity and justice. At the same time, a widespread distrust of the national level was extended. However, this crisis shows with stark transparency the importance of the latter. Given the magnitude of the threat we face, a global and articulated response would be reasonable and expected. But the truth is that events have ended up sharpening the perception of the profoundly national character of social life. This is not new, although it has remained rather in the shadows. As empirical research has shown, the most relevant experiences that individuals have and that lead to knowledge and know-how in the social world are mainly national. Individuals' deepest senses of dependence are linked to the national scale. But this was not sufficiently taken into account by contemporary theory.

COVID-19 has contributed to revealing the profound and radical importance of the national level, mainly due to the role that states have taken in this crisis. It is on them, on their resources, on their current agendas and on their previous actions that the destinies of the populations in different countries depend. Mortality and the strength of health services are inversely proportional. The deaths of many will challenge states that had managed resources for the sake of macro-stability, whose winners are precisely the most powerful economic actors, or that had used those resources in less than virtuous ways according to criteria not necessarily related to the population's well-being. In short, states that betrayed their public character to benefit the private sector. But, for the moment, as is often the case in circumstances where survival seems to be at stake, it is towards national scales that the redemptive and saving hopes of the population are directed.

But this strengthening of the national scale is also and above all related to the strategies for tackling the crisis and what they mean for people. Not only have border closures been widespread, but also, in many cases, resort to the nation and nationalist feelings has been the main tool for appealing to citizens. In addition, a kind of honorary competition between nations, defined by the number of deaths and the flattening of curves, has been established. On the other hand, assumptions about the 'character traits of national cultures', a highly suspicious concept long neglected by sociology, have played a decisive role in defining the management of the crisis. Confidence in the disciplined obedience of citizens in the case of Japan made it possible for them to be in public spaces at a time when other countries were compulsorily confining cities and towns. The assumption of the transgressive character of inhabitants in Peru defined and made admissible a very long and early total lockdown.

There are several risks. A widespread feeling of mistrust has grown stronger. The xenophobia suffered by Chinese citizens abroad, especially at the beginning of the pandemic, is a good example. Fear gives rise to the ferocity with which the closure of borders is defended, and to the legitimacy of the most brutal exclusion 'for the good of the nation'. A new common sense seems to have settled in. The open and uncovered explanation of the competition between nations allows behaviours worthy of stories of pirates or gangsters (countries stopping planes and confiscating medical material; negotiations in which the most powerful make it impossible for the weakest to access respirators or medical implements). The foreseeable closure of the great nations, in productive-strategic terms, in the future, today seems a necessary and justified consequence, but it constitutes a real threat to the most fragile and poorest countries in the world.

The challenges are not few. Because of space, I will limit myself to mentioning one: that the importance of the national scale in people's lives (and in their ordinary, everyday struggles) does not necessarily result in the register of the common becoming narrower. If history is the result of various disputes, perhaps one that we must urgently pursue today is the recovery of the dignity of the foreigner in times of fear; the expansion of solidarity towards the international in times of scarcity; the expansion of the consciousness of our common humanity in times of uniqueness.

However, there are potentialities. One of them is that critical thinking can recognize the relevance of the national scale to the ways in which people perceive themselves and orient themselves in the social world, as well as to the construction of the social bond. An opportunity to admit that demonizing the national scale, or evading it through an elusive game that goes from global to local, does not help, because it leaves critical thinking out of tune with the experiences, imaginaries and conceptions of a vast majority of the population (a mistake that is paid for dearly if we think about the several extreme-right parties in the world). The possibility of understanding that, more than throwing away the nation, the relevant task is to resignify it.

The individual and the collective: the individual as a threat

Perhaps one of the most frequent appeals in this time of pandemic is to individual responsibility. The importance of the individual as a base for the solution seems to be evident to everyone. We appeal to the moral dimension of individuals in the use of their freedom; their capacity to moderate their freedom on the basis of their responsibility towards the collective. Perhaps this health crisis, like few events before it, has highlighted the degree to which the processes of individualization have expanded.[1] They have been radicalized in regions of the world where they have a long history, such as in Central Western countries. But they have also spread to many other regions of the world. Of course, on this path, the idea of the individual and the characteristics of individualization have taken on different meanings and values. However, in all cases, this crisis has revealed the extent to which these processes have radically transformed the ways in which collective problems are addressed. The effects of individualization put new conditions on the possible and efficient ways of appealing to people and their commitment towards the collective.

Taking into account these phenomena of individualization when thinking about the social bond is of extreme urgency. This is the case in Latin America, a region in which the elites have historically privileged tutelary forms in their relations with the rest of society, depriving them of individual autonomy by diverse means. In such a context, the strengthening of individualization is a major factor in destabilizing traditional ways of conceiving the social bond. Nevertheless, there have not been enough studies and reflections in this field. The main reason for this—and this occurs not only in Latin America—is the erosive action of a premise.

The individual has often been conceived, even or perhaps especially by critical thinking, as a threat. This has been expressed in the association between the individual and egoism; the individual and transgression; the individual and the anti-collective; the individual and anti-solidarity, or in its most contemporary version, in the idea of the individual as pure expression of a neoliberal subjectivity that distances him or her from the idea of the common. Through these associations, what has been underlined is the distance between the notion of the individual and that of the common. A conception like the previous one is highly problematic. It has difficulty grasping what this crisis (and those to come) challenges, and answering the question of how to face situations that require high degrees of collective coordination and solidarity in a world of strong individualization.

Of course, a reading that links the individual to selfishness or reduces the individual to a mirage destined to sustain mechanisms of domination is not completely wrong. The development of this pandemic has provided us with enough examples. On one hand, food hoarding was a massive and widespread reaction; the violent protection of territory against potentially infected people made headlines in many countries; the individualistic assertion has led to the expansion of the violent use in ordinary interactions of moral superiority as a weapon of imposition on others. On the other hand, the strengthening of individual responsibility has allowed the responsibility for political decisions to be reduced and the structural effects to be watched over; the strengthening of the myth of the transgressor individual has served to vindicate the policies of state protection and those of the ruling class.

This reading, then, is not wrong, but it is insufficient. A large contingent of the population has restricted their access to public spaces, even without being obliged to do so by the state authorities. Many strongly individualized individuals have submitted themselves to very large renunciations for the protection of others.

In short, the risk of remaining in a critical reading and at a distance from the individual is that it prevents us from seeing that we are facing irreversible and expanded processes of individualization and even singularization, and that this implies a profound rearticulation of the relationship between the individual and the collective. It makes us see ordinary people as enemies, since it is in them and from them that the making of the world and its transformation takes place or will take place. The challenge that this crisis presents us is clear, although perhaps not simple: how to think in the future about a strongly individualized individual who is the foundation of the collective; how not to forget that it is the individual, the same one that critical thinking looks at with suspicion, who is the skeleton and the very heart of the social bond. To begin to respond to this, it is indispensable to abandon the conception of the individual as a threat.

Social regulation as domination

In the COVID-19 crisis, influencing people's behaviour has been presented as one of the most crucial goals. Although the metaphor of war used by several rulers has been questioned, and rightly so, the truth is that there are true similes with moments of war and other catastrophic events. The need for the widespread mobilization of the population and its behaviours, habits and customs in a new direction in an abrupt and accelerated manner becomes urgent. Therefore, these situations underline the importance of social regulation, authority, leadership and other mechanisms to guiding the population's behaviours. At times like these, the issue of obedience and compliance with rules is placed at the centre of strategy building. The tension between freedom and security is renewed. The importance of the value of survival restructures the hierarchy of these values. The boundaries between what can be considered undue control and the demands of control for the common good or the survival of the collective become indiscernible.

This crisis and the prospect that we will have to face other catastrophic situations in the future reveal another challenge for social sciences and critical thinking. Both have been prolific in studying and discussing the risks of control and the forms of domination it entails, but they have been much less productive in providing clues about what are the features of acceptable social regulation; on how to define the question of social regulation today in an acceptable way, a way that takes into account our values and normative principles such as freedom, autonomy or privacy. The usual association in critical thinking between social regulation and domination has prevented a serious discussion of the former. We have not sufficiently discussed how to solve problems of social coordination or reproduction in the context of a complex, individualized, more horizontal and more distrustful world.

In the absence of a reflection on this question, the confusion is greater. An example illustrates this: The crisis has allowed us to see with transparency the struggle between three great ways of conceiving how to obtain the obedience of the population. First, there are *de facto* strategies of control, in which compliance is the result of the action of devices or mechanisms. In them, the question of the relational power exercised is veiled behind the cold efficiency of platforms, apps or figures. Second, there are strategies of a relational type strongly based on intersubjective models, which appeal to a reflexive and strongly argumentative dimension, but which are inevitably sustained in the last instance, in view of their failure, by a repressive and punitive component. Third, there are also forms of the exercise of authority based explicitly on imposed punitive models that make coercion their main support. The most critical and progressive positions, given the lack of reflection on the point, have ended up defending one or the other in a disorganized manner.

Chile decided first for the strategy of using selective quarantines in different areas of Santiago. Left wing parties and the more critical and progressive political sectors, clamoured very early for an immediate greater closure. In the name of life and protection a total mandatory quarantine was demanded on a discourse in which economy and life were billed as enemies.

In a country with a fragile labour relationship, with a significant percentage of informal work and with a middle class characterized by extreme vulnerability, this demand did not seem to take into account the existence of broad sectors of the population for whom this total confinement very early on was simply unfeasible if related measures were not taken, such as deliveries of food and medicines and access to monetary support, all of which require a very high level of logistical preparation. The most critical sectors demanded extremely severe penalties for violators of the confinement rules, most of whom were not the usual powerful people, although there were many of those, but rather vulnerable populations whose survival is highly threatened. The representatives of critical and progressive thought promoted a model of repressive and punitive control, the same that they themselves have often denounced, a model that did not take even the slightest consideration of issues such as freedom or the structural situation of economic vulnerability of these populations (and thus Marxism stopped considering the economy as progressivism left aside the question of freedom).

The risks of not taking into account the problem of social regulation are enormous. They are, of course, as we have just seen, those of maintaining old repressive and totalitarian forms of securing regulation. But they are also those of naively collaborating with the drift of factual forms of imposition of power and control, or those of strictly defending freedom without taking into account the problem of how to solve social coordination or simply the limits imposed by social life in complex societies. *But the heart of all these risks is not having responded yet to the challenge that this crisis reveals. This is to say, the need to endorse a deep, self-critical and radical reflection on how to resolve the tension between freedom and control. How to tackle the ill-famed but indispensable question of social regulation.*

Conclusion

The challenges ahead are enormous. As is the uncertainty that we will have to face without theoretical and conceptual certainties to give us security. But this is human destiny. History, as it has been reiterated, is a result of disputes to give meaning and direction to events. To be part of these disputes, in moments of deep crisis such as the one we are experiencing, requires the humility to accept our blind spots, the courage to face them and the strength to overcome them. Social sciences and critical thinking are deeply connected with these requirements of courage, strength and, especially, humility.

Note

[1] The individual is placed at the axis of the idea of society at the same time that there is an expansion and deepening of the mandate towards the cultivation of individualities.

31

A Sociology for a
Post-COVID-19 Society

Sari Hanafi

The dark times of the COVID-19 pandemic call to mind how I felt during the long hours of waiting in front of Israeli checkpoints during my time working in Ramallah and living in Jerusalem between 2000 and 2004. The waiting for the waiting's end, being controlled and oriented by others, the rule of non-rule, became a suspended violence. This deprivation of a temporal existence (a process of change, an ontological time in anticipation, and one beyond my control) reduced my being to, as Heidegger would put it, a linear time, wherein I did not feel a 'spacio-cide' (Hanafi, 2013) but a 'chrono-cide'. Today, with its imposed alienation of time and its disruption of the life of half of humanity, which includes being under lockdown and even curfew, feels like those days in Ramallah and Jerusalem. The current disruption will change, at an unprecedented rate, how we eat, work, shop, exercise, manage our health, socialize and spend our free time. This virus has changed the direction of the wind. As Arundhati Roy eloquently put it:

> Unlike the flow of capital, this virus seeks proliferation, not profit, and has, therefore, inadvertently, to some extent, reversed the direction of the flow. It has mocked immigration controls, biometrics, digital surveillance and every other kind of data analytics, and struck hardest – thus far – in the richest, most powerful nations of the world, bringing the engine of capitalism to a juddering halt. Temporarily perhaps, but at least long enough for us to examine its parts, make an assessment and decide whether we want to help fix it, or look for a better engine.[1]

The surreal atmosphere of the COVID-19 pandemic has exposed fault lines in trust among human beings, among countries and between citizens and governments, and it is pushing us to raise big questions about ourselves, our social relationships and life generally. And this crisis is not just limited to public and environmental health or the economy – what we are witnessing is a moment of truth regarding the crisis of late modernity and its capitalist system on a broad, overarching scale. We will not be able to simply revert to 'business as usual' after we get through this crisis, and the social sciences should work to both analyse and actively engage in addressing these new realities. Tasks are of two sorts: ones that are urgent for now, and others that are important for tomorrow.

First, in order to unpack the social origins and to understand the magnitude of the COVID-19 impacts, to understand how the upward curve of infection can be flattened, to gain insight as to how to deal most effectively with the consequences of social distancing, and to properly study the measures required to alleviate the consequences for those who have lost their work, it is urgent to foster collaboration among scientists in all fields. We need not only medical labs but also sociological ones. The International Labour Organization estimates that as many as 25 million people could become unemployed, with the loss of workers' income reaching as much as $3.4 trillion USD (Ryder, 2020). Second, we need to understand the conspiracy theories and fake news around COVID-19, and to seek ways of mitigating the increasing discrimination against foreigners and refugees, including rising stereotypes against Chinese and those being accused for 'bringing the virus'.

One year ago, I wrote a piece that offered recommendations regarding possible new directions for global sociology (Hanafi, 2019), which included a call for supplementing the current postcolonial approach with an anti-authoritarian one, and a call for taking into account the new features of our postsecular society. In this chapter, I want to place further emphasis on three tasks for sociology: to build multilevel focuses that branch from community to humanity; to take an active approach in fighting against the diseases of the *Anthropocene* and the *Capitalocene*; and finally to set a better agenda for recognition and moral obligation.

Multilevel focuses: from community to humanity

First, COVID-19 has made it very clear how truly interconnected the world is, transforming the image of a global village from a metaphor into a reality. But we still need to generate *more global solidarity and more humanistic globalization*, and to do so successfully requires a *multi-scale conceptualization*. Gilles Deleuze argued that the left (and with it most social scientists, with the exception of orthodox economists) perceives the world in terms of relationships that begin from the most distant, and move inward. Social inequality, for instance, has been understood as a large, global phenomenon of exploitation whose relationship can be traced in, towards imperialism and colonialism. Because of this, most social scientists call to address the existence and structures of imperialism and colonialism in order to properly address the suffering of the affected (abstract) social classes. Contrary to this are identity politics movements (that is, some Islamic movements, and far-right-wing and conservative movements), which view relationships as beginning from a close point, moving to the most distant. They believe in community work and in family and neighbourhood relationships. For instance, Trump supporters do believe in his capacity to address the social inequalities faced by forgotten communities of rural White Americans. Faith-based organizations in Lebanon are currently the most proactive NGOs dealing with families who lost their job during the curfew.

I see our post-COVID-19 sociology as one capable of reinventing how it has traditionally commanded its focus to create methods that use multi-scale focuses, rethinking the importance of the family, community and of the ethics of love, hospitality and caring, and then scaling up to the level of the nation state and humanity as a whole.

Struggle against the Anthropocene/Capitalocene

COVID-19 is a disease not only of globalization but also of the *Anthropocene*. The creed of human consumerism is depleting resources that our earth cannot renew, and this virus is but one (albeit significant) episode of this consumerism.

Voracious consumerism is induced by what the French sociologist Rigas Arvanitis called the *mythological access to happiness*, which ultimately serves as an effective accelerator for more health troubles, epidemics, deaths and disasters. Examining these multi-scale relationships cannot be done without reconnecting the individual, society and nature. Addressing climate change and the political-economic system cannot be done without raising public awareness of the relationship of people to the earth and to humanity. Jason Moore (2016), proposes the notion of the *Capitalocene*, considering that capitalism is organizing nature as a whole: it is world-ecology that joins the accumulation of capital, the pursuit of power and the co-production of nature in successive historical configurations.

This multi-scale approach requires reconnecting the economic to the social, and connecting these to the political and to the cultural. Neoliberal and speculative capitalism is not just about economics, it is also a system of power and a system of culture, and these interrelations mean that even democratic systems are not always successful in preventing collusion between political and economic elites or the domination of wealthy lobbies (Pleyers 2020).

We need to revive Karl Polanyi's (2001) concept of social embeddedness. Polanyi introduced three forms of integrating society into economy: exchange, redistribution and reciprocity. Our social sciences thus should rethink these three terms seriously, as the market (a place of exchange) needs to be moralized, which includes establishing firm societal control against all forms of speculation. Redistribution cannot be done without taking significant measures to prevent the concentration of wealth from being held by a minority of companies in each sector, without establishing heavy taxation on high levels of capital and wealth (Piketty, 2014) and without moving to a slow-growth economy and its corollaries (including the need for cheap and low-carbon public transportation, seeing public services as investments rather than liabilities, and for increasing the security of the labour markets).

We are aware that the struggle for the environment is inseparable from our choice of political economy and from the nature of our desired economic system – and these connections between human beings and nature have never been as immediately or intimately connected as they are now. There is an acute crisis of rapid growth that was expressed very clearly by former president of the United States Ronald Reagan when he said: 'There are no such things as limits to growth, because there are no limits to the human capacity for intelligence, imagination and wonder' (see Bourne, 2018). For the American economist James Galbraith and the German sociologist Klaus Dörre (2019) this growth was based on the assumption regarding the long-term stability of the fixed costs of raw materials and energy, and when these costs were revealed to be unstable, financial speculation intensified and profits shrunk, and it generated distributional conflicts between workers, management, owners and tax authorities. Taking all of this into consideration, the authors suggest 'a consciously slow-growing new economy that incorporates the biophysical foundations of economics into its functioning mechanisms' (Galbraith and Dörre, 2019). I will add that we also need to think about the serious social effects of digitalized forms of labour and the trend of replacing labour with automatons. Even if digital labour partially reduces the unemployment rate, the lack of social protection for digital labourers will have tremendous effect in the future generation.

Politics of recognition and moral obligation

Polanyi (2001) defined social embeddedness as the mutual exchange of goods or services as part of long-term relationships, where reciprocity, moral obligation and concerns are added to contractual relations. I would qualify this reciprocity in two ways. First, reciprocity requires politics of recognition (Honneth, 1996) between groups and/or networks who accept the identity of the others, which work in line with the paradigm of pluralism and multiculturalism. Second, functioning reciprocity is dependent on the strength or weakness of the moral obligations in social relations. Alain Caillé (2008) pushes an anti-utilitarian hypothesis, whereby the desire of human beings to be valued as givers means that our relationships are not solely based on interest alone but in pleasure, moral duty and spontaneity. But the sense of moral obligation can also be weak. French philosopher Bruno Latour explains that, while people may not necessarily be ignoring climate change, they do not feel as though they belong to the land in which they live, and, in turn, may move quickly to other places as an individual exit strategy.

Post-COVID-19 sociology will only have meaning if it is armed with a utopia, or 'real utopias' as Wright (2010) would put it, as, even if is it not fully realizable, it will direct our actions. There is no ethical life without utopia, and the difference between clerical preaching and a sociologist's utopia is that the latter does not necessarily denounce the anti-utopian vision of others, and may seek to work with those who believe in it. This sociology should thus appreciate the Maussian gift relationship and the moral obligation to – and push for – connecting the social sciences to moral philosophy. It is important to rethink the construction of otherness, not only with regards to who is perceived as the adversary and why that may be, but with regards to how we care about *the Other*.

Here serious ethical discussion could tame the pursuit of our own self-interest. This is the sense of Paul Ricoeur's (1992) aphorism 'The ethical life is achieved by aiming to live well with others in just institutions', where, in other words, the ethics of love, hospitality, care and solicitude with and for others may be included in institutional frameworks to ensure and reinforce social justice and democracy. This is in line with the 'convivialist manifestoes' and Paulo Henrique Martins' contribution in this book in Chapter 37. To remind us how to think responsibly regarding freedom, and how to foster and encourage meaningful relationships with our 'other' fellow human beings, sociology should go back to these and other salient insights of philosophers such as Emmanuel Levinas, who, simply and astutely explained, 'avant cogito, il y a bonjour' (before *cogito*, there is hello).

Conclusion

Taking sociology to task has always been an integral reflection of the International Sociological Association. This global crisis may have prompted fresh strategies to reinforce exploitation, dispossession and our neoliberal capitalism, and increased the reach of our greed and selfishness, but it has also given us an opportunity to explore and provide new ways of understanding and reclaiming our social justice and humanity. I have attempted here to sketch some thoughts for a post-COVID-19 politics of hope that may signal to the possibilities for transcending our neoliberal and speculative capitalism, for reconnecting individuals, societies and nature and for embedding the economy in on social relationships, cultural values and moral concerns.

Let me finish it with a positive note that here in Lebanon, my colleagues at the American University of Beirut have measured a reduction in air pollution by 36 percent, and even the reduction of the noise pollution has invited our birds to sing along the board of my home window, all with the intimacy of self-reflection. During this confinement I rewatched the film *Love in the Time of Cholera*, reflecting on the beauty of creating love for the sake of it. Maybe one day another Gabriel García Márquez will write *Love in the Time of Corona*.

Note

[1] Roy, A. (2020) 'The Pandemic Is a Portal', *Financial Times*, [online] 3 April, available from: https://www.ft.com/content/10d8f5e8-74eb-11ea-95fe-fcd274e920ca

References

Bourne, R. (2018) 'The earth's resources are limited, but human ingenuity is infinite', *The Telegraph*, [online] 6 December, available from: https://www.telegraph.co.uk/business/2018/12/06/earths-resources-limited-human-ingenuity-infinite/

Caillé, A. (2008) 'Beyond self-interest (an anti-utilitarian theory of action I)', *Revue Du MAUSS*, 31(1): 175–200.

Galbraith, J. and Klaus, D. (2019) 'The choke-chain effect: Capitalism beyond rapid growth', *Global Dialogue*, 9(1).

Hanafi, S. (2013) 'Explaining spacio-cide in the Palestinian territory', *Current Sociology*, 61(2): 190–205.

Hanafi, S. (2019) 'Global sociology revisited: Toward new directions', *Current Sociology*, 68(1): 3–21.

Honneth, A. (1996) *The Struggle for Recognition: The Moral Grammar of Social Conflicts*, Cambridge, MA: MIT Press.

Moore, J. (ed) (2016) *Anthropocene or Capitalocene? Nature, History, and the Crisis of Capitalism*, Oakland, CA: PM Press.

Piketty, T. (2014) *Capital in the Twenty-First Century*, Cambridge, MA: Belknap Press.

Pleyers, G. (2020) 'Interconnected challenges of the 21st century', *Global Dialogue*, 10(1).

Polanyi, K. (2001) *The Great Transformation*, Boston, MA: Beacon Press.

Ricoeur P. (1992) *Oneself as Another*, Chicago: University of Chicago Press.

Ryder, G. (2020) 'COVID-19 has exposed the fragility of our economies', *International Labour Organization*, [online] 27 March, available from: https://www.ilo.org/global/about-the-ilo/newsroom/news/WCMS_739961/lang--en/index.htm

Wright, E.O. (2010) *Envisioning Real Utopias*, New York: Verso.

32

The Paradox of Disturbance: Africa and COVID-19

Elísio Macamo

Many are concerned about what our world will look like when the dust settles on the current pandemic. Will it be the end of capitalism? Is it the threshold of a new international relationship? Is it the time of a new Anthropocene that does not exercise its power over nature to the detriment of all other species? It would be so good if the answers to any of these questions were relevant to the African continent. But they are not. This does not entail the idea that the continent is not part of the world. Nor does it mean that the continent will be spared any negative consequences that come with the post-COVID-19 era.

It is more because, for the continent, what comes after, if anything changes at all, it will not change Africa's place in the normal order of things. Africa will continue to be the continent seeking to situate itself in a world that it has helped to build, not a world that it built for itself. This is the true meaning of Africa's integration into the world through colonization. The continent has been forced to participate in building a world made to measure for others. What we call development is, in fact, the vain effort that Africa makes to take ownership of whatever is left for it in a world crafted in this manner. In other words, Africa is because it is not; that is, what defines Africa is all that it cannot be in this world. The continent is a residual category.

The pandemic has demonstrated this. The virus is, for all intents and purposes, something natural. In this sense, there is nothing intrinsically bad or good about it. Calling it a pandemic is part of the way human societies react to the perceived danger it poses. In this sense, defining it as a pandemic reflects the way certain people or communities have 'socialized' the virus, effectively characterizing it as a major threat to social and economic integrity.

This characterization allows certain measures to be taken to protect society from the effects considered negative.

The social transformation of the virus into a pandemic has imposed on Africans, at least theoretically, a definition of the situation that is alien to the problem it represents for Africa. In other words, this transformation has universalized an ethical problem that is actually provincial. In Europe, and in the developed world in general, dealing with the virus has become a choice between protecting as many human lives as possible and/or keeping the economic fabric intact. Confinement, under these circumstances, imposed itself as the 'best' solution to this ethical dilemma by reconciling the two. In Africa, however, the dilemma is not posed in the same way. If we want to be brutal, it is a choice between letting many people die while protecting the economic and social fabric and/or letting many people die without protecting the economic and social fabric. If this sounds Malthusian, that is because it might indeed be Malthusian. The question, however, is what the exact meaning of this Malthusianism would be.

At this point, I would like to insert a long excerpt from an older publication (Macamo, 2011) on the notion of *disturbances*, in which I make use of an old literary genre (*dialogus mortuorum*) to approach the problem of the application of social science concepts in non-European countries by using the example of the examination of catastrophes. Ludwig Wittgenstein seems to me to be the ideal interlocutor in this respect, because he deals more than almost any other philosopher with the question of the relationship between philosophy and truth, and in particular the extent to which language extends or blocks our perception of reality. It will allow me set the stage, but also swiftly bring me into the point I wish to make in this brief chapter. Here we go.

A *dialogus mortuorum* between an African ancestral spirit and Ludwig Wittgenstein

Unfortunately, the following interview did not take place. However, if it had taken place, it would have been between an African ancestral spirit and Ludwig Wittgenstein, the master of the deep and flawless sense. What is at stake in this conversation is the meaning that is revealed when we look at the world. The world in turn allows us to make clear statements. The conversation takes place with Wittgenstein because only he can understand the significance of the statement that one should keep silent about what one cannot speak of. The condition of possibility for this conversation is not a physical one, which in Wittgenstein's view can be described as non-existent and thus, so to speak, as reality, but it is the conversation over all the things about which he is silent. Yet these are things that somehow have the potential to be part of the world.

African ancestral spirit:	Well, Mr Wittgenstein, not being properly understood can be the punishment for disturbing the certainties of others.
Ludwig Wittgenstein:	What's that 'sulphur'?[1] And what is this superscript after the word?
African ancestral spirit:	No sulphur, Mr Philosopher, but a fact, if I may freely quote you, of course. I mean, I have only referred you to one fact and suggested how the facts contained therein are connected. I mean that there are people who claim to know what the world looks like. They get their authority from science. By virtue of their beliefs, these people know what is right or wrong in the world. And if there are other people who lead their lives in a way that is difficult to categorize, they feel misunderstood. That's what I meant. The superscript, that is Mr Macamo.
Ludwig Wittgenstein:	I don't get it.
African ancestral spirit:	What now, the fact or the superscript?
Ludwig Wittgenstein:	Both. Why is the sum of the facts you have listed a fact and what does this Mr Macamo have to do with the superscript?
African ancestral spirit:	Well, Mr Macamo is a footnote, I mean, this conversation is not taking place in reality, but we are being used by him for purposes that only he understands. He is the glass, and we are the brain, or vice versa. Whatever! He lets us say things that he wants to say to the scientific world about his research. He uses these superscript numbers to make things more precise, that we can use in our 'conversation'. It's best to ignore him. Now, the issue at hand, it's a long story, and it's what we're going to discuss. You know, there are scientists in the non-European region who claim that we are a Western invention …
Ludwig Wittgenstein:	Wait a minute, please, who's *we*?
African ancestral spirit:	We are the people who are not Europeans. The 'rest', so to speak. In any case, what these scientists mean by this is that the Europeans and North Americans have an idea of us

which they can assert as the truth with their technological, economic and political superiority. It is not necessarily the truth, but it is the only way to render us visible.[2] You don't really need to understand this, this is the talk of our children, who think they can resist the West by deconstructing it.

Ludwig Wittgenstein: *Deconstruct?*

African ancestral spirit: Anyway, so, what I'm really interested in is the relationship between the norm and the reality …

Ludwig Wittgenstein: Wait, wait a minute! What makes you think you can discuss these things with me? I mean, what makes this Mr Macamo think I'm qualified to discuss such things?

African ancestral spirit: Well, who knows, I mean, I guess you're suited for that because you once wrote interesting comments about Frazer's *The Golden Bough* that our creator found to be true.[3]

Ludwig Wittgenstein: Our creator?

African ancestral spirit: Mr Macamo …

Ludwig Wittgenstein: Uh-huh. But when I wrote those notes, I wasn't thinking about norm and reality.

African ancestral spirit: But, I mean, the subject was implied in it. You have rightly pointed out that the same natives who are confronted with irrational thinking according to Frazer – for example, because they stick needles into a doll and think that they are actually hurting a person – that these natives not only imagine their houses but also build them; when they are hungry, they do not imagine that they are full, but eat …

Ludwig Wittgenstein: Well, that. Yeah, you're right. With that I wanted to point out, on the one hand, that language does not necessarily reflect reality; but on the other hand I wanted to affirm that there is a difference between reality and the world, whereby the truth of our statements is not exhausted in the extent to which they are consistent with the world.

African ancestral spirit:	Right. Because there is a problem with the way in which the social sciences deal with worlds with which we are not familiar. By familiarity, of course, I don't just mean knowledge of certain facts but also the possession of the appropriate vocabulary that can be used to talk about them. I think there is a tension between Western familiarity on the one hand and the realities that are possible outside the Western experience on the other.[4]
Ludwig Wittgenstein:	For an ancestral spirit, you speak in a very complicated manner. But I see your point. Your statement reminds me of my seventh sentence in the *Tractatus*: 'What you cannot speak of, you must remain silent about.' I dedicated it to my friend, David H. Pinsent.
African ancestral spirit:	Exactly. But it is precisely this inability to talk about what one cannot say anything about that characterizes the relationship between a Western-style social science and the non-Western object. The non-Western object is disturbing.
Ludwig Wittgenstein:	That's what you're getting at!
African ancestral spirit:	Yes. I am interested in the question of the significance of the experience of phenomena that are made by people and in areas that are outside the experiential space of a representative of Western social science. How can one talk about it? Can one? ... Following your lead, I would like to put forward the thesis that the non-Western world has the potential to be 'disruptive' because it evades explanation. Social science as a permanent fixture consists not only in describing reality but also in thinking about the terminology that makes descriptions possible. The more appropriate the conceptual apparatus describing reality appears, the greater the certainty can become that the reality described by the apparatus is not only historically conditioned

but actually corresponds to the order of things. Forms of appearance which reality can take on and which are not covered by the semantic fields of the conceptual apparatus can be quite disturbing. That is in my opinion a perspective on the concept and the phenomenon of 'disturbance' that is worth looking at more closely.

Ludwig Wittgenstein: Jesus Christ, you're driving heavy projectiles through the place!

African ancestral spirit: But still within the framework of what you have written yourself. You once said that understanding goes hand in hand with alienation.[5] By this I mean that 'disturbance' is a term that is full of preconditions and at the same time has no consequences. It is therefore filled with preconditions because it implies a natural or normal order which has only mockery, ridicule and sometimes even hatred and violence for certain events which do not fit into the order. It is often the case that it is not the order that is the problem but the conceptual apparatus with which this order is made perceptible. This terminology seems to me to be inflexible, because it declares the reality, which it can perceive and classify, to be the normal case. A disturbance is not conceivable without a normal case. If I may stick to the concept of order, I can consider that in sociology a stately order has been declared the normal case. This has led to the fact that generations of sociologists and Africa researchers have been educated to add derogatory adjectives to everything that does not fit into this concept: We speak of a weak, broken, collapsed and criminal state in Africa, to name but one example. The term 'disturbance' is also momentous because it cannot exist without the idea that there is a normal case. It therefore promotes, as a rule, a normative attitude, according to which, in the case of disorders, one deals with them with the aim of eliminating them.

Ludwig Wittgenstein:	I understand. David Hume, a so-called *long-dead White male* like me, would have said the following: *No ought follows from an is ...*
African ancestral spirit:	Exactly. Earlier I said that we are misunderstood because we disturb the certainty of the social sciences, confuse the norm with reality and presume to be able to explain everything, instead of first sounding out the limits of our own concepts. So we want to explain, that is, to show that something does not fit, why it may be justified to call this something disturbing. The angry non-Western academic notices that this attempt to explain does justice to neither the reality that has been declared normal by social science nor the disturbing events; it ends up being an attempt at rescuing the concept. It is an act of desperation that we are witnessing here, that is, a science that tries to save face confronted by fierce resistance offered by reality.
Ludwig Wittgenstein:	All right, I had already established this when I pleaded in my interpretation of language that we give priority to description.[6] But please tell me what you are getting at! Why do village elders always disguise their statements in riddles? Get to the point!

Back to the beginning

I claimed that the social transformation of the virus into a pandemic imposed a definition of the situation at odds with the real actual significance of the problem in Africa. This is the problem of norm and reality explored in the imaginary dialogue. Our language and, in particular, the language of the social sciences leave us very few options for describing the problem in ways that might be meaningful to Africans. If we say, as we should, that the pandemic renders visible Africa's precarious condition, we will be casting the continent in the usual manner as a problem to be solved. If we take comfort from the relatively mild consequences of the pandemic so far, we incur the risk of promoting a complacent and irresponsibly nativist attitude to a problem that has not yet run its course. There is a sense in which the pandemic exposes the fissures cracked open by a global system of inequality, the recognition of which does not empower Africans to make any change in their condition. They can only describe those fissures.

This leaves us with a paradox. It is the *paradox of disturbance*, that is, the condition of facing up to a disaster affecting the global structures which undermine one's own standing but being unable to exploit the disaster to one's advantage. As many have convincingly argued, the COVID-19 pandemic is a critical commentary not only on global structures but also on how they distribute the costs produced by their dysfunction. There does not seem to be any adequate vocabulary to address this paradox in meaningful ways for Africa. Africans are not to blame for this, of course. This is a description of the circumstances under which the continent was integrated into the world. These circumstances have confined Africa to the role of a residual category of the world. Africa is defined by all that it is not. The most radical manifestation of this condition is even the apparent impossibility for the continent to socially transform the virus into a genuine African problem. The confinement measures taken everywhere point to this difficulty. The foreign virus resists domestication by imposing alien solutions to the local havoc it is likely to wreak.

Notes

[1] Wittgenstein called 'sulphur' the illusion of the explanation that captivates people before they have understood what the meaning of a word is.

[2] Some concise examples from different regions: Said (1978), Mignolo (2005), Mudimbe (1988). Interestingly, all authors refer to Michel Foucault and his idea of a knowledge order with a claim to power.

[3] Wittgenstein commented on the book *The Golden Bough* by James Frazer in 1931. Some comments that did not find their way into the final manuscript include the following: 'I now believe that it would be right to begin my book with remarks about metaphysics as a kind of magic ;-) However, I must neither speak the word of magic nor make fun of it ;-) Of magic, the depth should be retained ;-) Yes, turning off magic has the character of magic itself here' (Wittgenstein, 1995, p v).

[4] This is basically a methodological problem. Jack Goody, the English ethnologist, has described it most succinctly by pointing out that empirical observations relating to all common terms should focus on the variables contained in the terms (Goody, 1996). Otherwise, there is a danger of making the conventional understanding of a term the measure of reality. In the study of slavery, for example, it is less helpful to use categorical differences such as slave and free man as a basis than to postulate different degrees of subjection, which can later help in the analysis to isolate the variable responsible for a particular relationship.

[5] Cf. Lölke (2001). Wittgenstein writes: 'I believe that the very reason why the undertaking of a declaration is misguided is because one only has to correctly compile what one knows, and not add anything to it, and the pacification that the declaration seeks to bring about is self-evident' (Wittgenstein, 1995, p 2; emphasis in original).

[6] Cf. Wittgenstein (2003) and Winch (1987).

References

Goody, J. (1996) *The East in the West*, Cambridge: Cambridge University Press.

Lölke, U. (2001) *Critical traditions: Africa. Philosophy as a Place of Decolonization*, Frankfurt am Main: IKO-Verlag.

Macamo, E. (2011) 'Afrika stört. Ein Totengespräch über Norm und Wirklichkeit in den Sozialwissenschaften', in J. Fleischhack and K. Rottmann (eds) *Störungen. Medien/Prozesse/Körper*, Berlin: Isa Lohmann-Siems Stiftung, 23–43.

Mignolo, W. (2005) *The Idea of Latin America*, London: Blackwell Publishing.

Mudimbe, V. (1988) *The Invention of Africa: Gnosis, Philosophy and the Order of Knowledge*, London: James Currey.

Said, E.W. (1978) *Orientalism*, New York: Pantheon Books.

Winch, P. (1987) *Trying to Make Sense*, Oxford: Basil Blackwell.

Wittgenstein, L. (1995) *Remarks on Frazer's Golden Bough*, Harleston: Rush Rhees.

Wittgenstein, L. (2003) *Philosophische Untersuchungen*, Frankfurt am Main: Suhrkamp Verlag KG.

33

We Are All Mortal: From the Empty Signifier to the Open Nature of History

Rita Laura Segato

May the pandemic illuminate the difference between what matters and what doesn't.

What is or is not the pandemic and where does it lead us?

A significant number of articles circulated during the first year of the pandemic, many of them written by influential authors. They attempt to examine two different aspects of the pandemic. One group makes bets on what may have been the origin of the virus, dividing itself between those who adhere to conspiracy theory and the others who, without necessarily knowing it, give continuity to what Marx already called the 'metabolic rift' or imbalance in the relationship between humans and nature. I will address here the other set of interpretations, devoted to understanding and analysing the *meaning* and use of the *pandemic in the future*. Each of them is derived from and presupposed by a political project and a system of values that they defend.

I see COVID-19 as Ernesto Laclau saw the figure of Perón in Argentina's politics: as an 'empty signifier', to which various political projects extended their discursive network. I also see it as an event that gives rise to a 'Rashomon effect', evoking here the way in which the theme of Kurosawa's classic film has been used in social sciences: the same crime described from four different perspectives of interest. But above all, I see it as an instance of what Lacan called the 'irruption of the real', the imaginary that traps our vision of the world or the grid through which we filter the entities that will be part of our perception in a fine cloth that wraps us. Beyond it lies the 'real', to use Lacan's term: nature as it is, including our own nature.

The virus is nothing but an instance of the unfolding of this other level, natural history, the unpredictable march of nature, its contingent unfolding, its drift. Organisms consolidate, last and disappear. Our species will also follow this uncertain destiny or, with improbable luck, will have the longevity of the cockroach, although it will be difficult, since the cockroach is characterized by requiring almost nothing. It is important to accept the idea that, even if this virus is a result of human manipulation in laboratories or, as it certainly is, a consequence of the abusive way in which the species has treated its environment, it is still an event of nature.

Why? Because we are part of that same nature, and even though we are capable, as a species, of manipulating microorganisms and provoking the advent of a new era such as the Anthropocene, we have our place there, we are part of that scene that we call 'nature'. Our biochemical interactions belong to and play a role in a scene all of which is interior to the great nest we inhabit, even if Western thought has pressured us to withdraw from that contained, interdependent and dependent position. To think this way is not easy for us, because we are inside the Cartesian logic of subject-object, head-body, mind-*res extensa*. The reification and externalization of life is our evil.[1]

By making that manoeuvre, Western thinking cancelled out two annoyances. One is the *temporality of life*, with its inherent lack of control and the limit it places on the attempt to manage it. Time, which is nothing more than the time of organisms, of the earth itself as a great organism and of the species itself as part of that great terrestrial womb, challenges the omnipotence of the West, its obsession with administering events, what I have elsewhere called its *neurosis of control*.

The other obsession of colonial-modern and Western thought is its placing us, as a species, in the position of omnipotence of the one who knows and can manipulate life, the Cartesian manoeuvre of formulating the res extensa, *life as a thing*, and catapulting us out of it. Therefore, in the face of this pandemic, we have the opportunity to save ourselves cognitively from this trap and to understand that, even if it is the effect of our interference, the virus that is making us sick is, in any case, a *natural event*, derived from that winding and unpredictable event that is time. And it is so because the virus results from an interaction within the realm of nature, of whose scene we are part. The jump of a virus from animals to humans must be read in this way, which places us in this position of being part of the natural world with its vagaries, which many times we believe to be dominated. A whole different availability for life and for the inevitability of death arises from a consciousness that accepts being a subordinate part of the natural order. Cartesian exteriority, far from being universal, leads to a faulty reading typical of the West, and has consequences.

One great theme is that of the future, also linked to the anarchic dimension of time. The three images of which I speak allow me to venture that a great *bewilderment* has occurred in the world in the face of this rare plague of archaic behaviour. In the face of this bewilderment, the three images I attribute to it (these being: the absence of meaning and intentionality of its own; its Rashomon-like provocation; and its radical reality independent of our bets) allow me to speak of a future battle for the imposition of an order on this bewilderment. Every teleological gamble hides a discourse of moral supremacy, and every discourse of moral supremacy has an authoritarian vocation.

The battle to narrate the future

Who, then, will have the *permission to narrate it* in the future, to use Edward Said's expression, or who will have the *right to narrate it*, using here the words of Homi Bhabha? These three theoretical figures then allow us to foresee that there will be a battle to decide which network of meanings, which discourses and which narratives will be capable of trapping the event that challenges us, in order to install the policies that will shape the world after. However, as I have already argued, the only utopia that has survived the successive 'revolutionary' failures in their attempt to reorient the path of the peoples is the absolute unpredictability of the future: we never know where or how the wind of history will blow. The only thing left for us to do is to play our part, in accordance with our convictions and responsibilities.

We have already seen the pre-announcement of the contest at the gates, and this text is also, inevitably, included. Many meshes of meaning have been stretched out to catch nature's time. Already, at the beginning, we witnessed the divergence of two well-known analysts, Slavoj Žižek and Byung-Chul Han: utopia and dystopia in confrontation at the same time, as omens.

From there, hundreds of attributions of meaning circulated in many texts, but the virus exceeds them in its uncertainty and the bewilderment into which it has plunged humanity. This is very important to consider because it leads us to the opening of history, to its unpredictability and to the acceptance of the implacable limits imposed on our capacity to control it, to order it. The virus testifies to the vitality and constant transformation of life, its irrepressible character. It demonstrates the vitality of nature, with us inside of it. It has shown a reality that exceeds us and overcomes all voluntarism. The West thus faces what constitutes the supreme difficulty of the colonial-modern world, because the goal par excellence of the Eurocentric historical project is domination, reification and control of life. To corner and block all unforeseen events, all improvisation has been its attempt and relative progressive triumph.

This virus and all those that preceded it and will come later present a freedom that makes this civilizing proposal tremble even more than death itself. An unknown freedom. This being the case, the order of the day could only be to retreat in order to 'take the fish out of water', to leave the new being without a host, until its dangerousness wants to 'take the curve', or a vaccine emerges from the hands of the role we represent in this great scene: the environmental scene. What we know works, more than control, is 'adaptation', flexibility and malleability of the behaviours and a capacity for response that is part of the same drama of which we are part. A great lesson is given by this tiny being to the West.

The initial undeniable impact of the virus was difficult to contain and conceal in the media discourse, because its appearance on the scene was frankly democratic. It attacked first and with great force the two greatest powers in the world, and the rich and comfortable Europe. At this very moment it is embarrassing the 'Big Apple' and the whole so-called developed world by showing that they lack what they seemed to have: security for their people and a capacity for mass and general care for their inhabitants. It attacked noblemen, high-ranking politicians and businessmen from powerful corporations. It generated surprising casualties among the cosmopolitan elites. Through the very lens of the media, it showed the world that, without a doubt, *we are all mortal*. It behaved like an immigrant around whom no one puts up fences. It led Henry Kissinger himself to talk about the end of US hegemony.

It is possible to say that, at least for a while, the virus, an event of nature, has given a lesson in democracy. In Latin America, meanwhile, it is possible to guess an expectant and barely interdicted terror, a half-truth about what we know may happen when the virus finally tears down the border that shields the inclusion of exclusion. In our continent, due to quarantine, exclusion penalizes those who live rigorously from day to day because of their need for daily income.

Returning to the 'futurology' practised by notable authors, the attempts to capture the meanings of the pandemic have included, so far at least, the following interpretations.

First, the virus will make it possible to tear down the neoliberal illusion and abandon selfish accumulation, because without solidarity and without supplier states we won't be saved. Without a state that guarantees protection and delivery of resources to those who have less, it will not be possible to continue life. The position, in this case, is that we will understand that it is necessary to place accumulation at the disposal of the people who need it to survive, and the rulers will be led in the future to disobey the fundamental precept on which capitalism rests.

The second circulating forecast could be described as 'Agambenian' and is pre-announced by dystopian science fiction. We are entering a laboratory of experimentation on a large scale that will allow spying on the world population through means of digital control and artificial intelligence with new infallible technologies. Everything will be informed by every living being and the threat of a state of exception of unknown magnitude will plague humanity.

Rulers like Trump and Bolsonaro seem to adhere, without stating it reflectively, to a third prediction related to the unsaid about the expected massacre when the virus crosses the great border with slums and favelas. A subtext of their discourse and action seems to agree with the extermination of the leftovers of the economic system, to bend to the law of survival of the strongest, of the most apt. A neo-Malthusian and neo-Darwinian social perspective is present here, a totalitarian ideology – in Hannah Arendt's definition of ideology – whose value affirms that whoever is not adapted to survival in certain circumstances, or whoever can harm the national project as defined by the perspective in power, must perish. The virus, seen from this ideology, fits in with the 'final solution' characteristic of totalitarianism: what is useless, in the sense that it does not serve an ideology, should not live. This position, which is ideological and responds to the political project of a sector of interests, should not be confused with an approach such as that of Germany, for example, which diverges from the strategy of rigorous quarantine and extinction of the virus through the absolute restriction of human hosts, and allows the movement of people betting on the natural decline of the infectious power of the virus through increasing human immunity. This last approach is not the same as the one proposed by the social neo-Darwinism, because the states that propose it, such as Germany and Sweden, offer greater medical care and equipment to reduce the lethality of the virus. Even so, doubts have already arisen about the bet on the natural development of human immunity, which will undoubtedly put the lives of many people at risk, and the countries that have adopted this strategy are abandoning it.

The fourth interpretation adheres to the importance of a warlike approach and a drift towards a fascist attitude. Thus, one trains to act on the basis of the existence of an enemy. The frenzy of the enemy rears its head. Any policy mounted on the assumption of the existence of a common enemy necessarily tends towards fascism. Enmity and warmongering become the raison d'être of politics. The virus allows the security forces to act within that perspective, and punitive and extermination logics are unleashed. A part of the population whose profile in politics and citizenship has these characteristics has been framed today in this reading of the pandemic. There are a number of examples of the expression of animosity and extreme aggression against neighbours who work in hospitals, whether they are doctors or nurses, against people who have come from abroad or people who are sick. Anger and hatred towards anyone associated with the plague is rampant among reactionary sectors of society, which will try, in the future, to impose that social order in the face of what they can define as a 'public threat': the sick, migrants, non-Whites, criminals, 'immorals' and so forth.

The fifth prediction is that, in the end, we will have to persuade everyone of – and impose on them – the idea that the earth, by whatever name it is called, will have shown us its limit and will have proved that the industrial exploitation of nature is leading us in a suicidal direction. Rich and poor, according to those who think this way, will have learned what the indigenous peoples have repeated to us so many times: 'The earth does not belong to us; we belong to the earth'.

A sixth position is that the virus has come to impose a feminist perspective on the world: to retie the knots of communal life with its law of reciprocity and mutual aid, to enter into the 'historical project of links' with its idiosyncratic goal of happiness and fulfilment, to recover the politicization of the domestic, to domesticate management, to make management equivalent to care and to make care its main task. That is what I have called in these days a 'maternal state', as differing from that patriarchal, bureaucratic, distant and colonial state that our history has accustomed us to distrust.

Disturbance of omnipotence and lucidity of precariousness

Let's be honest, all these bets can be perfectly convincing, depending on which historical project you adhere to and which interests you represent. They are all equally interesting and smart, but they are all omnipotent, in the sense that they intend, beforehand, to win in the roulette of time. They all suffer from the control neurosis of the West in its effort to frame history in a predictable direction. They show the inculcated *inability to be*, evoking here inevitably the rescue of the power of time in its flow undertaken by the Argentinean philosopher Rodolfo Kusch, when he substituted the Heideggerian being for the Andean *being standing*.

Problems that already existed have been exacerbated and have become more visible, have emerged and torn a surface that previously did not give them access. The historical project of capital, and its structure manifested in what I have called the 'historical project of things', as opposed to the 'historical project of links', had effectively banned the consciousness of finitude. It needed to place death on a distant planet. But today we have a great media funeral, hundreds of coffins shamelessly exposed. It is possible that this diverts our desire in another direction from what we are used to: What importance could the marks have, before the presence of Death in the neighbourhood? Let's make ourselves comfortable. Anyway …

It turns out, moreover, that plagues are always biblical, pedagogical and instructive. Suddenly, it is possible to ask oneself if the institutional order and the economic plant to which it was responding were not fictional, if the universe we inhabited was not already suffering from an unsustainable precariousness. More than the deaths that it causes, since we have already seen many deaths, but they have not stopped the world, it is the bewilderment, lack of control and unpredictability that the microscopic creature has introduced that come to disturb the credibility of the system. For example, it has come to demonstrate that reality can be changed practically 'in one stroke' by the president. Here there is a *citizen pedagogy*: nothing is immovable; everything can be altered with enough political will. In terms of life management, we can see that it is possible to transform the world into a great laboratory in which a marvellous experiment is carried out. And that is what makes the owners of the planet feel uncomfortable.

Let no one come and tell us now that 'it is not possible to try other ways of being in society' or other ways of managing wealth: production can be stopped, just as trade can be stopped. We are witnessing a phenomenal act of disobedience without being able to guess what the exit route will be. The world has been transformed into a vast laboratory where an experiment seems to be able to reinvent reality. It is suddenly revealed that capital is not a machine that is independent of political will. We are now faced with the evidence that the owners of wealth and their managers have always sought to hide: the key to the economy is politics, and *the laws of capital are not the laws of nature*.

We are facing an unusual state of exception which, conversely, has tightened the lever that suspends the operation of the great power plant that we confused with the divine order: a pseudo-divine order, an imposture whose perfect metaphor is the famous biblical golden calf, the false god that disoriented the people of Israel in their journey to Canaan; a great plague came about by placing a false god in the place of the true one. Capital is the false god; Mother Earth is the true one. And these are the myths in the great episteme of the species: they always guide us in reading the present.

The here and now: recovering the fabric of communal reciprocity

Protecting life, taking care of it in a here and now, however it develops, in an absolute present, is all that matters. Not so, the prognoses and declarations of moral principle and intention, for, as I have argued elsewhere, in this apocalyptic phase of capital the discourse of moral persuasion has become innocuous in the face of the *pedagogy of cruelty* that has inoculated our hearts and consciences with the most effective antidote that cancels the empathic perception of the suffering of others.

Moreover, future guidelines based on a supposed general idea of goodness are risky: in the face of any flaw in the clause we have established, the whole construction will crack; any disappointment, and the structure we have carefully built will seem to collapse. Working on prediction is dangerous, for we have no clear data about the present or the future. We do not know precisely what threatens us. What is important is to learn how to be, to take care as much as possible and to resist the moving ground under our feet. I have suggested elsewhere that politics in a feminine key is better suited to this type of contingency in which saving lives is all that matters.

On more than one occasion I have presented the state as the last stage in the history of patriarchy. I have said that when the male political task ceases to be one between two political tasks, and the space where it is executed ceases to be one between two spaces – the public and the domestic, each with its own style of management – to become an encompassing public sphere and the unique agora of any discourse that claims to be endowed with politics, that is, to be capable of impacting the collective destiny, at that moment, the position of women, now kidnapped in the capsule of the nuclear family, collapses to the quality of margin and rest, expropriated from all politics.

However, it occurs to me that the *Albertian approach*, its way of speaking to us, is, at least in this circumstance, a domestic management of the nation. 'Maternal', I have said publicly, because the maternal and paternal are independent of the body in which they are deposited, as the useful and vilified category 'gender' has taught us for some time, a great formulation of feminism that has allowed us to de-essentialize and de-biologize roles and sexualities. At the beginning of the pandemic, Alberto Fernandez asked us to unite, generating an uncommon experience in my home country, Argentina. He asked us to generate community, to put aside discord and to try to reinitialize in order to face the unknown, saying that he will protect us and that he will consider material needs in their inequality.

That is why I have said that he seemed to embody, at the beginning of his government, a maternal state, that is, a domestic management, as an innovation. I cannot fail to recall here the two notions of homeland to which Jean Améry's wonderful essay *How Much Home Does a Person Need?* refers: the patriarchal, warlike, defensive, walled-up homeland, and the maternal, hospitable, host homeland. Nordic languages have two different words for them: *vaterland* or *fatherland* on one hand, and *heimat, homeland*, on the other. It is essential to emphasize this event, the Albertian difference, because by theorizing, we not only describe the events but we also prescribe them, make them be, give them reality, encourage them towards a path. We have to identify and name the novelties that appear in the unknown scene of the present.

More than a fantasy of the future, we must pay attention to what is in fact there, the proposals and practices that emerge, what people are concretely doing and inventing. What is happening here and now around us and among us? Again: politics from a feminine perspective, as I have said on other occasions, is topical and not utopian, practical and not bureaucratic. In this vigil, ways of sustaining life that were in the background are slowly being rekindled. We are realizing that at least part of the capacity for subsistence must necessarily remain in the hands of the people themselves. The memory of 2001 resurfaces in Argentina. Our own *space odyssey* unhappily archived. A very great sense of loss is experienced when we realize that, at the moment when the state efficiently retakes the reins of the national economy and the period of great need is overcome, that entire popular economy disintegrates. In the famine of 2001 collective structures emerged, individualism receded and the country went through a mutation that is still felt today. But when the problem of immediate material needs was resolved, nothing promoted the permanence of those operative structures that had been created.

I have defended the notion that the good state is a state that restores community jurisdiction, protects production and local and regional trade and is capable of setting off on an amphibious path: it cannot remove itself from the global market because the resources for its public policies come from its dividends, but neither should it abandon the self-sustainability of communities, food sovereignty and the local, rooted trade, which, as in the present case, is once again crucial for survival. A good state travels between the two paths and shields the more fragile one, so that its knowledge, its own trade circuits, its technologies of sociability and its products are not lost, nor is its autonomy. We see again today how the very small vegetable gardens in balconies, corridors, galleries and patios, the exchange of their products between neighbours, resurface around us; the government proposes community quarantines in neighbourhoods that are closed as communes; the collectives take up their role again, they make collections, they organize themselves so that people can eat, and my neighbours in Santelmeña ask me every day what I need. Let us not forget the millions of Hindus 'walking home', a place that no one should ever be forced to leave. We see the anxiety of returning to the land everywhere, and we have an obligation to understand this visceral, atavistic movement of returning home.

The problem that remains is how to guarantee that this experience is recorded in the discourses of post-pandemic time and remains audible so that the fantasy of normality and inalterability that captured us is not brought back; how to retain the experience of a desire that, at least during this interval, was freely directed towards other forms of satisfaction and fulfilment. There will be skilful forces, very well instructed, studying the subject in order to close that memory, banish it, leave it well closed, and in this way guarantee the continuity of a 'normality' that the pandemic had interrupted. How can we be prepared so that forgetting does not happen? How can we prevent the loss of experience accumulated from happening again?

Note

1   I thank my daughter, Jocelina Laura de Carvalho Segato, for the countless hours of conversation about the cognitive and epistemological errors of speciesism.

34

The COVID-19 Pandemic and
the Crisis of Care

Karina Batthyány

COVID-19, like all pandemics, disrupts our customary ways of living. It is a health crisis that has revealed what feminist currents have long considered central for rethinking a project centred around life: that we are all interdependent. A the same time, the rapid spread of COVID-19 and the institutional measures implemented in most countries to produce social isolation have underlined one of the weakest links in our society: care.

People need goods, services and care to survive. Care is relational and interdependent, and all of us have required or will require care at some moment in our lives, just as all of us have cared for or will care for someone in the stages of our existence. People need food, clothing, shelter, assistance, support and company, in that we all experience injury, illness, early childhood and probably old age.

In spite of this, however, one of the lessons to be learned from the COVID-19 health emergency refers to the invisibility of care. We wonder how the changes proposed by national measures are affecting individuals' daily lives. The situation presents an opportunity for us to ask in this chapter (and in fact this has also been asked by certain members of the media and policymakers) about what has happened to care in the framework of a health emergency.

Complexity and women

For a structural problem of this magnitude, solutions are obviously not simple. An historical approach has been to ignore the centrality of care, assuming that the incorporation of women into productive work will redistribute the workload on its own. Evidence proves, however, that the result has been a double workload for women. We know from the study of gender and care that the so-called productive economy is supported by the work of caregiving (neither recognized nor paid), often invisible. As we know, in Latin America, women perform approximately 80 percent of unpaid caregiving and most paid caregiving. A large part of total care, therefore, is provided by women.

In homes around the world, most unpaid work is carried out by women and girls. But in our region, imbalance in the distribution of domestic tasks and personal caregiving is much worse than in other places. If we analyse the total time devoted to unpaid work in the home, women in Latin America and the Caribbean contribute 73 percent, and men the remaining 27 percent. In contrast, the contribution of men is 44 percent in Sweden, 38 percent in the United States, and 39 percent in China.

Some of the proposed measures in the current crisis assume isolation in domestic settings and a search for individual care solutions within each household: individual solutions mediated by resources of diverse types. Such measures return to the inside of the home and the solutions that each home devises.

The need to close educational and caregiving establishments has revealed that workdays are not compatible with the care of children, teenagers and dependent adults. If we consider the supervision of children's schoolwork at home, the amount of unpaid caregiving at home increases exponentially.

Instructions issued for the total social isolation of individuals over 60 or 65 years of age, depending on the country, remind us that, in our region, thousands of members of this segment of the population lack networks of support, caregivers and resources.

Informal work and women

According to figures from the International Labour Organization, 126 million women – about half of the female population – perform informal work in Latin America and the Caribbean. This statistic translates into consequences that include employment instability, low incomes and the absence of essential mechanisms of protection in a crisis such as the one we are currently experiencing.

Many countries in my region, Latin America, register extremely high levels of informal work. In Bolivia, Guatemala and Peru, 83 percent of all women have informal employment, with no type of social security coverage or protection provided by labour legislation. In the region as a whole, almost 40 percent of working women are employed in commerce, restaurants, hotels or domestic work. In the economic crisis that has been unleashed by the current health emergency, these sectors are the most affected, and the jobs they contain are the least protected. How can these women possibly stay at home? How can these women possibly remain in their productive role if their dependents are confined at home?

Almost one-fourth of all employed women in the region provide care in households other than their own. In spite of past efforts and achievements in formalizing their employment conditions, most of these workers are in very precarious employment conditions, without access to social security. Most of them have continued to work despite recommendations for the general population to stay at home; in some cases, they have been sent home, but without pay.

Caring at home

We should also remember that in Latin America, one-half of all physicians and more than 80 percent of nurses are women: the highest percentages in the world. This occupational segregation by gender is not accidental, as it is influenced by the gender norms that make health professions socially acceptable for women: an extension of work in the home.

In the current crisis, part of the unpaid domestic work that exposes women to the greatest risk of infection is their role in caring for the sick at home. The Pan American Health Organization (2021) has stated that 80 percent of the population's healthcare is provided at home, and various national studies have concluded that such care is provided primarily by the women in those homes. With the pandemic, demands will increase for the care of the sick and the elderly.

To solve the care crisis, we need a new idea of public administration that understands that personal interdependence is part of community life. The solution is not simply a more equal distribution of caregiving between men and women. Rather, the importance and value of caregivers must be recognized and provided by society, with the participation of the state.

The COVID-19 emergency draws new attention to the issue of the social organization of care. In addition to supporting all measures and actions that emphasize people rather than the market in dealing with the pandemic, we must be able to implement an emphasis on care, and not on the market, as the central organizing axis of community life. The crisis has made manifest that now is the time to begin thinking about new forms of social organization in general, in which the social organization of care plays a central role.

Faced with governments that implement different measures, individuals who cannot be cared for by members of the population at greatest risk (such as the grandmothers who provide a large part of childcare), poor wage-earning women without job protection and collapsed medical services, we must think urgently about new ways of managing care.

The crisis of care will have another and no less dire consequence: the difficulty for women of joining or continuing in the workplace under the same conditions as men. Taking into account that the greatest economic repercussions of this emergency will be suffered by unprotected, informal workers who work by the day, we can affirm that the pandemic will probably make women poorer and more vulnerable.

We have seen this outcome before in situations involving natural disasters. How will the state approach the consequences of the loss of employment, given the overwhelming need for care? What measures can be implemented by the state, by companies and by workers to promote co-responsibility in domestic work and care in situations of confinement at home?

Conclusion

The only total, effective response to national crises is provided by universal, public and free institutions in common and collective locations. Yet in the current situation of alarm, governments in general have called on individual responsibility to deal with a structural crisis, revealing the fragilities of public systems for serving dependent individuals. The inability of states and governments to discern the structural dimension of care causes great concern.

Women will continue to be those most affected by unpaid caregiving, especially in times of crisis. As we've mentioned, due to the overloading of health systems and the closure of schools, the work of caregiving has fallen mainly on the shoulders of women. Measures are needed to break away from traditional patterns and prevent disproportionate burdens for women.

We must determine ways to distribute the crisis so that not only women sustain the functioning of society in critical moments. This implies constructing, among other elements, an alternate view of our model of interaction, an alternative view based on the real – not simply formal – and irrevocable equality of men and women. A return to the political dimension of daily life is the road to be taken. In the COVID-19 pandemic, the crisis of care has been revealed once again, although not the central concern of those now implementing measures to slow the spread of infection.

References
Pan American Health Organization (2021) *Gendered Health Analysis. COVID-19 in the Americas*, Washington, DC: PAHO.

PART VI

Post-Pandemic Transitions and Futures in Contention

35

Global Chaos and
the New Geopolitics of Power
and Resistances

Breno Bringel

We are living in a moment of *global chaos*. Chaos does not mean the complete absence of some kind of order, but suggests a level of turbulence, fragility and contemporary geopolitical uncertainty in the face of multiple 'global risks' and possible destinations. Unpredictability and instability become the norm. This refers not only to greater volatility in the face of threats, but also to the dynamics of political forces and contemporary capitalism.

The world order that emerged with the fall of the Berlin Wall sought to expand formal democracy in the world (despite how often the major powers destabilized and interrupted it whenever they thought it was necessary) hand in hand with neoliberal globalization, in a kind of 'global social-liberalism' (Domingues, 2019). A narrative of global 'prosperity' and 'stability' was created confining democracy to neoliberal capitalism. This strategy was being challenged even before the pandemic, in light of the prospect that the international market can hold up well even with authoritarian drifts, neo-fascism and constant violations of individual rights.

The pandemic exacerbated this scenario, but also opened up new possibilities. As a new historical and geopolitical turning point seems to emerge, it would then be necessary to discuss some of the main emerging geopolitical trends and patterns, as well as the contentious scenarios in dispute at the global level. That is the focus of this chapter. On the one hand, I will seek to outline some of the main reconfigurations of the geopolitics of power, including the process of (de)globalization and systemic accommodation. On the other hand, I will analyse the redefinition of the geopolitics of resistances and alternatives since the beginning of the pandemic, seeking to explore, in a relational way, the role of social movements and its dispute of meanings and horizons among social, political and economic actors.

New trends in global power: neither de-globalization nor the end of capitalist globalization

I suggest that we are not facing the end of globalization and the emergence of 'de-globalization', as many authors have proposed, although we are possibly facing the end of capitalist globalization as we know it. The degree of radicalization of the territorial and financial expansion of capital during the last decades has been made possible by the creation of an agreement championed by the West with the United States at the helm (even as its hegemony is on the decline) which has allowed for the creation of a dominant narrative of growth. This was attuned to the unlimited expansion of transnational companies and to the approval of diverse groups that hold power and national and international organizations.

Its unfolding took place, as is well known, by removing all barriers in accordance with a grammar of deregulation, flexibilization and liberalization that secured neoliberalism's place around the world while destroying nature, the environment and social life. With it came a process of cultural struggle to entrench neoliberal globalization as a model that was not only economic but also societal.

Despite intense criticism of the alter-globalization movement, the emergence of a wide range of resistance movements and the extent to which the 2008 crisis uncovered the most tragic and lethal dimension of financial capitalism and globalization, the political response was not an alternative to this model but a radicalization of it. The losses were shared with the entire population and states applied adjustment policies and austerity while bailing out the banks, which in turn privatized the benefits. Capitalist globalization was thus able to follow its course of accumulation and plunder, deepening the extractive model.

The recent scenario, amplified in times of pandemic, seems to be a little different: among the different sectors of the right and extreme-right, 'anti-globalists' and nationalist positions emerge everywhere, whether in the core of the system, in the 'emerging powers' or in peripheral countries, seeking to reorganize capitalism in a more closed and authoritarian way. There is no single strategy. In fact, Reyes and Bárcena (2020) show how the three main hubs of capitalist globalization have followed different strategies in recent years. The Trump administration in the United States promoted protectionist policies,[1] while at the same time strengthening the trade war with China, which, like the European Union, seeks to strengthen global economic chains, although in different ways: in the first case by pushing an ambitious plan of economic expansion, in which the new Belt and Road

Initiative stands out; in the second by encouraging trade negotiations and bilateral investments.

Meanwhile, international trade, privatizations and capital flows may stumble over more public regulations proposed by different actors; dependence on inputs and products from other countries (visible in the pandemic with masks or respirators, but in reality extending, in many cases, to essential products) is prompting many countries to revise their policies, thinking about self-sufficiency or, at least, about reducing dependence.

Strategies for specialization and internationalization of production, on the other hand, are being reworked. Central states and transnational companies are reorganizing and increasing investments in technologies such as robotization and artificial intelligence. The world, therefore, seems to be moving, at least in the short term, not towards de-globalization, but towards a *more decentralized, reticular and ultra-technological capitalist globalization.*

Global value chains will change their directions in the face of the post-pandemic recession, although they will certainly continue to carry a lot of weight. The supranational institutional framework designed to facilitate the logic of accumulation may lose weight in the face of a more complex economic and political plot of accumulation in cities and in hierarchical networks.

Not everything is new. The pandemic may also accelerate and consolidate geopolitical changes and trends that have been triggering over the past decade. This is the case with the relative strengthening of China, which, even if it does not become a new hegemon in the short term, will play a more decisive role in the world system. Conversely, the gap between the centre and the periphery—or the Global North and Global South—tends to increase even more, due to both the centrality of technological development and the economic recession, which is always accompanied by a known macroeconomic prescription that is harmful to the countries of the Global South.

These scenarios and trends reinforce the fact that the current geopolitical order is predictably marked by greater rivalry in the interstate system and distrust between political and economic actors, but also by the deepening, on the part of dominant actors, of global militarization, which could strengthen *systemic chaos.* It seems unlikely that a new global governance of health can emerge, both because of the faltering role of the World Health Organization and because of the lack of commitment from the states themselves. International and multilateral organizations of all kinds have also failed to cope with the tragedy of the pandemic, either through silence, inability or incongruity. That is precisely why they need to reinvent themselves.

Most of the regional blocs have been weakened and, in some cases, dismantled and are without moral authority in the face of the pandemic. This is especially the case for the European Union, which, during the global health crisis, missed the opportunity to establish itself as an alternative both to the failure of the US's response to the pandemic but also in the face of the centralized and authoritarian Chinese model. Cracks and asymmetries within the bloc appeared again, making internal coordination and external projection difficult.

On the other hand, those regional projects that some years ago tried to project themselves in Latin America as counter-hegemonic regionalisms, such as UNASUR, CELAC and ALBA-TCP, went almost silent in the pandemic and were not large enough to build any relatively well-articulated supranational political response. In cases where they minimally functioned, as with the Asia-Pacific Economic Co-operation Forum (APEC), this occurred mainly through the objective of exchanging information and coordinating policies to stimulate trade and business. Thus, in some cases the pandemic may lead to the definitive burial of some regional projects. In others, regionalism will be reorganized as a result of broader geopolitical and geo-economic changes.

Contentious scales: virus contention and social protests

During the pandemic, national sentiments were mobilized, and a kind of 'transitional health Leviathan' (Svampa, 2020) emerged. With it came, in most cases, social and health protection policies, but also the military in the streets, states of emergency whereby everything was suspended and the establishment of a dangerous warlike narrative.

It turns out that permanent surveillance, from the most classic forms to digital tracking and the use of drones, control and management of big data (see Milan and Treré's contribution in Chapter 9 of this volume), new facial recognition devices and other sophisticated forms of social control, is deepening and not just to fight against the virus. Power concentration adopted to combat COVID-19 may even be necessary to enable public healthcare and 'protection' of the population. However, there is a very thin line between this and authoritarian practices.

The state responses were diverse, also varying according to the profiles of their political regimes (see the Part I of this volume). Nevertheless, the importance of the state and the national sphere coexisted with a strong appreciation of places and the local scale. All over the world, local initiatives have appeared, seeking to generate dynamics of mutual aid and to build neighbourhoods and communities to provide collective responses from below, based on people's daily needs. Given the difficulty of protesting in the streets at the beginning of the pandemic, much of the analysis of resistance in times of COVID-19 has tended to emphasize the crucial role of digital activism, but also the creativity of social movements in generating spaces and innovative proposals, as Donatella della Porta argues in her contribution in Chapter 16 of this book.

The press, as usual, tends to pay attention only to the most visible aspects of citizen action and social movements, such as flash mobs, *cacerolazos* (pot-banging protests) or online petitions. Although this has been an important part of the collective actions during the pandemic, it is essential to also note what happens under the surface, such as the self-organization and protection of workers who have had to continue working, either because they cannot survive without their income or because their jobs fall within what are considered 'essential services'.

Despite the restrictions and difficulties inherent to protests, uprisings can always occur through some catalytic event, even at unlikely times like during a pandemic. This was the case with the brutal murder of an African American man, George Floyd, by a White policeman in Minneapolis on 25 May 2020, which unleashed a wave of anti-racist protests not seen in the United States since the struggles for civil rights (see the complementary contributions of Bandana Purkayastha, John Krinsky and Hillary Caldwell, and Nara Roberta Silva in Chapters 8, 23 and 24 respectively).

Although it is common to hear that the elderly population is the most vulnerable to COVID-19, recent events have made it clear that being African American in the United States or Black in Brazil, and in so many other countries with strong structural racism, also means that you belong to a *high-risk social group*. In other words, the chances of dying from racism are greater than from COVID-19, which leads to a relative reduction in the costs of protest in times of pandemic.

Beyond material and immediate needs, the commitment of many groups and collectives to the community and to the reconstruction of social ties in times of deep individualization of society has been significant. They have also sought to bring to light care-work inequality, the defence of public services, solidarity and food and energy sovereignty. The lockdown of a third of the world's population has also served to spread a message that feminist movements have long insisted on: that the body must also be considered as a scale. In sum, social movements are challenging our societies in everyday life, as they place key questions at the centre of social life and personal experiences.

But the local scale was not only important in a transformational, non-institutional and, in some cases, anti-institutional sense. In those countries that failed to push forceful measures throughout their national territory, there was fierce dispute with local and regional leaders who, along with unofficial initiatives, took on the institutional lead in the fight against the pandemic. In other cases, progressive and leftist municipalities have also sought to promote collaborative care platforms, or have directly taken over the reins of crisis management.

This 'new return' of places and their importance to social resistance and social movements in times of COVID-19 cannot lead us to fall back into what had seemed to be overcome but which are once again widely circulating today: a new kind of division between the "local" and the "global", as if the global scale is the place of capitalism and the local scale the locus of resistance. As I have insisted (Bringel, 2015), in the past two decades the most *globalized* social struggles were the more *localized* ones. In other words, territorialized movements are the ones that have managed to internationalize more successfully.

This has been the case, for example, with the peasant and indigenous movements in Latin America since the 1990s, but also with the several experiences gathered around the alter-globalization movement and global and environmental justice struggles. However, the emergence of what I have defined as a new 'geopolitics of global indignation' (Bringel, 2013) during the last decade seems to have led to a lower intensity of organizational density among social struggles around the world.

That protests expand globally, or rather, through different countries, does not mean necessarily they are globalized in a strong sense – that they articulate with solid ties and build a truly global response to the capitalist world system. On the one hand, it is important to distinguish between global actions and global movements. On the other, taking into consideration emerging youth activism and new political cultures, it would be necessary to deepen the debate on the changes in the 'social movement form' and in the reconfigurations of contemporary activism. Although they continue to coexist with more traditional formats, they force us to question previous lenses used to grasp cognitive, generational and identity dislocations, with important repercussions on practices of resistance, political articulations and conceptions and horizons of social transformation.

Geopolitical scenarios and the struggles for the future

In the contemporary political debate, three different projects seem to dispute the direction of the post-pandemic world. The first one is that of *business as usual*, focused on GDP growth, predatory developmentalism and the search for new market niches to lift economies out of the crisis, including adjustment policies that require, once again, the sacrifice of the majority to maximize profits for the few. Second, we have *green capitalism,* usually associated with hegemonic ecological transitions, labelled or not as a 'Green New Deal', which initially emerged a decade ago in the United Kingdom, and has gained more prominence in recent years from the proposal of Democratic representatives in the United States to generate social and economic reforms to transform the energy sector. It has also spread very quickly since the beginning of the pandemic, with diverse appropriations by companies, international organizations and the European Union, which is creating its own 'European Green Deal'. And, finally, the *paradigm shift towards a new socioeconomic and ecological matrix*, proposed by several actors, ranging from scientists' communities and progressive religious movements to grassroots environmental movements and many anti-capitalist sectors that see degrowth, *buen vivir* ('good living') and more disruptive measures as the only possible alternative to neoliberal capitalism.

These projects seem to open up three possible scenarios, which do not occur in a 'pure' mode and can be interwoven in multiple ways, although all have their own logic: the *recovery* of the most aggressive logic of economic growth; the *adaptation* of capitalism to a 'cleaner' model, although socially unequal; or the *transition* to a new model, which implies a radical change in the ecological, social and economic matrix. In view of these projects and scenarios, it is essential to glimpse the implications of each of them.

The implementation of 'business as usual' implies an even greater strengthening of militarized globalization, of the biopolitics of authoritarian neoliberalism and of a model of destructive despoliation that would lead, predictably, to even more catastrophic scenarios, including wars and the deepening of the eco-social crisis. Terms such as 'return to normality' or even 'the new normal' justify and ensure this type of scenario, based on the anxiety of a large part of the population to recover their social lives and/ or employment.

In the case of adapting to a green capitalism, deep geopolitical and geo-economic adjustments seem likely. According to this vision, a 'green makeover', as a process that began with the 'adjectivation' of development as 'sustainable', is no longer enough. The situation now requires going a step further. And we know that, if capitalism accepts it, it does so not necessarily for the protection of the environment and for a radical change but because this may be a way to maximize profits. The new strategies of coexistence between the accumulation of capital and the environmentalist imaginary may give more room for autonomy to local politics, but it will also deepen North/South inequalities and environmental racism.

However, it is necessary to be fair: This predominantly 'adaptive' scenario is still strongly disputed. On the one hand, an important part of the dominant collectivities, especially in the North, understands that it is a path to follow. On the other hand, political forces that defend social justice and sustainability seek to stress it in various ways, towards a rupture and an integral reconfiguration. This is the case of proposals that claims for the 'decolonization' of the rationale of the Green New Deal regarding the South, or that critically discuss their assumptions, but ground them in other realities such as Latin America, Africa or Asia, as a basis for essential North/ South democratic dialogues.

Finally, the third scenario is the most difficult, but also the most necessary. The environment cannot be, once again, a banner for the saving of capitalism, but must be for the saving of humanity and the planet. It is the social movements themselves, the territorial experiences and a diversity of popular and political-intellectual struggles that drive this scenario, stretching the limits of the narratives of green capitalism. The transition towards a radical change in the eco-social matrix is a goal of several activists, communities and social movements today in both the Global North and Global South.

At this critical juncture, it is essential to create broad democratic and transformative platforms that bring together activists, committed citizens and social organizations that seek to prevent the destruction of ecosystems and the multiple inequalities brought to light by the COVID-19 crisis. There is not one recipe, but a multiplicity of routes to escape from capitalist globalization and to articulate a new globalization of trans-local movements. Many are already underway and seek to reinvent transnational solidarity and internationalism, expanding future horizons.

This is, for example, the spirit of countless proposals for popular eco-social transition. It's also what led to the creation of the Latin American Ecosocial and Intercultural Pact in June 2020.[2] One of the key points of this platform is the articulation of redistributive justice with environmental, ethnic and gender justice. To this end, concrete proposals, which also spread in other forums (such as solidary tax reform, cancellation of states' foreign debts and a universal basic income), are combined with broader horizons associated with building post-extractivist societies and economies, strengthening community spaces, care and information/communication for society.[3]

Moving in this direction will require sacrifices and drastic changes ranging from the personal sphere (changing habits, reducing consumption or reducing travel) to macro-policies (that make possible the relocation of food and a change in the food system or a radical decline in sectors such as oil, gas and mining), as well as in labour relations and social life as a whole. It also implies territorial resistances that seek new forms of articulation, connection and intelligibility within the global map of emerging struggles. Or, in other words, it will require developing, from the struggles of our time, a *global movement* that can challenge the directions of this *new alter-globalization moment*. Only then will we move from a destructive globalization to a 'pluriverse' one (Kothari et al, 2019). Only then will other possible worlds emerge.

Notes

[1] Biden must seek to overcome populist nationalism with internationalist liberalism, which supports free trade and embraces globalization. However, it is not simply a question of restoring the Obama administration's foreign policy, since the internal political tensions are multiple and the world is quite different today.

[2] More information about this initiative can be found here: https://pactoecosocialdelsur.com/

[3] In a recent text published in *Foreign Policy in Focus*, John Feffer tried to synthesize some public debates of the Southern Ecosocial Pact on how to build post-extractivist futures: https://fpif.org/building-a-post-extractivist-future-for-latin-america/

References

Bringel, B. (2013) 'Brazil within the geopolitics of global outrage', *Global Dialogue, Magazine of the International Sociological Association*, [online] 1 July, available from: http://globaldialogue.isa-sociology.org/brazil-within-the-geopolitics-of-global-outrage/

Bringel, B. (2015) 'Social movements and contemporary modernity: Internationalism and patterns of global contestation', in B. Bringel and J.M. Domingues (eds) *Global Modernity and Social Contestation*, London: Sage, 122–38.

Domingues, J.M. (2019) 'Social liberalism and global domination', in H. Cairo and B. Bringel (eds) *Critical Geopolitics and Regional (Re) Configurations: Interregionalism and Transnationalism between Latin America and Europe*, London: Routledge, 49–62.

Kothari, A., Salleh, A., Escobar, A., Demaria, F. and Acosta, A. (eds) (2019) *Pluriverse: A Post-Development Dictionary*, New Delhi: Tulika Books.

Reyes, L.G. and Bárcena, L. (2020) '¿Ha empezado el fin de la globalización?', *El Salto*, 3 June.

Svampa, M. (2020) 'Reflexiones para un mundo post-coronavirus', *Revista Nueva Sociedad*, April.

36

Denialism, 'Gattopardism' and Transitionism

Boaventura de Sousa Santos

The COVID-19 pandemic has called into question many of the political certitudes that seemed to have been consolidated over the past forty years, especially in what is known as the Global North. The main certitudes were the following: capitalism's final victory over its great historical competitor Soviet socialism; the primacy of markets in regulating not only the economy but social life as well, with the consequent privatization and deregulation of both the economy and social policies and the reduction of the state's role in regulating collective life; the globalization of the economy based on comparative advantages in production and distribution; the brutal flexibilization (read precarity) of labour relations as a precondition for an increase in employment and economic growth.

Taken together, these certitudes made up the neoliberal order. It was an order that fed on the disorder in people's lives, especially in the lives of those who reached adulthood during those decades. Let us just remember that the generation of young people who entered the job market in the 2000s have already gone through two economic crises, that of 2008 and the current pandemic crisis. But the pandemic has meant a lot more than that. More specifically, it has shown that it is the state, not the markets, that has the capacity to protect citizens' lives; that globalization may put the survival of citizens at risk if each country fails to produce the essential goods it needs; that casual workers are the ones most severely hit because they find themselves without any source of income or social protection as soon as they lose their job – an experience the Global South has long been familiar with; that many people have again started playing with the idea of social democratic and socialist alternatives, not just because the ecological destruction brought about by capitalism's infinite expansion has reached the limit but also because it turned out that the countries that did not privatize or decapitalize their labs (Russia and China) seem to have been the most effective of all in terms of producing vaccines and the most fair in distributing them.

It is no surprise that financial analysts at the service of those who created the neoliberal order now predict that we are entering a new era – the era of disorder. This is only understandable, given that they are incapable of imagining anything outside the neoliberal playbook. Their diagnosis is very lucid and their concerns are real. Let us look at some of the main outlines.

Over the past thirty years, the wages of workers in the Global North have stagnated while social inequalities continued to increase. The pandemic has only worsened this scenario, which is very likely to result in much social unrest. During this period a class struggle has, indeed, been waged by the rich against the poor, and the resistance of those who so far have been defeated could erupt at any moment. Empires in their final stages of decline tend to choose cartoonish characters as their leaders, such as Boris Johnson in England or Donald Trump in the US, and all they do is precipitate the end. In the wake of the pandemic, the foreign debt of many countries will be unpayable and unsustainable, a fact the financial markets do not seem to be aware of. The same will happen with household debt, especially among the middle class, given that this was the last resort of many families in the attempt to maintain their standard of living. Some countries have opted for the easy path of international tourism (the hospitality and catering industry), a typically face-to-face activity that will certainly suffer from permanent uncertainty in the future. China has made progress towards again becoming the world's leading economy, a position it held for centuries until the beginning of the 19th century. The second wave of capitalist globalization (1980–2020) is over and nobody knows what will come next. The era of social policy privatization with an eye to profiteering (namely in the area of medicine) seems to have reached an end.

Such (sometimes bold) diagnoses suggest that we are about to enter a period marked by options that will be more decisive and less comfortable than those we have been faced with in recent decades. I foresee three main paths.

Denialism and gattopardism

The first I call denialism. It does not partake of the dramatic nature of the assessment offered, nor does it see the current crisis as a threat to capitalism. On the contrary, it believes that capitalism has only grown stronger because of the crisis. After all, the number of billionaires kept rising during the pandemic, with some sectors even increasing their profits as a result of it (as was the case with Amazon or communication technologies like Zoom). There is recognition that the social crisis is going to get worse; in order to contain it, all the state needs to do is reinforce its 'law and order' system and increase its capacity to suppress social protests – which have already started to be felt and will certainly keep erupting – by expanding its police forces, retraining the army to target 'domestic enemies', strengthening digital surveillance and expanding the prison system. In this scenario, neoliberalism will continue to dominate the economy and society. Admittedly, we will be dealing with a genetically modified neoliberalism, if it is to defend itself against the 'Chinese virus'. A neoliberalism in times of exacerbated cold war with China, mind you, and therefore mingled with a measure of nationalistic populism.

The second path, gattopardism, is the one that most directly serves the interests of those sectors who recognize that some reforms will be necessary if the system is to continue to function, in other words, if the return on capital is to continue to be guaranteed. I call this option gattopardism, an allusion to Giuseppe Tomasi di Lampedusa's 1958 novel *Il Gattopardo*: change is necessary if everything is to stay the same; that is, if that which is essential is to be preserved.

Thus, for instance, the public health sector has to be expanded and social inequalities have to be reduced, but no thought is given to changes in the production system or the financial system, the exploitation of natural resources, the destruction of nature or consumption patterns. This position implicitly sees that denialism may gain the upper hand and fears that this may end up making gattopardism unfeasible. The legitimacy of gattopardism rests on the forty-year coexistence between capitalism and democracy – a low-intensity, well-tamed kind of democracy, wary of jeopardizing the economic and social model while still ensuring a number of human rights that make radical rejection of the system and anti-systemic insurgency more difficult. Without the safety valve of reforms, whatever social peace there is will cease to exist, thereby making repression inevitable.

Transitionism

There is a third position, which I call transitionism. For the time being, it only inhabits the anguished non-conformity now mushrooming in multiple places: in the ecological activism of urban young people worldwide; in the sense of outrage and the resistance of peasants and of the indigenous, Afro-descendant, forest and riverine populations faced with illegal invasion of their land and with being abandoned by the state when the pandemic hit; in the calls for recognizing the relevance of all the care-related tasks carried out by women, be it in the anonymity of households, in the context of the struggles of popular movements or at the head of governments and health policies in various countries; in the new rebellious activism of a host of artists, poets, theatre groups and rappers, mainly from the periphery of large cities, which has been aptly called artivism.

This is the position that views the pandemic as a sign that the civilizational model that has been dominant in the world since the 16th century has come to an end and that a transition to a different civilizational model or models needs to begin. The current model is based on the unfettered exploitation of nature and human beings, on the notion of infinite economic growth, on the primacy of individualism and private property and on secularism. This model has produced impressive technological advances, but it channelled the resulting benefits to a few social groups while causing and legitimizing the exclusion of other, actually more numerous social groups, by way of three principal modes of domination: worker exploitation (capitalism); racism, with its legitimizing of massacres and of the plundering of races viewed as inferior, as well as the appropriating of their resources and knowledge (colonialism); and sexism, with its legitimizing of the devaluation of care work performed by women and of the systemic violence against them, both in the domestic and public sphere (patriarchy).

At the same time that it exacerbated inequalities and discrimination, the pandemic clearly showed that unless we change our civilizational model, new pandemics will continue to plague humankind, causing unforeseeable harm both to human and non-human life. Given that the civilization model cannot be changed overnight, it is imperative that we start designing transition policies. That's why I use the term transitionism.

Although transitionism is still a minority position, it holds a more promising future for human and non-human life on the planet, and therefore deserves greater attention. Based on it, it is possible to foresee that we are about to enter an era of paradigmatic transition which in turn will comprise several transitions. Transitions occur when a dominant individual and collective way of life that is the product of a given economic, social, political and cultural system begins to find it more and more difficult to reproduce itself, at the same time that more and more unequivocal signs and practices indicative of new, qualitatively different ways of life start to sprout in its midst.

The idea of transition is a profoundly political one, in that it presupposes the co-presence of two alternative, possible horizons, one dystopian and the other utopian. From the point of view of transitionism, doing nothing – a characteristic of denialism – does entail a transition, but a regressive one. In fact, it amounts to a transition to a hopelessly dystopian future, one in which all of today's evils and dysfunctions will increase in number and intensity, truly a future without a future, because human life will become unliveable, as is already the case for so many in our present world.

On the contrary, transitionism points towards a utopian horizon. And since utopia is unattainable by definition, transition is potentially infinite, but no less urgent. If we do not start right away, tomorrow may be too late, according to the warnings coming not only from climate change and global warming scientists but also from peasants, who are the ones bearing the brunt of the dramatic effects of extreme weather events.

The most salient feature of transitions is that you never know for certain when they begin and when they end. Viewed from the future, our present times may very well be assessed very differently from the way we see them today. It may even be that the transition will be seen as having already started but having been constantly blocked. The other main feature is that a transition is barely visible to those who live through it. Such relative invisibility is the flip side of the semi-blindness with which we have to live during transition times. These are times of trial and error, of progress and setbacks, of persistent and ephemeral change, of fads and obsolescences, of departures in the guise of arrivals and vice versa. Transition is not fully identifiable until it happens.

Conclusion

Denialism, gattopardism and transitionism are soon going to clash with one another, and most likely the clash is going to be less peaceful and democratic than one might wish. One thing is certain: The time for major transitions has been inscribed on the skin of our time and may even disprove Dante's line. Dante wrote that '*che saetta prevista vien più lenta*' (foreseen, an arrow comes more slowly). We are seeing the arrow of ecological catastrophe coming towards us. It is coming so fast that at times it feels like it has already pierced us. Even if we succeed in removing it, it will not be without pain.

37

COVID-19, the Gift and Post-Neoliberal Scenarios

Paulo Henrique Martins
(Translated by Marco Aurélio de Carvalho Silva)

The events we are experiencing were somewhat predicted due to growing systemic, social, ecological, political and economic imbalances as previously stated by critical authors of anthropocentrism such as Chakrabarty (2009) and Danowski and Viveiros de Castro (2014). However, there was no clear idea as to how and when events would rush themselves into opening the prospect of a civilizational change of unpredictable outcomes. Theoretical criticism valued the political contestation of neoliberalism provoked by the transnational mobilizations of bolder movements such as feminism and youth activism. However, it did not intelligibly contemplate an immediate rupture through a bio-human vector as formerly predicted by ecological anthropology.

One could not possibly foresee a scenario of a pandemic turning the tide, displacing neoliberal agendas and the myth of the market, disclosing the strategic role of the state and public policies in institutional regulation at national, regional and global levels and finally rekindling the prospects of social and community pacts in solidarity. Naturally, the urgency of the moment shifts attention to health actions in general and public health in particular, with impacts on both real and economy. In parallel, it is possible to observe changes in routines, habits, actions of mutual aid and gestures of solidarity with the most humble.

These changes reveal the strength of the gift, that is, of the free obligation of donation, reception and retribution observed by Marcel Mauss (1999) in his famous *Essay on the Gift* of 1924, which was updated by contemporary interpreters gathered at MAUSS (Anti-Utilitarian Movement in the Social Sciences), founded in France in 1981. The luminous signs of the gift, involving individuals, families and destitute communities that seek to recompose the modalities of solidarity at interpersonal, group, institutional and political levels, are presented as an important political outlet at the current time.

Several intellectuals are already moving forward, devising a theoretical critique of the pandemic. However, most of these comments are focused on academic exercises of analytical patterns that had already been developed before the crisis. Many of these analyses do not clearly point out the places of rupture and the gaps that give room to both conservative reactions and democratic innovations that can happen in a new civilizational sphere. Therefore, we should carry out a forecasting exercise regarding the trend of events in order to understand the possible scenarios in the post-crisis period with the exhaustion of neoliberalism.

Before and after COVID-19: continuities and ruptures

Let us think of the scenarios of continuities and discontinuities regarding mentalities, dreams, values, beliefs and institutions. I believe that these scenarios should start taking into consideration the loss of legitimacy of the market as a regulator of economic and social life. The belief in the primacy of a self-regulating market capable of managing institutions is based on a legend: that the market would replace state regulation for its instrumental effectiveness, both in national societies and in the international sphere. The misconception of this 'Market thesis' is demonstrated by the way in which the financial market has been shrinking, on the one hand, and how state intervention has been expanding, on the other.

In fact, the return of the state as a central agent to confront COVID-19 and to reactivate economic, political and social life is a challenging point. This return is taking place to the extent that only the state apparatus has the capacity to regulate various conflicts, to issue currency in its territory and to generate expanded social protection policies.

Simultaneously, there is a revaluation of spontaneous solidarity actions taking place within both the civil society and the physical and virtual communities at national and international levels, reactivating the paradigm of the gift as a political, social and institutional regulator. It encompasses the possibility of recreating the traditional mechanisms of organization of social and community pacts based on solidarity associations between people in urban and rural areas. This possibility constitutes a stimulus for the moral empowerment of individuals in the organization of their institutions and everyday practices.

In any scenario, there is an imponderable factor: the impact in space and time of the effects of the COVID-19 crisis on national societies and populations and on migrants, exiles and refugees. This impact has been demanding public and social political actions that organize the life of communities in local, national and transnational territories. Political and institutional reactions induce the most general changes at a global level, on the one hand, and the stimulation of horizontal solidarity practices involving individuals, families, social groups and institutions of co-operation and social support on the other. The particularities of the cases must also be taken into account. China has managed to control the pandemic process because it has a centralized political structure and a Confucian culture of valuing the hierarchies of authorities that are very particular. This mode of vertical management of social life works in authoritarian states, but its implementation in democratizing societies can generate repressive and politically destabilizing actions.

Most Western countries need to adopt more dialogic initiatives to obtain citizens' consent and to implement health actions. The prospect of overcoming the viral crisis in the short or middle term does not necessarily mean overcoming the catastrophic potential contained in the neoliberal model of unlimited wealth accumulation. In any case, we should consider that this tragic collective experience opens up new possibilities for reorganizing power systems and political, economic, cultural and moral structures. The temporal discontinuity impacts on the psychological understandings of humans about life and death. It reinforces both pathological and self-destructive tendencies and opens collective sensitivity to the understanding that the force of group action can generate collective processes more important than individualistic strategies.

Major scenarios for the future

Taking due care of the limits of prospections, we can foresee two main scenarios. If the immediate strategies for overcoming the crisis generated by COVID-19 are not successful, we will certainly have a more pessimistic scenario, pointing to chronic recession processes with impacts on the lives of organizations and people. This scenario could be very bad for democratic struggles. It may favour authoritarian regimes as right-wing leaders take advantage of fear and hopelessness to impose verticalized power structures. The dictatorial way out is a haunting ghost on the horizon of societies weakened by repressive experiences, as now seen in the case of Hungary.

In contrast, we can consider more pro-democracy outlets if health strategies can contain or, at least, mitigate the effects of the virus, and if civic and community mobilizations contribute to strengthening citizens' feelings of belonging to a specific place, which had been fragmented by the commodification of the world. New agendas of social and community movements will be favoured so that they can anticipate events, creating devices of resistance against authoritarian and dictatorial tendencies.

Breno Bringel (2020) suggests that the pessimistic and optimistic positions at the beginning of the pandemic can be unfolded in three main scenarios (see also Chapter 35): a) 'recovery', the business-as-usual scenario, focuses on the growth of GDP; b) 'adaptation', for example the Green New Deal, which drives a new green capitalism; and c) 'transition', indicating the change of paradigm towards a new economic and eco-social matrix.

Boaventura de Sousa Santos also foresees three scenarios somehow similar to those of Bringel. Reflection on scenarios can then enable democratic projects to be strengthened by avoiding authoritarian centralism and dictatorial adventures. The exercise of solidarity is a good way to motivate public opinion to position itself in its classist, corporatist, identity-based, ethnic and religious diversity, allowing a new level of organization of plural, participatory and representative experiences. We can witness this fact in some European and Asiatic societies that are already starting to relax their restrictive measures. In the case of Brazil, COVID-19 has displaced the agenda of the extreme right that was preparing a dictatorial coup under Bolsonaro and his allies. It allows us to visualize the recomposition of democratic forces.

Possible developments: state, market and society

In the short term, we may imagine some unfoldings in three directions: a broadening of the role of the state in the organization of public welfare policies and the protection of employment and business; resistance from market forces, with major banks and financial institutions betting on the rapid overcoming of the pandemic so as not to give up their financial and rentier privileges; diverse reactions from social groups and individuals to organize civic actions that strengthen the community spirit and the practice of spontaneous donations between individuals and communities.

Different ways of organizing power in the management of institutional, economic, political, cultural and community life have emerged. The resurgence of spontaneous and supportive initiatives advocated by the gift, which were being fragmented by consumerism, is an encouraging sign that can help to remove people from the lethargy and hypnotic outbreaks fuelled by political and religious fanaticism. Only in this way can we foresee a reorganization of civil society and communities that express practices aimed at a new humanism.

COVID-19 as an extraordinary event

The effect of the virus has two sides: pathological and emotional. It spread mainly among travellers and wealthy individuals, generating an inevitable panic within the middle and wealthy classes that assumed they were protected from the poor, the unemployed and the excluded. They believed that they could continue to enjoy consumer society in an unlimited way, even at the expense of social misery. COVID-19 is acting, then, as an extraordinary political event in the spaces of the crowds that are multiplying in the vacuum of disorganized civil society. It accomplishes what the radical liberal and environmentalist movements have failed to accomplish.

What scenarios can we imagine for politics, society and culture? The answers to this question can be seen in practice and in the short term owing to the strengthening of state action in containing the pandemic and to the spontaneous mobilizations of social groups and national and transnational governmental and non-governmental organizations. Here we can imagine these possibilities:

- The strengthening of authoritarian states that have great planning capacity and relatively accommodated populations, such as China.
- The strengthening of the social welfare state in those societies, such as European ones, which have a strong tradition of social and political participation.
- The strengthening of peripheral welfare states, whether in the authoritarian and dictatorial form or in the form of enlightened oligarchies that seek to build left-wing populist discourses. It is possible that, in peripheral societies, the social catastrophe witnessed in mass deaths of individuals will lead, in the medium term, to the strengthening of oligarchic regimes willing to restore populist practices with eventual support from religious fundamentalism and traditional political power.
- The deepening of the systemic rupture with the liberation of new modes of global and national governance open to the intensification of democratic practices, in solidarity with and driven towards the mass inclusion of individuals who had been excluded from the neoliberal model. We can visualize the liberatory perspectives generated by the emergence of new affective and moral solidarities among vulnerable populations as well as the creation of new political and social institutions aimed at managing the liberation of the gift in community spheres. For Sari Hanafi (in Chapter 31 of this book), 'it has also given us an opportunity to explore and provide new ways of understanding and reclaiming our social justice and humanity'.

The left needs to quickly reassess the mistakes generated by the renunciation of a more comprehensive democratic project at the end of the 20th century. The belief that the rupture of neoliberalism would come from within has proven naive and impossible under the utopian limits of traditional liberalism. In this direction, a proposal to explore the potential of a convivial democracy founded on horizontal gifts is deemed paramount. That is, a democracy that implies exchanges of goods and services in solidarity and of reciprocal kindnesses based on the sharing of new moral values and new affective dispositions (Caillé, 2015). It can emerge as the condition for the emancipation of solidarity-based economies and new policies of care that will re-establish the value of the human as a whole as the basis of a new political culture.

At this first moment of the crisis, the focus of attention is still on the hope that public policies that are merely welfare-oriented or aimed at preserving employers and employees and the interests of large firms will suffice to ward off the damage done by COVID-19. But, if the issue is not resolved in the short term, a major change in the power-standards paradigm will be needed in order to gain another understanding of the human. A new civilizational paradigm that enables us to reinvent the economy and social life from an ethical, ecological and political project legitimized by community and convivialist experiences must emerge with the end of the Anthropocene era. Therefore, there is a new fact that rises from the bankruptcies of the market and of the centralizing state: that resulting from the strength of gift systems, of spontaneous and convivialist solidarity occupying the spaces of regulation of social life.

This new agenda opens up with post-neoliberalism and must contemplate the conditions for structuring a new economy, a new society and a new human being. As Mauss pointed out, it is fundamental to understand agonism not as mutual destruction but as a communitarian ritual that favours the alliance between individuals and social groups.

References

Bringel, B. (2020) 'Geopolítica de la pandemia, escalas de la crisis y escenarios en disputa', *Geopolítica(s) Revista de estudios sobre espacio y poder*, 11.

Caillé, A. (2015) *Le convivialisme en dix questions*, Paris: Le Bord de l'Eau.

Chakrabarty, D. (2009) 'The climate of history: Four theses', *Critical Inquiry*, 35(2): 97–222.

Danowski, D. and Viveiros de Castro, E. (2014) *Há mundo por vir? Ensaio sobre medos e fins*, Florianópolis: Desterro.

Mauss, M. (1999) *Sociologie et anthropologie*, Paris: PUF.

38

Post-Pandemic Transitions in a Civilizational Perspective

Arturo Escobar

The COVID-19 pandemic is a turning point in the usual ways of living and doing things, fostering a space for deep collective reflection on the societies we have been building.[1] For a long time, the world elites told us that the market and the great machine of capitalist accumulation cannot be stopped. But it turns out that they can – that it is possible to activate the emergency brake when life is deemed to be at risk. The crisis calls on us to consider that what is at stake is a *new historical project of society*, as well as a *different model of life*, which allows us to relearn to co-exist with human beings and with all living beings in a mutually enriching way. For that, it is necessary to listen to this historical voice of the earth, instead of giving in to the desire to 'return to normality', that is, to the social horror and 'terricide' (the killing or destruction of the earth) that we had come to consider as normal.

It would be impossible to account for all the ideas and proposals that are emerging motivated by the global pandemic and the responses to it. Each one of us will be able to draw our own map of these narratives from our particular physical, cultural, existential and political location. In a longer text (Escobar, 2021) I organize them into two large groups: those that focus on the relationship between the pandemic and capitalism; and those that understand the pandemic through a civilizational view, that is, from the perspective of the relationship between the pandemic and the crisis of humanity. They are not mutually exclusive – capitalism has a clear civilizational dimension, and all civilizational change has to address the question of capitalism and the economy as one of its main concerns. In this chapter, I will concentrate on the latter, discussing some provisional conclusions that have appeared from the encounter with three dimensions of contemporary thought: transitional discourses, in many parts of the world; 'sentipensante' (feeling/thinking) activisms and movements; and certain academic debates.

The recommunalization of social life

This first principle begins with a resounding *no* regarding individual solutions to the crisis; they obscure its roots and promote the stigmatization and alterization of particular groups. It is increasingly important to actively and explicitly resist the ever more efficient individualization of subjectivities imposed by modern capitalism in its global phase. (With its obsession with creating subjects who see themselves primarily as individuals making decisions in terms of markets, globalization has entailed an uncompromising war against everything that is communal and collective.)

History teaches us that human experience is place-based and communal, carved out at the local level. Not only that, in its best expressions, the communalitarian condition of existence resonates with the radical interdependence of everything that exists and the symbiotic co-emergence of living beings and their worlds, resulting in communalitarian entanglements that make us kin to everything that is alive (Gutiérrez Aguilar, 2018). Oaxacan activists refer to this dynamic as the *condicion nosótrica de ser*, the *we* condition of being. If we see ourselves as interrelated, *nosótricamente,* we cannot do otherwise than adopt the principles of love, care and compassion as ethics of living, starting with home, place and community – this not in order to isolate ourselves but to prepare for greater sharing rooted in autonomy, for communication and *compartencia* ('sharing').

The relocalization of social, productive and cultural activities

Human history has always seen movement, flows, regroupings. Delocalizing pressures, however (often times imposed by force, as with the various experiences of enslavement throughout history and with today's dramatic dispossession of peoples and communities for extractivist projects) increased exponentially with the development of capitalism and even more in the age of development and globalization. Given their high social and ecological cost, we need to oppose these pressures; the pandemic is fostering a new awareness that they are not inevitable when life is at stake. As Gustavo Esteva (forthcoming) states, the crisis re-establishes fully the importance of the local and the role of real people, many of whom are abandoning the roles assigned to them by society in order to re-communalize.

It is imperative to relocalize multiple activities in order to regain those rooted in the local. Food is one of the most crucial areas; it is also one of the domains in which there is greater communalitarian and relocalizing innovation, that is, innovations that break with the patriarchal, racist and capitalist way of living; the emphasis on food sovereignty, agroecology and urban gardens are instances of this renewed will. These relocalizing activities, even more so if they take place on an agroecological register and from below, would enable transformations of national and international production systems, revaluing the commons and reweaving ties between country and city. Emphasis is placed on relocalization on the basis of a series of active verb-strategies: to eat, to learn, to heal, to dwell, to build, to know. This involves a significant reorientation of the worlds we inhabit.

The strengthening of autonomies

Autonomy is the political correlate of recommunalization and relocalization. Without the former, the latter two would only go half way or might be reabsorbed by newer forms of delocalized reglobalization. There has been a vibrant debate on *autonomía* in Latin America since the Zapatista uprising of 1994. Autonomy is thought of at times as the radicalization of direct democracy, but also as a new manner of conceiving and enacting politics, understanding politics as the inescapable task that emerges from the entanglement of humans among themselves and with the earth, oriented towards reconfigurations of power in less hierarchical ways, on the basis of principles such as sufficiency, mutual aid and the self-determination of the norms of living. All of this requires thinking about strategies of 'overturning and flight' in relation to the established orders of capitalist modernity and the state (Gutiérrez Aguilar, 2008, p 41).

These areas point to the creation of dignified lives in the territories, rethinking the economy in terms of everyday practices of solidarity, reciprocity and conviviality. There are many clues for this project among those groups who, even during the pandemic, have continued to be dedicated to the production of their own lives, constructing instead of destroying, reuniting instead of separating. These are tangible and actionable principles of 'dream-designing' (*disoñación*) and redesign required for a selective but substantial de-globalization. We can intuit the end of globalization as we know it, or at least the beginning of a globalization in different terms, such as according to the paradigm of *cuidado*, or care (Svampa, 2020) – in which case, it might not be called globalization – and an impetus towards the pluriverse, or a world where many worlds fit.

This could be seen as an antidote to a type of globalization that destroys everything, to a normative middle-class way of life marked by agonizing consumption, to the profound dependence on digital technologies, to bodies grafted with ubiquitous digital technologies, whether cell phones, laptops, earphones, apps or 'Alexas', that subvert our personal and collective autonomies with our complicity and seemingly to our liking.[2]

One final comment: To relocalize, recommunalize and strengthen autonomies necessarily involves the reconstitution of the naturalized concept of the economy; on the one hand to decentre it, that is, to see it as one of the most influential civilizational onto-epistemic operations of capitalist modernity, which separated the economy from the rest of life, assigning it the central role in society (Quijano, 2012), and on the other hand to undertake in earnest the task of constructing other economies on the basis of relationality, centred on livelihoods, the commons and the reproduction of, and care for, life.

There is much to be done along this crucial path. To paraphrase Bolivian historian Silvia Rivera Cusicanqui (2018), we can say that there is no decolonization without de-alienation and de-economization, without decolonizing labour and markets. We find clues for this endeavour in popular economic practices that, operating in multiple worlds at the same time, interweave processes of communalization with capitalist processes, thus de-globalizing economies through their 'persistent disobedience to capitalist markets' (Rivera Cusicanqui, 2018, p 66), albeit in a tense and contradictory way (Gago, 2015). Contemporary movements in defence of the commons, social and solidarity economies and degrowth point in one way or another in this same direction.[3]

The depatriarchalization, de-racialization and decolonization of social relations

The worlds, ontologies and civilizational projects associated with patriarchal capitalism are seemingly immune to attempts at dismantling them. Its power assemblages are strongly naturalized in our desires and subjectivities and in the concrete designs of the worlds that we inhabit and that entrap us. It is necessary to go through them, day in and day out, in order to etch out other ways of inhabiting the world. We are reminded of the stakes at hand by the Latin American feminist dictum that there is no decolonization without depatriarchalization and de-racialization of social relations.

To depatriarchalize and de-racialize requires repairing the damage caused by the heteropatriarchal White capitalist ontology, practising a 'politics in the feminine' centred on the reappropriation of collectively produced goods and the reproduction of life (Segato, 2016, 2018; Gutiérrez Aguilar, 2017). In places inhabited by racialized and ethnicized women, such politics involves following the peaceful routes they travel as they reconstitute their territories and maintain dignified lives, as the Afro-Colombian philosopher Elba Palacios suggests in her work with poor Afro-descendant Black women in Cali, Colombia. 'In their territories, women give birth to life and to modes of re-existence', says this activist-researcher (Palacios Córdoba, 2019, p 143); the women teach us that 'to re-exist means much more than resist'; 'it involves the creation and transformation of autonomy in defence of life, through a sort of contemporary urban maroonage that enables them to reconstitute their negated humanity, reweaving communities in the historical diaspora' (Palacios Córdoba, 2019, p 150). This feminist and antiracist optic is essential to understanding and strengthening the processes of recommunalization and relocalization in many places (see also Lozano, 2019; Hartman, 2019 for the historical experience of young Black women in the US).

The depatriarchalization and de-racialization of social existence imply repairing and healing the tapestry of interrelations that make up the bodies, places and communities that we all are and inhabit. This emphasis is particularly well articulated by the diverse movement of communitarian feminism led by Mayan and Aymaran activist-intellectuals, such as Gladys Tzul Tzul (2018), Julieta Paredes (2012), and Lorena Cabnal. Tzul Tzul highlights the potential of the communal as a horizon for struggle and as a space for the continuous reconstitution of life. Her perspective is absolutely historical and anti-essentialist; it designates the complexity of thinking from and living within in *entramados comunitarios* (communitarian entanglements), with all the forms of power that traverse every community.[4]

From this perspective, the reconstitution of life's web of relations in a communitarian manner is one of the most fundamental challenges faced by any transition strategy; as stated by Argentinean anthropologist Rita Segato (2018): 'We need to advance this politics day by day, outside the State: to re-weave the communal fabric as to restore the political character of domesticity proper of the communal,' she says, and continues

> To choose the relational path is to opt for the historical project of being community. ... It means to endow relationality and the communal forms of happiness with a grammar of value and resistance capable of counteracting the powerful developmentalist, exploitative, and productivist rhetoric of things with its alleged meritocracy. *La estrategia a partir de ahora es femenina.* (the strategy, from now on, is a feminine one; p 106, emphasis added)

I believe this is a feminist and radical relational politics we should fully endorse.

The liberation of the earth

We arrive, finally and necessarily, at the earth (Gaia, Pachamama, co-emergence, self-organization, symbiosis). For nearly two decades, the Social and Communitarian Minga of the Nasa indigenous people of Northern Cauca in the Colombian southwest has been articulating a powerful project around the concept-movement of the liberation of Mother Earth, as part of their strategy of 'weaving life in liberty'. As they say, earth has been enslaved, and as long as she is enslaved, all living beings on the planet are also enslaved. Their struggle involves both the active recovery of lands and a different mode of existence. The struggle comes out of Northern Cauca, but it is not Northern Cauca's struggle. It comes from the Nasa people, but it is not the Nasa people's. Because life itself is at risk when the earth is exploited in the capitalist way, which throws the climate, the ecosystems, everything out of balance. As they hasten to clarify, it's a project for everybody, since we are all earth and pluriverse. 'Every liberated farm, here or in any corner of the world, is a territory that adds to re-establishing the balance of Uma Kiwe [Mother Earth]. This is our common house, our only one. Yes, indeed: come on in, *the door is open*.' What does it mean to accept this invitation, whether in the countryside or in the city, in the Global South or the Global North? The liberation of Mother Earth, conceived from the cosmocentrism and cosmo-action of peoples-territory such as the Nasa, invites us to *disoñar* ('dreamagine') a different design of the world, one propitious to the reconstitution of the web of life with the entire more-than-human range, the sustainment of the territories and to communalized forms of economy, wherever we are.[5]

The liberation of Mother Earth, as an imaginary for peoples and collectives, wherever they happen to be, is not as utopian a project as it might seem. For historical reasons, Latin America has been preparing for this fundamental project at many levels, generating little by little an entire onto-epistemic and political space where the earth-centred struggles, knowledges and critical thought all converge. This convergence has become more noticeable in the wake of the multiplicity of struggles triggered by resistance to the brutal extractivism of the past few decades, which would be impossible to summarize here. Let me just mention that Latin American environmental thought has been articulating a cogent and forceful *apuesta por la vida* (a betting, or critical perspective, on life), in the conviction that the devastation of the planet is not an inevitable destiny.

The earth question has attained an incredible urgency, powerfully expressed by environmental philosopher-activists such as Mexican Enrique Leff (2014) and Colombian Ana Patricia Noguera. For Noguera, to the 'geometries of atrocity produced by a calculating world', Latin American and Abya-Yalan environmental thought responds with a 'geo-poetics of weaving-dwelling' geared towards original modes of inhabiting the planet (2020, p 271). There is, in these expressions of environmental discourse, as in indigenous, Black, peasant, feminist and ecological struggles, an entire archive of categories and practices with which to think about paths to concrete transitions.

Notes

[1] This chapter has its origin in the webinar 'Coronavirus and disputes for the public and the common in Latin America', organized by ALAS, CLACSO and ISA, 15 April 2020.

Thanks to Breno Bringel, Geoffrey Pleyers and Pablo Vommaro for the invitation to participate in this forum, as well as to the other speakers. My special thanks to Gustavo Esteva, Elba M. Palacios C., María Campo, Patricia Botero, Lina Álvarez, Xochitl Leyva, Rita Segato, Marilyn Machado M., Vilma Almendra, Manuel Rozental, Mario Blaser, Alfredo Gutiérrez, Alberto Acosta and Eduardo Gudynas, as well as the members of the Global Tapestry of Alternatives.

[2] The challenge of de-digitalization and of the slowing down of the intensification of the virtual is enormous; as a recent Spanish text put it, 'Digital life cannot be a permanent substitute for real life, and the surrogate debates that take place today on the internet will never be able to replace the presence in flesh and blood and the live dialogue.' See: https://ctxt.es/es/20200501/Firmas/32143/riechmann-yayo-herrero-digitalizacion-coronavirus-teletrabajo-brecha-digital-covid-trazado-contactos.htm

[3] We may quote Vaneigem, the situationist, to bring home the civilizational stakes in rethinking the economy: 'The economy is everywhere that life is not. ... Economics is the most durable lie of the approximately ten millennia mistakenly accepted as history. ... There is only one terror: For most people it is the fear of losing the last illusion separating them from themselves, the panic of having to create their own lives. ... Civilization was identified with obedience to a universal and eternal market relationship. ... *Nature cannot be liberated from the economy until the economy has been driven out of human life. ... As the economy's hold weakens, life is more able to clear a path for itself*' (Vaneigem, 1994, pp 17, 33, 36; emphasis added).

[4] Contrary to common thinking, indigenous communitarian formations are not homogeneous but plural; neither do they suppress personal expression: 'The communal does no place limits on the personal, it rather potentiates it. The communitarian entanglements provide the grounds on which personal and intimate lives are sustained' (Tzul Tzul, 2018, p 57), even if the organization of life, of politics and of the economy is realized collectively and every family has to engage in these practices.

[5] There is an extensive Nasa archive on the liberation of Mother Earth. See: NASA ACIN (2010) 'Libertad para la Madre Tierra', [online] 28 May, available from: http://www.nasaacin.org/libertar-para-la-madre-tierra/50-libertad-para-la-madre-tierra; 'NASA ACIN (2010) 'El desafío que nos convoca', [online] 28 May, available from: http://www.nasaacin.org/el-desafio-no-da-espera ; Pueblos en Camino (2016) 'Lo que vamos aprendiendo con la liberación de Uma Kiwe', *Pueblos en Camino*, [online] 19 January, available from: http://pueblosencamino.org/?p=2176 ; Almendra, V. (2012) 'La paz de la Mama Kiwe en libertad, de la mujer sin amarras ni silencios', 2 August, available from: http://pueblosencamino.org/?p=150. See also 'Libertad y alegría con Uma Kiwe: Palabra del proceso de Liberación de la Madre Tierra', http://liberemoslatierra.blogspot.es/1481948996/libertad-y-alegria-con-uma-kiwe-palabra-del-proceso-de-liberacion-de-la-madre-tierra/. I must emphasize that the movement for the liberation of Mother Earth is currently divided and, at the same time, heavily repressed by landowners and government forces. For a full account of the movement and the situation, see Escobar (2020), Chapter 3.

References

Escobar, A. (2016) *Autonomía y diseño: La realización de lo comunal*, Cauca: Editorial Universidad del Cauca.

Escobar, A. (2018) *Otro posible es posible: Caminando hacia las transiciones desde Abya Yala/Afro/Latino-América*, Bogotá: Editorial Desde Abajo.

Escobar, A. (2021) 'El pensamiento en tiempos de pos/pandemia', in O. Quijano (ed) *Pandemia al Sur*, Buenos Aires: Prometeo Libros.

Esteva, G. (forthcoming) 'El día después', in O. Quijano (ed) *Pandemia al Sur*, Buenos Aires: Prometeo Libros.

Gago, V. (2015) *La razón neoliberal*, Buenos Aires: Tinta Limón.

Gutiérrez Aguilar, R. (2008) *Los ritmos del Pachakuti. Movilización y levantamiento indígena-popular en Bolivia*, Buenos Aires: Tinta Limón.

Gutiérrez Aguilar, R. (2017) *Horizontes comunitario-populares*, Madrid: Traficante de Sueños.

Gutiérrez Aguilar, R. (ed) (2018) *Comunalidad, tramas comunitarias y producción de lo común*, Oaxaca: Colectivo Editorial Pez en el Árbol.

Hartman, S. (2019) *Wayward Lives, Beautiful Experiments: Intimate Histories of Social Upheaval*, New York: Norton & Company.

Leff, E. (2014) *La apuesta por la vida*, Mexico City: Siglo XXI.

Lozano, B.R. (2019) *Aportes a un feminismo negro decolonial*, Quito: Abya Yala.

Noguera, A.P. (2020) 'Ethos–cuerpo–tierra. Diseños-otros en tiempos de transición civilizatoria', in A.P. Noguera (ed) *Polifonías geo-ético-poéticas del habitar-sur*, Manizales: Universidad Nacional, 271–300.

Palacios Córdoba, E.M. (2019) 'Sentipensar la paz en Colombia: Oyendo las reexistentes voces pacificas de mujeres Negras Afrodescendientes', *Memorias: Revista Digital de Historia y Arqueología desde el Caribe colombiano*, 38: 131–61.

Paredes, J. (2012) *Hilando fino desde el feminismo comunitario*, La Paz: DED.

Quijano, O. (2012) *Ecosimías. Visiones y prácticas de diferencia autonómica/cultural en contextos de multiplicidad*, Popayán: Editorial Universidad del Cauca.

Rivera Cusicanqui, S. (2018) *Un mundo ch'ixi es posible*, Buenos Aires: Tinta Limón.

Segato, R.L. (2016) *La guerra contra las mujeres*, Madrid: Traficantes de Sueños.

Segato, R.L. (2018) *Contra-pedagogías de la crueldad*, Buenos Aires: Prometeo.

Svampa, M. (2020) 'Reflexiones para un mundo pos-Coronavirus' in P. Amadeo (ed) *La fiebre. Pensamiento contemporáneo en tiempo de pandemias*, Buenos Aires: Editorial Aspo, 17–38.

Toro, C. (forthcoming) 'Aprendiendo de saberes y haceres: Los nadies en tiempo de pandemia', in O. Quijano (ed) *Pandemia al Sur*, Buenos Aires: Prometeo Libros.

Tzul Tzul, G. (2018) *Sistemas de gobierno comunal indígena*, Mexico City: Instituto Amaq.

Vaneigem R. (1994) *The Movement of the Free Spirit*, London: Zed Books.

39

The World That Is Coming: Pandemic, Movements and Change

Geoffrey Pleyers

Many committed intellectuals and activists share a similar conviction: the pandemic has revealed the limits of the corporate capitalist system and the damage it has caused through neoliberal policies, austerity and the fast destruction of nature. Movements for social justice and progressive intellectuals claim the crisis should be treated as a moment of rupture that will bring significant changes into our lives, our societies and our world. Scholar-activists and movements have drawn countless scenarios for 'alternative futures'. Most see in the pandemic crisis the confirmation and the deepening of crises they have denounced in earlier work, framing it as the crisis of corporate globalization, capitalism (Amadeo, 2020) or the Anthropocene (Kothari, in Chapter 21 of this book), or as a civilization crisis (Escobar, in Chapter 38 of this book).

Dozens of opinion articles and petitions have circulated stating that we need to build a fairer society after the pandemic, with more robust public services and access to healthcare for all, universal revenue and better working conditions. This chapter highlights the importance of the battle for the interpretation of the pandemic and the crisis it has generated. However, it is essential to get rid of the illusions underlying some of these stances and the simplistic view that the crisis will bring about social change by itself, that the world will change 'because it simply can't go on like this'.

Opening new horizons

Opening new horizons of possibility has always been a crucial role for social movements. While the dominant actors impose the idea that 'there is no alternative' to their world order, social movements challenge them, claiming that 'another world is possible'. They introduce dissents, debates and reflexivity into a world order that is taken for granted, contributing to social change, to the ability of a society to transform itself, 'to produce itself' more conscientiously, as sociologist Alain Touraine would say.

This role is even more important in times of crisis. Crises break up routines and 'business as usual'. They provide opportunities to reflect individually and collectively on our values and aims. The COVID-19 pandemic has deeply shaken our daily lives and many of the 'certainties' of our geopolitical, economic and social system. Forced to implement a lockdown to limit the virus's dramatic spread, the defenders of the dominant world order frame the 'return to normality' as the purpose of a 'national unity'[1] that gathers policymakers, corporations, workers and the whole population in a common struggle against COVID-19. Activists insist on the opposite, that what is presented as 'normality' is not the only way and is actually part of the problem. 'Nothing could be worse than a return to normality', claims Indian activist Arundhati Roy.[2]

In the heat of the pandemic, progressive movements have had some success in spreading arguments far beyond activist circles, at least in Western European democracies. After years of austerity in public services, governments spend lavishly to mitigate the effects of the pandemic and of the economic crisis. State interventionism in the economic sector is rising, and several governments argue for a relocalization of the production of 'essential goods'. Those who used to promote budget cuts in public hospitals took part in the daily handclapping to support nurses and medical doctors.

Until early March 2020, French president Emmanuelle Macron implemented austerity plans in public hospitals and refused to attend to the claims of nurses and medical doctors who conducted the longest strike in the sector in French history. In his two speeches to the nation at the beginning of the lockdown in March 2020, Emmanuel Macron's perspective was very different. He described the public hospital workers as 'national heroes'. The state increased the hospitals' budget during the crisis, and the president swore that there would be major changes in public policy, explaining that 'the day after the pandemic will not be like the day before':[3] 'We will have to question the model of development that our world has been committed to in the past decades'.[4] A fervent defender of free trade, the president now talks about 'economic sovereignty', provides massive loans to key 'national corporations' and even considers nationalizations. The pandemic may even succeed where one of the longest general strikes in French history has failed: in getting rid of the major neoliberal pension reform.

Three lessons from the global financial crisis

Such a change of stance echoes declarations by another French president in the early aftermath of the global financial crisis. On 23 October 2008, Nicolas Sarkozy declared that 'the ideology of the dictatorship of the market and public powerlessness has died with the financial crisis'.[5] Alter-globalization activists could not say it better; at the 2008 European Social Forum, they shared the conviction that 'the [financial] crisis has proven us right. Now governments will have to take into account our arguments and stop neoliberal policies'.

The aftermath of the global financial crisis took a very different path. A few years after the crisis, the dominant narrative put the burden of the economic crisis on European welfare states, paving the way to austerity policies across the continent. It led to a decade of social crisis, and increased inequalities that set the ground for historic rises of right-wing populists. In most European countries, austerity policies targeted public services and the public health sector, limiting its efficiency to cope with today's pandemic.

Three lessons may be drawn from the aftermath of the global financial crisis when it comes to social change. The first one is that, no matter how large it is, a crisis itself will not generate social change. The latter depends on the capacity of social actors to highlight the questions spawned by the historic situation and to advance alternative political visions and economic rationality (Pleyers, 2010). Social actors play a major role in raising public awareness, proposing an alternative political and economic rationality and pushing towards a concrete implementation of alternative policies and behaviours. There is no predetermined way to get out of the pandemic. Social agency during the crisis and its aftermath may thus have significant impacts on society, economics and politics.

A second lesson is that good arguments and facts are not sufficient to shape the outcomes of the crisis. Sociologist of science Raymond Boudon (1989) demonstrated that the 'truth' of economic theories has more to do with their capacity to forge a provisional consensus than with their always highly debatable scientific validity. Likewise, the COVID-19 pandemic is at the same time a series of facts that no one can deny and a social reality that is reinterpreted very differently by social actors. It is often embedded in a pre-existing narrative and strengthens previous convictions and worldviews. Facts and sciences are not shared references but are subject to reinterpretations by ideologies and populist leaders who mistrust science. Habermas's faith in a deliberative public space is challenged in a time of very fragmented public space, social media, fake news and populist leaders.

Hence – and this is the third lesson – the battle over the meaning of the crisis is crucial. The actors who will shape the dominant narrative of the crisis may shape the policies to tackle the pandemic but also lay the ground for new policies in economic, social and democratic matters. As leading Latin American scholar-activist Arturo Escobar put it, 'It is crucial at this stage to have narratives about other ways of lives, and to have them ready'[6].

Civil society organizations and networks of movements counterbalance the government messages of national unity. Each sector of the popular or progressive movements frames the pandemic in its own meta-narratives focused on its historic claims and worldview that act as a 'master frame' (Snow and Benford, 2002) in its work to produce a meaning of the crisis. Some show the pandemic from different standpoints, from the favelas in Brazil (see Chapter 11 of this book) or the deficient social housing in New York City (Krinsky and Caldwell, Chapter 23 of this book). Others develop gendered and intersectional perspectives on the pandemic, showing that women and minorities particularly suffer from the virus and from the lockdown and cope with most of the crucial tasks of caring in families, communities and public hospitals.[7] All over the world, progressive intellectuals link the pandemic to the ravages of capitalism ('Capitalism is the true virus' has become a trending slogan on social media) and with the ecological crisis. Latin American progressive movements and intellectuals frame the crisis in their meta-narrative which has surged from the confluence of indigenous, feminist, ecological and social justice movements over the last decade: 'The crisis reveals the deep social, political and ecological crises we are in. Behind the sanitary crisis, there is a crisis of civilization' (see Sagot, Chapter 10 of this book).

Movements and countermovements

Progressive movements are, however, not alone in this battle to shape the meaning of the COVID-19 crisis. They confront two kinds of 'countermovements' (Polanyi, 1944): reactionary movements and a capitalist elite that defends corporate globalization, 'a social movement for global capitalism' (Sklair, 2002). The years that followed the global financial crisis showed the ability of the actors who defend corporate globalization and capitalism to impose their narrative of the crisis. In just a few years, they managed to shift the meaning of the crisis and the focus of policymakers from the collapse of global financial capitalism to the excesses of over-indebted welfare states, paving the way for a decade of austerity policies.

Today, the actors that seem better able to seize the opportunities opened by the crisis and the rupture of economic dogmas may be on the same side. In many countries, the COVID-19-crisis bailout has channelled historic amounts of public money (over 500 billion dollars in the first bailout budget in the US) to large corporations. While activists claimed the crisis should be an opportunity to build a different economic model and reduce greenhouse gas emission, oil companies received their share of public money to cope with the crisis and governments set up massive bailouts and loans for the airlines.[8] Naomi Klein (2008) has shown how capitalist elites have taken sudden crises as opportunities for imposing neoliberal policies. The COVID-19 crisis may be no exception. This scenario is already being repeated in Ecuador with the COVID-19 crisis, with measures taken by the government to reinforce neoliberal policies during the confinement (Ramírez, 2020). Elsewhere, while most governments have extended their budget to cope with the sanitary crisis, the economic and debt crises that will follow may be seized as an opportunity to shrink social policies.

Reactionary movements also draw on the pandemic. Conspiracy theories spread all over social media, giving rise to an unprecedented 'infodemic'. Such discourses embedded the crisis in a broader 'war of cultures' narrative that blames migrants, the 'multicultural society' and 'cultural Marxism' for the pandemic. In several cities, far-right activists set up neighbourhood solidarity initiatives during the COVID-19 outbreak to support their 'own people'. At the same time, they target migrant workers, foreigners or slum dwellers for spreading the virus. Far-right activists protested against the lockdown even when the pandemic was at its peak. In the United States,[9] rallies against the stay-at-home order and business closure started in Michigan on 15 April, and have taken place in most state capitals, with the support of Donald Trump. In Brazil, the president himself participates in protests against the sanitary measures imposed by the state governors.[10] In Germany, protesters include anti-vaccine activists, anti-Semites, ultra-liberals and conspiracy activists who frame the lockdown as the first step of a coup imposed by Angela Merkel.[11] Meanwhile, conservative neo-Pentecostal churches claim 'faith, not science will save us'[12] and bring their support to state leaders who plead to reopen the temples during the lockdown.

Racism has surged in all regions of the world, against migrant workers in India and China, against Asian Americans in the US, against minorities and poor people accused of spreading the pandemic and all over the world against refugees. The United Nations general secretary has issued an alert on what he frames as a 'tsunami of hate and xenophobia, scapegoating and scare-mongering' unleashed by the COVID-19 pandemic. 'As speculation swirled about where the virus originated, Guterres said migrants and refugees have been vilified as a source of the virus and then denied access to medical treatment. And journalists, whistle-blowers, health professionals, aid workers and human rights defenders are being targeted'.[13] As poor people suffer higher risks of infection due to precarious work and housing, they became the target of a 'racism of class' that often combines with ethnic racism against minorities and people of colour.

Social movements are not the only actors striving to shape the meaning of the current crisis. Governments have portrayed themselves as the key players in the pandemic. They have massively invested in media and public communication seeking to impose their narrative and defending their management of the crisis. China's Communist Party carefully monitors its image as an efficient government able to deal with the crisis, control the pandemic and arrest anyone who dares to challenge this narrative or criticize the crisis management of Xi Jinping.[14] In Hungary, freedom of speech has come under further threat from COVID-19 'emergency measures' that allow Prime Minister Orban to rule by decree and threatens authors of 'false information' with up to five years in prison.[15] This power game to shape the narrative is not exclusive to authoritarian states and populist leaders. The French government is particularly vigilant about public discourses on its crisis management. On 16 April, a woman was detained for four hours under police custody, accused of 'insult to a person holding public authority' for hanging a banner, 'Macronavirus, when will it stop?', at her house.[16]

Many governments tend to hide their initial failure to deal with the virus early on by placing the blame on individual citizens who do not comply with the lockdown. In terms of biopolitics and social control, the border between democracy and authoritarian regimes has been partly blurred. The way the pandemic has been managed may pave the way for a new authoritarian era, with biopolitics grounded in new technologies, artificial intelligence and increasing interventions by police forces.

A fragmented battlefield

The battle over the societal meaning of the pandemic crisis is taking place all over the world. However, it is a highly fragmented debate, at least at three levels. First, it takes place in a complex and highly fragmented media space. Social media opens spaces for expression and the spread of alternative information and meanings. However, it also fragments the public space. Each political orientation will overload its social media followers with news and analyses that strengthen their worldview. Mainstream media and television channels remain influential in manufacturing opinions and consent. In most countries, the pandemic has lowered polarization and political conflicts, as the population unite against a common threat. The opposite has happened in Brazil and the United States: the pandemic strengthened the polarization of society, as each pole interpreted the crisis following its worldview and conducted electoral campaigns against the other stances.

Second, this battle over meanings is taking place on different bases in each country and world region. On one side, the experience of the pandemic is very different in countries and neighbourhoods where a majority of workers depend on the informal economy as compared to in European welfare states.

On the other side, progressive movements and committed intellectuals in each region interpret the crisis according to the meta-narrative they have built in previous years. For instance, Latin American movements and committed intellectuals see it as the mark of a 'civilizational crisis', a narrative that is less diffused in the Global North. International networks of popular movements aspire to bypass these divisions by opening spaces for 'global dialogue for systemic change' and building international analyses.[17]

Third, the outbreak takes place in a tense geopolitical context (Bringel, 2020; Chapter 35 of this book) that redefines diplomatic alliances and the relations between governments and their citizens. This panorama is not without consequences for social movements. Liberal democracy is far from being the only regime or even a common horizon. Activists engage in this battle over meaning in very different circumstances and at very different risks in authoritarian or liberal regimes. However, COVID-19 arrived after a decade of increasing repression of protests and movements, both in authoritarian and liberal regimes.

Conclusion

Will today's progressive movements succeed where others failed a decade ago, in the aftermath of the financial crisis? There is no easy path that leads from the pandemic to a better, greener and less unequal world. Once new horizons have opened, it is only the beginning of a struggle to assign meaning to the crisis. The fact that a fairer, more equal and sustainable world is urgently needed is, however, not sufficient to rebuild the world in different ways after the COVID-19 pandemic.

The COVID-19 outbreak is a battlefield for alternative futures (Pleyers, 2020). Progressive, capitalist and reactionary movements compete to impose their narratives and shape policies and society, while governments urge to return to the pre-pandemic 'normality' and massively invest in diffusing their own narrative and advertising their management of the crisis. Shaping the meaning of the current crisis and opening new horizons for powerful visions of alternative futures is a major stake and will have a dramatic impact on society, the economic system and the daily lives of billions of people, as well as on the environmental crisis.

Notes

[1] Emmanuel Macron's first public address on the virus was entitled 'A united France is our best asset in the troubled period we're going through with COVID-19. We will hold. All together.': https://www.elysee.fr/emmanuel-macron/2020/03/12/adresse-aux-francais

[2] Roy, A. (2020) 'The Pandemic Is a Portal', *Financial Times*, [online] 3 April, available from: https://www.ft.com/content/10d8f5e8-74eb-11ea-95fe-fcd274e920ca See also Bizberg, in this book.

[3] See: https://www.elysee.fr/emmanuel-macron/2020/03/16/adresse-aux-francais-covid19

4   Macron, E. (2020) *Adresse aux Français*, 12 March, available from: https://www.elysee.fr/emmanuel-macron/2020/03/12/adresse-aux-francais

5   Sarkozy, N. (2008) Déclaration de M. Nicolas Sarkozy, Président de la République, sur les mesures de soutien à l'économie face à la crise économique internationale, 23 October. https://www.elysee.fr/nicolas-sarkozy/2008/10/23/declaration-de-m-nicolas-sarkozy-president-de-la-republique-sur-les-mesures-de-soutien-a-leconomie-face-a-la-crise-economique-internationale-a-argonay-haute-savoie-le-23-octobre-2008

6   Intervention in the CLACSO, ALAS and ISA online seminar "Coronavirus y disputas por lo público y lo común en América Latina", 9 April 2020. https://youtu.be/pOFQlsesLf8

7   Hirsch, A. (2020) 'After coronavirus, black and brown people must be at the heart of Britain's story', *The Guardian*, [online] 7 May, available from: www.theguardian.com/commentisfree/2020/may/07/coronavirus-black-brown-people-britain-ethnic-minorities

8   See: https://stay-grounded.org/savepeoplenotplanes

9   Vogel, K.P., Rutenberg, J. and Lerer, L. (2020) ,The Quiet Hand of Conservative Groups in the Anti-Lockdown Protests', *The* New York Times, [online] 21 April, available from: https://www.nytimes.com/2020/04/21/us/politics/coronavirus-protests-trump.html

10 Waldron, T. (2020) 'Brazil is the new epicentre of the Global Coronavirus pandemic', *Huffington Post*, [online] 20 May, available from: https://www.huffpost.com/entry/bolsonaro-brazil-coronavirus-pandemic_n_5ec5662ac5b6dcbe36022e5a

11 Baumgärtner M., Bohr, F., Höfner, R., Lehmann, T., Müller, A.K., Röbel, S., Rosenbach, M., Schaible, J., Wiedmann-Schmidt, W. and Winter, S. (2020) 'The Corona Conspiracy Theorists', *Der Spiegel International*, [online] 14 May, available from: https://www.spiegel.de/international/germany/the-corona-conspiracy-theorists-protests-in-germany-see-fringe-mix-with-the-mainstream-a-8a9d5822-8944-407a-980a-d58e9d6b4aec

12 Michelle, B. (2020) 'Can faith healing work by phone? Charismatic Christians try prayer to combat the coronavirus', *Washington Post*, [online] 3 April, available from: https://www.washingtonpost.com/religion/2020/04/03/supernatural-healing-christian-faith-coronavirus-pandemic

13 United Nations (2020) 'UN Secretary-General Denounces "Tsunami" of Xenophobia Unleashed amid COVID-19', United Nations, [online] 8 May, available from: https://www.un.org/press/en/2020/sgsm20076.doc.htm

14 Davidson, H. (2020) 'Critic who called Xi a "clown" over Covid-19 crisis investigated for "serious violations"', *The Guardian*, [online] 8 April, available from: https://www.theguardian.com/world/2020/apr/08/critic-xi-jinping-clown-ren-zhiqiang-covid-19-outbreak-investigated-china

15 Hungarian Helsinki Committee (2020) 'Free Media and Human Rights Defenders Needed More Than Ever', HHC, [online] 31 March, available from: www.helsinki.hu/en/emergency-law-gives-carte-blanche-powers-to-government

16 Polloni, C. (2020) 'Pour des banderoles au balcon, la police à domicile', *Mediapart*, [online] 16 April, available from: www.mediapart.fr/journal/france/160420/pour-des-banderoles-au-balcon-la-police-domicile

17 See: https://systemicalternatives.org/2020/04/29/global-dialogue-for-systemic-change

References

Amadeo, P. (ed) (2020) *Sopa de Wuhan*, La Plata: ASPO.

Bringel, B. (2020) 'Geopolítica de la pandemia, escalas de la crisis y escenarios en disputa', *Geopolítica(s)*, 11: 173–87.

Klein, N. (2008) *The Shock Doctrine*, New York: Waterstone.

Kothari, A., Escobar, A., Salleh, A., Demaria, F. and Acosta, A. (2020) 'Can the coronavirus save the planet?', *Open Democracy*, [online] 27 March, available from: www.opendemocracy.net/en/oureconomy/can-coronavirus-save-planet

Pleyers, G. (2010) *Alter-Globalization: Becoming Actors in the Global Age*, Cambridge: Polity.

Pleyers, G. (2020) 'The pandemic is a battlefield. Social movements during the COVID-19 lockdown', *Journal of Civil Society*, 16(4): 295–312.

Polanyi, K.(1944) *The Great Transformation*, Boston, MA: Beacon Press.

Ramírez, R. (2020) *Dictaduras democráticas, autoritarismo neoliberal y revueltas populares en tiempos de COVID-19*, Mexico City: CELAG.

Sklair, L. (2002) *Globalization: Capitalism and Its Alternatives*, Oxford: Oxford University Press.

Snow, D. and Benford, R. (2002) 'Master frames and cycles of protest', in A. Morris and C. Mueller (eds) *Frontiers in Social Movement Theory*, New Haven, CT: Yale University Press, 133–55.

Touraine, A. (1973) *La production de la société*, Paris: Seuil.

Index

References to endnotes show both the
page number and the note number (75n14).